WORKS ISSUED BY THE
HAKLUYT SOCIETY

———

THE EXPEDITION OF THE *ST JEAN-BAPTISTE*
TO THE PACIFIC, 1769–1770

SECOND SERIES
NO. 158

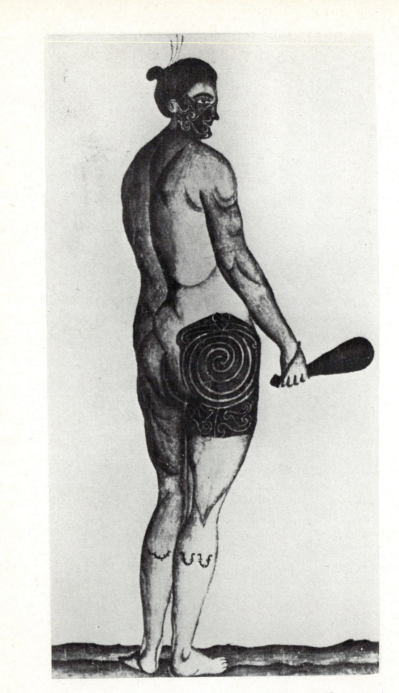

Plate 1. Ranginui, Maori chief, by Pottier de l'Horme (frontispiece)

THE EXPEDITION
OF THE *ST JEAN-BAPTISTE*
TO THE PACIFIC
1769–1770

From Journals of Jean de Surville
and Guillaume Labé

Translated and edited by
JOHN DUNMORE

THE HAKLUYT SOCIETY
LONDON
1981

ISBN 0 904180 11 5

Printed in Great Britain at the
University Press, Cambridge

Published by the Hakluyt Society
c/o The Map Library
British Library Reference Division
London WC1B 3DG

British Library Cataloguing in Publication Data

The expedition of the *St Jean-Baptiste* to the
    Pacific, 1769–1770. – (Hakluyt Society second series; 158)
    1. St Jean-Baptiste *Ship*
    2. Pacific area
    I. Surville, Jean de II. Labé, Guillaume
    III. Dunmore, John
    910′.09164   DU20

ISBN 0-904180-11-5

CONTENTS

ILLUSTRATIONS

PREFACE

The expedition of the *St Jean-Baptiste* has been known marginally for many years in connection with the rediscovery of the Solomon Islands and the early history of New Zealand, but it usually warranted little more than a brief mention, and the broader pattern of the voyage was never clearly outlined. In each case it seemed that the ship emerged out of darkness and disappeared into the fog. Judgements passed on it were simplistic or perfunctory. Yet the *St Jean-Baptiste* was a complex expedition, representative of a significant attitude towards British hegemony; it fitted into the framework of intensive exploration which began in the Pacific in the 1760s, and it was related to the voyages of Bougainville and Boenechea, and indirectly to subsequent French expeditions; its role in helping to establish the existence and longitude of the Solomons was recognised twenty years later and has not been challenged since; its reports on a variety of places, from eastern Malaysia to New Zealand, and its bitter first-hand experience of the policy of exclusiveness in Spanish South America, will retain their value. It was necessary for at least some of these aspects, which have been dealt with fragmentarily and to a greater or lesser degree in scattered publications, to be brought together in a coherent and logical manner, by the publication of at least one of the expedition's Journals.

The obvious one to choose was the captain's. Unfortunately Jean de Surville was drowned on the coast of Peru, and the image his Journal would give on its own would thus still be incomplete. The complementary Journal is clearly that of Guillaume Labé, his second-in-command but also one of the partners in the undertaking. Labé took over command at Surville's death, dealt with the irritatingly slow and unsympathetic Spanish authorities, and brought the ship back to France. The voluminous journal of Pottier de l'Horme starts in June 1769, omitting the first two months of the voyage which formally began with the ship's departure from Bengal, and has a three-year gap, corresponding to the period spent in Callao. The accounts written by Monneron, the ship's clerk, are summaries of events, written as reports to the French authorities and the main financial backers of the venture.

Although the work of these two participants has been drawn upon where required, the two main shipboard journals, Surville's and Labé's, together give an adequate overall and detailed picture of the voyage.

Nevertheless, publishing the complete text of both journals, with the minutiae of daily manœuvres against unfavourable winds down the Straits of Malacca and of the eventless crossing of the southern Pacific — at least eventless if one overlooks the frequent deaths carefully and sorrowfully recorded by Labé — presented certain problems, and it was decided to limit publication to the most significant section: from the arrival at the Batan Islands to the departure from New Zealand at the beginning of 1770. For those who wish to consult it, the complete text of both journals is held, in typescript form, by the Alexander Turnbull Library, Wellington, New Zealand.

My thanks are due to a number of institutions and individuals who have assisted in this enterprise over a number of years. Financial assistance was made available by the New Zealand University Grants Committee, Victoria University of Wellington, and Massey University, Palmerston North. The Alexander Turnbull Library, Wellington, provided help on numerous occasions; the Archives Nationales in Paris as well as the Archives de la Marine were unfailing in their courtesy; the National Maritime Museum, Greenwich, helped with additional information. The Rockefeller Foundation, New York, through its Bellagio Study Center, assisted in providing those precious commodities: quiet and time.

Among individuals, the personality of J. C. Beaglehole stands out, both as a model and as someone who considered the undertaking not merely worthwhile but essential and overdue. The late H. F. Buffet, who pioneered Surville studies, is owed a debt of gratitude as is his counterpart in New Zealand, the late R. R. D. Milligan. Miss Beauchesne, Archivist of the Port of Lorient, placed her encyclopaedic knowledge untiringly at my disposal. Encouragement and help over the years has been received from Admiral M. R. de Brossard, Father O'Reilly of the Société des Océanistes, and successive French representatives in Wellington. Others who helped to track down obscure references in various parts of the Pacific are thanked in specific footnotes; if they are not, may their cooperation be now acknowledged collectively here. Finally, I should like to thank my wife for her support, and her belief that there is nothing strange in sharing more than ten years of one's life with a shipload of officers and men who sailed across the deserted Pacific more than two centuries ago.

INTRODUCTION

I. THE PARTICIPANTS

(i) *The Officers and Crew*

Jean-François-Marie de Surville was born in Port-Louis in Brittany on 18 January 1717. Port-Louis, formerly known as Blavet, acquired its name in 1616 when it was rebuilt and fortified on the orders of Louis XIII; it had had a long history as a naval port, but its fortunes began to wane during the eighteenth century when the port of Lorient (named after a ship, *L'Orient*, built across the estuary by the French India Company) started to acquire importance as a commercial centre. Surville was born in the Rue de la Pointe, a few doors away from the house where Julien Crozet, who sailed with Marion Dufresne to New Zealand, was born eleven years later.

The Surville family, as the name indicates, came from Normandy. His great-grandfather, Jean de Surville, was born near St-Lô and subsequently moved to St-Pierre-de-Sémilly, where the grandfather, Michel, was born; his father, Jean, was the eldest of eight children; he moved to Port-Louis in 1695, thereby founding the Breton branch of the family, of which there appear to be no direct descendants today. Jean was 'Receveur des fermes du Roi' – which means he was collector of taxes for the district – he was also the *Intendant*'s agent in Port-Louis, a controller of the hospital, a banker and a trader. It is clear, therefore, that the family was well-to-do and influential. His first wife, Marie Barbe, was the daughter of a local shipowner of considerable means; his second wife, the explorer's mother, was Françoise Mariteau de Roscadec, again the daughter of a local shipowner and the niece of Bréart de Boisanges, a director of the *Compagnie des Indes Orientales*. Of their nine children, six survived – four girls and two boys.

The eldest, Catherine, married at the age of seventeen Louis Guyont de la Motte who had taken over the post of collector of taxes when Jean de Surville died in 1719. Françoise and Thérèse each married captains of the India Company, Louis de Canivet and Nicolas de

Frémery, and Elizabeth-Ursule entered the order of the Bon Sauveur of Saint-Lô founded by her aunt Elizabeth a few years earlier. Jean-François' elder brother, René-Louis, born in 1710, entered the service of the India Company at the usual early age; he went to China as first ensign in the *Fulvy* in 1738–9 and again as second lieutenant in the *Neptune* in 1741–3 under his cousin Bréart de Boisanger, and once more in 1745–6 in the *Philibert*, commanded by his brother-in-law Nicolas de Frémery. Appointed post-captain in 1747 he commanded first the *Aimable*, then a succession of vessels until 1759 when he was killed on the *Centaure*, which ship his younger brother then took over. His son was Hughes-Jean-Marie who came under the protection of his uncle and sailed with him to New Zealand.

Surville went to sea at the age of ten and entered the service of the Indian Company. We find him in April 1740 second ensign in the *Hercule* sailing for Bengal; in October 1743 he went to China in the *Dauphin*, but the War of the Spanish Succession intervened and he was taken prisoner by the English on 5 February 1745. Freed a few months later he reached France on 12 February 1746 and joined the *Bagatelle* in April, only to be again taken prisoner; this time he was not able to return to France until July 1748. He joined the *Duc de Béthune* as first ensign in October and sailed for the Ile de France and the Ile de Bourbon, where he bought some land, probably in the early 1750s. He is credited with introducing to the islands in 1753 the mangosteen and several varieties of cinnamon trees. By then he was a second lieutenant sailing for Bengal in the *Reine* (February 1752 to July 1753). The following year he obtained his own command – the *Renommée*, going to India and China, transferring in February 1755 to the *Compagnie des Indes* in which he sailed back to France from Pondicherry.

The Seven Years' War broke out soon after Surville returned to India with the *Duc d'Orléans*. He joined the squadron of the Comte d'Aché, whose captains included Marion Dufresne and D'Après de Mannevillette. They fought at Cuddalore and Porto Novo, Surville being wounded and receiving the Cross of St Louis on 30 March 1759. In December of that year his brother René-Louis was killed in action and Surville took over command of the *Centaure*, of seventy guns, in which he sailed to Madagascar to fetch supplies for the Ile de France. Given a commission in the royal navy as post-captain he transferred to the royal ship, *Fortuné*, of sixty-four guns, and served as flag captain to D'Aché's successor, Amiral de St-Georges. When the war was over he sailed home with the Cambrésis regiment and a number of civilians, but the ship foundered off Fish Bay, east of the Cape of Good Hope: he was nevertheless able to reach Capetown without loss, even succeeding in saving the cargo. He returned to India in the *Duc de Praslin* in April 1764. Back in France in July 1766, he began planning a series of trading voyages in Eastern waters which he had already discussed with Law de Lauriston, whose deputy he had been appointed in connection with the restoration and rebuilding of Pondicherry.

The *St Jean-Baptiste* was built in Nantes for Law, Chevalier and Surville who obtained supplementary funds from several Lorient merchants. He sailed in the new ship from Port-Louis on 3 June 1767, reaching the Ile de France in November and the mouth of the Ganges in March 1768. He left in April for Ceylon, although the monsoon was unfavourable, sighted Ceylon in July, but decided against landing and veered north for Madras which he reached at the end of the month; on 4 August he sailed again, calling at various trading posts and taking a load of salt at Binganapali for Chandernagore which he unloaded in September.[1] The next months were spent on preparations for the major expedition the three partners were planning, the garbled news of the rediscovery of Tahiti by Wallis having reached French India and led to a change of emphasis from a voyage to China to a voyage into the Pacific. Two lieutenants, Jacques Bourde de la Villehuet – Surville's nephew by marriage – and Alexis de la Vigne-Buisson, were paid off and replaced by Guillaume Labé and Pottier de l'Horme. The expedition sailed on 3 March 1769. Surville was drowned off Chilca in Peru on 7 April 1770.

Surville married Marie Jouanneaulx in Nantes in September 1750. They had two children, Jean-Louis and Jean-François, who both served as officers in the army; the latter wounded at the siege of Pondicherry in 1778 died of his wounds at the Cape; Jean-Louis rose to the rank of captain in the Artois regiment, but had no descendants. Marie de Surville received a pension from the king and is recorded as still living at Port-Louis in 1789 at the outbreak of the Revolution.

The character of Jean-François de Surville is a complex one. Much of what we know of him comes to us from Guillaume Labé who was irascible and prejudiced and, one can go so far as to say, closer to the stereotype of the old sea captain. Labé's comments are a mixture of grudging admiration and petty criticism. Undeniably, Labé suffered because Surville did not confide in him enough – and yet Labé had

[1] *Extrait du journal de voyage...de Bengal à Ceilan et côte Coromandel, contre mousson,* Marine 4JJ 108, no. 161.

invested in the venture a sum which for him was considerable – but the expedition had to be shrouded in secrecy if the suspicions of the English, to say nothing of the Dutch and the Spanish, were not to be aroused. There was more to the captain's attitude than a concern for security, of course; Surville was in charge, he had had a distinguished career which included a period in command of royal ships, he was one of the main partners and, as a report in his personal file states, he was "a great sailor, a fine soldier, suited to great enterprises, active, witty, firm and determined, a man attentive to details'.[1] The pettiness of Labé's complaints is evidenced by the protracted row over the chickens as early as 19 August 1769: 'As we already had some sick aboard, our surgeon wanted some chickens to give them. There was a disagreement over this. The result was a strong reply that since they were needed for the sick this was quite acceptable but they would no longer be served at the officers' table. We expect this is one of our captain's jokes.'[2] But it was no joke, as Labé plaintively points out on several occasions. Was it a sign of stubbornness on the part of Surville, or was the captain concerned, as Labé was, about the quality and amount of supplies taken on board for such a long voyage? Or does it reflect what was undeniably an important trait in his character – a real concern for his men, carried to a degree that was exceedingly unusual among merchant captains in the eighteenth century? Time and again we find him postponing some manœuvre or shortening sail to avoid tiring his men or to give those in danger of falling sick some opportunity to rest at night.[3] He showed a rare understanding of the subsistence level of the Maoris' economy and took care not to make unreasonable demands on their meagre reserves of food.[4] His gifts of animals and seeds to them, at a time when food stocks on board were dangerously low, are further examples of his generosity, not unmixed with an element of rashness or at least some optimism about a more profitable landfall in the not too distant future in the Pacific. Labé certainly disagreed with the captain's attitude: 'Mr Surville is too considerate towards them. They do not deserve it. They are scoundrels and great thieves.'[5]

Surville's attitude towards the young Solomon Islander and the Maori taken by the expedition reveals the same element of kindness. Indeed his treatment of them is nothing short of astonishing – he had them at his table, exempted them from any work and saw that they

---

[1] Colonies C2.289:8. [2] Labé, *Journal*, 24 August 1769.
[3] E.g. *Journal*, 12, 21, 25, 27, 31 October, 26 December 1769, 10 January 1770.
[4] See entries of 23 and 26 December 1769. [5] *Journal*, 23 December 1769.

did not suffer from the shortage of food. Not surprisingly, Labé was critical of the whole thing: 'Mr Surville treats [the Maori] very well, has him eat at the officers' table and sleep in the quarter-deck cabin, as well as the little kaffir taken in Port Praslin. They are the first to be served at table and with the best, which means almost nothing is left.'[1] Admittedly, this solicitude, which did not extend to the same degree to the Bashi islanders, may have been due to a desire to preserve the health of natives from little known areas, who could later provide him with useful information about their countries and their resources, but much the same results could have been obtained by a different approach. Against Surville's treatment of Lova and Ranginui we have to set his kidnapping of them. In a period of slave trading and press-ganging, the charge is not so serious as it would be today, and in Maori society revenge or *utu* was normal: the Maoris had stolen the yawl, some form of vengeance was to be expected and not necessarily against the actual individuals who had committed the offence; that some action on Surville's part was expected is clear from the Maori's cautious attitude towards him. This is not to exonerate the Frenchman from an act which was the result of tiredness and exasperation, but it has been built up out of all proportion over the years and has cast a shadow over his name ever since.

The difference between Labé and Surville in their attitudes towards native people is shown by the latter's comments of 29 December. Congratulating himself on good relations with the Maoris, Surville says: 'This proves that it is better to become accepted by gentleness and patience than by strength and violence, which moreover seem to me rather unjust towards people who are in their own country and have never thought of coming to disturb you in yours.'

There is no gainsaying his enthusiasm for exploration and his eagerness to learn more about the countries of which, obviously, he could only explore the coastline – his journal provides ample evidence of this.[2] In taking his three hostages from the Bashi Islands and repeating his action in the Solomons and in New Zealand, he was, like a botanist gathering leaves or a geologist chipping rocks, a scientist collecting anthropological specimens which he treated with all the consideration his circumstances allowed.

Surville's character led to his death. Unwilling to wait a day longer for help for his men, he decided to go ashore across the stormy Chilca Bar which a more cautious Labé had already rowed to but found too

[1] Ibid., 4 January 1770.   [2] E.g. entry of 6 November 1769.

dangerous to cross. The attempt was generous but rash, and it cost him his life.

Guillaume Labé was a native of St Malo, although his date of birth is not known. He does not appear on the registers of the French India Company, not even among the petty officers among whom were recruited many of the ships' officers who served in Eastern waters in the *vaisseaux de la côte*. Yet it is clear from internal evidence that he had spent many years in the East: he comments on 2 February 1770 that he suffers from the cold, 'having spent so many years in very hot climates' and on 10 May 1773 that he had left France for the last time in 1752; his report on Trengganu mentions that he was in Bengal in 1744; and, on the admittedly slender evidence that the syndicate agreed to pay his wife a pension in rupees, rather than in French *livres*, it appears that he had settled in India, rather than the Ile de France.

There can be no doubt that he was a man of experience and of some seniority. Surville was glad to have him on board and shows on several occasions that he regarded him highly, both as a man and as a sailor. That he was a man of substance is shown by his financial commitment to the enterprise and by his final remarks, on 23 August 1773, that he had lost 58,000 *livres*.

His journal, rich in comments, many of them critical, gives the impression that he played Sancho Panza to Surville's Don Quixote, and that he was not many years younger than the captain himself. It is probable that he was in his forties and that he had gone to India as a relatively junior petty officer on a merchant ship, and had amassed a fair fortune through a combination of trade on land and of coastal merchant ventures dating back to the late 1740s.

Prior to his joining the *St Jean-Baptiste*, he had served as first officer in the *Concorde*, which he left for reasons of ill health in early 1768; this vessel, earlier known as the *Merry*, belonged to the India Company between 1762 and 1767 when it was apparently renamed and sold to 'Moors' – she is recorded as arriving in Surat in 1769 after refitting for delivery to her new owners. After his return to France in 1773, Labé was taken on as a *capitaine de brûlot* (fireship captain) as a 'blue officer', one of a large group of merchant navy officers who were granted temporary and on occasions permanent appointments in the royal navy when the need arose. This appointment suggests that he had distinguished himself as a privateer during the Seven Years' War, as the grade of fireship captain was reserved for 'those captains of merchant ships or corsairs who, quite apart from a recognised level of experience in navigation, had carried out a brilliant feat of arms during a war'.[1] However, he saw no action and we find him on 7 April 1775 sailing for India as captain of the merchant vessel *Le Boynes* owned by Jean-Baptiste Chevalier, of Chandernagore.

Gruff, down to earth, pessimistic, Guillaume Labé nevertheless had a kind heart. We find him cursing the ship's suppliers, cursing himself for having been foolish enough to join such an ill-equipped expedition, complaining about not being consulted by Surville – and possibly tricked into investing his money in the project – about some of his fellow officers and especially the chaplain, about the construction of the ship, about the weather, the treacherous islanders, and indeed about most things, including some which seem to us rather petty. But he was generous with the men, visiting the sick daily and giving them small 'douceurs' – jam, sweetmeats, wine – from his dwindling store; and his comments on the Bashi islanders, even though he thought Surville should have kidnapped a few more, show sympathy and friendliness towards them. On the other hand, his rage against the Spanish and especially against the 'infamous' Demetrius Egan knows no bound and at times reaches the ridiculous. It was a combination of exasperation and rigid determination that led him to restore order with blows from his stick when, on the voyage home, the Spanish crewmen began to grumble.

For much of the voyage Labé was a sick man. His health had already troubled him when he was serving in the *Concorde*, his years in the East had affected him, and on top of the privations on board the *St Jean-Baptiste*, the shortage of food and water and the stench of scurvy, he had been severely wounded in the Solomons. He had soon lost the enthusiasm which the syndicate had infused in him and did not share for very long the vision which sustained the captain through so many difficulties. Davis Land might or might not exist: what really mattered was trade. We note how carefully he records their first, and as it turned out their only commercial transactions at Trengganu. His natural pessimism soon found more than enough to feed on as the voyage proceeded.

Of his knowledge of eastern seas there can be no doubt. His comments appear almost as soon as the expedition sailed and on most occasions, making allowance for his gloomy disposition, they are justified. Certainly, they are coloured by the uncertainty in which he

---

[1] Article 15 of an order-in-council of September 1764, quoted in Aman, *Les Officiers bleus dans la marine française au XVIIIe Siècle*, p. 108.

found himself about the real aims of the voyage. Surville knew that in him he had an officer of wide experience and utter dependability; it is more than likely that he took note of many of Labé's views, although to preserve his own position he seldom openly acknowledged it. The captain's journal, not by any means overfull of comments about his officers, makes it abundantly clear that he held Labé in high regard – and, grumbles notwithstanding, the reverse is also true: 'I have lost a real friend', Labé wrote when the shattering news of Surville's death reached him. From then on, it was his duty to cope with the multiplicity of problems the drowning created and to bring the ship and the crew safely home. And this with a rare determination and typical skill, he carried out.

Pierre-Antoine Monneron was the twelfth child of Antoine Monneron (1703–1791), a lawyer and salt tax inspector of Annonay in the Vivarais, and of Barbe Catherine Arnaud (1718–1792), a relative of Dupleix. He was born in Annonay on 26 January 1747 and was therefore only twenty-two when he sailed with Surville.

However, his relative youth should not lead one to underrate his importance as Law and Chevalier's representative on board – which Labé seems to have done until after Surville's death. Antoine's offspring numbered twenty, of whom seven travelled abroad and four, including Pierre, became *députés*. Several were influential in eastern trade matters. One, Paul-Méraut, born in 1748, sailed with La Pérouse and was drowned with him. Another, Charles-Claude-Ange (1735–1799) entered the office of Dupleix's brother, later transferred to the *Compagnie des Indes* and eventually became a member of the Pondicherry *Conseil Supérieur*, a post he held at the time of the Surville expedition. Jean-Louis (1742–1805) went out to Pondicherry with Charles and was the author of a *Mémoire en faveur des colonies françaises des Indes* (1790). Both were elected *députés* during the early years of the Revolution, the fourth brother to join them being Joseph-François-Augustin (1756–1824).[1]

Pierre-Antoine was involved in a number of commercial ventures with his brothers, and was presumably selected for the *St Jean-Baptiste* expedition because of his connections; after his return he continued working for the family firm, but remained in touch with the court and Indian affairs.

[1] See on the Monneron family: Bouchary, *Les Manieurs d'argent à Paris à la fin du XVIIIe Siècle*, III, 181–247; Luthy, *La Banque protestante en France*, II; Sen, *The French in India*; and Nicod, 'Monneron aîné' in *Revue historique du Vivarais*, IX.

At the conclusion of the 1778–1783 wars, Bussy appointed him to negotiate the restitution of France's territories in India; in 1790, following the outbreak of the Revolution, we find him preparing a case for the National Assembly on behalf of the citizens of Pondicherry. By then, the Monnerons had established a powerful commercial organisation with branches in France, India and the Ile de France. Their fortune was claimed by their opponents to amount to fifteen million *livres*, leading Pierre-Antoine to deny this in a leaflet published in Paris in 1791: *Réponse de M. Pierre-Antoine Monneron, député de la colonie de l'isle-de-France*. But disaster was lying in wait for them. The Monnerons were granted a licence to issue *petits assignats*, small copper coins that were issued through their Paris offices and their provincial branches; but inflation destroyed the value of the *assignats* large and small, and Monneron et Cie were forced into bankruptcy in March 1792.

Pierre-Antoine was first reported to have taken his own life, but he had in fact fled to Marseilles, where he embarked for India where he hoped, as he wrote in 'Mon Odyssée,[1] to retrieve 'a fairly considerable fortune dissipated in the space of three years by a blind trust in a few false friends'. He seems to have been only partly successful, for we find him later imprisoned in Jeddah and appealing for help from the French Ambassador in Constantinople. He attempted to return to India in 1802 but disappeared, presumed drowned, in the Persian Gulf.

Jean Pottier de l'Horme – as he appears in his voluminous Journal – may have been a grandson or great-nephew of Joseph Pottier, sieur des Ormes, second-in-command of the *Grande Reine d'Espagne* which carried out a circumnavigation in 1711–1714, the heyday of French trade with Spanish South America. The name is also found variously spelt as de l'Orme and Delorme.

He was born in St Malo, the likely date being 8 July 1738, the son of Jacques Pottier. He sailed to India at a relatively early age and became an 'officier de côte', serving on French India Company ships in eastern waters. We find him sailing as such, with the rank of lieutenant, in the *Ajax* on 5 October 1764 from the Ile de France, arriving in Lorient on 6 May 1765. He returned to Mauritius at the beginning of 1766 with his wife, Marianne Le Garoux, as passengers in the *Condé*. They arrived on 15 June 1766 and Pottier subsequently joined the India Co. ship *St Charles* as second lieutenant. He may have served in that ship on previous occasions, as she had been a 'vaisseau de côte' since 1756.

[1] Reprinted in *La Revue de Paris*, August 1907, pp. 569–96.

In spite of his erratic spelling, Pottier was far from uneducated. On arriving off the coast of Peru on 5 April 1778 he quoted in his Journal two lines from Voltaire's play *Alzire*:

> Cette contrée aux malheurs féconde
> Qui produit les trésors et les crimes du monde.[1]

His Journal is very long, filled with minute details about winds, the temperature and the ship's course, but also with a number of observations on the places the French visited – eight pages on Trengganu, ten on the Bashi Islands, seventeen on Port Praslin in the Solomons and twenty-four on New Zealand.

He gives few details, however, about life on board and the misfortunes of the *St Jean-Baptiste* which are not recorded, in a more direct manner, by Surville and Labé, very little information about his fellow officers and practically none about himself. One obtains the impression of a serious-minded officer, devoted to his duties, a reliable, human observer who kept himself to himself to the extent that this was possible in a small and mostly overcrowded ship.

Hughes-Jean-Marie de Surville was the captain's nephew. Born in Nantes, he had been appointed second ensign in 1764, largely as a posthumous tribute to his father, René-Louis de Surville (1710–1759) who had displayed great bravery in a naval engagement on 10 September 1759 (Archives Nationales, Marine, (2.289, f.33).

Hughes is recorded as sailing from Lorient for India as second ensign in the *Duc de Praslin* on 22 April 1764, being then recently turned 20. The ship returned on 20 July 1766 from Port-Louis.

There is no Journal by him in existence, and we may presume that he did not keep one. His relations with Labé were stormy – no doubt he considered that his family links with the deceased captain entitled him to some special consideration – and he deserted with the chaplain, Villefeix, during the night of 9 September 1771. The intention of the two fugitives was to prospect for gold: when they were arrested near Lima on 6 October they were found in possession of the usual prospectors' impedimenta of pickaxes and shovels. Time must have weighed heavy on the Frenchmen in Peru, with little else to do than

---

[1] 'This country, fertile in misfortunes, which produces the world's treasures and its crimes.' Appropriately, *Alzire* is set in Peru, in the sixteenth century, and a leading character is a harsh Spanish governor. The play, first produced in 1736, was one of Voltaire's greatest successes. The extract should read 'cette rive, en malheurs trop féconde' – 'this shore, all too fertile in misfortunes' (Act I, sc. i); the slight inaccuracy shows that Pottier did not have a copy on board.

await Monneron's return from his diplomatic mission in France, with little money and the constant chafing of shipboard discipline. Yet one wonders whether Hughes had not been sent out in the *St Jean-Baptiste* so that his uncle could keep an eye on an unruly youngster.

He deserted a second time during the night of 4 to 5 January 1772 and is heard of no more, except for an appeal three years later by Monneron for part repayment of a loan of 1749 *livres*. This appeal was addressed to the Navy in the hope that a total of some 1269 *livres*, arrears of pay held by the naval treasurer at Lorient to the credit of Hughes de Surville, could be paid over to Monneron. Although it was unlawful for officers to lend money to others, an exception was made, after the matter had been referred to Labé, on the grounds that the exceptionally long and arduous voyage had created a special situation and that a refusal would have been unjustifiable. Labé confirmed that the 1749 *livres* had been spent on necessities: 'linen and clothes in the local style'. That Monneron was successful in obtaining the 1269 *livres* was based on the official view that young Surville's desertion deprived the lender of any other legal recourse.

René Charenton, was the son of Jean and Perrine Charenton and was born in Lorient in 1730. He is first recorded as sailing for India in April 1749 in the *Auguste*, a ship of the French India Company, with the rank of third *pilote* and emoluments of 22 *livres*. He was back in France in January 1752; on 21 May, he sailed for Senegal as *pilote* at 25 *livres* in *Le Cerf*; he sailed again for Senegal, on 3 May 1753, this time in the *Cybèle*, at 36 livres. He made a third voyage to Senegal in *Le Petit Chasseur*; on 30 November 1753, as first *pilote* at 45 *livres*.

His career was therefore a very successful one for a young man in his early twenties, with rapid advancement, and he gives the picture of a man of promise and ability. He next made two voyages to India, the first in 1755–1757 in the Company's frigate *Danaë*, the second in the *Baleine* from March 1758. His next voyage was less fortunate: he was taken prisoner on 7 October 1760, and he spent 1761 and 1762 as a prisoner of war in England. He was repatriated by way of Cherbourg in early 1763 and sailed for India in April 1764. He joined the *St Jean-Baptiste* in Pondicherry on 30 May 1769 at 120 *livres* and served, faithfully and efficiently until the very last when, on 5 April 1773, a mere two days before the ship was to sail home from Peru, he deserted.

What his reason was, we do not know. Was he enticed by some Peruvian shipowners anxious to use his skills? Did he believe that Peru held greater prospects for him than did the French merchant navy now that the French India Company had been dissolved? Had he formed some liaison ashore? Whatever it was, he waited until the very last, when Labé, all his preparations made for the long awaited voyage back to Europe, would be in no mood to delay and he vanished silently and finally.

Amable Lorry was born in Nantes in 1750. He was therefore a very young officer who joined the *St Jean-Baptiste* in 1767, firstly as an unpaid *volontaire*, then as a supernumerary ensign at 50 *livres*. He proved his worth, was appointed second ensign at 80 *livres* then, on 9 April 1770, the day when Surville's death was confirmed, he was promoted to first ensign at 95 *livres*. He is recorded as serving as ensign in the privately owned merchantman *Le Dauphin* which left France for China on 21 March 1775, apparently landing at the Ile de France where he seems to have settled, because on 31 May 1777 he sailed from there in the merchant vessel *Les Trois Amis* for China and signed off when the ship was back in Mauritius on 21 April 1778.

François Avice was born in Cancale in 1749. He had sailed in *La Marie* from Bayonne to Miquelon off the coast of Canada at the age of fifteen, and in *Le Hardy* on various voyages from 1765 to 1768, making his way to the Ile de France, where he joined the *St Charles* and then the *St Jean-Baptiste*, firstly as a *volontaire* at 21 *livres*, then in the reorganisation which following the final desertion of Hughes de Surville as second ensign at 80 *livres*. After the return of the expedition to France in 1773, he sailed back to India, joining the *Ville de Lorient* as an unpaid ensign on 4 February 1774.

The surgeon, *Pierre Dulucq*, was born, according to the Muster Roll, in Ste Boisse (more correctly St. Boès) in Béarn, in the foothills of the Pyrenees. The name is not uncommon in the district. He was born in 1738 and is first recorded in 1764 when he joined the *Penthièvre*, a French India Company ship, as assistant surgeon, sailing from Lorient on 21 February and returning on 14 June 1765. He then joined the *St Jean-Baptiste* in 1767 at 45 *livres* as chief surgeon, his assistant being Jean Le Clère Hamon, from Nantes, who was drowned 'in a pond in Bengal' on 26 April 1768 and replaced by Antoine Terradec, from Rochefort. On 1 September 1768 Dulucq's monthly pay was raised to 80 *livres*, and he completed the voyage at this rate, being paid off in Lorient on 20 August 1773 – the higher rate would seem to be motivated by the greater responsibility involved in a voyage of exploration: certainly, few ship's surgeons would have faced greater burdens and met with greater hardships, and one can hardly begrudge him the 5105 *livres* payable to him at the end of the voyage.

Jean de St Paul, who joined the *St Jean-Baptiste* in Pondicherry on 28 June 1769 with a detachment of 24 men may be that same Captain de St Paul, then in the service of the French India Company, who sailed from Lorient in the *Berryer* on 2 February 1762 for the Ile de France, arriving on 14 June 1762. He would have remained for several years in the Ile de France, which had a strong garrison, and subsequently went to Pondicherry where the main bulk of French troops – some 400 to 500 men and officers – were stationed from 1765 on. A Lieutenant-Colonel de St Paul, of the Pondicherry regiment, is listed as a passenger in the private vessel, *Le Superbe*, sailing with his two sons, François and Jean-Baptiste, from St Malo on 15 April 1783 for the Ile de France.

Hibon de Villemont deserves a brief mention: his part in the expedition was limited to the voyage from Chandernagore to Pondicherry. He was another of the 'officiers de côte', men who had settled more or less permanently in India or the Ile de France and served in ships of the French Indian Company.

He came from the *Saint-Charles*, as did a number of the *St Jean-Baptiste*'s complement, but signed off at Pondicherry on 15 May. He was still there a year later for we find him joining the Company merchantman *Marquis de Sance* on 16 June 1770, signing off at the Ile de France a month later, on 27 July.

Mention must also be made of *Martin Hérigoyen*, a young man who joined the *St Jean-Baptiste* in Pondicherry and is listed as a passenger. He was in all probability a *volontaire*, without emoluments at this stage in his career. In his position, he had none of the small advantages, such as a private store of wines, jams and dried fruit, that the officers enjoyed, and he was not strong enough to resist the strains of the voyage; he was one of the first whites to die – on 9 November 1769, not long after the ship finally left the Solomons.

★ ★

As for the crew, the vast majority came from Brittany, and not surprisingly from the coast. The areas around Port-Louis, Lorient, and Nantes, supplied fewer than the ports along the northern coast – St Malo, St Servan, Dinan, Paramé and the small villages that surround them. Western Brittany was the home of a number of them – Brest, Quimper, St Pol de Léon – but only a few came from inland Brittany, mostly from Rennes. These together totalled just under a hundred.

There were a couple of Normans, one man from Provence, and a sprinkling of men from parts of non-maritime France, such as Dauphiné, Périgord, Savoy, Orléans and Paris. A handful of foreigners also served on board, one each from Brussels, Luxemburg and Prussia. Where the information is available, it indicates, as one would expect, that the soldiers came from a variety of backgrounds – from Toulouse, Paris, Orleans, Burgundy, even from Italy, but not from seaports.

Most of the men were in their mid-twenties, the petty officers in their thirties or forties. Undoubtedly many of them knew each other: the considerable number who came from such relatively small towns and villages as St Méloir, Pleurtuit, St Enogat, Châteauneuf de Faou, suggests that they may have been related or that they grew up together. The consequent poignant effect on these places of the high number of deaths that occurred during the voyage can easily be imagined and gives an added dimension to the tragedy.

As the voyage proceeded the condition of the men worsened. Whatever small extras by the way of food, wine or tobacco some may have been able to afford to bring on board were soon used up; nor were there other facilities, or ports of call where they could buy supplies or replace items of clothing. By the time the *St Jean-Baptiste* reached South America, the crew must have been, not merely emaciated and sick, but literally covered in rags. Their standard form of dress was at the best functional and rudimentary, with little space available on board to store any personal effects. A recent work describes them as follows:

> They were dressed in a seamless shirt tied at the neck by a small cord. A broad woollen scarf protected the neck. In cold weather they wore a thick jersey over this shirt with a long woollen cape with a hood called a *mante*. They worked barefoot and barelegged as their breeches did not reach below the knee. When the weather was rough they put on a type of leather or oilskin boots and clogs stuffed with straw. Their head was covered with a tall pointed woollen bonnet which came down over their ears, enclosing their hair, which they took care to keep long and thick if for no other reason than to avoid being taken for former convicts.[1]

By comparison, the officers wore a coat, waistcoat and breeches, usually blue in colour, with gold braid, but it is clear from the monetary transaction which took place between Monneron and Hughes de Surville in Lima that by that time the officers' clothes were also in a bad state.

[1] Picard *et al.*, *Les Compagnies des Indes*, p. 201.

(ii) *The Backers*

Jean Law, Baron Lauriston, was born in 1719. His father was William Law, the brother of the famous Scotsman John Law who established the *Banque générale* and the Mississippi scheme during the Regency of the Duc d'Orléans. William had four children; Jean's brother Jacques-François, Comte de Tancarville, who died in 1766, was the father of Jacques-Alexandre Law de Lauriston who became one of Napoléon's generals and a Count of the Empire.[1]

The collapse of John Law's *système* did not spell disaster for the family. Although John died in exile, the Duchesse de Bourbon, who had succeeded in getting out at a profit before it was too late, took William's family under her protection. Jean himself inherited the title, as John had no male issue. Both he and his brother went out to French India – we find Jacques taken prisoner by Lawrence at the 1752 siege of Trichinopoly.[2] Jean went out at the age of 23 and by 1754 was in charge of the factory at Kazimbazar. After the fall of Chandernagore in March 1757 some of the garrison escaped to Kazimbazar, fled to Bhagalpur, and took service under Ali Gauhar, the future Shah Alam II, to harrass the victorious British. Law, it is apparent, was no strategist, but a brave soldier. 'He was taken prisoner after the battle of Gayá in 1761, fighting gallantly, it is true, atoning to some extent by his personal valour for his many faults as a general and a leader'.[3]

Sent back to France in 1761, Law was promoted to the rank of colonel and given the Order of St Louis. In 1764 he was appointed Governor of the Indian settlements returned to France by the peace treaty; he arrived in Madras on 29 January 1764, took possession of Karikal and of Pondicherry, and at once set about the task of reorganising the administration and rebuilding the city and its defences.

Although the liquidation of the French India Company and the freeing of the eastern trade resulted in a division of responsibilities in India, with the *Intendant* supervising finances and trade and the Governor dealing with political issues, Law seems not to have been inhibited in any way from backing commercial ventures like that of the *St Jean-Baptiste*. According to Luthy,[4] Law and Chevalier were still business associates in 1775 – 'ce consortium...constitue à lui seul une petite Compagnie des Indes'. His term as governor ended in 1777.

[1] La Chenaye-Desbois, *Dictionnaire de la noblesse*.
[2] Priestly, *France Overseas*, p. 193.
[3] Malleson, *History of the French in India*, p. 475.
[4] *La Banque protestante en France*, II, 453–5.

Jean Law was the author of a number of *mémoires* on French India, including the lucid, if at times biased, *Mémoire sur quelques affaires du Grand Mogol*, and *L'Etat général de l'Inde en 1777*. He had married in 1755 his sister-in-law Jeanne Carvalho; they had one daughter, and his branch of the family died with her.

Jean-Baptiste Chevalier, Seigneur de Caunan, from Vendômois, was appointed governor of Chandernagore in July 1767. Chevalier, a colourful and determined person, had served at the French factory in Dacca before the oubreak of the Seven Years' War. One's opinion of his character depends on one's point of view. He was motivated by the desire to defend and if possible extend the French sphere of influence in Bengal against the encroachment and suspicions of the British in Calcutta.

'His intricate understanding of the political situation in northern India, together with his passionate attachment to France, made him an opponent worthy of a Clive or a Hastings' is the judgment of one modern historian[1] who also praises his vigorous leadership. He was, by and large, unsuccessful, certainly in his more grandiose schemes. The days of Dupleix were over, never to return, and the next war with England put an end to all of France's aspirations. Thenceforth, the French remained in India purely on sufferance. Consequently Chevalier has been judged less sympathetically from a different viewpoint:

> [He had] an optimism sometimes bordering on facile imaginativeness and with a blind patriotism which on occasions brought him ridicule even from his compatriots. He kept himself in constant touch with the Princes of north India and with the French military adventurers scattered all over the sub-continent, intrigued at every *Darbar*, and never doubted for a moment that it was possible for France, even at that late hour, to drive the English out of Bengal with the help of some of the Indian princes...Although the British in Bengal considered him as their most dangerous enemy, to his own countrymen he remained a ridiculous figure who merely put forward fantastic projects.[2]

He eventually had to flee from Chandernagore in July 1778, but was arrested three weeks later at Cuttack; released on parole, he returned to France in 1779 to find that he had lost much of his political influence. There were suggestions in 1781 and again in 1782, possibly prompted

---

[1] Kennedy, 'Anglo-French Rivalry in India and the Eastern Seas', p. 87.
[2] Sen, *The French in India*, pp. 112–13.

by himself, that he should be sent as ambassador to the court of the Moghul, but nothing came of it, and he lost credibility when France realised that the power of the emperor was only a sham and that any alliance with him could not have any tangible results.

Chevalier, like Law, was very wealthy. He lived at Goretty, the residence built by Dupleix, outside Chandernagore itself, which he transformed into 'a great palace, the architectural beauty of which was an object of admiration to all and where came every week-end the Governor and members of the Calcutta Council.'[1]

II. MOTIVES AND AIMS OF THE EXPEDITION

No copy of the instructions has been found. There is none in the archives of the Marine where the various journals are held, none in Surville's personal file, and if a copy exists among the papers of Law de Lauriston or Chevalier it has not come to light. The only known copy was destroyed as dangerously incriminating by Labé and Monneron after Surville's death off the coast of Peru.

We should not anyhow expect the kind of detailed instructions that were issued to Kerguelen or La Pérouse, because unlike these official voyages the expedition of the *St Jean-Baptiste* was a privately organised commercial venture, literally *à l'aventure* as the sixteenth-century explorers put it, in search of a new land and the trade it might bring.

Furthermore, Surville himself was a leading partner in the triumvirate that backed the expedition. He knew what was involved, as he had been privy to all the discussions and a moving force in the undertaking, possibly its main instigator. All that was really needed was a partnership agreement which laid down the financial outlay and the proportional sharing of eventual profits, together with a broad outline of the voyage.

A similar situation is found in the case of Marion Dufresne's expedition to the Pacific of 1771–2. His voyage was also a private undertaking, his only links with the French authorities being the return of the Tahitian Ahu-toru to his native island and financial assistance to enable him to proceed. Thus when he was killed in New Zealand, and his second-in-command examined his papers to ascertain what should be done to achieve the aims of the voyage:

'We found only some very detailed notes in the guise of instructions from the civil administration of the Ile de France which, while leaving M. Marion master of his activities and his exploration, simply set out

[1] Ibid., p. 87.

the best way of carrying out his observations, and of directing them towards objectives likely to be the most useful to our colonies and in general to the advancement of human knowledge.'[1]

Surville's officers were no better informed. On 26 August 1769 Labé complains that he was not consulted on the route to be followed after their departure from the Bashi Islands; less than a month later, on 23 September, he again confides to his journal his dissatisfaction – 'I have no idea what M. Surville proposes to do, as he has never spoken of his plans'. After their departure from the Solomons, the same plaint occurs, on 8 and 10 November. The next day he speculates on whether the captain is endeavouring to reach Hoorn Island. Surville did discuss the desirability of making for New Zealand on 24 November, and Labé promptly agreed; but on 26 February 1770 an entry in the latter's Journal makes it clear that Labé knew little about a search for Davis Land, since he writes that 'it seems' that Surville is making for the latitude of 'the so-called Land of Davis', an island in whose existence Labé patently did not believe.

If Labé knew little about the real aims of the voyage, we can assume that other officers, Pottier de l'Horme, Avice, Dulucq, St Paul, knew even less. Monneron was in a different position as the representative of Law and Chevalier, with some, relatively obscure connections with Pondicherry bankers such as Delessert; but even he was a subordinate. His summary accounts of the voyage do not help us to reconstruct the actual instructions, because they were written at the conclusion of the voyage – the 'Rédaction abrégée' makes this obvious, and the title 'Extrait du Journal' is not to be taken as an indication that Monneron kept his own log: as a ship's clerk he was not required to.

Labé's Journal, as we have seen, only illustrates the lack of knowledge of the first officer, even though he had invested what was for him a very considerable sum. The introductory section does suggest a relatively precise itinerary: Pondicherry to Malacca, the China Seas and the Philippines, a voyage of discovery in the Pacific, both north and south, then to New Guinea and New Zealand, with the return journey by way of Manila, China and Batavia. The problem is that Labé's Journal is a copy, which includes items inserted after the event and that, for instance, the call in New Zealand seems, from the internal evidence of both Surville and Labé's logs, to have been forced on the French by circumstances, rather than planned. Nevertheless the section taken as a whole gives a fair impression of what was envisaged. The

---

[1] Crozet, *Nouveau Voyage*, pp. 123–4.

comparable section in Pottier de l'Horme's Journal is far less informative: 'Journal of the voyage around the world...containing the relation of the discovery of a considerable extent of land east of New Guinea [and] the circumstances of the landfall and stay in New Zealand'.

Pottier does on two occasions refer to 'instructions'. When Surville gathered his officers for a meeting after their departure from New Zealand, he read a clause forbidding the expedition to sail to Spanish America;[1] and on 6 March 1770 Monneron read a clause urging 'the officers to display the utmost constancy and firmness, so necessary in a voyage of exploration' and sought their views on the search for Davis Land then in progress.[2] The first clause is to some extent contradicted by a plan for a voyage to Acapulco which Labé found and burnt on 11 April 1770. Neither of Pottier's statements alters the view that specific instructions containing a precise itinerary probably did not exist: if they had, then either Labé or Monneron would have found them. Pottier in fact confirms the state of affairs when, after Surville's death, he notes that Labé's new role as leader of the expedition is likely to be a difficult one because 'M. de Surville told none of the officers anything about his intentions or his instructions'.[3]

There is however sufficient indirect evidence to enable us to reconstruct the motives and aims of the voyage.

The basic factor was trade, an alternative form of employment for Surville, following the collapse of the French India Company and the anticipated abolition of its monopoly. The finances of the kingdom after the Seven Years' War were in desperate conditions and the hard-pressed *contrôleurs des finances* had more serious problems on their hands than shoring up the 44-year-old monopoly. It was in fact suppressed in August 1769 and the Company itself was dissolved in April of the following year. The government could do little more than try to cushion the blow for those who had spent years in the Company's service. Some officers and men entered the royal navy, others were given every facility to work for private shipowners:

His Majesty, wishing to ensure that, for as long as the operations of the India Company shall be suspended, the officers of the said Company may continue to be employed, not merely on voyages to various parts of India, China and the seas beyond the Cape of Good Hope, but also for any other destination...orders...that the

[1] Pottier, *Journal*, p. 245.   [2] Ibid., p. 283.
[3] Ibid., p. 313.

Captains, first and second lieutenants of the India Company shall be allowed to command ships sent out by His Majesty's subjects to the places where the India Company customarily traded...or to any other destinations.[1]

Surville and Labé did not wait until the last minute to make arrangements for their future. The future role of France in the East after the war was obviously uncertain, and could not fail to raise misgivings in the minds of traders and administrators alike. Law de Lauriston, sailing to India in 1765 in the *Duc de Praslin*, commanded by Surville, must have held long discussions with him during the voyage about political and commercial prospects.

It was obvious that capital would be needed: the moribund French India Company had always suffered from inadequate funds. The addition of Chevalier, rich and intensely patriotic, gave the proposed three-man syndicate far greater stability. Law and Chevalier were wealthy and well connected, and Surville – while he also contributed some capital – had the necessary experience.

After his return to France in July 1766, Surville obtained from the directors of the Company permission to trade in the area covered by its crumbling monopoly. In addition, keeping a final semblance of control over matters, they appointed him their agent and deputy to Law in Pondicherry.[2] This meant little, since the Company was to lose its charter and go into liquidation within three years, but it gave Surville added status and, what was of more immediate value, a greater element of credit-worthiness, for we find him borrowing 50,000 *livres* from two Lorient traders, Bourgeois and Gallois, who had lent considerable sums of money to the Company.[3]

This sum, added to his own 60,000 and the amount made available by Law and Chevalier, enabled Surville to have built the *St Jean-Baptiste* in Nantes – or possibly to take over from the Company the partly completed ship. There is some doubt about what actually happened, but it seems clear that when Surville sailed from Port-Louis in June 1767 the syndicate were effectively the owners, with the hapless Bourgeois and Gallois as ill-secured creditors.[4]

---

[1] Archives de Brest 1-L: 46. Registre des ordonnances No. 8, 13 November 1770.
[2] A notarial copy of the agreement was sent to the Lorient office in May 1767. (Archives du Port 1 P298, 1.24/61).
[3] They appealed for repayments of various sums in 1773 and subsequently, with a separate plea for repayment from the syndicate.
[4] The closing muster roll refers to the '*St Jean-Baptiste* armé à L'Orient le 3 Juin 1767 par la Compagnie des Indes' (Archives du Port de Lorient, Désarmement 14 No. 14), but by the date of this document the Company had been dissolved, and the reference should be read in the light of Surville's appointment as the Company's agent. The legal imbroglio is apparent at every turn.

The *St Jean-Baptiste* after her arrival in India began to trade along the coast as planned, going in particular to Ceylon, and carrying cargoes of rice and salt. In October she was the subject of a protest by Chevalier over an incident in the Ganges when she was stopped and illegally searched by sepoys (Archives des Colonies C2 209 fo. 114, 27 Oct. 1768). A few months later, Law reported to the Minister of Marine that the next voyage was to be to the Philippines: 'The ship *St Jean-Baptiste*...which arrived in India a year ago...is back in Bengal being readied for the Manilas by Surville, Chevalier and other interested parties. I expect her here next month'.[1] But by then something of far greater importance was already being planned; on 30 December, Chevalier sent the first report on the proposed expedition to the Ministry of Marine:

I must now outline the reasons which decided me to leave on the vessel the *St Jean-Baptiste* the European crew she had brought from Europe and even thought it necessary for the good of the service to strengthen it as much as I could. This vessel, as you are aware, My Lord, has been built for two purposes, one being to trade in time of peace and the other to carry out raids against the enemy in time of war...to capture privately-owned English ships and even those of the English Company and therefore cause great harm to their trade as soon as news is received of a declaration of war...

But a second motive which is no less important is a plan for a bold voyage she is about to undertake, and which it is my duty to advise you about, on account both of its importance and of its novelty. The suggestion has been inspired by the English following a strange discovery they have just made and which foreshadows a success as strange as it is remarkable.

One of their ships, recently arrived at the Cape of Good Hope from the South Sea, was driven by the winds towards an island which did not figure on the charts. Although they have taken every precaution to prevent its latitude from being known, nevertheless certain people from the ship have been so enthusiastic about this discovery that they were unable to stop themselves from gossiping, and this is what in broad terms we have learnt:

This island, according to reports, must be situated in approximately 102° west of the Paris meridian. We suspect that it may be the one seen by the Englishman David in 1686 which is marked on the French

[1] Law to de Boynes, Colonies C2 100 fo. 46, 10 February 1769. The expression 'les Manilles' should be interpreted to mean eastern seas as far as Japan, as may be seen from Chevalier's letter, *infra*.

chart. However, the English say that it is not shown on any of theirs. Whatever it is, the adventure is worth attempting and its success could become too important for our nation for me not to be in honour bound to sacrifice everything to make it succeed. In the instructions which I am giving M. de Surville, of which I have the honour to enclose a copy,[1] you will see in detail the plan of this affair and the manner in which we are proposing to carry it out. Should fate not grant us the success we hope for, we may still be recompensed through the attempt which M. de Surville has been instructed to make to open the trade with Japan and share it with the Dutch. For too long they have enjoyed its fruits alone and fooled the public with their fables in order to discourage people from attempting to discover the real facts. The worst that can happen is to fail in both these enterprises, but what harm can it do? At the most a trading loss or rather reduced profits because it is certain that, as a last resource, the sale in Manila of the goods that make up the cargo must repay the costs and expenses of the shipowners.[2]

This document reveals the syndicate's hopes of breaking the Dutch monopoly of the Japanese trade and confirms Labé's view that the voyage of discovery would terminate with a call in Manila. It adds the element of political rivalry which now assumes growing importance and is one more facet of Law and Chevalier's attempts through the decade up to 1778 to expand French trade in the farther East through French trading posts in Manila, Cochin China and Cambodia,[3] as well as Pegu, the Andamans and Mergui.[4]

Chevalier's report is confirmed from a number of sources, the first being Monneron whose 'Extrait du Journal' begins: 'Messrs Law, Chevalier and de Surville, who were the owners, intended to trade in Eastern waters, but they altered this plan on account of news which had spread about the discovery of an island in the South Sea by an English vessel. What came to their knowledge was so extraordinary that it deserved all their attention and viewing this affair from a political point of view, they did not hesitate to complete their arrangements for a second voyage to take possession of this island.'[5]

[1] The copy is not attached.
[2] Chevalier to the Minister, Archives Nationales Colonies C2 99 fos. 254–5, 30 December 1768.
[3] 'The favourite project of de Lauriston and Chevalier entailed a sweeping commercial agreement with Spain which would enable the Company to exploit the China and South American trade through a base in the Philippines.' Kennedy, 'Anglo French rivalry', p. 267. See also p. 268 on Cochin China.
[4] Ibid., p. 271.   [5] Monneron, 'Extrait du Journal', p. 2.

Rochon, who was later to give one of the few printed accounts of the expedition, adds some interesting details:

> I was in Pondicherry in August 1769 when the rumour spread that an English vessel had found in the South Sea a very rich island where, among other peculiarities, a colony of Jews had been settled. The account of this discovery...became so well known that it was believed in India that the purpose of de Surville's voyage...was to search for this marvellous island.'[1]

What and where was this 'marvellous island'? Chevalier quotes only a reputed longitude: 102° west of Paris or approximately 100° west of Greenwich. Monneron confirms this location – '700 leagues approximately west of the coast of Peru'[2] – but he adds a latitude, namely 27 to 28° south. There are unhappily no rich islands – indeed practically no islands at all – in this area. Easter Island fits the location more than the other alternatives, which are Pitcairn, Ducie, Rapa-iti, San Ambrosio, San Felix and Sala-y-Gomez. Easter Island had been discovered by Roggeveen nearly fifty years earlier and there had been no glowing reports then or since about it; similarly Pitcairn discovered by Carteret in July 1767 had not given rise to reports of great potential wealth and was uninhabited.

Chevalier's mention of an English vessel which had called at the Cape of Good Hope in 1768 after discoveries in the Pacific can only be a reference to Wallis and the *Dolphin*. Carteret arrived at the Cape on 28 November and remained until January: his stay does not appear to have given rise to exaggerated reports[3] and it is obvious that whatever information had reached Pondicherry – probably by way of the Ile de France – must have done so during the middle months of 1768.

The reference to David in Chevalier's letter – the other clue to the identification of what triggered the Surville expedition – clinches the matter. A Frenchman will pronounce the letter a in the same way, whatever the syllable in which it is found: David (especially as the correct name is Davis) will be very similar phonetically to Wallis, and whatever French agent at the Cape notified Law could easily have mistaken or misspelt the name of the English captain.[4] Thus, into

---

[1] Rochon, *Voyages aux Indes orientales*, p. 233.
[2] 'Relation abrégée', p. 1.
[3] The log of the French India Company ship *Villevault*, captain Maugendre, which arrived at the Cape on 31 December 1768, records flatly on 6 January the departure for England of 'an English frigate which has sailed round the world'. A.N. Marine 4JJ 108.
[4] Maugendre, of the *Villevault*, reporting the arrival at the Cape of Bougainville's *Boudeuse* on 9 January spells the name 'Boquainville'. Ibid.

Wallis' real discovery of the island of Tahiti was infused almost a century of past speculation about an island or continental mass known as Davis' Land.

It was in 1687 that Edward Davis, in the *Batchelor's Delight*, came across a stretch of land about which he told William Dampier:

> Davis told me that after his Departure from us at the Haven of Rea Lejo...he went, after several Traverses, to the Gallapagoes, and that, standing thence southward for Wind, to bring him about Tierra del Fuego, in Latitude of 27 South, about 500 leagues from Copayapo, on the Coast of Chile, he saw a small sandy Island just by him; and that they saw to the Westward of it a long Tract of pretty high Land, tending away to the North West out of sight. This might probably be the Coast of Terra Australis Incognita.[1]

This final sentence gave great importance to what otherwise might have been a fleeting reference to some minor island. Davis Land lay in that region of the Pacific where the fabled southern continent was still expected to be found. Over the centuries Terra Australis had become endowed in the imagination of many with truly fabulous wealth. In Davis Land the imaginary riches of the fifth continent mingled with the gold and silver mines of Spanish America. Monneron, the clerk, the man who represented business interests, expressed this traditional view when he wrote, 'it was a natural thing to believe that it was much richer than the other countries because it was situated...by the southern latitude of 27 to 28 degrees, which is that of Copiago, where the Spanish obtain gold in enormous quantities.'[2]

If the members of the syndicate had been able to consult another account of the discovery, by the *Batchelor's Delight*'s surgeon Lionel Wafer, they would have hesitated about identifying Wallis' island, a reputed 102° west of Paris, with Davis Land:

> Accordingly, we went [from the Galapagos] again for the Southward, intending to touch no where till we came to the Island of John Fernandino...we steered South and by East, half easterly until we came to the Latitude of 27 Deg. 20 Min. South when, about two hours before Day, we fell in with a low sandy Island.[3]

Now the Galapagos are in 90° 30' west of Greenwich, and anyone sailing south by east could hardly reach a landfall so far to the west;

---

[1] Dampier, *A New Voyage round the World*, p. 352.
[2] Monneron, 'Extrait du Journal', p. 2.   [3] Wafer, *A New Voyage*, p. 125.

even tacking against south-easterlies and struggling against the currents would scarcely have brought the *Batchelor's Delight*, bound as she was for the south-east, to a point much further west than her original longitude. Far more likely, sailing from the Galapagos to Tierra del Fuego or Juan Fernandez, the *Batchelor's Delight* sighted the small islands of San Felix and San Ambrosio, which lie in 26° south, within 30′ of the position assigned by Wafer to Davis Land, and astride 80° west of Greenwich. Some years later, the astronomer Pingré expressed the plausible view that the copyist or the printer had let slip an error 'and that the small island is not 500 leagues distant from Copiapo, but only 150'.[1] Carteret and La Pérouse considered the slip to have been in substituting 'leagues' for 'miles' which amounts to the same thing and confirms the identification of Davis Land with San Felix and San Ambrosio.[2]

A phonological slip may have led the French to prick up their ears at the sound of Wallis and revive the rumours of Davis Land, but something more was needed to arouse their energies to the extent of fitting out the *St Jean-Baptiste* in great secrecy and regardless of cost. Political rivalry was of the essence. Bougainville had attempted to establish a French settlement in the Falklands which would, when the need arose, serve as a defence post against British penetration from the east, particularly if France and Spain could remain united against British expansionist policies. As it turned out, the Spanish were not anxious to share the responsibility for guarding the eastern Pacific, and Bougainville's settlement was abandoned.

In the west, the best France could do was to hold on to its few Indian settlements and base its defensive strategy on the Ile de France – which as became apparent during the Revolutionary and Napoleonic wars was an effective policy, the island proving a troublesome thorn in the side of the British so that it was eventually conquered and never allowed to revert to French ownership.

An island of real value in the central area of the Pacific, or a stretch of land which might prove to form part of the famous southern continent, was a prize of such strategic value that, as Monneron and Chevalier stated, prompt action and sacrifices were warranted. The British had discovered it: they could be forestalled by the French when it came to taking actual possession of it.

A consideration of great significance was the reported presence of

[1] Pingré, *Mémoire sur les découvertes*, p. 69.
[2] See H. Carrington's summary of this point in *The Discovery of Tahiti*, pp. 274–7.

a friendly and civilised people. This offered a possibility for trade and for a treaty of friendship. George Robertson, master of the *Dolphin*, reported that white-skinned people were to be found in Tahiti. 'This Race of White people in my opinion has a great resemblance to the Jews, which are Scaterd through all the knowen parts of the world.'[1] This kind of rumour is a very likely one to have percolated back to Pondicherry, far more so than precise details about latitude and longitude, because the officers of the *Dolphin* would have been circumspect and tight-lipped, whereas the men, in the taverns of Cape Town, would have gossiped and romanced freely, and been more likely to have been overheard by spies in the pay of the French. Rochon confirmed some years later that this particular information had reached Pondicherry: 'a very rich island where, among other peculiarities, a colony of Jews had been settled.'[2]

Jews or some white race suggested inevitably some degree of civilisation and greater possibilities of trade than with a more primitive people. The value of an eventual treaty was correspondingly enhanced. Above all, years of speculation and wishful thinking about a southern continent added to the importance of the discovery, for if Wallis had found Davis Land, and as some believed it was a part of the southern continent, then he had stumbled upon a land that could approach in importance what Columbus three centuries before had unwittingly brought to the knowledge of European man.[3] Tahiti itself was to become the centre of a cult, linked to the Rousseauist view of the natural perfection of man uncorrupted by civilisation, and overlaid by all the Romantic trappings of the exotic south Pacific – an image that never died out but has survived into the modern age of the tourist industry. Tahiti became symbolic of a lost paradise. To understand how rumours of wealth and of a strange and enviable civilisation could have been spread in Cape Town we must try to imagine the reactions of Wallis' sailors 'aching from scurvy, turning from hard salt beef, weevily biscuit and water that stank'.[4]

[1] See Carrington, *The Discovery of Tahiti*, p. 228; McNab, *From Tasman to Marsden*, pp. 33–4. White men in various parts of the Pacific have long been the subject of speculation. John Campbell's map of Dampier's discoveries in New Guinea includes a mention of Jews living there, 'suspected to be a Remnant of the Ten Tribes of Israel'; see *The Journals of Captain Cook* (ed. J. C. Beaglehole), I, p. lxxvii, note 1. For a theory on Spanish castaways, see R. Langdon, *The Lost Caravel*.

[2] Rochon, *Voyages aux Indes Orientales*, p. 233.

[3] The story of the southern continent is too complex and length to discuss here. It goes back to Claudius Ptolemy and was not laid to rest until after Cook's voyages. Numerous navigators, from Magellan onward, had sought for it. A good French summary may be found in A. Rainaud, *Le Continent austral*; valuable in English is L. C. Wroth's *The Early Cartography of the Pacific*.

[4] Beaglehole, *The Journals of Captain James Cook*, vol. I, p. xciv.

This was an island lived on; as the *Dolphin* coasted the northern shore the ship-board eyes saw a multitude of houses; as she dropped anchor the bay was alive with canoes; a multitude of brown and naked skins seemed to laud an amicable sun. It was a balmy season, the Polynesian June...under the bright day the air was soft and caressing as the water; and after the day came the quick dark, flooding over the heights, the sombre tree-filled valleys, the cascades, the sand still warm beneath the coconut boles while above the islands of all that sea floated the thousand archipelagoes of the stars. Sailors...may well be forgiven for thinking themselves imparadised. So almost suddenly, so overwhelmingly, was the idea of the Pacific at last to enter into the consciousness, not of seamen alone but of literate Europe...For Wallis had not merely come to a convenient port of call. He had stumbled on a foundation stone of the Romantic movement...The unreal was to mingle with the real, the too dramatic with the undramatic; the shining light was to become a haze in which every island was the one island, and the one island a Tahitian dream.[1]

At the very time when these sailor's reports were reaching Pondicherry and Chandernagore, Bougainville in the *Boudeuse* was arriving in Tahiti. The French, equally weary after their hard and slow crossing, were closer to Rousseau's philosophy, and fell correspondingly greater victims to the charm of the islands. Bougainville named it New Cytherea, even though after a time and as a result of talks with Ahutoru, the Tahitian who had joined his ship, he began to have doubts about the real nature of the island paradise. But his officers were enraptured: the *volontaire* Fesche wrote of 'a superb land with the finest climate' and that there was not 'in the world a happier nation than the Tahitian one'.[2] The expedition's naturalist, Commerson, was even more enthusiastic, and more attracted by the philosophical implications. In Commerson's eyes, Tahiti displayed 'the state of natural man, born essentially good, free from all preconceptions and following, without suspicion or remorse, the gentle impulse of an instinct that is always sure because it has not yet degenerated into reason'.[3] Others, such as the surgeon Vivès, taking a philosophical position diametrically opposed to the Rousseauists, wondered how such a civilisation could have developed without the influence of Europe.[4]

---

[1] Ibid., pp. xciv–xcv.
[2] Fesche, *La Nouvelle Cythère*, p. xxx.
[3] Letter to the astronomer Lalande, reprinted in the *Mercure de France*, November 1769. See Corney, *The Quest and Occupation of Tahiti*, vol. II, pp. 461–2.
[4] Vivès, Journal, B.N., N.A.F. 9407: 76, p. 101.

There is, however, no evidence of any influence of this later voyage on the Surville expedition. Bougainville reached the Ile de France on 7 November 1768. The astronomer Véron disembarked, intending to proceed to Pondicherry where he hoped to observe the transit of Venus, due on 3 June 1769. It is hard to believe that by early 1769 the French in India had no knowledge of Bougainville's discovery, in spite of such uninformative reports as Maugendre's quoted earlier. There is but one mention of Bougainville in the papers of the expedition, a marginal note by Monneron, but we know that his account was written after the completion of the voyage. We can safely assume that the syndicate did not identify Bougainville's island with Wallis's, having already satisfied themselves that the English vessel had found Davis Land and therefore in all probability Terra Australis, a discovery of greater value than a mere Rousseauist paradise. Furthermore, by the time the news reached Chandernagore, the *St Jean-Baptiste* was ready to leave and may even have already sailed down the Ganges. Whatever Surville may then have heard in Pondicherry was not enough to make him change his plans: according to Bougainville and his compatriots, the Tahitians were friendly, the women extremely so, but they were not rich; nor was the island such as to suggest that it was associated with a continent or particularly suitable for a naval or a commercial outpost.

Davis Land it was therefore to be, in approximately 27 degrees of latitude south – if information had been received about the Bougainville expedition which had included Tahiti's latitude, it would have been that the island was in 16 to 18 degrees south and strengthened the syndicate's belief that Tahiti was not what they were seeking. As for the longitude, it was assumed to be some 500 to 700 leagues from the coast of South America. In that area of the Pacific only a scattering of unimportant and isolated islands can be found. As we shall see, when he traversed those seas Surville kept to a somewhat higher latitude, usually the mid to high thirties: this strengthens the view that he was interested in a significant discovery – a continent rather than an island – since by sailing south of 27° he would be more likely to strike Terra Australis of which Davis Land was believed to be a northerly outlier.

To sum up, the motives were related to Chevalier and Law's long-term policy of promoting French trade in Eastern waters, largely by finding new outlets and establishing new posts, and of countering whenever possible the constantly growing influence of Great Britain. Surville shared this view, but in addition needed employment following the collapse of the French India Company. The garbled reports from Cape Town brought in the element of Davis Land and its assumed connection with the fabled Southern Continent; the consequence was a sense of urgency and a considerable increase in the original investment; it changed the plans from a search for trading opportunities with known countries such as Japan and the Philippines, to a voyage of general exploration in the Pacific, essentially *à l'aventure*. The bets were nevertheless edged by an anticipated return to Manila or Canton, where the sale of the cargo would cushion the losses that could be expected if the expedition discovered nothing of value.

The element of secrecy is explained by the wish to forestall the British, although it might seem odd that an investor like Labé should have been kept in the dark – but as a captain in the employ of the India Company he would have on numerous occasions sailed ships simply as instructed, without being privy to the Directors' overall plans.

III. THE SHIP: COST AND CARGO

Guillaume Labé frequently complained that he was not informed of the syndicate's plans for the voyage of exploration and in particular the search for Davis Land, in spite of his investment of 50,000 *livres*, or an estimated eventual loss of 58,000; but this sum, however considerable it appeared to him, represented less than two per cent of the total involved.

The list of goods sold by auction in Lorient on 8 November 1773 produced the sum of 2,420,525 *livres*, including 44,330 *livres* in respect of 'goods from Europe'.[1] It should be noted that the list included '1096 items in a perished condition which reached 500 *livres*', while frequent references during the crossing of the south-east Pacific to drying out bales affected by water leaking into the hold support the assumption that the cargo would under normal circumstances have fetched at least two and a half millions. As against that, we have the possibility that, as the great bulk of the cargo came from India and Ceylon, its actual cost may have been considerably lower than the sum it realised at auction. Patriots and visionaries though Chevalier, Law and Surville may have been, they were also shrewd businessmen with a long experience in the India trade.

To the cost of the cargo must be added that of the ship and the

---

[1] Registre de la vente de la cargaison du *St Jean-Baptiste* du 8 Nov. 1773 à Lorient. Archives du Port R. 41. The tax levied on the transaction for poor relief was 2,637 *livres*.

equipment. The *St Jean-Baptiste* was a ship of 650 tons and 36 guns (26 twelve-pounders and 10 six-pounders). As she was to serve a dual purpose – trade in peace time, privateering in wartime – she may have been more expensive to build and equip than a conventional merchantman. Labé refers to 'a considerable quantity of firearms' and the auction register mentions '100 musquets and bayonets as is'. It was because the *St Jean-Baptiste* was more costly than expected that Surville had to borrow 50,000 *livres* from Bourgeois and Gallois: 'His funds and those of M. Chevalier were not sufficient to equip the ship, and therefore he approached Messrs Bourgeois and Gallois who together provided him with a total of 50,000 *livres*'.[1] They add that this original and inadequate sum was 300,000, which suggests that Surville needed 350,000 *livres* before he could sail. Although too much credence must not be placed on the two businessmen who may have been told no more than Surville thought they should know, a sum of this magnitude to build and outfit a ship of 650 tons and stock it adequately for the voyage to India, to pay the customary advances to officers and sailors – in most cases six months' pay – and to load trade goods for India, is far from excessive.

In 1768 Labé was brought in and contributed his 50,000 *livres*. Money was also lent by the Delessert brothers, bankers and traders,[2] one of whom lived in Chandernagore.[3] As the voyage was likely to be a long one, provision needed to be made for supplies and to pay the officers and crew. The pay-off summary at the end of the Muster Roll, dated 24 August 1773, shows a total of 273,468 *livres*. This amount includes 90,896 *livres* for the Spanish sailors taken on at Lima to complement the crew for the return voyage, leaving 182,572 *livres* – to which, however, we should add advances paid prior to the departure, which bring the total outlay under this heading to well over 200,000.[4]

Labé's estimate that a round three million *livres* was invested can be accepted; whether half of this was lost is more difficult to assess. Some, like Surville and the unhappy Bourgeois and Gallois lost everything; others, such as Chevalier who had provided the real lion's share of the money, were luckier.

What would this sum mean in modern terms? It is unwise to try

[1] Appeal, 14 August 1779.
[2] Mentioned in introductory paragraphs in Labé's Journal.
[3] Reference to a Delessert of Chandernagore, in whose house French traders in Bengal used to gather, is made in Luthy, *La Banque protestante en France*, vol. II, p. 438n.
[4] Récapitulation, Désarmement, Archives du Port de Lorient 14, No. 10. It should be pointed out that the Désarmement covers the period 3 June 1767 to 20 August 1773, so that the Recapitulation applies to the voyage from Lorient and the time spent trading between India and Ceylon, and provides additional evidence of the complexity of the financial tangle.

to equate costs across a gap of two hundred years. Voltaire in his *Dictionnaire philosophique* of 1764 states (in an article on 'Feasts') that a silk weaver in Lyons supported his wife and eight children on 45 *sous* a working day, or 639 *livres* a year. If we assume this to be the average annual earnings of a skilled worker we might reach the conclusion that the investment in the *St Jean-Baptiste* was nothing short of astronomical. Yet the captain was paid 240 *livres* a month or 2880 a year, Labé 160 a month or 1920 a year, and sailors averaged 300 *livres* a year. If we allow for the fact that the men were fed and housed on board, the silk weaver's wages fall into a reasonable perspective: the cost of the *St Jean-Baptiste* expedition was undeniably very high.

The French *livre* was subject to frequent fluctuations as a result of wars and financial crises; in 1768–9, following the disastrous Seven Years' War, France's financial situation was unenviable. We can assign a value to the *livre* of less than one shilling or five modern pence, which would place the cost of the expedition at around £150,000 in eighteenth-century values, and Labé's own investment at some £2,500. If we bear in mind that Cook's voyage of 1768 cost less than £10,000 and Kerguelen's voyage of 1773 some 340,000 *livres* and La Pérouse's of 1785 in the region of 635,000 *livres*, we get an idea of the extent of the capital invested in the Surville expedition.

The difference was obviously in the value of the cargo. The other expeditions carried mostly trinkets for barter transactions with natives: the *St Jean-Baptiste* was meant to trade, if not with 'White men' or 'Jews', at least as a last resort with Manila. If we estimate the value of the cargo at say 2,600,000 *livres* – since it fetched over 2,400,000 at auction – we are left with a basic 'voyage of exploration' cost in the region of 300,000 to 400,000 *livres* or £15,000 – which, after due allowance is made for all the extra costs involved as a result of the arrest of the ship in Lima for a period of three years, makes the voyage of the *St Jean-Baptiste* reasonably comparable with the cost of the voyage of Cook's *Endeavour*.

How good the *St Jean-Baptiste* herself was is a matter of opinion. Surville, who bought her or supervised the construction, had few complaints. Certainly, there were weaknesses. The rudder found broken in Malacca was clearly unsatisfactory,[1] but the captain was satisfied with the ship's performance during the storm in Doubtless Bay.[2] The members of the syndicate had praised the *St Jean-Baptiste* on her arrival in India as the best ship that had ever been seen there,

---

[1] 'Apparently the timber was too green when it was made'. Surville, Journal, 3 July 1769.   [2] See Surville, Journal, 29 December 1769.

but while Labé admitted that she carried her canvas well[1] he had few other favourable comments to make and many complaints.

Indeed, if one listens to Labé, the ship was a disaster and the builders and chandlers a pack of rogues. She was badly tied, she leaked, she strained as soon as the wind rose; stowage space was inadequate and ill-designed; supplies were inadequate for a long voyage. The criticisms are numerous,[2] but once she left Malacca the St Jean-Baptiste was almost constantly at sea, with no opportunity for a careening, a refit, or the purchases of spares. For eight months, she sailed through storms, tropical calms and uncharted seas, with an increasingly sick crew and a dire shortage of food, her men continually making do, patching, sewing, repairing, with even items like needles or caulking tar running short. It was little wonder that by February and March 1770 she leaked and her sails tore almost daily.

The cargo, in addition to the usual stock of provision, dried meat, dried biscuits, flour, rice, wine and, in the earlier part of the voyage, livestock, consisted largely of goods from India and Ceylon. The auction records list cinnamon from Ceylon, cloves, pepper, nutmegs, mace; printed cloth from Madras, Pondicherry and Mazulipatnam; handkerchiefs from Kazimbazar, from Bengal, from Palicat, including handpainted ones; Bengal gingham; camlet; blue and white guinea cloth from Mazulipatnam; embroidered Bengal cotton cloth; taffeta from Madras; cretonnes; cloth from Kerabad; shirts plain and with trimmings; tablecloths and napkins; embroidered cuffs; carpets from Constantinople; cambric; barber's towels; muskets and bayonets; and 300 bottles of brandy from France and the Basque country.

Which books and charts were on board can only be surmised. There was in all probability a copy of the *Encyclopédie*, or at least such volumes as had been published between 1751 and 1767 – because it is from this famous work that Surville obtained the name 'Assassins' which he gave to the Solomon Islands.[3] Similarly internal evidence makes it likely that a copy of the Abbé Prévost's *Histoire générale des voyages*, first issued in 1753 and reprinted in a revised edition five years later, was on board. The small library collected for a voyage of exploration must have included as many available accounts of earlier expeditions as the organisers could find. Surville had on board an account of Dampier's voyages and obviously also one of Tasman's since he read it and

---

[1] Labé, Journal, 3 February 1770.
[2] See for instance entries of 13 November and 7 December 1769, 6 January, 21 January, 24 January 1770. [3] See his Journal entry of 24 October 1769.

discussed it with Labé. Whatever was available on Davis – and it was little enough – would have been added. It is probable therefore that Surville had on board a copy of Charles de Brosses' important *Histoire des navigations aux terres australes*, published in two volumes in 1756. Whether he had Melchisédech Thévenot's *Recueil de voyages* of 1681, or his *Relation* of 1696, Coréal's *Recueil de voyages dans l'Amérique méridionale* of 1738, Oexmelin's *Histoire des aventuriers* of 1688, Feuillet's account of his voyage to South America in 1707–12 or Frézier's of 1712–14, is more arguable, but Labé's introductory comments certainly show that he was familiar with Frézier's *Relation du voyage de la Mer du Sud*.

The French had D'Après' invaluable *Neptune oriental* which contained practically all the information available on the problems of navigation in eastern seas; his charts included Vaugondy's 'Carte réduite de la Mer du Sud' – since it is reprinted in de Brosses' book and contains a mention of Gente Hermosa which Labé refers to – and Maurepas' chart, far less reliable, since Labé compares it unfavourably with D'Après'.[1] Philippe Buache had had printed a 'Carte Physique de la Grande Mer' in 1744, but no mention is made of it in the Journals: it had been superseded by Vaugondy's. In addition, Pottier mentions that he had on board a copy of Bellin's 'Carte Réduite des mers comprises entre l'Asie et l'Amérique' which appeared in his *Hydrographie françoise* of 1756 and probably also his *Petit Atlas maritime* of 1764.

It should be borne in mind of course that much of the Pacific was unknown, that the information which appeared on the charts was often misleading guesswork, and that the term 'charts' is in itself a misnomer if we think of them in the sense of modern navigational charts: they were in practice large-scale maps of the Pacific. Many of the comments made by Surville, Labé and Pottier are for the information of others who might sail after them, – and this even in the relatively known waters of the Malacca Straits – part of a constant gathering of knowledge to which all responsible officers, whether on a voyage of exploration or merely a mercantile one, were expected to contribute. It was largely for this reason that logs and journals were required to be deposited with the Ministry of Marine, a wise policy in its day and one for which posterity, for different reasons, must also be grateful.

[1] Labé, Journal, 23 August 1769.

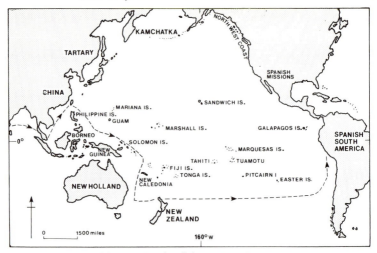

Map 1. Track of the *St Jean-Baptiste*

IV. THE VOYAGE

The voyage of the *St Jean-Baptiste* can be divided into five sections, each one culminating in a prolonged call – from the Ganges to Trengganu, to the Bashi Islands, to the Solomons, to New Zealand, to Peru. The expedition disintegrated so completely in Callao that the final stage, Peru to France, can be regarded as forming part of the aftermath; furthermore, returning to Port-Louis was not in the original plan formulated by Surville and his partners.

1. *The Ganges to Trengganu*

Although Surville and his officers spent some time in Chandernagore, the French settlement headed by their wealthy partner Jean-Baptiste Chevalier, the voyage proper began, as the Journals make clear, *Au nom de Dieu*, from the mouth of the Hooghly on 3 March 1769, making first for Yanaon, another of the few remaining French settlements in India, where a further thirty-five bales of textiles were taken on board, together with some bullocks and kids. The stay lasted nine days, the French leaving at midnight on 29 March for Mazulipatnam where the French had a commercial agent, a Monsieur Mangin, who provided forty-five bales of assorted merchandise, mostly handkerchiefs and cloth, and further food supplies; but other goods which Surville

34

expected had not arrived, and he sailed on the morning of 17 April, having spent a moderately profitable fortnight in the port.

At this point, we find Labé, who had only recently joined the *St Jean-Baptiste*, making his first adverse comments on the cargo and the arrangements made for the voyage. Later, he would criticise the ship as well saying, 'The builder will answer before God, as well as those who supervised the work, for the lack of solidity of the ship' (Journal, 24. 1. 1770). But while Surville may himself have had some misgivings about the provisioning of the ship – something he had to live with, since there was an element of urgency in sailing to forestall the English in 'Davis Land' – he would not have agreed with Labé about the suitability of the *St Jean-Baptiste* for a long voyage, as he had bought the ship himself in France and had sailed in her for two years: and indeed, considering the length of the circumnavigation and the stresses she had to undergo during the voyage through the Pacific, we cannot support Labé's strictures.

Continuing to Pondicherry, the main French port on the eastern coast of India and the residence of the second leading partner in the venture, Law de Lauriston, the French were driven, in bad weather, as far south as Trincomalee Bay, in eastern Ceylon. They veered north to drop anchor in Pondicherry roadstead on 5 May.

Firewood and water were taken on, together with a further hundred bales of trade goods and some supplies which went some way towards meeting Labé's criticisms. He had handed Surville a list of what he considered was required, but Pondicherry was not able to provide everything. Ropes would have to be obtained from Malacca, and live pigs and poultry were inadequate substitutes for preserves and similar provisions essential for a long voyage. The ship was too cluttered as it was: Labé had to be satisfied with filling up his own cabin with a personal store of supplies. 'I am expecting to meet many troubles and hardships', he confided to his journal.

Finally, in the early hours of 2 June 1769, the *St Jean-Baptiste* sailed from Pondicherry with a brisk south-westerly breeze. The ship's complement had been increased by the arrival of twenty-three marines and of one stowaway, a boy who had been told by one of the sailors that the *St Jean-Baptiste* was homebound.

The Nicobar Islands were sighted within eight days – it was a swift crossing soon to be balanced by an irritatingly slow progression down the Straits of Malacca. The Nicobars are strategically situated by the entrance to the Straits, and European powers kept a jealous watch on them. There was a rumour in India that the Danes had recently established a base there; Surville was to ascertain whether this was true, but by the time the islands were sighted, at dawn on 10 June, the *St Jean-Baptiste* was already to leeward. The matter was not of sufficient consequence to justify tiresome manoeuvring and Surville continued on his way.

The Straits lay ahead: the painful struggle against winds and tide began. The expedition had taken eight days to cover the more than 1000 miles from Pondicherry to the Nicobars: it would take nineteen days before the next 700 miles, to Malacca, were covered.

Malacca had been under Dutch control since 1641. The Governor, Thomas Schippers, made the French welcome, allowing them to buy supplies from local merchants and from the port stores, but at exorbitant prices. Soon, however, the atmosphere cooled: Malacca was to some extent an advance post of the Dutch East Indies, and its officials were sensitive to political moves in and around the Malayan peninsula. Rumours that the *St Jean-Baptiste* was contemplating trading among the Dutch islands, brought by an English ship which arrived on 10 July, led to an immediate change of attitude on the part of Schippers who had no wish of being accused of having helped potential challengers to the Dutch trading monopoly. Surville assured him that he was not bound for 'questionable places', but there was little point in staying much longer. On 14 July the French sailed out of the port and continued their struggle against tide and contrary winds towards the southern tip of Malaya.

The voyage almost ended then in disaster. A sailor dropped a lighted candle in a brandy cask and fire was prevented only with difficulty from spreading through the ship. A few days later, 23 July, the *St Jean-Baptiste* anchored off Pulo Tioman to obtain water; one of the anchors became trapped in coral and could not be retrieved. It was the first of a series of such losses which was to plague the expedition.

Soon after this, the expedition reached Trengganu where the only significant commercial transaction of the entire voyage took place, meticulously recorded by Labé. The stay itself is described in the officers' journals[1] and provides a valuable picture of the town and the court. There were prospects for any French merchantmen that might call there in search of new markets in the period following the economically disastrous Seven Years War.

[1] See Dunmore, J., 'French visitors to Trengganu in the eighteenth century', *Journal of the Royal Asiatic Society, Malaysian branch*, XLVI, (1973), 145–159.

2. *Trengganu to the Bashi Islands*

In the evening of 1 August, the French set out for the South China Sea, making first for Pulo Condore which was sighted on the 6th. On the afternoon of the 8th a sail was noticed far away to the NNE; it was seen again on the 9th, its position indicating that it was south-bound; on the 10th it was seen no more. It was the last ship they were to meet for seven months.

Surville now abandoned all pretence of trade in the China seas: his men noted that he neither veered east towards Manila nor north-west towards Canton, but made instead for the Bashi Channel between Luzon and Formosa. The Philippines were sighted on 17 August – distant mountains at first, then Cape Bojeador, followed soon after by the Babuyan Islands low on the horizon.

On the 21st the *St Jean-Baptiste* dropped anchor off the Batan or Bashi Islands, the latter name given to them by William Dampier after the *bashee* drink which he and now the French sampled with appreciation. Apart from this, they obtained water, goats, pigs and vegetables, but the islands were poor and could not supply the extra provisions which Labé was anxious to lay in for the hazardous voyage ahead. Welcoming and happy though the islanders were, their way of life was far from that idyllic state which some French philosophers, simplifying Jean-Jacques Rousseau's theories of social evolution, expected to find in primitive societies. Those who achieve freedom from the vices and restrictions of civilisation, commented Labé, must suffer greater discomforts through the lack of the material benefits of civilisation.

But on 22 August three men deserted, and Surville was unable to make the islanders understand that he wanted them returned. A gift of three pigs was no substitute for the missing men. He had two dozen islanders arrested out of those who thronged the decks, then released all but three. On the 23rd he sailed, going south-east into the Pacific.

The Bashi kidnapping is an episode of some importance in estimating Surville's character, for two similar charges would be laid against him later in the voyage. Each time anger played its part, but it cooled quickly and was replaced in this case by the double purpose of learning more about the islands and of replacing the three deserters. The intention was to return them later to their homes, since it was part of the original plan to sail back to Pondicherry by way of the Philippines. This turned out to be impossible, but the treatment they received – in an age when negroes were being shipped out of their homelands under appalling conditions, and the European poor often fell victim to the kidnappings of the press-gangs – was far from inhuman. Surville sought to console them with gifts, and they received in fact more attention than the average seaman on board. Two were to die of scurvy, but so were many of the crew. To Surville, they were men who came from a little-known country where one day the French, through the knowledge they would gain, might decide to set up a fragile foothold, establishing a presence in a part of the world where so far only the Spanish and the English, and at times the Portuguese, had been able to trade. The three men would learn French, he would question them about their country and its resources, and through them he would discover far more than any other traveller had done. This was the reasoning which led him to keep these hostages, and to repeat his action in the Solomons and in New Zealand. Posterity would condemn him as a kidnapper and blackbirder; but for Surville this was the first step in a long voyage of discovery.

3. *The Bashi Islands to the Solomons*

Rounding the north of Luzon into the Pacific was a leap into the unknown. French charts of the area were few and unreliable. Islands were shown, but their longitudes were rarely correct, if not downright fanciful: this, coupled with the unreliability of the dead reckoning method which in the absence of chronometers was all the French could really depend on, meant that the *St Jean-Baptiste* was truly sailing *à l'aventure*. The Philippine Sea is in fact a vast void. Surville's ESE course would lead him to the western Carolines – to the Palaus or the Yap group. On 7 September, Labé estimated that he was in the middle of the Carolines, but their point of departure from the Batans was incorrect, Dampier's longitude of a century earlier being 3° out, and the equatorial calms caused the ship to drift into a position that could not be estimated with any hope of accuracy. As Surville said on 7 September, 'as far as my longitude is concerned, I am not altering it, for fear of altering it the wrong way'. He was trying to make for St Andrew's or Sonsorol Islands but passed to the north, in the wide gap between them and the Palaus. It was one of many occasions when luck proved to be against him and even the law of averages kept him out of sight of land.

As Labé feared, food began to run out and sickness made its appearance. The signs of scurvy were unmistakable, and morale fell daily as the great sails hung limply and heavily over the decks, no breeze rose to lessen the heat and the ship at times did not even respond to the helm. From the 24th to the 30th the total distance covered was barely eighty miles. Somewhere to the north lay the Carolines, to the south lay Papua New Guinea and New Zealand – but in between, where the *St Jean-Baptiste* wallowed and struggled, there was only sea. Cockroaches bred in the steamy darkness below decks where growing numbers of sick were now crowded in the dark heat filled with the smell of their sweating bodies and of their vomit, while down in the hold rats gnawed at the cargo.

October brought relief by way of showers and a stronger breeze. It was still necessary to proceed with caution, especially at night, as the French had no idea where they were. Finally, on the morning of 7th, they sighted a coastline stretching from SE to WSW. The nearest land seemed to be an island, to which they gave the name of 'Ile de la Première Vue'. It was in fact the southern tip of Choiseul Island in the Solomons. Surville had been close to the group for some days: overcast weather had prevented him from sighting Bougainville Island and the northern coast of Choiseul, for when land was finally seen it was no more than twenty miles away, and the high ranges inland could easily be discerned once the clouds lifted.

Surville was not certain whether what he had reached was the labyrinth of islands it seemed to be or a 'continent', but he inclined to the second alternative. Consequently, not wanting to become trapped in what he suspected was a wide bay to the south-east, he sailed north and avoided the dangers around Manning Strait between Choiseul and Santa Isabel. Visibility was still hampered by showers, but he did sight a 'terrible gulf or perhaps a passage' – which was Manning Strait – before veering south towards land. His men were now in such a bad condition that he kept manœuvres to a minimum and tried to anticipate the squalls which added to their discomfort. It was imperative to land somewhere to rest them and obtain supplies of water and fresh food. On 13 October the *St Jean-Baptiste* dropped anchor in a broad sheltered channel formed by Gagi Island and several islets, to the north-west of Santa Isabel. The anchorage was named Port Praslin, after César de Choiseul, duc de Praslin, Minister of Marine (it would have been a more charming coincidence had Port Praslin actually been on Choiseul Island); the name remains to this day, as does Surville's own name, given to one of the islets.

The problem of finding water was complicated by the number of natives who clambered aboard or thronged the shore. Labé went with a party ashore which was attacked, the sergeant of marine dying of his wounds a few days later and Labé himself suffering a blow below the groin, which festered and was to trouble him for many months.

Surville was greatly incensed by the attack – he mentions it several times and gave the island group the name of Arsacides, after the Assassins of the thirteenth century. Now on their guard, the French succeeded in refilling their water casks and one young islander was kidnapped, a youth whom Surville was to treat so well that Labé was to grumble about it, and who was eventually to reach France ahead of the *St Jean-Baptiste*, accompanying the ship's clerk, Monneron, on his mission to Paris. But fresh food was far more difficult to obtain and the frequent torrential showers did little to restore the health of the men. On the 21st the French sailed out of Port Praslin to continue ESE along the coast of Santa Isabel.

By bestowing the name Arsacides on the islands, Surville showed that he did not identify them with Mendaña's discovery. With their inaccurate plotting of the route and the sketchy charts at their disposal, the French were not even certain whether they had passed to the east or the west of New Britain, and they referred to the land they saw as 'the land of the Papuans'; but by November Surville began to suspect that he might be off a coast that had some relationship with the Solomons, possibly being an extension of that archipelago. Labé was convinced that they had sailed east of New Britain. Pottier de l'Horme believed that the captain had been seeking to reach the latitude of the Solomons, while Monneron was to speculate later that the land they had visited was part of the island group seen by Bougainville, and that there were similarities between the land of the Arsacides and the description Figueroa gave of Mendaña's Santa Isabel. It was left, however, to professional geographers to piece all the information together and to place the Solomon Islands firmly and finally on the map of the south-west Pacific.

4. *The Solomons to New Zealand*

Surville sailed ESE as the land was running thus and he wanted to keep it in sight. He could see a high range of mountains far away to the SW, which was the hinterland of Santa Isabel. On the 26th he sighted a small island so far from the rest and therefore so unexpected that he called it 'l'Ile Inattendue': it was Gower Island discovered by

Carteret two years before. He did not call there, rejecting the possibility that the islanders might be more hospitable than those of Port Praslin. Canoes did come from the larger island of Malaita, bringing fruit for barter. Ulawa lay ahead and, more optimistic now, Surville altered course towards it, to seek 'a few refreshments, a few greens for our sick...whose number grows daily', but Labé, going ahead in the yawl, found himself threatened again, and the St Jean-Baptiste sailed away towards San Cristóbal and three small islands which the French named The Three Sisters, as they are still known today. They sighted Ugi Island, then Santa Ana and Santa Catalina, at the eastern tip of San Cristóbal, which they named the 'Iles de la Délivrance' to mark the end of what had been a long chain of disappointments. On 7 November, Surville wrote in his Journal 'left the land of the Papuans'. He had turned what is now Cape Surville, the eastern end of San Cristóbal and, still on a SSE course, entered the Coral Sea.

The route led directly to the New Hebrides and Banks Islands, while the long island of New Caledonia stretched like a net across to the south. It seemed inevitable that Surville should find within a short time some island where his crew could find a respite, yet Fate again played a cruel trick. After four days of sailing almost in a straight line towards the New Hebrides, until he was eighty miles off them and would have sighted them within twenty-four hours, he altered course for the south-west.

Once again, wrong longitudes had foiled his plans. On the 9th he had estimated that the ship was close to Taumako which was shown on charts – including the latest, Dalrymple's of 1767 – as being NNE of Espiritu Santo. The logical step was therefore to veer SSW in order to find this land which Quiros had discovered and where he had hoped to found a Spanish colony. The relationship between Taumako, which is part of the Duff group, and the New Hebrides is, however, a north-to-south one, and the St Jean-Baptiste sailed away from her hoped-for landfall.

There was a chance that the French might have sighted the jagged hills of New Caledonia which rise to almost 4000 feet in the northern region, or been slowed and attracted by the reefs and islands that surround its north-western tip, for they were sailing in a fairly straight line towards it; but the currents drove them further to the west and nothing was sighted. On 22 November Surville consulted Labé; together they read Tasman's account, for the Dutchman was the only one known to have penetrated in these waters, and they agreed that the only course, seeing the grave condition of the crew, was to make for New Zealand. Tasman had been attacked by the Maoris, but however unfriendly the inhabitants might be, the French had no alternative than to seek refuge somewhere on the coastline Tasman had traced in the little-known southern Pacific.

The route involved sailing south to at least 35°. The only nagging doubt was whether, taking the unreliable longitudes into account, they were not already to the east of New Zealand. To guarantee against this frightening possibility, they sailed south and south-west. This took them through Brampton Reefs and west of Lord Howe Island, possibly to within a hundred miles of the Australian continent. On 4 December, having passed 33° south, the *St Jean-Baptiste* altered course ESE and E for New Zealand. On the 12th land was sighted due east: the expedition was just south of Hokianga harbour.

Surville hauled along the sandy coast, looking for a suitable anchorage. He would find none on the inhospitable west side of New Zealand's northern peninsula: so-called Ninety Mile Beach provides no shelter. Soon the weather worsened, obscuring the land. A gale blew up which enabled the French to reach the northern tip of the country and to turn North Cape without delay. It was that very gale which blew James Cook away from the land as his *Endeavour* was battling her way north along the east coast. The two ships sailed out of sight of each other, probably at a distance of some thirty miles, and the historic meeting between the first two European expeditions to sail to New Zealand in 127 years never took place.

Surville's eyes anyhow were on the coast, not towards the open sea where the unthinkable English ship was. He was seeking the anchorage which his crew so desperately needed. The northernmost point of New Zealand, now known as Surville Cliffs, had nothing to offer: the south of North Cape little that could guarantee safety. On 17 December, however, the *St Jean-Baptiste* reached a wide bay, which Cook had named Doubtless Bay, to which Surville gave the name of Lauriston Bay after the Governor of Pondicherry and backer of the expedition, Law de Lauriston.

He dropped anchor near a cove in the shelter of Knuckle Point, the northern headland of Doubtless Bay. To his relief, the Maoris welcomed then with every sign of friendship, save a little anxiety in the background about the purpose and probable length of the stay. The sailors were fortunate in finding some greens, rich in vitamins, which quickly· restored the health of most of the crew. There was little exploration of the hinterland – apart from the headland itself with its coves which the French surveyed most of the area consists of low sand dunes and marshland – but the accounts of Maori life and settlements, contained in the journals, provide valuable information about pre-colonial Maori life. To cement relations with the New Zealanders and repay them for their hospitality, Surville presented them with a couple of hogs, a cock and a hen, wheat, peas and rice.

Lauriston Bay was what Surville had been seeking to refresh his men, but it was not satisfactory as a harbour. Already on the 19th and the 22nd Surville had changed the anchorage in the hope of coming closer to the land and finding better shelter; but his final anchorage, if more convenient, was no safer. On the 27th a storm drove the *St Jean-Baptiste* towards a cluster of rocks, the anchors were not holding, and Surville had great difficulty in saving the ship. The cost was a broken rudder, damage to the mast and sails, and the loss of two anchors – which have only recently been recovered.

On the 31st as he was preparing to leave, Surville sighted the yawl which he had thought lost in the storm. He hastened towards the shore where it had been washed up; but by the time he got there the boat had gone. A trail across the sand indicated that Maoris had dragged it over the dunes to a small river where, in spite of all Surville's efforts, it remained hidden. Weary and angry, Surville captured a local chief, Ranginui, and had him taken aboard to join his other captives from the Bashi Islands and the Solomons. As was the case with the others, especially the young Solomon Islander, Surville treated his prisoner exceedingly well, but Ranginui died of scurvy three months later, and his capture and death have weighed heavily on Surville's memory.

There was now no alternative but to leave the bay. It was not a safe haven, the crew had largely recovered, and the Maoris were likely to seek revenge and attack the French. Surville gathered his officers together, read them a clause in his instructions which forbade him from breaking the policy of Exclusiveness by calling at any Spanish settlement in America, and asked their advice. All agreed that the condition of the ship, dwindling supplies, the loss of 62 men and the frail condition of many of the others, made a call at any European settlement imperative. The prevailing westerly winds, compared with the slow and danger-strewn route to Manila or the Dutch Indies, meant that only South America offered a chance of survival. It was worth the risk. The *St Jean-Baptiste* sailed out of Doubtless Bay during the evening of 31 December 1769, on an easterly route, bound for the South American coast, 5000 miles away.

5. New Zealand to Callao

The journey across the Pacific, the first to have been made from west to east in such latitudes, brought the *St Jean-Baptiste* into unknown seas, zigzagging between 34° and 40° North. The weather was often stormy, the ship straining greatly, the sails tearing frequently, imposing further strain on the crew. Labé, still not cured of the wound he had sustained in Port Praslin, rapidly relapsed into despondency, but in late February he was told by Surville that his instructions included a search for Davis Land, the supposed position of which they were now approaching.

More than a week went by, with no sign of land. Scurvy had reappeared and, as the sailors had no reserves of strength, it made rapid progress. Water, firewood, food, were all in short supply. On 6 March 1770 Surville once again called his officers together. They were unanimous that they should make for South America without any delay. 'We could no longer amuse ourselves looking for Davis Land', he recorded in his Journal.

On the 12th they sighted a sail in the distance: it was the first European ship they had seen for seven months. On the morning of the 24th – the day the Maori died – land was seen to ENE. It was Mas Afuera, the westernmost of the Juan Fernandez group. Surville continued on his westward course, hoping to send boats ashore on Mas a Tierra, the other and larger island of the group, but the weather was stormy and the two boats he wanted to despatch would have left the *St Jean-Baptiste* dangerously undermanned. He sailed N and NE intending to make for Peru, where the main Spanish authorities resided.

The coast of South America was sighted on 4 April; the landfall was not far from the present town of Lomas. Conditions on board were now truly desperate. The meagre quarters of the ship's surgeon were totally overtaxed; there were no berths for the sick who lay on heaps of dirty tow; although they were feverish, water was rationed. Thus, when the *St Jean-Baptiste* dropped anchor off the small town of Chilca, Surville could not wait for the sea to moderate. Labé tried to cross the bar in a boat, but turned back. The captain himself then tried, dressed in full uniform with his Cross of St Louis and his sword so as to impress the local Spanish and overcome any reluctance on their part to assist foreign sailors. He wrote a message for help, which he enclosed in a bottle, tying it round the neck of a Pondicherry lascar who was a strong swimmer. The Indian managed to struggle ashore, but the boat capsized by the bar. Surville, weighed down by his clothing, was drowned, together with the two sailors who had accompanied him to man the boat.

Labé took the ship to Callao on the 9th, where he obtained confirmation of the captain's death and began the endless series of negotiations with the Spanish authorities.

Jean de Surville was buried by the local priest in Chilca's old cemetery which was closed and replaced by a new larger one at the end of the nineteenth century. Investigations in the 1960s did not reveal the presence of any tombstone – and indeed French records do not mention any expenditure of this kind. The parish registers were burnt during the Peruvian–Chilean wars, and the old cemetery as well as the old Chilca church was destroyed by the major earthquake of October 1974. Not even in local traditions is there any memory of a Frenchman being buried locally. The remains of Surville have therefore disappeared as completely as if he had been buried at sea – a not inappropriate destiny for a man who had spent the greater part of his life at sea and who had finally sacrificed it in a foredoomed attempt to get help for his men.

Shortly after the *St Jean-Baptiste* dropped anchor in Callao a guard was put on the ship. In October 1770 Monneron went to Paris in the hope of hastening her release. He returned in August 1772. The expedition finally sailed from Peru on 7 April 1773 with sixty-three Spanish sailors to make up, in part, for the deaths and desertions. After an uneventful voyage the *St Jean-Baptiste* finally reached Port-Louis in Brittany on 20 August.

V. THE AFTERMATH

1. *The voyage home*

The *St Jean-Baptiste*, now released from her long period of inaction, sailed from Callao on the evening of 7 April 1773, exactly three years after her ill-fated arrival.

Labé was in command and determined to stand no nonsense from anyone. Pottier de l'Horme was his first officer, assisted by Lory who however was not in good health. They were helped by former warrant office René Le Mire and the former 'volontaire' François Avice, both appointed second ensigns. Charenton had disappeared two days earlier, Hughes de Surville and Villefeix had long since gone, but the surgeon Dulucq was still on board as was Captain de St Paul. Monneron had returned from France, and a Spanish chaplain, Brother Miguel Tenoro, a native of Peru, had been taken on to replace Villefeix.

To make up for the losses through deaths and desertions, sixty-three Spanish sailors were signed on, causing an early clash with the captain through insisting that they be paid in advance. The authorities had reservations about the ability of the French to pay the men their due on arrival in France, and supported the complainants, the port captain supervising the transaction in person. In addition, to make sure that the French did not attempt to sell contraband goods, the *St Jean-Baptiste* was followed for a time by a small coastal vessel, modestly armed with two guns and two soldiers.

Once clear of the land, the ship sailed SW with a fair breeze. Pottier's Journal gives little more than the usual navigational details, but Labé records that on the evening of the 15th he was affected by a high fever which forced him to remain in his cabin for several days and did not leave him for a week.

He nevertheless kept an eye on things and had a number of Spanish sailors put in irons for gambling on deck, after which the others were 'quiet but lazy which is the original sin of their nation'.[1] The ship however was averaging almost 30 leagues a day, although the winds turned and forced Labé to tack NW and SW. By the end of the month, the *St Jean-Baptiste* was in 36°40′, almost the latitude of Concepcion. Labé had had more trouble with his Spanish crew: they complained that the food was not of the kind they were used to, 'several tried to raise their voices, I fell upon them with great blows of my stick and had the leaders punished and the others put in irons. They are now as quiet as lambs'.[2] By 10 May the French were approaching the fiftieth degree of latitude and Labé was complaining of the cold. A report that land had been seen in the east caused him to veer west and 'waste time' because although he did not really believe he could be so close to the coast of Chile, he could not take any risks. The weather was constantly overcast with occasional hail, showers and snow.

In late May the *St Jean-Baptiste* began to veer south-east towards Cape Horn. There was no intention of sighting land: a wide sweep was made round Tierra del Fuego, down to 58°6′ on 31 May and then north-east and north. A week later, the Falklands were in sight to the east and the north-west, snow-covered and unappealing. Labé corrected his position from them and sailed north and north-east with a fresh gale which enabled him to cover up to 60 leagues a day. On the 23rd

---

[1] Labé, Journal, 19 April 1773.   [2] Ibid., 26 April 1773.

he reckoned himself to be 65 leagues to the south-west of Ascension. There was little to report. During the night of 8 July the French crossed the Equator. Supplies of fresh food must by now have run out for scurvy reappeared: Labé recorded the first death on the 13th – one of the Spanish sailors. A few days later Captain de St Paul fell victim to a high fever and more scurvy cases were reported. On the 20th St Paul was 'in great danger'; he began to improve on the 25th, by which time there were five scurvy cases. Labé thought of his own health, impaired by the hardship of the voyage and the wound he had sustained in the Solomons, which had left 'a kind of fistula, as it still weeps at times.'[1]

On 1 August a small English vessel hove into sight, en route from New York to the Guinea coast. Labé hailed her, anxious to know whether he would find Europe at peace or at war when he arrived. In anticipation of reaching western waters he had supervised gunnery practice himself a few days previously, there being no one on board with adequate experience. Learning that Europe was at peace, he altered course towards the Azores.

Another of the Spanish sailors died, on the 4th, of a hernia. The next day Labé lists six men as being affected by scurvy and suspects that they had been in poor health when they signed on in Callao 'with a fever that has not left them since our departure.'[2] A few days later twelve men were on the sick list, five of scurvy, the rest of a fever. There was no sign of the Azores; instead on the 12th a French ship appeared, on her way from Gorée in West Africa to Le Havre. They checked longitude, found them roughly equal and went on their way. The next meeting was with an English ship from Bristol, bound for Cadiz. Making a comfortable 35 to 40 leagues a day, the St Jean-Baptiste was now entering busy shipping lanes and rapidly nearing the French coast. The health of the men was improving: the sick list was down to eight by the 15th, all reported to be 'in a fairly good condition'.

The coast of Brittany was in sight at 10 a.m. on 17th August – the islands of Glénan with the coastline behind. In the evening the St Jean-Baptiste dropped anchor off the Ile de Groix. Monneron went ashore in a small boat to give news of their arrival and seek a pilot for the final stage up the estuary to Lorient. It had started to rain and the winds were variable. Progress into port was slow and marred by a minor grounding which necessitated the removal of the guns and caused the loss of a day. Finally the ship was tied up, on Monday 23

---

[1] Ibid., 28 July 1773.   [2] Ibid., 5 August 1773.

August 1773, and Labé could write in his log, 'Non plus ultra', and Pottier in his, 'It is here that ends the voyage which has been marked by sufferings and exhaustion'.

2. The legal tangle

After the ship had tied up, Labé had a number of matters to attend to: the paying off of the crew, which was completed on the 24th, and handing over the cargo, which he did without delay 'to M. Quatrefage, agent for M. de Rabec, who is the legal representative of M. Chevalier, the chief partner'. Labé also handed over a detailed inventory, 'including the ship fittings, equipment, food, etc.'. Soon after this, Rabec himself arrived, Labé showed him the ship's accounts, obtained a receipt, and left. Rabec then organised the auction. Taking into consideration the need to check and catalogue the cargo and advertise the auction, he wasted no time. The sale gathered 87 buyers and brought in 2,420,525 *livres*.

Labé went to see Mme de Surville in Port-Louis, and gave her the captain's clothes – a suit of velvet with gold braid and crimson silk – his Cross of St Louis, a lock of his hair cut off by the Spanish authorities as evidence of his identity and death, the books he had on board, and a few other personal effects. But there was no money. Her dowry of 60,000 *livres* had been added to Surville's own resources to finance the expedition in its early stages. The legal tangle arose out of arguments about the date when the voyage to the Pacific had really begun. The muster roll suggested that it had started in 1767 when the *St Jean-Baptiste* sailed from Nantes; if that were so, then the first investors would share equally with those who had financed the 1769 voyage. The counter argument was that the voyage to Davis Land was a separate venture which dated from the time news had come of a mysterious British discovery, and that those who financed it were the only legal claimants to the proceeds of the auction. The latter argument apparently prevailed, leaving Chevalier, Law, Labé and the Pondicherry bankers with a valid claim to the remaining assets. Those who had joined from the start were in a position of unsecured creditors, and technically some of them, like Bourgeois and Gallois, were Surville's creditors.

Rabec, it should be noted, was Chevalier's agent in France, and Chevalier was officially listed as the 'principal armateur'. To the extent that Law contributed to the 1769 expedition, he would have had a legal claim, and as a close associate of Chevalier's he may have been able to use moral or other forms of persuasion to obtain a larger share. Labé expected no more than fifty per cent back and he may have got just that. The Pondicherry bankers Delessert Brothers may also have seen half their loan moneys returned. But for Surville and those who had helped him in 1767, there was nothing. To save Mme de Surville from utter destitution, the Crown granted her a pension of 500 *livres*;[1] she was still being paid shortly before her death during the 1789 Revolution; her eldest son Jean-Louis, a captain in the Régiment d'Artois had asked that the pension be made reversible to him in the event of her death, but the Revolution swept these privileges away, and the family died out in the early nineteenth century.[2]

The legal arguments went on for years through various tribunals. The liquidators of the French India Company had more important matters to see to; their original financial commitment, if there had been one, was relatively insignificant. Legal documents have scattered in various holdings: among the papers of the Company's office in Lorient and Paris – a mass of reports and correspondence which unfortunately contains many gaps – in the files of the Amirauté de Port-Louis in Vannes, in those of the lawyers representing the interests of the various parties. A reconstruction of the financial structure of the expedition would give an interesting, but extremely complex picture of the efforts made in the wake of the Seven Years' War by such men as Surville and Law to fill the vacuum left by the collapse of the French India Company, but it would for this single expedition span over least twelve years and, one may suspect, even more.

That the situation was still in dispute ten years after the *St Jean-Baptiste* had sailed from Pondicherry is evidenced by the appeal made on 14 August 1779 by Bourgeois and Gallois for leave to sue Chevalier's agent before the Admiralty tribunal at Vannes:[3]

14 August 1779.
To their Lordships,
The Admiralty Judges of Vannes,
      Messrs Bourgeois and Gallois, traders in Lorient, make this humble request,
— Stating that in 1767 they were associated in a maritime business venture initiated by the late Mr Surville, captain of a vessel of the India Company.

[1] Archives Nationale, Marine C7 314, Morbihan, 3042.
[2] Surville to Marshall de Charac, 13 August 1786, Arch. Nat. Marine B4 316.
[3] Turnbull Library, Wellington N.Z., Miscellaneous MS W 14. This document was obtained through an official of the French Embassy, having been purchased from an antiquarian, which suggests that some of the papers relative to the commercial aspects of the expedition have been scattered and, one may assume in some cases, lost.

— This officer having arranged this venture in India with Mr Chevalier who financed it to the extent of three hundred thousand *livres*,

— When he arrived in France, he had a ship built called the *St Jean-Baptiste*.

His funds and those of Mr Chevalier were not sufficient to fit out the ship, and therefore he approached Messrs Bourgeois and Gallois who, together, provided him with a total of fifty thousand *livres* to the extent of which sum they became his partners and associates with the same rights in the company as had, proportionately, Mr Chevalier and himself.

— This venture prospered while it was under the command of Mr de Surville, an officer whose experience and honesty were universally recognised. After his death during the expedition, misfortune followed misfortune. His ship, after being held up for four years in a foreign port, finally arrived in France, where it was received and laid up by Mr de Rabel [*sic*], who sold the cargo and performed other customary operations.

Given these facts,

Messrs Bourgeois and Gallois presented a claim in order to recover part of the proceeds of the sale in proportion to their holdings. Having experienced various delays and difficulties which they were not expecting, attachments were issued against the holders of the company's funds, and were placed in their hands, with the proposal that arbitrators be named to determine their differences. This just and honest procedure was not followed, and they were thus obliged to have recourse to judiciary processes to obtain what they had requested in vain.

These facts considered,

Should it please their Lordships to summon to their first session, in due time, Mr de Rabel, who laid up the ship, the *St Jean-Baptiste*, and sold her cargo, as well as all other necessary persons, to be condemned:

And whereas the suppliants are partners in the said venture, for them to be paid, in proportion to their holding, part of the proceeds of the above-mentioned sale; and that they who refuse or oppose this be condemned to pay damages and interest on costs, other rights being reserved, as well as any new legal action in favour of, or against any person.

Request for leave to appeal at Vannes, this 14th day of August 1779.

VI. RESULTS

1. *The Elimination of Davis Land*

As a commercial venture, the voyage of the *St Jean-Baptiste* was a disaster, largely because the expedition was held in Lima for so long and thereby prevented from crossing back to the Philippines and to China and disposing of the cargo before it deteriorated further and the arrears of pay accumulated to disastrous heights. Even so, the ship needed expensive refitting before an east to west crossing of the Pacific could be contemplated – and supplies and spares would have been expensive to buy in Peru: it is significant that when Labé wanted to buy an anchor from the naval store the price asked by the Spanish was so outrageous that he had one made privately of copper.[1] But from the point of view of Pacific exploration, of geography, of ethnography, the voyage of the *St Jean-Baptiste* was valuable. Its role has been constantly underrated, because Cook's voyages overlapped with it and while the French, enmeshed in arguments over the Spanish policy of Exclusiveness in South America, waited for release, others were joining in the exploration of the South Seas. Had the ship been able to proceed promptly to France or back to India, the status of the expedition in the annals of Pacific exploration would be quite different. Once again, the commercial side, paramount in the eyes of Labé, Monneron and Chevalier, undermined its other aspects.

The first contribution to the map of the Pacific which can be credited to Surville, at least indirectly, is the final elimination of Davis Land. Belief in it had never been strong, but it had nagged away in the mind of geographers, linked as it was to the elusive Southern Continent. Carteret in 1767 had made a determined attempt to find it by sailing towards Juan Fernandez and then west of San Felix and San Ambrosio, before veering west to pass south of Easter Island. At the same time Wallis was sailing some twenty degrees further west and then veering westward to pass north of Easter Island. Between them, they had cut off a mighty slice of the south-east Pacific, sighting no continent or land of any kind. Not many months later, Bougainville traversed the same area in search of the fabled land and saw nothing. The story should have been laid to rest by now, but the arrival of the *St Jean-Baptiste* in Callao sparked off a further expedition in search of the low sandy island with its higher land in the distance.

[1] Labé to Viceroy, 4 August 1773; Labé to Minister of Marine, Lorient 25 August 1773. Misc. correspondence Arch. Nat. Marine B4 316.

Strictly, the Spanish should have been satisfied with the French's reports on their fruitless search. The *St Jean-Baptiste* had sailed much further south than Carteret, Wallis or Bougainville; they had crossed in latitudes east of New Zealand where no one at the time, not even Cook, had ever penetrated, and thus eliminated the possibility of a continental Davis Land from vast tracts of uncharted ocean. It seemed pointless to spend more time and money on further investigations.

Yet the Viceroy, Don Manuel de Amat, believed that if the French still considered it politically important enough to risk a fortune on searching for land relatively close to the Spanish possessions, then Spain should take steps to look for it too and take possession of it. He had obtained permission from Madrid to equip an expedition to establish Spanish sovereignty over any islands that could properly be claimed to fall within the Spanish sphere of influence. The voyages of Wallis, Carteret, Bougainville and Cook, all coming within a short span of three years, posed a real threat to the policy of Exclusiveness; winds of change were blowing over the Pacific, and the Spanish were beginning to feel uncomfortable.

On 10 October 1770 two ships, the *San Lorenzo*, 74 guns, and the *Santa Rosalia*, 36 guns, sailed from Callao under the command of Felipe Gonzalez 'for a secret expedition which it is believed is the discovery of Davis Land'.[1] The instructions were modelled on the information Surville had: to seek Davis Land, one should sail along the 27th degree of latitude. Such a course could only lead to Easter Island which is in 27° 10'. Gonzalez took possession of it, a document being drawn up which he had signed by several islanders. After a stay of six days, the expedition sailed on towards the west, found no other land and returned to Peru.

By 28 March 1771 the ships were back, Labé was shown the charts and reports and was told Davis Land had been rediscovered. 'This discovery caused a great sensation', he reported, but rejected all suggestions that it could be anything but Easter Island. The Viceroy remained convinced: he had rediscovered Davis Land and that was the end of it. Others in Lima began to have doubts as they read Roggeveen's account of Easter Island and compared it with Gonzalez's. Reports by now were arriving of Tahiti as seen by the British and by the French; his earlier confidence now totally shaken, the Viceroy sent the *Santa Maria Magdalena* (now the *Aguila*) under Domingo Boenechea, to both islands, leaving him the option to go to either first, in order

[1] Labé, Journal, October 1770.

52

to establish a settlement and ensure Spanish sovereignty. Boenechea shared the view that the so-called San Carlos Island of Gonzalez was not the mysterious Davis Land but Easter Island, and that all the evidence pointed to Tahiti as more significant and more attractive. Circumstances prevented him from ever calling at Easter Island, the myth of Davis Land finally died out, even the Spanish losing interest,[1] and the attempted colonisation of Tahiti by Spain petered out within a short time.

2. The Rediscovery of the Solomon Islands

Probably the most valuable single contribution made by Surville's expedition was providing conclusive evidence on the question of the Solomon Islands. On 7 January 1568 Alvaro de Mendaña, sailing from Callao, had discovered Santa Isabel; within a few weeks the Spanish expedition had added to the list of discoveries: Malaita, Guadalcanal, the Florida group, Choiseul and much of New Georgia. As a group they became known as the Islands of Solomon, an appellation which suggested great wealth and some element of mystery – appropriately, because their actual position became a matter for argument and doubt. Mendaña, on a second voyage in 1595, was unable to find them; Quiros in 1605 was no more successful. In time the islands disappeared from some maps or were scattered across the entire spread of the Pacific in others.

On Vaugondy's chart of 1756 which Surville used, the Solomon Islands are placed to the north-east of Tonga and roughly to the north of the Samoa group. As late as 1768, John Callander, admittedly in a work largely pirated from de Brosses' *Histoire des navigations* of 1756, mentioned the uncertainty of their latitude (which was nothing compared with uncertainty as to their longitude) and suggested that their existence might be 'a fiction'.[2] Dalrymple, in 1770, brought the Solomons back to New Guinea, attempting a synthesis based on a study of the earlier charts, an approach which however required him to question the latitudes given by the Spanish, which had in fact been reasonably accurate.[3] His views were accepted by others, such as

---

[1] Navigators kept a perfunctory lookout for it. La Pérouse sailed across its reputed location, just to make certain, and saw no sign of any Sandy Island (Milet-Mureau, *Voyage de la Pérouse*, p. 75). Dalrymple, as late as 1773, still believed Davis had discovered Easter Island (*A Letter from Mr Dalrymple to Dr Hawkesworth*). But it ceased to be a matter for serious speculation after the voyages of Surville and Gonzalez.

[2] Callander, *Terra Australis Cognita*, III, 711.

[3] 'This error in latitude... has prevented it from being observed that the Solomon Islands, discovered in 1567, are in fact New Britain.' *An Historical Collection*, I, 19.

Thomas Forrest who, nearly ten years later, added the description of New Britain by Carteret to the scaffolding of evidence being erected and suggested that the location of the Solomon Islands off the eastern tip of New Guinea had become almost unchallengeable.[1] But Alexandre Pingré, whose *Mémoire* of 1767 Surville may have read, but which was really intended for geographers and astronomers, believed that the Solomons were much further east.

While geographers pondered and speculated, explorers sailed into the Pacific. In August 1767, Carteret skimmed along the north of the Solomon group, and discovered Ndai, Kilinailau and Buka. In June 1768, Bougainville discovered the large island which now bears his name, as well as Vella Lavella, the Treasury Islands, and sighted Choiseul and Shortland Island. And in October 1769, Surville sailed to Choiseul, called at Port Praslin in Santa Isabel and proceeded along to Malaita, Ulawa and San Cristobal.

Neither of these realised that they had effectively rediscovered the lost Solomons. Surville, using Vaugondy's chart, was inevitably misled by it, but his information was essential if the geographers were to solve the puzzle.[2] It should come as no surprise that the geographers in question were French: the Arsacides, as Monneron reported, was a continent or an archipelago of very considerable size. The journals of the *St Jean-Baptiste* deserved careful scrutiny, but they were available only to the French – and admittedly the Spanish, but in a limited diplomatic context. Knowledge of the expedition does not seem to have been widespread at first: attention primarily focussed on the commercial aspects. Thus seven years elapsed before a geographer, helped by an enlightened naval administrator, drew up a memoir arguing that Surville's Arsacides and Mendaña's Solomons were identical.

Jean-Nicolas Buache de Neuville, born in 1741, had studied under his uncle Philippe Buache (1700–1773) and joined the Dépôt des Cartes et Plans where he came under the influence of Fleurieu, a practical sailor who had been involved in testing Berthoud's and Harrisson's chronometers and was appointed director of ports and arsenals in 1776. In January 1781 Buache presented to the Académie des Sciences a memoir on the Solomon Islands, 'Mémoire sur l'existence et la situation

---

[1] Forrest, *A Voyage to New Guinea*, p. viii.

[2] His failure to identify the Solomons himself has been criticised as negating his achievements: 'Surville...is lauded...for rediscovering the Solomons although failing...to identify them as Mendaña's mid-16th century discovery'. Helen Shawcross, review article, *Journal of the Polynesian Society*, LXXV, 2 (1966), p. 257. This is somewhat like suggesting that Columbus did not really contribute much to the discovery of the American continent because he thought he had reached India.

des îles de Salomon.'[1] This communication, which led to his election to the Académie, reexamined all the available evidence and pointed out that the early maps had all placed the Solomons off New Guinea; this, he argued, obviously reflected the contemporary opinion of cartographers. It was not until the mid-seventeenth century that they began to place the islands further east until, in despair, some had left them out entirely. Mendaña's widow, Buache pointed out, had spent only two days searching for the Solomons after her departure for Santa Cruz; this could suggest that Mendaña had told her they were not far to the west of it. She had given up too soon, and since her day only two men had sailed between Santa Cruz and New Guinea — Bougainville and Surville — while one, Carteret, had crossed the northern area; and all three had sighted islands, some of them very large, and obviously part of an archipelago. The reports by Bougainville, but more especially by Surville, on the customs and appearance of the natives tallied with Mendaña's description of the Solomon Islanders.

The case was well argued, but as yet it was only a theory and, as theories often do, it led to a bitter controversy. Alexis Rochon found it hard to accept,[2] while others, such as La Borde dismissed it out of hand.[3] La Pérouse was asked to seek confirmation — understandably since Buache and Fleurieu drew up his instructions — but he never reached the Solomons and the question remained open. Someone else sailed instead into the uncharted space between New Guinea and Santa Cruz: an Englishman, John Shortland, and he approached it from the south, making a landfall on San Cristobal and sailing west to Guadalcanal and the Russell Islands. It was August 1788. He passed through Bougainville Strait to the north of Bougainville Island and continued north to the Dutch East Indies. To the land he believed he had discovered he gave the name of New Georgia. As a navigator, Shortland deserves credit, but the editor of the narrative of his voyage, Stockdale, put forward claims on his behalf which the French could not let pass: 'the points seen and described by the French discoverers are very few, and for the knowledge of the form and bearings of the rest of the Coast...we are indebted entirely to the researches of our own countrymen'.[4]

The first Frenchman to respond was Jean-Baptiste de la Borde, not a professional geographer but a man of culture, a musician, a courtier,

---

[1] It was reprinted by Fleurieu in his *Découvertes des François*.
[2] Rochon, *Voyages aux Indes orientales*, p. 232.
[3] La Borde, *Histoire abrégée*, p. 7.
[4] Stockdale, *The Voyage of Governor Philip*, pp. 200–1.

an author of travel and other books. He put his protest in the form of a communication which he read to the Académie on 21 April 1790. He did not believe that Surville had rediscovered the Solomons, but that the Arsacides and Bougainville's various islands formed part of one very substantial archipelago or 'continent' and that the French discoveries, far from being 'very few', were very many. The title of his *mémoire*, which he published shortly after, makes his attitude quite clear: *Mémoire sur la prétendue découverte faite en 1788 par des Anglois d'un continent qui n'est autre chose que la Terre des Arsacides découverte en 1768 par...Bougainville...et en 1769 par Surville* – indicating that he believed both Frenchmen to have discovered jointly a large land mass.

To La Borde's chagrin, Buache read a similar paper four days later, and with Fleurieu set to work to answer Stockdale in a more reasoned and final manner. Fleurieu's book *Découvertes des François en 1768 et 1769* included in its title the firm statement that the English had subsequently visited and renamed the archipelago: *et reconnaissance postérieure des mêmes terres par des navigateurs anglois qui leur ont imposé de nouveaux noms.* Fleurieu gave credit where it was due, producing a synthesis of the contributions of Carteret, Bougainville, Surville and Shortland in a coordinated chart and reprinting Buache's original *Mémoire* to remind his readers of the geographer's earlier deductions.

What clinched the matter was the detailed description of the islands and their peoples given by the Spanish and the French is their respective journals. Monneron had already dropped a hint in his 'Extrait' when he wrote, 'One finds, however, in the Voyage of M. de Bougainville that he sighted part of the same land',[1] but he had also reported that the Arsacides natives made 'great use of a plant they call Binao which takes the place of bread' and added a marginal note to the effect that Figueroa, who wrote an account of the Mendaña expedition, had stated that 'a resin called Venau' was the principal food of the inhabitants of Santa Isabel.[2] The extent to which Fleurieu drew on the reports of the Surville expedition in connection with the islanders' customs and artifacts, and the information supplied on the flora is freely acknowledged.[3] They enabled him to present a case which was basically unanswerable. Mendaña has indeed discovered an important cluster of major islands, Carteret had come close to relocating them, Shortland could lay claim to part of New Georgia; the rest incontrovertibly belonged to Bougainville and Surville.

---

[1] Monneron, 'Extrait du Journal', marginal note, p. 35. [2] Ibid., p. 53.
[3] Fleurieu, *Découvertes des François*, pp. 230–1, 308–9.

Thus was the problem of the Solomons finally solved. With Cook's contributions in the south-west, the map of the Pacific could for the first time take on a definitive appearance. The mysterious islands which had beguiled cosmographers for so long could now be finally set down in their appropriate place, while the rumours of their great wealth, which had caused them to be named after Solomon, could be laid to rest with the ghosts of Davis Land and of Terra Australis. It had been Surville's destiny to help rediscover a land which many believed did not exist while losing his own life on a fruitless search for an imaginary island.

3. *New Zealand*

As far as the French knew, no European had ever set foot on New Zealand soil and the only encounter with its inhabitants had been Tasman's unhappy one of 1642. In fact James Cook had landed on the east coast of the North Island on 8 October 1769, while Surville was just reaching the Solomons, and by then the first Maori had already been killed.

Cook remained until March and his reports on the country and its inhabitants were lengthy and detailed. Nevertheless the information brought back in the French journals gives a valuable picture of the life and customs of a Maori community in the pre-European contact period, as much – and probably more – than one could expect from a group of officers on a non-scientific mission and in a poor state of health.

The influence of these reports on French attitudes towards New Zealand is hard to assess. Little was known in France about them until late 1771 and even then it was restricted to a small circle. By then, the reports of the Cook expedition were becoming available – the first French translation of the *Voyage* appeared in 1772. Surville's comments did not suggest that there were serious possibilities for trade; the inhabitants lived a fairly wretched existence, subsisting on fish and a few crops, their clothes were the skins of animals or made of flax and feathers; the villages, although well planned for the purpose of warfare, gave no indication of prosperity or comfort; there were no articles for barter except a few artifacts of value only as 'curiosities'.

When Marion Dufresne came to New Zealand for a more prolonged stay in 1772, he and a number of his men were ambushed, killed and eaten. That unhappy episode had the further effect of turning the French away from New Zealand, and almost seventy years elapsed before, spurred by thirty years of active British interest in the islands, they made a belated and rather perfunctory attempt to establish a settlement in the South Island.

Some have tried to lay the blame for Marion Dufresne's death on the kidnapping of the Maori chief Ranginui by Surville. The tradition of *utu*, revenge or blood payment, did indeed form part of Maori life; but to link the two suggests a unity of purpose between different and often warring tribes that did not exist, and it overlooks the fact that Marion Dufresne had been welcomed and well treated for five weeks before the attack took place. There were other, far more complex reasons for Marion Dufresne's death, and the simplistic answer of men like the Abbé Rochon, who viewed New Zealand as he did France – as a unified country with its honour to defend against insults or attacks anywhere on its territory – is untenable.

Time had to elapse before Surville's contribution to our knowledge of pre-colonial Maori life was appreciated. The reports of the expedition – comments by Surville himself, by Labé, Pottier de l'Horme and Monneron – lay ignored for many years, overlaid by comments about Maori savagery and by a growing body of information coming forward from English missionaries and administrators. But the latter were biased or at least coloured by predetermined points of view and by the need to impress men of influence in London or Sydney. When approaches to Maori culture seemed to suggest a degree of heretical sympathy, the reaction was violent, as was the case with the unfortunate missionary Thomas Kendall. Similarly it took time – and many lives – before some understanding was reached of Maori systems of land tenure, tribal relationships and defensive strategy. It was not until the mid-nineteenth century that serious and dispassionate studies were made of New Zealand's first inhabitants. By then, of course, the effects of European settlement had changed the original culture almost beyond recognition: a new generation had grown up and the survivors of the old had withdrawn into themselves. The journals of the Surville expedition provide a rare series of comments on pre-colonial life, with the added element that they emanated from a cultural background that was quite different from that of the English commentators and observers who provide us with the bulk of what we know of pre-colonial Maori life.

VII. TEXTUAL NOTES

1. The Journal of Surville is a holograph log in three foolscap books (*cahiers*) held in the National Archives in Paris, Section Marine, reference 4 JJ 143 file 24. The last 28 pages of the third cahier are blank.

The handwriting shows character and a generous nature: the writing is open and sweeping, but controlled. Legibility is hampered at times by water stains which have caused the writing of adjoining pages to show through; this is a particular problem at the beginning and end of each *cahier*. The ink has faded to a rusty brown, but the quality of the paper was good.

The interpretation of words, rather than sentences, has caused occasional problems, either because of obliterations or mis-spellings. Although not an uncultured man, Surville like so many others in his day is a poor speller. He was a practical man, he went to sea at the age of twelve, and his education, at least in respect of literacy, was basic. His vocabulary is extensive, but particularly with proper nouns, the spelling is erratic. The problem of standardisation arose in his case as it did with Labé's Journal. The solution chosen was to keep to the first spelling of a name, whatever different forms may be found subsequently; this procedure has not been followed, however, in some cases where a mis-spelling would merely cause confusion, especially when a different spelling of the same name occurs in Labé's Journal. Liberties of this kind have been kept to a minimum and explained in a footnote where necessary.

Capitalisation found in the original has been ignored in the translation where it will be found only as required by normal rules of grammar. One obvious reason for this is that in a translation certain linguistic structures are totally transformed, so that to allocate a capital letter somewhere in the English equivalent merely because Surville used a capital in the French is impossible to justify. For the same reason, punctuation has been corrected or inserted to the extent that English practice would require, although care has been taken to adhere to the original wherever possible.

Taking these factors into account, the translation has been kept as close as reasonable to the original. A totally literal translation would give a wrong impression: a rendering into elegant prose would similarly betray the style of the original. What has been attempted is a compromise – a readable account in a style that aims to preserve the flavour of Surville's own.

The Journal represents a daily report on the events of the day, counting from twelve midday to twelve midday. The log was normally written up in the early afternoon after the ship's midday position had been established. Unless a view of land and a reliable chart were available to pinpoint the ship's position, it could only be determined by dead reckoning, with only the latitude being checked – and this on condition that the weather was not overcast. The abbreviation Est. (for *Estimé*) has been retained as a convenient form for a latitude or longitude estimated by dead reckoning. Surville set down his daily calculations as an arithmetical sum; this layout has been simplified into a running paragraph. On a number of occasions, lengthy lists of sounding were given in the log; this also has been simplified by giving the first and last sounding only, with the word 'to' in square brackets.

Courses, or the estimated distance covered in the previous twenty-four hours, are based on dead reckoning. The formula used gives the estimated direction plus the distance in degrees and minutes which is then converted into leagues at 20 leagues (60 miles) per degree. Thus, the entry of 24 August records that the *St Jean-Baptiste* travelled 115′ which, converted at the rate of 20 leagues per degree, gives a distance from the point of departure of $38\frac{1}{3}$ leagues or 115 nautical miles.

Bearings, courses and positions have been given in the French style. This involves thirty-two divisions of the compass by rhumb lines giving an angular difference of 11°15′. Thus a reading of N$\frac{1}{4}$NE will give a difference from North of 11°15′, the next bearing NNE giving 22°30′, and so on.

The Journal of Labé is a manuscript copy held in the National Archives in Paris, Section Marine, under the same reference as Surville's, but file 22. It is signed by Labé as a true copy and dated 26 April 1774.

The original was kept by Labé – 'resté entre mes mains' – and is not available; thus the Journal presents all the problems deriving from a transcription by someone who was not present during the events that are referred to; Labé's original mis-spellings are compounded at times by the copyist's own errors into unrecognisable nonsense – on occasions the copyist has tried to solve a difficulty by merely imitating what appears in the original, i.e. drawing it. Furthermore the small precise handwriting is not easy to read, especially when towards the end of a page he begins to cram the text in a attempt to complete a whole day's entry on it.

Labé's syntax is engagingly erratic. He was clearly a less well educated man than the captain; when his feelings are involved his grammar and his construction of sentences suffer; he wrote, if not quite in the way he spoke, at least fairly close to it. Consequently, in spite of the occasional restoration work an adequate translation requires, his personality and his reactions come through quite clearly.

The Journal, like Surville's and Pottier's, is basically a shipboard log, rather than a narrative. The left-hand side of the page is ruled in columns in which are entered hourly the direction and strength of the wind, the weather, the estimated route, adjustments to the sails and any other items relating to the ship and the courses. The main text gives the midday positions, the distance travelled during the twenty-four hours, and general information about the ship and her progress. It is this text which is reprinted, the tables being omitted as being raw data on which Labé based his narrative, except where information of significance appears in them and nowhere else, in which case it is given usually as a footnote.

The same procedure has been adopted with regard to the style of the translation, the spellings, proper names, bearings, and the presentation of the ship's course in a running paragraph, as in the case of Surville's Journal. Cross-reference between the two has been kept to what was felt to be a reasonable minimum.

Several separate but overlapping summaries of the voyage are believed to have been made by Monneron. The clerk was sent to France on 26 October 1770 to obtain the release of the impounded vessel and he also had to keep the syndicate advised. One under reference 4JJ 143:23 is an 'Extrait du journal de Guillaume L'abé [sic], premier Lieutenant sur le Vaisseau le St Jean Baptiste...parti de Pondichéry en 1768 pour les Terres Australes', a title which is puzzling with its incorrect date and the bland reference to Terra Australis. In the same file is found the 'Extrait du Journal' signed by Monneron and dated Paris 4 October 1771. A further copy, 'Rédaction abrégée' exists under reference B4 316, which contains the Spanish translation of Surville's Journal by Don Juan Lacombe. A further 'Extrait du Journal', believed to be by Monneron, is held in the Bibliothèque Nationale, Nouvelles Acquisitions Françaises, under references 9436–9437, while an additional version is held in the Service Hydrographique de la Marine under the reference B 5708.

Scattered though these may be, they are due to the fact that Monneron was faced by the need to supply a concise narrative of the expedition to the various departments and individuals he approached.

The Ministry of Marine would have required a copy, as would the Ministry of Foreign Affairs which was involved in negotiations with Spain through France's ambassador in Madrid; the liquidators of the French India Company and Chevalier's representative in France, Monsieur de Rabec, and indeed Law and Chevalier themselves, would have been anxious to know, as speedily as possible, what had happened to the *St Jean-Baptiste*. If Monneron retained his own working copy, we can therefore assume that six *Rédactions abrégées* or *extraits* from the journals were made in 1771. There may easily have been more.

They do not tell us a great deal that we cannot find out from the two main Journals – Surville's and Labé's – or from other reports. Similarly Lacombe's translation, of which we can expect several copies to have been made, one initially for the Viceroy of Peru, one for the authorities in Spain, and one for the French in Paris (the translation in the Archives Nationales is patently the work of a copyist), is uninformative. There has been little profit in seeking clues in the Spanish version to obscurities or illegible passages in Surville's original Journal: it was found that in such cases Lacombe simply paraphrased the sentence loosely or avoided the problem by skirting around it.

Pottier de l'Horme's Journal is held with Surville's and Labé's in the Archives Nationales, Marine, under reference 4JJ 143 file 25. The handwriting is firm and flowing; the Journal is tidy, well set out and legible, but it consists to a large extent of tables, carefully drawn and providing the usual information about winds, courses and the working of the ship on a hourly basis. The courses and observations are shown separately with equal neatness.

Observations made by Pottier at various ports of call show the mind of an intelligent spectator, serious and conscientious. His spelling, however, is more erratic than his fellow officers', with occasional archaisms. His various comments have been published at intervals, for example in McNab's *Historical Records of New Zealand*, vol. II and in *The Journal of Pacific History*, vol. IX, the latter periodical giving a faithful rendering of the original spelling. It takes up 388 foolscap pages and includes a number of sketches and small drawings, but it does not shed much light on the origins of the expedition or relations between the various officers, or indeed on shipboard incidents other than matters of daily routine. One obtains the clear impression that Pottier, who was not involved in the commercial or political side of the expedition, kept himself very much to himself.

THE JOURNAL
OF SURVILLE

[*Surville's log opens with the entry of 3–4 March 1769 with his departure from the mouth of the Hooghly River, in Bengal. It is interrupted from 3 May to 2 June, the period of his stay in Pondicherry. Following the relatively speedy crossing to the Straits of Malacca, the* St Jean-Baptiste *struggled to Malacca and Trengganu. Both these stays are described in detail in the entries of 30 June and 29 July to 2 August.*

Surville then made for the Philippines, sighting Cape Bojeador, the north-eastern extremity of Luzon, on 18 August. The entry of 21 August describes his arrival at the Bashi Islands, north of Luzon, by which the expedition is to enter the Pacific Ocean. The ship anchored in the pass between Ibahos and Sabtang, referred to in the text as the islands of Bashi and Monmouth.]

Monday 21 August 1769

From the time of the altitude reading and the last bearings taken yesterday we kept to the courses shown in the margin, to reach the anchorage. We were taking soundings at every moment but found bottom only when we were well in between Bashi and Monmouth. We came across violent currents and whirlpools which would certainly have swung round any other ship than ours. At 1.45 the southernmost point of Bashi bore W when we found ground at 27 f. rotten coral.[1] The next throw of the lead 20 f. same ground, the next as quick 17 f., then 16. Then I just bore away along the reef without hauling in any further. I had the sails taken in and dropped anchor promptly in 14 f. same ground as above. I could have hauled along a little further N without coming in towards the reef but a squall blowing up forced me to anchor for fear of being driven off and losing the bottom: when you haul in to pass between these 2 islands Bashi and Monmouth you think the entire pass is closed by breakers and that there is no way through. But as you near these breakers they gather towards the side

[1] Fathoms. The French *brasse* was equal to five to six (French) feet, roughly the equivalent of two stretched-out arms (cf. bras). In modern terms a *brasse* is equal to 1·62 m or 5′ 3¾″.

of Bashi and look like nothing.[1] The island is surrounded by a very steep reef, so that to land we had to seek a little pass opposite a small sand dune in the NE approximately of the island, a little before [you reach] a point of the reef, which seems to advance quite a distance into the pass.

We have anchored in latde. N20°17′ and Dampierre had anchored in 20°20′.[2] He was N of the reef point I have just mentioned and in the NNE of the island and not the NE as he claims. He had anchored in 7 f. clear sandy bottom. Where we were, if we had anchored in such a depth, we would have anchored among the reefs themselves. We were better sheltered than Dampierre, only we should have been 1 or 2 cablelengths further N but without being any nearer the reef: there the ground would have been a little better as well as the shelter. Anyhow I warn those who may take it into their heads to come here to well hatchell their cable on account of the blocks of white coral found at intervals, and also when they come from the W, as soon as they have turned Cape Bojador to gain fast the latitude of the Bashi Islands which are clear, because the sea is extraordinarily rough in this passage and there are currents which, during calms, could carry you between the islands of north Luson which are not safe.[3] This is what I felt during the calm, I stemmed NE and even N when the wind allowed me without, for more than 15 h[ours], being able to clear one of the islands, the fourth. Moreover the sea is so rough that I think any other vessel than ours would have been carried off course and been unable to answer the helm, and that towards the island itself without being able to pass under the lee where perhaps one might find an anchorage. That is what I do not know. The bearings of our anchorage are: the southernmost part of Bashi Island we can see bore WSW3°C distant ¾ of a league[4]

[1] Marginal note: 'There are a few dangers when you come up between these two islands on account of the currents and the whirlpools. In addition the winds were bothering me a little when I entered.'

[2] William Dampier spent from 6 August to 3 October 1687 among these islands: 'The sixth day of August we arrived at the five Islands that we were bound to, and anchored on the East side of the Northernmost Island in 15 Fathom, a Cable's length from the Shore. Here, contrary to Expectation, we found abundance of Inhabitants in sight; for there were 3 large Towns all within a league of the Sea; and another larger town than any of the three, on the backside of a small Hill close by also; as we found afterwards. These Islands lie in 20 d. 20 m. North Lat. By my Observation, for I took it there, and I find their Longitude according to our Drafts, to be 141 d. 50 m. These Islands having no particular Names in the Drafts, some or other of us made use of the Seamens priviledge, to give them what Names we pleased.' *A New Voyage Round the World*, p. 421.

[3] There are strong tide rips on the Kalayan Bank over which the *St Jean-Baptiste* passed during the night of 19–20 August, and in the Balintang Channel between the Babuyan and Batan groups.

[4] The league, usually abbreviated to l. in the journals, was equal to approximately 3 nautical miles.

or 1 l., the reef is two cable lengths from land and continues all along the coast as far as N¼NW3°W. From the moment we entered the pass between the two islands a quantity of small boats full of islanders followed us and some of them made sign to us to make for Monmouth Island. Their gestures were first made with their hands or with a paddle, but thinking this was not sufficient they came straight across our track, made [signs] with their hands at first, then suddenly turned their boats and stemmed towards the place where they wanted us to be and repeated this all the time adding their voice to these actions. But there is no anchorage in that part of Monmouth except close inshore among the rocks.

As I had no time to lose I could not spare any time to look for a place to get water. On Bashi Island you can find it only in wells far from the shore and even then beyond hillocks where it would be impossible to roll the barrels. Mr Labé, my first officer went all along the side of Monmouth which is close to us without finding a suitable place to get it, except behind a reef breaker where he got with extreme difficulty 8 barrelfuls and where he told me one risked losing one's boats and he himself had been forced to swim to land and re-embark.

I obtained from Bashi Island 17 pigs and 15 or 16 kids. The pigs cost me one piastre and one knife each, the kids 2 or 3 knives according to their size. The islanders themselves brought the pigs sometime from one league away for one knife or a drink of wine each, giving them afterwards the empty bottle.

I had in the end to trust them, if not I would never have finished. I suddenly gave to one who came up to me more than did the others ten piastres and ten knives, making him understand that I wanted ten *Baboui* which is the name they give to pigs. He set to at once to get them for me. Some were brought during the evening, most of them up to the ship's boat where they loaded them themselves, and the next morning they brought me the remainder to the ship in their own boats.

Three men deserted here, part of the crew of our longboat. They had certainly planned their escape because when they went ashore they had their [spare] clothes with them. I do not know whether the islanders were party to it or whether they hid in some hole without showing themselves until after the ship had sailed, but it is certain that they appeared never to understand anything when I showed them three men and made signs to show they had fled [and] that they had to be brought back to me. They could see I was displeased, which puzzled them. They then hastened to bring me the remainder of the pigs they owed me and then asked me whether this was satisfactory, by using the word *Mapia* which is what it means, but I at once signified that it was not and I showed them three sailors, gesturing to show they had run away and that they had to be brought back. They did not seem to understand me. Finally I decided to arrest 24 or 25 of those who were on board and have them tied up, and I began again my gestures to these because all the others had fled. After making many gestures which we thought they had at last understood I had most of them released and kept only 6 as hostages. Those I had released seemed to have understood us so well that they asked us for ropes to tie up our men, and we gave them some. They then called their boats which were standing a great distance off and which indeed came to get them. They left, leaving us to understand that they would bring back our men, but nothing appeared. However, several boats came back, some of which brought goats and pigs which they wanted to give me, making signs for me to release their friends. In the end, seeing that I was only wasting time which was all the more precious to me because I had not been able to obtain water in these islands, I decided to release three of the six islanders I had retained. I gave each of them a six-foot length of cloth and they hailed a boat which came to take them off.[1]

The one I had given ten piastres yesterday morning to buy pigs has been bold enough to return on board since I had some arrested and to come into the quarter deck cabin where I showed him his friends tied up. He did not appear very put out by it; but then passing his hand over my back to caress me while showing me the pigs he had brought, saying his word to ask if I was pleased (Mapia), but as I made a sign to indicate the opposite and displayed some impatience showing him three sailors I needed, he went away fairly precipitately with some signs of fear. Nevertheless after this another boat came up with the sole intention of trading. They displayed at first a great deal of fear as they came alongside, but then got bolder and climbed on the fore and aft gangway where I bought everything they had, paying fairly well so that they left very satisfied.

Finally having spent nearly 24 h[ours] waiting for my three men and

---

[1] Unless they identified them as the cause of the kidnapping and understood that they were under Surville's orders and had disobeyed him by staying ashore, the islanders may have regarded the three deserters as welcome settlers. When Dampier visited the islands, the natives gave indications that they would welcome Europeans; a storm had blown up, forcing Dampier to put to sea for a while, leaving six of his men ashore; he found on his return that they had each been offered 'a young Woman to Wife, and a small Hatchet, and other Iron Utensils, fit for a Planter, in Dowry; and withal showed them a piece of Land for them to manage. They were courted thus by several of the Town where they were.' *A New Voyage Round the World*, pp. 438–9.

the tide being favourable to leave the two islands, I unmoored and sailed, taking our three prisoners who began to weep when they saw the ship sailing beyond their islands. Their tears lasted only a moment, after which they remained quiet and lay down as if to sleep, but I had shirts and pants brought which I got them to wear. Then they began to laugh, saying Mapia which meant that this was good. As I had had their hands tied up again after dressing them for fear they might throw themselves overboard, and in addition had them watched by the soldiers because one had already jumped with his hands tied and had thus reached one of their boats,[1] they made such pressing requests to be untied that I released them and they remained quiet. There are however two who seem still a little sad over their involuntary departure, as for the 3rd [he] seems very gay.

These three islands are as well farmed as any land I have seen. There are excellent figs, very large and very good potatotes, yams, coconuts; they also grow sorghum and a kind of small bean which they eat boiled. They have maize but do not appear to me to cultivate it very much. There are almost no trees on Bashi Island and even fewer on Goat Island.[2] If the small number of trees they have give fruit, it was not the season for it, for we saw none. There are guavas. The Bashi is a kind of [?] which is fairly good but not as good as Dampierre says.[3] On land the women came up to us freely as the men. They were the ugliest that I have seen among such people. Their legs are decorated with glass beads. They put much more on one than on the other.

Thursday 24 August 1769

We sailed at 3 yesterday afternoon with a good westerly breeze. We first made S to get free of the pass. At 4 sailed S$\frac{1}{4}$SE, and at 4.15 E$\frac{1}{4}$SE. The S point of Monmouth Island bore then NE2°N, the northernmost

---

[1] This was one of the original twenty-five.

[2] Dequey Island.

[3] 'Their common Drink is Water; as it is of all other Indians: Beside which they make a sort of Drink with the Juice of the Sugar-cane which they boil, and put some black sort of Berries among it. When it is well boiled, they put it into great Jars, and let it stand 3 or 4 days and work. Then it settles, and becomes clear, and is presently fit to drink. This is an excellent liquor, and very much like English Beer both in colour and Taste. It is very strong, and I do believe very wholesome: For our Men, who drank briskly of it all day for several Weeks, were frequently drunk with it, and never sick after it. The Natives brought a vast deal of it every day to those aboard and ashore: For some of our Men were ashore at work on Bashee Island; which Island they gave that name to from their drinking this Liquor there; that being the Name which the Natives call'd this Liquor by...and indeed by the plenty of this Liquor, and their plentiful use of it, our Men call'd all the Islands, the Bashee Islands'. Dampier, *A New Voyage Round the World*, p. 431.

of Bashi N$\frac{1}{4}$NW4$\frac{1}{2}$°W, the southernmost of the same island NW$\frac{1}{4}$N4°N. At 5.30 appears an island bearing SE$\frac{1}{4}$S3°E.[1]

At 6 p.m. the island that bore SE$\frac{1}{4}$S3°E at 5.30 stretches to the SE$\frac{1}{4}$S4°S. The south point of Grafton[2] bears WNW distant about 4 l., the south of Monmouth NNW5°W 8 to 9 l., the NE bears N$\frac{1}{4}$NE3°N distant 9 to 10 l., a point [which forms] about the middle of the same island N. Until the said hour we steered E$\frac{1}{4}$SE making 1$\frac{1}{2}$ l. an hour. I take my point of departure at 7.30 p.m., reckoning myself N and S of Monmouth and Grafton. At 1.30 a.m. the wind rose, the sea became very rough, one roller came from the NE, another from W to WSW. At three lowered the mizzen tops as well as the fore topsail on account of the wind being right aft. At 7.30 took in the mizzen tops and took in all reefs. The ship is labouring heavily.

Courses E$\frac{1}{4}$SE2°30'S 115' or 38$\frac{1}{3}$ leagues. Lat.N about 20°, diff. S 25', Est. N19°35' observed 19°49', diff. N14'. Long. E of Monmouth 1°42'.[3]

Friday 25 August 1769

We spent the whole night with the topsails close reefed and the mizzen, sometimes the mizzen topsail close reefed. At 6 a.m. I let out two main and fore topsail reefs and 1 mizzen top. At 7.30 hauled aboard the mainsail tack. The sea was frightful. It is beginning to moderate.

Courses SE 114' or 38$\frac{1}{6}$ league. Lat. N 19°49', diff. S 1°22, Est. 18°27, observed 18°26'. Long. E of Month. 1°42', diff. E 1°22', Est. E 3°04'.

The ship has been cruelly strained by the rolling and so have the masts; consequently one of the shroud chains snapped.

Saturday 26th

We have had very fine weather since yesterday. There is a swell but rising aft so that the ship does not strain. We have continually sailed all canvass out except at 11.30 this morning when, the weather clouding over a little, we took in the topgallants, staysails and standing jib.

Courses SE 89$\frac{1}{4}$' or 29$\frac{9}{12}$ leagues. Lat. N 18°26', diff. S 1°03', Est. N 17°23', observed 17°34', diff. N 11'. Long. E of Monmouth 3°04', diff. E 1°03', Est. E 4°07'.

---

[1] Balintang Island, in the channel of that name, between the Batan and Babuyan groups.
[2] Batan Island.
[3] Marginal note: 'I left N and S of Monmouth 118°49' east of Paris, difference E 1°48', estimated position East 120°37'.' The correct longitude of the island is 119°37' east of Paris.

We sighted a comet during the night. It is bearded, is not bright and rose in the [blank].[1]

Sunday 27th

We have had fair weather, but weak breezes. At 1 we were compelled to haul in the topgallants on account of the calm and the swell, the sea still being rough. At 6 this morning we let them out again.

Courses SE¼S4°E 59' or 19⅔ leagues. Lat. N 17°34', diff. S 47', Est. 16°47', observed 16°46'. Long. E of Monmouth 4°07', diff. E 36', Est. E 4°43'.

The sea is still swelling and rises from different sides. This worries the ship, especially with the weak breezes.

Monday 28 August 1769

We have had clouds and gusts, but no rain, although sometimes we had cause to lower the main and fore topsails and clew up the mizzen topsails.

Courses SE¼S 111' or 37 leagues. Lat. N. 16°46', diff. S 1°32', Est. N 15°14', observed 15°11, diff. S 3'. Long. E 123°48', diff. E 1°04', Est. E 124°52'.[2]

Tuesday 29th

Yesterday we were under the 4 main sails; 1 o'clock under the main and fore topsails. At 2 p.m. let out the mizzen topsail. The sea was rough. At 5 let out the standing jib and mizzen. Strong gusts blew from 8 to midnight. At 8.30 we had hauled in the mizzen topsail. At 6 a.m. the sky was cloudy everywhere, treble reefed the main and fore topsails. At 10 o'clock clewed up the mizzen topsail and the standing jib as well as the mizzen. At 11.30 set the standing jib and stay sails. The weather seemed to be undecided during the whole morning as to whether it would set fair or not.

---

[1] This comet was discovered by Charles Messier (1730–1817) and first sighted by him in Paris on 8 August 1769. It has a very large orbit of uncertain period and has not been observed since. As Messier discovered a number of comets of which this is the fifth, an appropriate designation would be Comet Messier (5). A description appears in S. K. Vsekhsytatskii, *Physical Characteristics of Comets*, published in Jerusalem in 1964. Less scientifically this is also Napoleon's Comet – he was born on 19 August 1769 – the subject of Messier's monograph *Grande Comète qui a paru à la naissance de Napoléon le Grand, découverte et observée pendant quatre mois*, Paris, 1808.

[2] Surville is changing to an estimated position east of Paris.

Courses SE$\frac{1}{4}$S2°30′E 114′ or 38 leagues. Lat. N 15°11, diff. S 1°32′, Est. N 13°39′. Long. E of Grafton [*sic*] 124°52′, diff. E 1°09′, Est. E 126°01′.

Wednesday 30 August 1769

At about 5 yesterday afternoon the sky clouded over and the weather became stormy. Continuous rain from 8 to midnight, lowered and hauled up again 3 times the main and fore topsails. At about 4 we had a very strong thunderclap right over us, all the others before and after were distant. From midnight to 4 o'clock the weather being worse than ever, we stayed under the foresail, and the main and fore topsails lowered. At 4.30 we hauled in the main and fore topsails, hauled aboard the main tack and let out the mizzen topsail. There was constant rain, but a steady settled breeze.

Courses SE30′S 72$\frac{1}{2}$′ or 24$\frac{1}{6}$ leagues. Lat. N. 13°39′, diff. N 52′, Est. N 12°47′. Long. E 126°01′, diff. E 52′, Est. E 126°53′. The sea is fairly smooth.

Thursday 31 Auguat 1769

The weather has been very fine. The comet appeared and much brighter and larger than the first day we saw it. It rose at 11.15.

Courses SE$\frac{1}{4}$E3°40′E 48′ or 16 leagues. Lat. N 12°47′, diff. S 24′, Est. N 12°23′, observed 12°21′, diff. over 3 days 2′. Long. E 126°53′, diff. E 43′, Est. E 127°36′.

For the last few days we have been followed by 2 birds which are perching on board and whose plumage is like a starling's.[1]

Friday 1 September 1769[2]

We have had almost nothing but calms during the 24 hrs, as may be seen from the log-board. In spite of that we have been compelled sometimes to reduce canvas when the ship, in spite of the helm, lay in the trough of the sea, on account of the flapping of the sails causing them to tear. We [were] at times unable to steer, especially from midnight until dawn when a storm rose up.

Courses SSW1°50′S 12′ or 4 leagues. Lat. N 12°21, diff. S 11′, Est. N 12°10′. Observed 12°10′. Long. 127°36′, diff. W 5′, Est. E 127°31′.

[1] The Micronesian starling (*Aplonis opacus*) is widespread in the Marianas and Carolines.
[2] Written '7bre'. In the same way, October is customarily spelt '8bre', November '9bre', and December '10bre'.

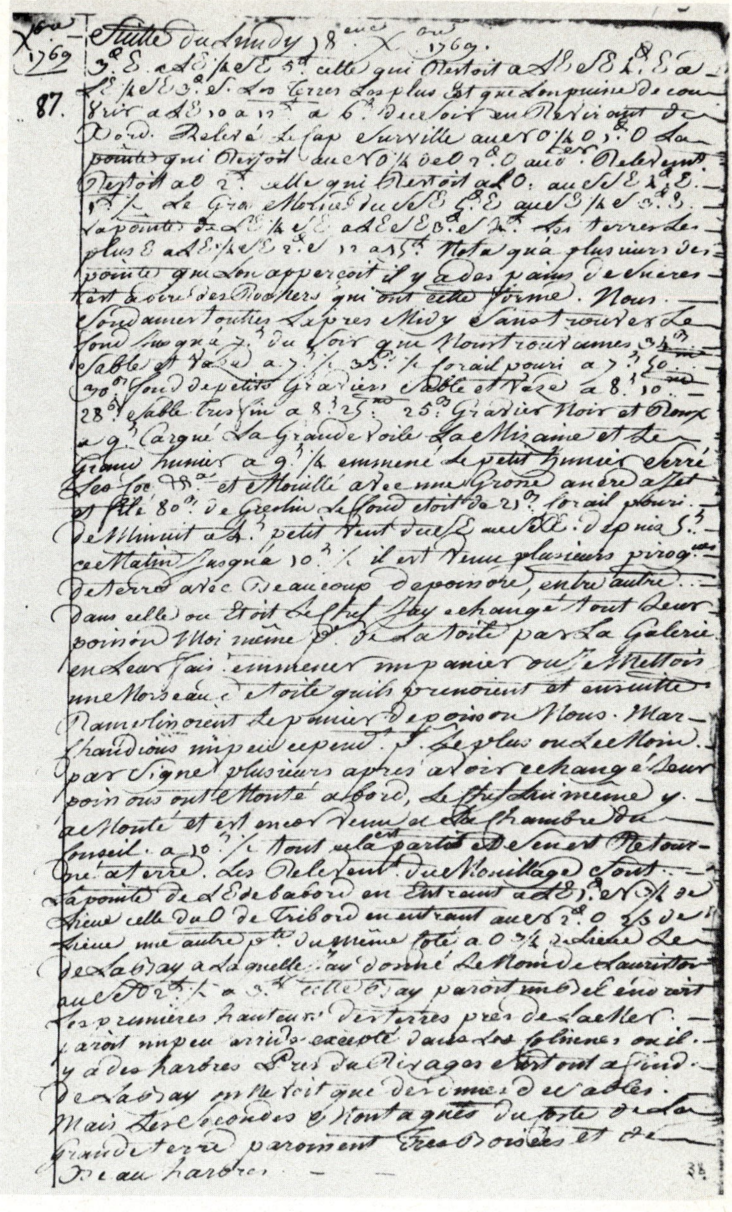

Plate 2. A page from Surville's Journal (18 October 1769)

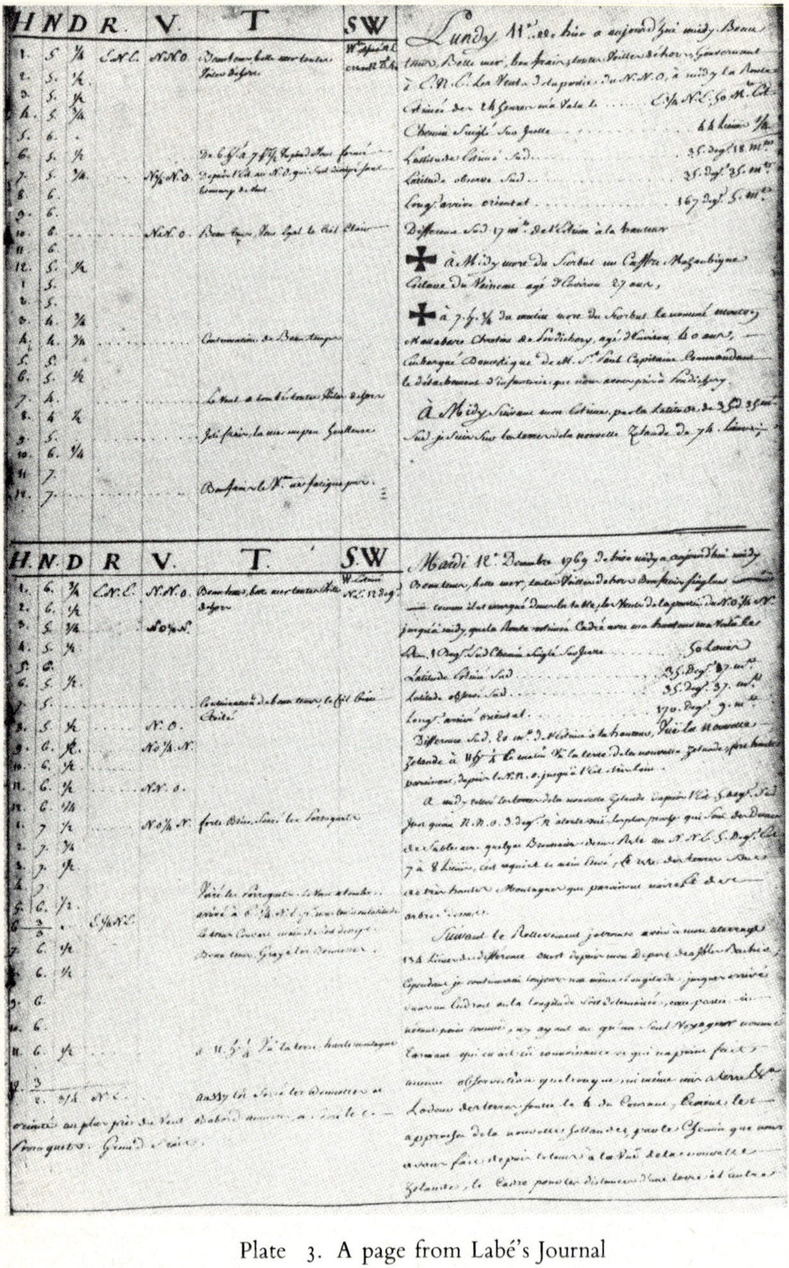

Plate 3. A page from Labé's Journal

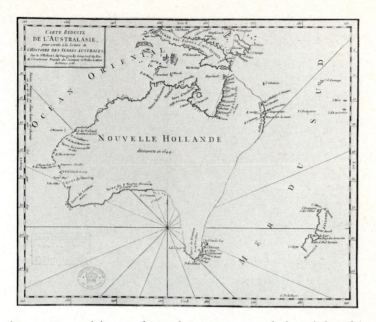

Plate   4. Vaugondy's map of Australasia, summarising the knowledge of the
area in the decade prior to the voyage

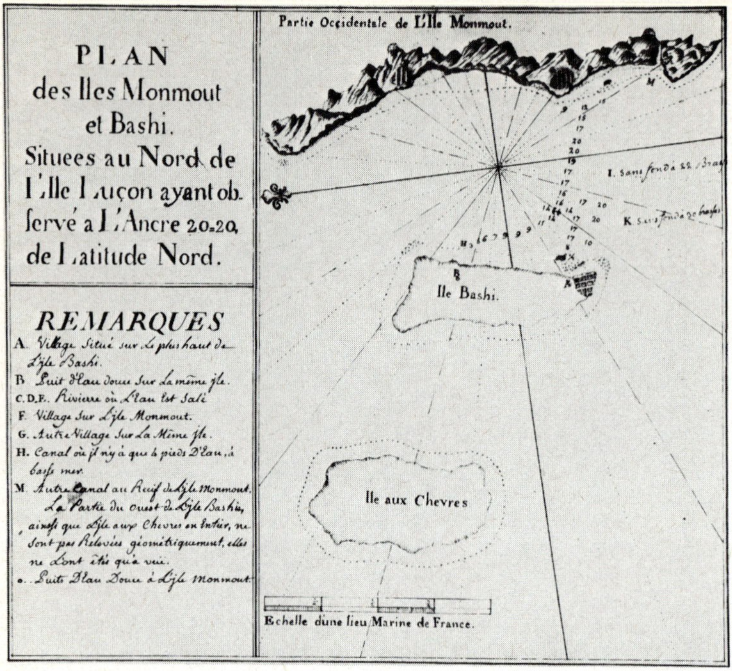

Plate 5. Chart of the anchorage, Bashi Islands, by Pottier de l'Horme

There was thunder and the horizon was overcast in the NE, but it cleared without reaching us.

Saturday 2nd

Last night at 6 seeing the weather turning squally I had all sails single-reefed. At 8 a stormy squall. Much thunder and lightning and little rain. Fairly good weather from 8 to midnight. At 6 this morning the weather improved, we let out the three topgallants. At 10 this morning we fixed new backstays to our topgallants. We let out jibs and staysails and hauled the mizzen taut. At midday exactly [?] the weather clouded again.

Courses S 93' or 31 leagues. Lat. N 12°10', diff. S 1°33', Est. N 10°3', observed 10°26', diff. S 11'. Long. 127°31'.

The sea has been very smooth.

Sunday 3rd

We had a fierce squall yesterday afternoon. We clewed up the mainsail and the fore topsail. At 3 I had all the reefs taken because the weather looked threatening. At 2.30 we brought aboard the main tack. All this bad [weather] has cleared. At 11 p.m. I let out two reefs. We still had squalls after midnight, but not strong. The winds were variable and squally in the morning.

Courses S¼SW3°15'S 41½' or 13⅚ leagues. Lat. N 10°26', diff. S 41', Est. N 9°45', observed 9°43', diff. S 2'. Long. E 127°31', diff. W 6', Est. E 127°25'.

The weather has been constantly overcast in patches, without much rain or wind.

Monday 4 September 1769

The weather has been very changeable, nearly always overcast, sometimes a light rain without wind. We changed course 3 or 4 times as can be seen, taking advantage of wind changes. We had no altitude.

Courses SE¼E3°E 37' or 12⅓ leagues. Lat. N 9°43', diff. S 19', Est. N 9°24'. Long. E 127°25', diff. E 32', Est. E 127°57',

Tuesday 5th

At about 4.30 yesterday afternoon I saw the weather was becoming overcast. I had all the reefs taken in and was well advised in this [for] we had a storm all night and violent gusts until midnight, then the rain continued without strong squalls, so that during the night we were first under the four main sails, then the fore and main topsails and the mizzen, then the mizzen and the main topsail, and about $\frac{1}{2}$ an hour under the mizzen but it was not necessary. At dawn the weather improved. I have even seen the sun piercing through just a little above the horizon. In spite of that the sky remained so overcast from that time that the sun did not reappear, but it was a sky with light scattered rain at times without gusts.

Courses SE$\frac{1}{4}$E4°E 47' or 15$\frac{2}{3}$ leagues. Lat. N 9°24', diff. S 23', Est. N 9°01'. Long. E 127°57', diff. E 41'. Est. E 128°38'.

Daprès' charts, which I have been using continually since Pondicherry, seem until now to be the best.[1] One must wait a little longer to decide the extent of their [reliability?].

Wednesday 6 September 1769

The weather never cleared all day yesterday. We could not see the sun even at sunset, which led me to wait for the moon to set to let out the reefs. Moreover we have everything out, jibs, staysails, mizzen, etc. At 9 o'clock everything was unfurled. Since that time the breeze has not stopped slackening and backing.

Courses SE$\frac{1}{4}$E32'E 64$\frac{1}{2}$' or 21$\frac{1}{2}$ leagues. Lat. N 9°01', diff. S 35', Est. N 8°26', observed 8°, diff. S since Sunday 26'. Long. E 128°38', diff. E 53', Est. E 129°31'.

Thursday 7th

We have had calm during these 24 hours and in the places where the ship is shown as sailing ahead she was doing so with so much leeway

[1] Jean-Baptiste Nicolas Denis d'Après de Mannevillette (1707–1780), son of a captain in the French India Company, had sailed for India for the first time at the age of 12 in the *Solide* commanded by his father. He then studied geometry and astronomy under Joseph Nicolas Delisle, the mathematician and geographer. He travelled extensively in African and Eastern waters. His main work is the *Neptune Oriental* (1745, 2nd ed. 1775), translated into English as the *East India Pilot* (London, 1782), but he was also the author of three lesser known books on matters of navigation in Eastern waters. Surville was probably using the *Neptune Oriental*, which included 77 maps and charts; his spelling of d'Après' name is retained in this translation.

that it can only be considered as drifting so that I do not know where the currents have carried us. I think it is to the NE. I am reducing none of my courses. They are not worth it.[1] I observed at midday 8°18′. That means I have lost 6 leagues North. As for my long^{de} I am not altering it for fear I may do so the wrong way: 129°31′.

The comet we have been seeing for some time has not been visible until now at the time of its rising. It rose at 1 a.m. to the E¼NE. We had all day seven sharks around the ship; we caught 6 of them. I have never seen so many caught in one day.

Friday 8 September 1769

We have had the finest light breeze in the world since yesterday 3 p.m. The night very clear and fine. From daylight only the sky became cloudy and from 9.30 till 10.30 we had heavy showers without wind. The little there was changed from a minute to the next from E to W and S. Finally at 10.30 the sky lightened and the wind settled SE to SSE but without any end to the rain.

Courses S2°W 40′ or 13⅓ leagues. Lat. N 8°18′, diff. S 40′, Est. N 7°38′. Long. E 129°31′, diff. W 2′, Est. E 129°29′.

We saw this morning a flock of small birds I do not know.

Saturday 9th

Courses S1°5′E 32′ or 8 leagues. Lat. N 7°38′, diff. S 32′, Est. 7°06′, observed 6°36′, diff. S 30′. Long. E 129°29′, diff. E 1′, Est. E 129°30′.

We have had fairly fine weather since yesterday, but very light breezes. Today we have seen no other birds than tropic birds[2] but we have seen a great number. We have 6 bales affected by water in the hold, due to the run-off of the heavy rains we have had these last two days. Fortunately there is no damage. We dried everything out and there was only one bale where the water had penetrated beyond the oil cloth and only a few lengths of cambaye were very slightly wet.

---

[1] The considerable easterly drift which resulted in the *St Jean-Baptiste* eventually reaching the Solomons is quite clear at this stage. Longitudes throughout September are quite unreliable. Passing between Palau and Yap, the French were sailing E and ESE south of the Carolines.

[2] There are two species of tropic-birds, the white-tailed (*Phaeton lepturus*) and the red-tailed (*Phaeton rubricauda*), both widespread in the south-west Pacific.

Sunday 10 September 1769

Throughout the afternoon yesterday the weather was very fine and the wind moderate. At 6.30 seeing the wind freshening and considering the short distance we have to cover before reaching St Andrew's Islands,[1] especially since I had 30′ diff^{te}. S at midday, I took in the topgallants. At 7 I had the staysails and the standing jib furled, finally at 9.30 having been forced to take in the main and fore topsails on account of passing squalls, I clewed up the mainsail and the mizzen, and once the squalls had passed we stayed under the topsails, single-reefed. Very soon after this we saw two large pieces of wood pass alongside. We then had more passing squalls which forced us to take in our fore and main topsails. At 4.45 we felt a squall, not well formed, rather a kind of gust, but very strong. That was the last. Until midday we had a fresh gale, but the weather fine.

At dawn, as we could not see St Andrew's Islands, I bore away SE waiting for a reading.

Courses SE$\frac{1}{4}$S1°S 94′ or 31$\frac{1}{3}$ leagues. Lat. N 6°36′, diff. S 1°20′, Est. N 5°16′, observed N 4°57′, diff. S 19′. Long. E 129°30′, diff. E 51′, Est. E 130°21′.

Monday 11th

The weather has been very fine since yesterday. Towards the morning, that is say since midnight numerous clouds have passed over without squalls, so we have had no wind from them. At dawn the E horizon was very black but evenly and with no appearance of squalls. This weather lifted gradually. A few light drops of rain fell, after which the sky cleared without squalls or wind, nor a wind change although this blackness moved from the E towards the W.

Courses ESE 96′15″ or 32$\frac{1}{2}$ leagues. Lat. N 4°57′, diff. S 37′, Est. N 4°20′, observed 4°08′, diff. S 12′. Long. E 130°21′, diff. E 1°30′, Est. E 131°51′.

---

[1] Surville, basing himself on the rather unreliable charts of the time, was making for St Andrew's or Sonsorol Island south-west of the main Palau group, which would have provided him with water and fresh fruit. Sonsorol was named St Andreas by Francisco Padilla who sighted it in 1710. The basic information on the Carolines was derived from an account by Fr Juan Cantova, published in *Lettres Edifiantes* in Paris in 1728 with a chart that remained in use until the cartographic advances of scientific parties in the nineteenth century rendered it obsolete. See Hezel and del Valle, 'Early European contact with the Western Carolines', *Journal of Pacific History*, v (1972), pp. 26–44.

Tuesday 12 September 1769

Very fine. Light breeze. The sea as in a strait. A few clouds did pass over during the night, but without giving anything. We took a few precautions with the sails and put them back soon after.

Courses ESE2°40′S 66¾′ or 22³⁄₁₂ leagues. Lat. N 4°08′, diff. S 28′, Est. 3°40′, observed 3°21′, diff. S 19′. Long. E 131°51′, diff. E 1°01′, Est. E 132°52′.

We have seen a few tropic birds and 2 or 3 *chevaliers*, these small birds that stay on the shore.[1]

Wednesday 13th

The weather has been less clear than on previous days. Numerous clouds passed over during the night without bringing any wind. This morning the weather is completely overcast, so that we have not had any altitude. We have sometimes furled some minor sails, but it was as a precaution; there has not been a single squall accompanied by wind. The wind has been often variable, but from 2 to ¾ only, which forced us to change the studding sails at every moment.

Courses E1°S 86½′ or 28⅚ leagues. Lat. N 3°21′, diff. S 2′, Est. N 3°19′. Long. E 132°52′, diff. E 1°27′, Est. E 134°19′.

The sea seems to me to have changed a little since this morning.

Thursday 14th

Yesterday afternoon we had everything out, studding sails and royals. At 4 o'clock a turtle passed alongside. At 7.30 there was a little fine rain but nothing else. At 8.45 a rainstorm without wind. As a precaution I had the topgallants, royals and studding sails furled. At 9.30 all that was put back. The weather remained cloudy with a fresh gale all night. There were a few wind changes and clouds without rain.

Courses E3°45′S 2′. Lat. N 3°21′, diff. S 6′, Est. N 3°15′, observed 2°57′, diff. S 18′. Long. E 134°19′, diff. E 1°19′, Est. E 135°38′.

I saw some seaweed this morning. We have also seen a gannet[2] and another land bird.

---

[1] This name is applied to a number of birds, including the Sandpiper. Both the Wood Sandpiper (*Tringa glareola* Linnaeus) and the Common Sandpiper (*Actitis hypoleucos* Linnaeus) are common in this part of the Pacific.

[2] 'The tropical species of this family are generally called boobies. They are robust seabirds, related to the cormorants, pelicans and tropic-birds.' Mayr, *Seabirds of the*

Friday 15th

At 1.30 yesterday a sudden shifting of the wind brought a strong squall, whereupon furled the mizzen topsail and the mainsail, then I had all the reefs taken in the topsails. The rain continued for a long while. No thunder. All this had cleared by the evening. I let out 2 reefs at 7 o'clock. The night was fairly fine. There was a squall at 2 but there was only a little rain. The topsails were taken in. From 6 to 8 variable breeze and light rain. At 10.30 fair weather. All sails out.

Courses E4°S 71′ or 23⅔ leagues. Lat. N 2°57′, diff. S 5′, Est. N 2°52′, observed 2°29′, diff. S 23′. Long. E 135°38′, diff. E 1°11′, Est. E 136°49′.

The sea is running a little higher than on previous days.

Saturday 16 September 1769

From 5 to 6 yesterday evening we had variable light squalls which however led us to be cautious with the sails. At 9.30 everything was set, studding sails included. The weather was fine during the whole night, but the strength of the breeze varies constantly from very weak to rather fresh, but not gusty. We saw last night 2 gannets, one frigate bird,[1] one gull[2] and a [?]

Courses E4°12′S 68′ or 22⅔ leagues. Lat. N 2°29′, diff. N 5′,[3] Est. N 2°24′, observed 2°05′, diff. S 19′. Long. E 136°49′, diff. E 1°06′, Est. E 137°55.

Sunday 17th

At about 3 o'clock yesterday afternoon a large round log, several pieces of bamboo and some gulf-weed[4] passed alongside. At 8 a gust right aft. Took in the topgallants and brought the topsails to half-mast

---

Southwest Pacific, p. 17. The French word, used by Surville and Labé, is *fou* – Crazy bird – a reference to the booby's tendency to perch on a ship within easy reach of sailors. There are three species of boobies in the South-west Pacific: the Brown Booby (*Sula leucogaster*), the red-footed Booby (*Sula sula*) and the Masked or Blue-faced Booby (*Sula dactylatra*). Of these the first is the most common.

[1] The two species found in this part of the world are the Pacific Man-o'-War (*Fregata minor* Ginelin) and the Least Man-o'-War (*Fregata ariel* Gray).

[2] If this was a true gull, it would indicate that land was indeed close since gulls are essentially coastal birds. 'There is only one gull in the S.W.P.' states Mayr (*Birds of the Southwest Pacific*, p. 21), the Australian Silver Gull (*Larus novaehollandiae*).

[3] Corrected in a marginal note. Part of these entries is obliterated.

[4] *Sargasso*. From now on, Surville and his men will continue to watch for these and other signs of the proximity of land: 'during the night we heard the cries of several birds, all these things are indication of the proximity of land'. Pottier, *Journal*, p. 93.

more as a precaution than as a necessity. The weather remains overcast and a thin rain continued falling until midnight. At 8.45 the topsails were back. At 2 a.m. put back the topgallants, at 3 the studding sails. Weather fair.

Courses E¼SE4°15′E 59′ or 19⅔ leagues. Lat. N 2°05′, diff. S 8′, Est. N 1°57′. Long. E 137°55′, diff. E 59′, Est. E 138°54′.

We have seen a few petrels, and last night at 8 when the gust blew up it was preceded by several birds who made themselves heard by their cries, but I was unable to identify them. Also, yesterday afternoon a shoal of bonito[1] passed alongside going apparently in a straight line, for they stayed only a moment near the ship.

Monday 18 August [sic] 1769

We have had fair weather but little wind.

We saw some birds, but not many. We saw several pieces of wood, large and small, and a snake.[2]

All the evening from 8 to 10 there were a few light showers with no wind.

Courses E¼NE4°12′E 32′, or 10⅔ leagues. Lat. N 1°57′, diff. N 4′, Est. 2°01′, observed 1°53′, diff. S 8′. Long. E 138°54′, diff. E 32′, Est. E 139°26′.

The sky is much clearer today than it has been recently.

Tuesday 19th

We have had fine weather since yesterday, although it clouded over a little during the night. Clear at daylight. At about 3 o'clock yesterday we saw a curlew which later let itself be caught at nightfall, having settled near a sailor;[3] it had settled a few times before on the water and flown off without difficulty. We have seen since dawn a quantity of gulf-weed go by, with large and small pieces of wood, and finally, at 11.30, a whole tree [with] roots and branches, stripped of its bark. We have seen fruit from those trees which grow on the seashore. Some cuttle-bones.

[1] Probably the *Sarda orientalis* which is common in this part of the Pacific.
[2] There are many species of sea snakes (*Hydrophiidae*). Surville many have sighted the yellow-bellied snake, *Pelamis platurus*, often seen on the high sea.
[3] Normally the curlew is a wary bird. This one was exhausted, as Pottier makes clear: 'He had been in poor condition for some time, which I estimate from his apparent thinness and exhaustion'. *Journal*, p. 94. Three species are recorded from this area: the Whimbrel (*Numenius phaeopus variegatus* Scopoli), the Bristle-thighed Curlew (*Numenius tahitiensis* Ginelin) and the Long-billed Curlew (*Numenius madagascariensis* Linnaeus).

Courses [blank]. Lat. N 1°53′, diff. N 19′, Est. N 2°12′, observed 2°12′. Long. E 139°26′, diff. E 1°06′, Est. E 140°32′.

Wednesday 20th

The weather since yesterday has been fairly fine and fresh. Only at about 11 o'clock this morning did the horizon cloud over in the S and SSW. We have continually seen pieces of wood since yesterday. Very few birds.

Courses E¼SE4°E 98′ or 32⅔ leagues. Lat. N 2°12′, diff. S 13′, Est. N 1°59′ observed 1°54′, diff. S 5′. Long. E 140°32′, diff. E 1°38′, Est. E 142°10′.

We have not seen the comet although the sky was quite clear.

Thursday 21st

The wind died down gradually from midday yesterday, so that at midday today we have almost none. We saw more pieces of wood yesterday afternoon and a few this morning, but not many, and no more gulf-weed at all. At 5 o'clock this morning we saw the comet rising; it was about 3° above the horizon.

Courses ESE3°E 59¼′ or 19⁹⁄₁₂ leagues. Lat. N 1°54′, diff. S 20′, Est. N 1°34′, observed 1°31′, diff. S 3′. Long. E 142°10′, diff. E 56′, Est. E 143°06′.

We have not seen any birds.

Friday 22nd

We saw some wood float by yesterday afternoon, and this morning we found ourselves in what was presumably a tideway for we saw a great many trees and some small pieces [of wood] and quantities of forest fruit. From 2 o'clock to sunrise there were light gusts but no breeze; moreover the weather has been very fine, merely too weak.

Courses SE¼E2°8′E 44′ or 14⅔ leagues. Lat. N 1°31′, diff. S 23′, Est. N 1°08′, observed 43′, diff. S 25′. Long. E 143°06′, diff. E 38′, Est. E 143°44′.

We have seen several gannets and some tropic birds. The equinox is causing strong currents.

Saturday 23 September 1769

It has been almost calm since yesterday. We had a little rain towards midnight, but without wind, and the sky cleared. Yesterday until evening we saw numerous tree trunks passing by and other pieces [of wood]. Today nothing.

Courses SE5°15′E 34¼′ or 11³⁄₁₂ leagues. Lat. N 43′, diff. S 22′, Est. N 21′, observed 10′, diff. S 11′. Long. 143°44′, diff. E 27′, Est. E 144′11′.

At the moment the calm is complete. Caught a shark at midday. No other appearing. Yesterday[1] we hauled in a tree trunk which we caught as it passed alongside. It is eaten into, but by rolling on the shore, not by worms, and the timber is light. I had it cut into logs and put aside to use as hawse-plugs or mast wedges.

Sunday 24th

The weather is too fine by far. One might call it dead calm. The atmosphere is heavy, one can hardly see the horizon and the heat is very great. We saw a large quantity of birds this morning, which at times perched, at other times sat on the water in flocks. We also saw a curlew. We saw a shark which was caught at once. We can see no wood today. It is true that we are not making any headway.

I have seen some of these small polyps which look like a kind of snake, some of which would have shed their skins and which usually drift in the water or else move very slightly, but [?] at times they go so quickly and as strongly as the snake itself, then they once again let themselves drift as if they were nearly dead.

Courses SE3°45′S 20′ or 6⅔ leagues. Lat. N 10′, diff. S 13′, Est. S 3′, observed S 7′, diff. S 4′.[2] Long. E 144°11′, diff. E 13′, Est. E 144°24′.

Monday 25 September 1769[3]

We had a day of calms until midnight. We made a little headway, after which I had the sails taken in as the ship was not responding and the movement was causing them to tear. We took advantage of this time to mend the [?] of the topsails, which needed it.

---

[1] The remainder of this entry is a marginal note.
[2] The *St Jean-Baptiste* presumably crossed the Equator during the night.
[3] With this entry, Surville begins a new *cahier* of 100 pages, which he heads up 'Continuation of [the] Journal of the ship *Le S. Jean Baptiste* September 1769'.

I am estimating my courses only until midnight, after which I make no reckoning.

Courses E¼S3°E5′ or 1⅔ league. Lat. S 7′, diff. S 4′, Est. S 11′, observed 12′. Long. E 144°24′, diff. E 3′, Est. E 144°27′.

We have seen a few birds.

Tuesday 26th

For two days we have had a dead calm. At times a light breeze rises here and there over the sea which allows the ship to answer the helm, nothing more. This morning a few little light clouds began to appear to the NW; they reached us and passed us without giving any more wind although they were low like the ordinary clouds [which accompany] very fair weather.

Courses SE8½′ or 2⅚ leagues. Lat. S 12′, diff. S 6′, Est. 18′, observed 16′, diff. N 2′. Long. E 144°27′, diff. E 6′, Est. E 144°33′.

We saw and caught a shark; 2 others had appeared earlier, but had merely passed by. We see neither birds nor wood.

Wednesday 27 September 1769

Courses SE¼E 1°45′S 17′ or 5⅔ leagues. Lat. S 16′, diff. S 10′, Est. S 26′. Long. E 144°33′, diff. E 14′, [Est.] 144°47′.

We have again had very feeble breezes from 6 p.m. We even had a dead calm during which I had the sails taken in and took the opportunity to mend during that time the [?] of our three topsails. At 10.30 there was a hint of wind. Finally at 11 the ship answered the helm and we made headway. Previously in spite of the helm, she stemmed from WSW to SE. We have been seeing numerous snakes these last 2 or 3 days.

Thursday 28th

Courses SE¼E2°40′E 14′ or 4⅔ leagues. Lat. S 26′, diff. S 7′, Est. S 33′, observed 36′, diff. S 3′. Long. E 144°47′, diff. E 13′, Est. E 145°.

We have had dead calms twice in the last 24 hours and moreover, as can be seen, we have made very little headway. We have seen birds of which several sat in a flock on the water.

We continue seeing snakes. Towards midnight I saw something fairly large passing alongside, but I was unable to see what it was. It did not appear to be a tree trunk. A swell has come up heavier than usual.

Friday 29th

We have had wretched weather. On two separate occasions we had dead calm, during which we were forced to take in everything to avoid tearing our sails to shreds through their flapping, as our ship was not responding, often being broadside on to the waves, without moving or being helped by the breeze, and therefore tossed about by the waves however small they were.

Courses SE5½' or 1⅚ leagues. Lat. S 36', diff. S 4', Est. S 40', observed 30', diff. N 10'. Long. E 145°, diff. E 4', Est. E 145°04'.

We have made so little headway that we have seen nothing except 2 sharks and some [?].

Saturday 30th

We had variable and gusty weather yesterday afternoon during which we twice altered course. There was not much wind in the gusts. At 5 a.m. the weather turned fair and we set all sails. At 2 this morning we had a fairly strong squall, not excessive. We had heavy rain. We shortened sail. At 3.45 we put back the topsails only. At 9 this morning we let out all the canvas. The sky remained cloudy until midday and my altitude is a little doubtful.

Courses ESE 3°20'S 46'. Lat. S 30', diff. S 20', Est. S 50', observed, doubtful 51'. Long. E 145°04', diff. E 41', Est. E 145°45'.

We can see numerous bonitos and tuna.[1] No wood or birds.

Sunday 1 October 1769

Here we are in a moment when things are very changeable which requires one to be on the lookout. The Equinox, the new moon, and the change of the monsoon from E to W south of the Line. The weather was very fair until midnight, after which the horizon appeared to be very dark from time to time, and that [blackness] rose up quickly, but the clouds had no consistency, they went away like a fog with no rain at all. We had gusts during the morning with no great strength.

[1] The tuna (*Thunnus thynnus*), possibly the long-tailed tuna (*T. tonggol*) which is rather more common in Indo-Pacific waters.

On the stroke of noon an insignificant little cloud caused us to miss the reading. We see neither birds nor wood.

Courses ES$\frac{1}{4}$E4°20′S 100$\frac{1}{2}$ or 33$\frac{1}{2}$ leagues. Lat. S 51′, diff. S 1°02′, Est. S 1°53′, observed, very doubtful 1°34′, it would be [a] diff. N 19′. Long. E 145°45′, diff. E 1°19′, Est. E 147°04′.

Monday 2 October 1769

We have had rain, thunder and squalls all [night] and so, as the weather seemed to me to be threatening this as early as yesterday I had all reefs taken in everywhere, on account of the night manœuvre and the little known locality where we are. The mainsail also stayed furled all night. This morning the weather lightened but it continued raining. At about 10 this morning I had two reefs let out.

Courses SE 73$\frac{1}{2}$′ or 34$\frac{5}{6}$ leagues. Lat. S 1°34′, diff. S 52′, Est. S 2°26′. Long. E 147°04′, diff. E 52′, Est. E 147°56′.

We can see neither wood, nor birds, nor fish.

Tuesday 3 October 1769

Yesterday afternoon we set the topgallants and the staysails, let out one reef in the mizzen topsail and set the mizzen topgallant. At 9 p.m. there were a few light squalls. We took in the topgallants. At midnight the weather was fairly fine. Took in the main sail to be better prepared. At 1.30 put back the topgallants.

Courses SE1°50′S 64′ or 21$\frac{1}{3}$ leagues. Lat. S 2°26′, diff. S 47′, Est. S 3°13′, observed 2°42′, diff. N in two days 31′. Long. E 147°56′, diff. E 44′, Est. E 148°40′.

Seen a type of curlew.

Wednesday 4th

At about 2.30 yesterday the wind became favourable again after a WNW squall with only moderate wind and rain. At 3 we set up the studding sails and at 4.15 we were forced to furl everything and haul down the topsails because of a squall. We took in all reefs. The wind dropped little by little and we put back all we could without letting out the reefs because the weather did not clear. At 3 o'clock this morning there was a little rain and not much wind. At 5 I let out two reefs and hauled up all the sails. At midday the weather was cloudy and we were unable to get a reading. There is a light rain without wind.

Courses SE$\frac{1}{4}$S4°12'E 55' or 18$\frac{1}{3}$ leagues. Lat. S 2°42', diff. S 43', Est. S 3°25'. Long. E 148°40', diff. E 34', Est. E 149°14'.

We can see nothing which gives an indication of land.

Thursday 5th

At 9.30 last night we took in the topgallants. From 10 to midnight the wind was gusty but not strong. At 2 it rose such that I had to clew up and take in the main and fore topsails after I had taken in all reefs. The wind was still blowing in gusts, but very strong. At 5 we hauled up the main topsail, at 6 the fore and at 8 the mizzen. We let out 2 reefs in the main topsail and one only in the fore on account of the wind right aft. The weather is still overcast and the wind fresh. The sea very heavy. We later set the topgallants. I saw a small turtle this morning and a small *chevalier*, [one] of these shore birds. There were rainshowers but which weakened rather than strengthened [the wind] until 11.45.

Courses SE$\frac{1}{4}$S2°40'E 87$\frac{1}{2}$'. Lat. S 3°25', diff. S 1°14', Est. S 4°39', observed 4°40'. Long. E 149°14', diff. E 44', Est. E 149°58'.

Friday 6th

Yesterday evening seeing that the weather was showing no indication of being fine, I had the sails reefed to spare our people during the night.[1] At 8 set the standing jib and stay sail. At 9.30 took all that in and the mizzen topsail. At 11.45 set the topgallants, staysail, standing jib and mizzen. From midnight to 4 o'clock fair wind although the sky was overcast. At 6 a.m. fine but calm.

Courses S$\frac{1}{4}$SE4°S 73' or 24$\frac{1}{3}$ leagues.[2] Lat. S 4°40', diff. S 1°12', Est. S 5°52'. Long. E 149°58', diff. E 9', Est. E 150°07'.

We see neither birds nor wood

Saturday 7 October 1769

We had let out a reef in the main topsail yesterday afternoon when the sea becoming rough I held fast for the fore topsail. At 2.15 the wind

---

[1] This is de Surville's first comment on the poor health of much of the crew, which had already been the object of critical comments in Labé's journal. Pottier states in his *Journal* under the same date: 'The rains we have had in recent days are causing sickness among the men. At present 15 are affected. It seems that Mr de Surville's intention is to reach the latitude of the Solomon Islands in order to call there so that they may recover and to obtain what refreshments we may find, for the crew are very tired of the sea.'

[2] Both Labé and Pottier estimated their courses as south and westerly rather than south with a slight easting as shown by Surville. This makes it likely that the *St Jean-Baptiste* sailed to the east of Tauu atoll which lies due north of Choiseul.

having freshened I let it out and set all sails. When the moon set there was a little squally shower with no wind. The sky was overcast and there were many lightning flashes. At 5.30 this morning we had sight of land from the SE to WSW.[1] At 6 o'clock sounded without finding bottom. At the said hour land bearing as follows: the nearest which has the appearance of an island bearing SE¼S distant 6 to 7 leagues. One can see low land beyond and off it stretching out to the SE. The land seems to continue as far as WSW, but there are clouds covering it so that one cannot know precisely how far it runs. But it seems that it all lies approximately SE and NW. At 8 o'clock one sees land which seems to be low lying, as far as SSE, the rest is hidden. The island that was the easternmost when we altered course and bore SE¼S bears S¼SE 5°S distant 9 to 10 l. At midday the said island through its easternmost point bears S¼SE, 9 l. We can see some low land far off to the east of it and 3 or 4 small islets.[2] Moreover we can see a continuous chain of mountains going on to WSW. The remainder is in the clouds. In this interval one sees a few headlands which could lead one to think they are islands, but we are not sure. There are even some lower ones between the large ones but all that is not clear, so that since it is all totally unknown to us we cannot judge correctly. What is certain is that it is a fine well-wooded land.

Courses S¼SE1°E 38' or 12⅔ leagues. Lat. S 5°52', diff. S 37', Est. 6°29', observed 6°55', diff. S 26'. Long. E 150°07', diff. E 8', Est. E 150°15'.

This land here has not been seen, I think, by anyone, because even in the Dutch accounts, when they sailed on a voyage of discovery to New Guinea I do not find that they ever reached the latitude we are in, since the first island we saw and which I will call from now on *Première Vue* is in approximately 7°20' according to today's reading and the bearings taken at midday.

Sunday 8 October 1769

At 2 yesterday afternoon sighted *Première Vue* Island through its easternmost point bearing SSE 2°S distant 7 to 8 l., the point of the

[1] Marginal note: 'Sight of the Land of the Papuans'.
[2] The island which was sighted first and which the French were to call *Première Vue* is Wagina, the easternmost of those adjacent to Choiseul Island in the Solomons. It rises fairly unevenly to approximately 200 ft. Further east are the Arnavon Islands in Manning Strait and a number of small islands and reefs at the western extremity of Santa Isabel – these are Surville's '3 or 4 small islets'. The identification of *Première Vue* is confirmed by Surville's estimated latitude for it of 7°21' – it lies between 7°23' and 7°28' south.

low land to the E of the said island SSE, the centre of another low land which has the appearance of several small islets SE$\frac{1}{4}$S1°E. At 2.30 the wind seemed to be setting NW with a light squall but it turned out calm. The currents are setting westerly from what we can see, but not very strong. At 6 *Première Vue* Island SSE 3°S and the high bluff to starboard of it which forms with it a kind of bay full of islets S 2°E.[1] The land stretches as far as WNW and is high. I think these are islands behind which we can discern a larger continent whose land is lower lying and stretches up to SE$\frac{1}{4}$S. From above one can also see a single island detached from all that bearing E. At sunrise *Première Vue* Island bore S$\frac{1}{4}$SE 4°S, the other high mountain to starboard of the kind of bay S 5°W, the most westerly land stretches out to W 5°N. At 8 o'clock the E point of *Première Vue* Island bears SSE 2°S. We sounded during the night without finding ground at 60 f., as well as this morning when we were making for the land. At 11 o'clock we saw the sea a greenish colour ahead of us. As soon as we reached this new water we sounded and found 27 f., immediately after 31 ditto, then no ground at 50 f. From there sighted land the easternmost bearing SE$\frac{1}{4}$E, the eastern point of *Première Vue* Island SE 5°S, distant about 3 l., the western point SE$\frac{1}{4}$S 2°E, the 1st islet of the bay SSE 5°E 3$\frac{1}{2}$ l., the 2nd SSE, the 3rd SSE 2°S, the 4th SSE 4°S, the headland at the entrance to the bay S$\frac{1}{4}$SE, the high bluff above which is the land nearest to us S$\frac{1}{4}$SW 3°W distant about 2 l., the most westerly land W. Sounded from then until midday without finding ground at 40 and 50 f. As soon as we had passed this shallow water the sea lost its changed appearance.

At midday the easternmost land in sight bore ESE 3°E, the eastern point of *Première Vue* Island ESE 4°S 2 to 2$\frac{1}{2}$ l, its most westerly point SE$\frac{1}{4}$S 4°E, a rock over which the sea breaks between it and the 1st island in the bay SE$\frac{1}{4}$S 2°S, this 1st islet SE$\frac{1}{4}$S 3°S, the 2nd SSE 1°S, the 3rd S$\frac{1}{4}$SE 2°E, the 4th S$\frac{1}{4}$SE 2°S,[2] the western point of the bay S 4°E, the high mountain above, which is still our nearest land, SW$\frac{1}{4}$S 3°S about 1 to 1$\frac{1}{2}$ l., a headland WSW, another headland which was set down at 11 o'clock as the most westerly W$\frac{1}{4}$NW 3°W, the most westerly land stretches out to WNW. We have had a light rain during the night, but in showers with no wind.

[1] This high bluff is Taura Peak which rises to 1950 ft and is the easternmost bluff of Choiseul Island. It forms with Rob Roy Island – which the French could not identify as a separate island without landing on it – a wide bay containing six small islands.

[2] The four islands listed as appearing in Taura Bay are Laina, Kakau, Sarima, and Bembalama; the rock could be a reference to Tamar which lies between Wagina and Laina, but reefs extend for some distance off the entire north-western shore of the former.

Courses SE¼E 15′ or 5 leagues. Lat. S 6°55′, diff. S 8′, Est. 7°03′, observed 7°12′, diff. S 9′. Long. E 150°15′, diff. E 12′, Est. E 150°27′.

Although in sight of land I cannot as yet alter my longitude because I do not know what land this is and I am still not certain whether I sailed E or W of New Britain.[1] It is certain that if what we are seeing has already been seen by someone the charts are quite wrong. I will be able to verify it later. I had planned to enter the bay formed by our *Première Vue* Island, but finding no bottom and seeing the sea breaking between the islets inside it, I was afraid that I might find a very bad [anchorage] and no doubt close to the land. Its NW aspect led me to give up this idea for fear of some untoward event. I am therefore standing off to sea and will try to find a better place, because we are in need of a short rest as much on account of the scurvy as for water.

Monday 9 October 1769

At 5 yesterday, the wind being calm and the currents bearing us away slightly, I sounded. We found 45 f. small round flat and broken shells and a few small pieces of red coral.[2] At that moment the eastern point of *Première Vue* Island bore then SE¼E 2°S distant about 2 l., the top of the mountain of the said point S 3°E. At 6 o'clock we sounded again and found 78 f., same ground as above. The easternmost point of *1ère Vue* Island bore then SE¼E distant 3 l. The summit of the mountain of the W point of the bay bore S¼SE 1°S. It is our nearest land, distant from us more than 2 l[eagues] or thereabouts. The most W land we can see bearing WNW. At midnight the middle of *1ère Vue* Island bore SE¼S, at 2.30 a.m. S 5°E. At sunrise the middle of *1ère Vue* Island bears

[1] This explains his first comment 'Sight of the land of the Papuans' on the 7th since by sailing west of New Britain he would have reached the coast of New Guinea. Pottier reflected the general uncertainty in his comments of the 7th: 'I find it very difficult to say what land is in sight. Here however are my conjectures based on the Mercator's chart of the austral lands, found in the Abbé Prévost's *Histoire générale des voyages*, page 198, volume 11. It seems natural to think that this is the bay formed by the coast of New Guinea and the western part of New Britain; but if we accept this theory we must challenge the latitudes Dampier observed since he places the northernmost part of New Britain in 2°20′S and its southernmost in 5°30′S, whereas I obtained 6°59′S which makes a considerable difference. My octant is a good instrument. If we assume that we are in the above-mentioned bay, the land which bore yesterday S to W¼SW is formed by Long Island, Brutante Island and Chevalier Root's Island; in that case where would Cape Closester and the west coast of New Britain be? It is true that only the eastern part of the latter is known. Or else we might be west of this island whose bight may be more considerable than is shown on this chart, but I repeat, everything is contradictory if our latitudes and Dampier's are correct and we are not in the said bight. If we are east of New Britain all the lands are wrongly marked since they run NE and SW.' *Journal*, p. 105.

[2] Blotted sentence. The word could be 'coquillages' (shells).

S$\frac{1}{4}$SE 3°S. We are discovering the low lands of the continent as far as SE 2°S. One can also see from the topmasts an island in the E and E$\frac{1}{4}$SE. The large bluff forming the starboard head of our bay bears S$\frac{1}{4}$SW 5°W, the westernmost land in view W$\frac{1}{4}$NW 4°W, hazy. At 8 sighted *1ère Vue* Island bearing S$\frac{1}{4}$SE. We have lost ground a little since 2 a.m. The low land which appears to me to be the large continent bears SE, an island or mountain E$\frac{1}{4}$S from above, the high mountain at the starboard head of our bay S$\frac{1}{4}$SW 5°W. The land we discover[ed] as the furthest W is not visible, it is hidden in cloud. At midday the most easterly island or mountain bears ESE 1°S; one can see several flat islets whose trees are drowned[1] appearing between the continent and us; the easternmost of the said [islets] bears SSE 1°E. The easternmost point of the continent which is still low lying bears SSE, a large bight in the said continent, one point of which bears S and the other S$\frac{1}{4}$SW 2°S, 5 islets bear from us in the opening of this bight the middle one S$\frac{1}{4}$SW 3$\frac{1}{2}$°S. The island of *1ère Vue* bears SW$\frac{1}{4}$S, the high starboard head of our bay SW, its W point SW$\frac{1}{4}$W 2°S, a 2nd point WSW 2°S. The most westerly land we can see bears W 5°N.[2] All the high and mountainous country stretching from *Pre Vue* Island up to the headland we have always called the most westerly land consists of a number of large islands behind which, at varying intervals, one sees the line of a great continent of low and level land, only a little higher in some parts. We lose sight of this continent from the point which we have set down as the most E, that is to say E and E$\frac{1}{4}$SE. There are flat and drowned islets off this continent, which indicates that there could be several shoals and shallows, so that I do not dare haul too closely along it. A further indication that this is a continent is that when the horizon clears a little on that side one can see a chain of high mountains well forward, dominating this low and level land which seems to be the finest country in the world, full of fine harbours and bays, but which one could approach only by wasting a great deal of time on account of the dangers which appear to line it and which one would have to survey before venturing near. I am very sorry that I have no time to sacrifice for this. Yesterday afternoon I had a boat lowered and sent Mr Labé, our first officer, to visit a little sandy bay in the island of *1ère Vue*, in the bay which it forms and where I had first wanted to go on account of our

---

[1] Meaning: 'seem to rise from the sea, the low land being below the line of the horizon'.
[2] All the foregoing gives a fairly clear impression of what Surville could see as he tacked north of Wagina Island: Santa Isabel far to the east, the Arnavon Islands and other low islets in and around Manning Strait, Wagina Island itself and the north-west coast of Choiseul.

sick; but he could not land, and not finding there a good anchorage even close inshore he saw simply that this small island, which was uninhabited, was filled with fruit trees giving out the sweetest smell, which is an indication that the rest of the country, which is much more attractive, is extremely fertile.[1]

Courses E¼NE 2°N 18', or 6 leagues. Lat. S 7°12', diff. N 4', Est. S [7°] 08', observed 7°07'. Long. E 150°27', diff. E 17', Est. E 150°44'.

We have had very little wind as can be seen from the table. There was a little rain during the night, but this morning when the wind veered N it poured without us having to haul in any sail.

Our longitudes of yesterday, Paris meridian:

Mine	150°27'
Mr Labé	151°12'
Mr Delorme	152°37'
Mr Charenton	151° —
Surville, nephew	152°32'
Mr Lauri	151°22'
Mr Monneron	151°39'
	——————
	1060°49'[2]

1060°49' of which one 7th [is] 151°15' to 16', being the average of all our longitudes, where for the present we must place our bay of 1ère Vue Island which is not accessible.

Tuesday 10 October 1769

I sounded at 6 p.m. yesterday 60 [f] without finding ground. The easternmost land in sight, having the appearance of an island bears ESE 4°E; a large mountain which the clouds allowed us to see, well forward in the land on what we could take to be a continent, ESE 1°E; from this island to SSE is an empty space, except for one islet to SE; this great emptiness forms a terrible gulf or perhaps a passage between two groups of islands.[3] The eastern point of another, smaller opening S¼SW 1½°W, the west point SSW ½°W distant 4 to 5 l[eagues] from the said land which is very low and level. Between these last two heads

[1] Much of Wagina is defended by coral formations. Landing anywhere from Wagina to Taura Bay would be hazardous. For a description of Labé's attempt to land, see his *Journal* under the same date.

[2] The range, from de Surville to Pottier de l'Horme, is therefore 2°10' or approximately 125 miles. The mean error is slightly in excess of 3°.

[3] This is Manning Strait which indeed provides a passage, albeit a dangerous one, between Choiseul and Santa Isabel. The island to SE referred to is the Arnavon group.

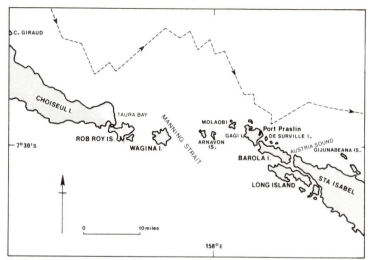

Map 2. Track of the ship in Manning Strait area

[are] 5 or 6 very low lying small islands, and a hill well forward inside this bight bearing SW¼W 2°S.[1] The island of *1ere Vue* bears from us SW¼W 2°S, the large starboard bluff of *1ère Vue* bay SW¼W 4°W, the most westerly head WSW 2°S, the two heads WSW 2½°W, the most westerly land we can see W 5°N. At midnight the island or mountain we could see in the east at sunset bears SE¼E 4°E. From 6 to midnight I sounded but we did not find bottom. Continued to sound every hour from midnight to 4 from 60 to 70 f. without finding bottom. At sunrise the land stretched from ESE 4°S to S¼SE 2°E. The one bearing ESE 4°E last night is what we see this morning bearing S¼SE 2°E and [it] has a long tail of tiny islands and drowned trees the furthest out to sea bearing S; *1ère Vue* island bears with the large bluff to starboard of the said bay SW¼W 3°W; the westernmost land in sight W¼SW 4°W and it is so far off one could take it for separate islands. At 8 this morning the land stretches from SE 2°E as far as SSE 3°S, what bore S¼SE 2°E at sunrise bears S¼SE 2°S, and the tail of drowned trees attached to it having the appearance of tiny islands S 2°W, the starboard bluff of *1ère Vue* bay SW¼W 3½°W. At 9.30 as altered course sighted the island which yesterday bore ESE 4°E. The land stretches from SE¼S as far as S¼SW 1°W. At midday, a chain of mountains or islands and islets lies

[1] The smaller opening referred to is Hamilton Channel which is obstructed by a number of reefs and islets.

from SE 3°E to SSW 1°W among which is included the one we could see last night bearing ESE 4°S, bearing now S¼SE 2°S, distant about 6 l. The high starboard bluff of *1ère Vue* bay which is also the most W land in sight bears WSW 1°S 10 to 12 l.

I must admit that I cannot tell whether everything we are seeing forms a kind of continent surrounded by an infinity of islands, some flat, the others mountainous, or whether it is only a mass of islands between which there sometimes remain some fairly wide spaces. I cannot yet form an opinion on whether I sailed E or W of New Britain. All that I think is certain is that no one has seen this before us.

Courses E¼NE 1°40′N 36′ or 12 leagues. Lat. S 7°07′, diff. N 8′, Est. S 6°59′, observed 7°06′. Long. E 150°44′, diff. E 35′, Est. E 151°19′.

The winds are extremely variable here and we have continual gusts which are then followed by calms, a dangerous occurrence in unknown waters.

Wednesday 11th

At 3.15 yesterday afternoon the weather began to cloud over so that I had all the small canvas taken in and the main and mizzen clewed up because the wind was threatening to shift. At 6 p.m. the starboard land S¼SW 1½°W distant 4 to 5 l., the easternmost point SE¼E 2½°E. At 8 o'clock, squalls, rain and wind, hauled the topsails upon the cap. From 8 to midnight sounded every hour at 60 f. without finding bottom. At 2 o'clock abundant rain, a little thunder. At 6 a.m. sighted a high land from SE¼E 3°S to WSW 3°W, some tiny islands as far as SE¼E 5°E, the nearest land S 5°E distant 5 to 6 l. There is also a small opening in this part but it is blocked or at least concealed by tiny islands. We cannot tell whether this would offer a place of refuge. The weather does not allow us to verify it. It is raining continually, but the squalls have lost their strength. We find it hard to keep a course with the small breeze they bring from one side then another, and so all we have done is tack about.[1] We are not taking bearings at 8 o'clock because not only have we hardly changed our position but the land is also very hazy. At midday, sighted the westermost land bearing WSW 3°W and the easternmost SE¼E. It is moreover the same land.

All the land we have seen so far is lined with small offshore islets which seem to have dangerous shallows which make them almost inaccessible, and time does not allow us to examine anything. We

---

[1] *Virailler*, a diminutive of virer, to change course.

cannot find the bottom, we often have calms and sometimes winds that drive us inshore. One cannot venture closer without running risks. There is no safety in sending boats in squally weather from such a distance, circumstances might prevent them from returning.[1] All this vexes me. The country appears to be well wooded, with the fine trees, but from the bluff in *1ère Vue* bay [to here] I have seen nothing cleared for cultivation, no smoke. We may be too far off.

Courses SE$\frac{1}{4}$E 22' or 7$\frac{1}{3}$ leagues. Lat. S 7°06', diff. S 12', Est. S 7°18'. Long. E 151°19', diff. E 18', Est. E 151°37'.

Thursday 12th

At 6 yesterday evening the easternmost land bore SE$\frac{1}{4}$E 2°S distant 7 to 8 l., the westernmost SW$\frac{1}{4}$W 5°S 6 to 7 l. At 5.15 seeing the sky still gave indication of rain I had the 2nd reef taken in the topsails to save the crew from getting wet at night during squalls, but fortunately I was wrong: the weather was fine all night. At 5 this morning I had this reef let out and unfurled all sails. At sunrise the most easterly land bore SE$\frac{1}{4}$S 4$\frac{1}{2}$°E, the most westerly SW$\frac{1}{4}$S 4$\frac{1}{2}$°S. At 8 o'clock the most W bore SW, an opening S$\frac{1}{4}$SE 1$\frac{1}{2}$°E, the most easterly land SE 1°E. At midday the most easterly land bore SE$\frac{1}{4}$E 2°E, the most westerly S$\frac{1}{4}$SW 3°W. What we took this morning for an opening is only a very small bight where the land rose as we got nearer. There still does not seem to me to be any place of refuge there. We sounded every hour throughout the night at 50 and 60 f. without finding bottom.

Courses E$\frac{1}{4}$SE 1°E 17' or 5$\frac{2}{3}$ leagues. Lat. S 7°18', diff. S 3', Est. S 7°21', observed 7°17', diff. N 4'. Long. E 151°37', diff. E 17', Est. E 151°54'.

Friday 13th

Yesterday afternoon finding myself only 1$\frac{1}{2}$ leagues from land I stood off to sea, but at 3.30 I returned to go out to sea only at sunset, so that I could sight a roadstead or port if there was one. At 5 I stood off, being far enough inshore. We could still see our large bluff in *1ère Vue* bay but only its summit bearing W$\frac{1}{4}$SW 3°W. I estimate it distant

[1] This is almost an answer to Labé's comment of the same date that two boats should be sent along the coast to seek an anchorage, and it may reflect a discussion on this issue between the two men. Pottier comments on the parlous state of the crew: 'It is high time for the sake of our crew to find a suitable place to anchor in safety, in order to transport them ashore and restore them as they are on the point of death and in great pain. The number of sick increases day by day. There are 27 scurvy cases today'. *Journal*, p. 113.

18 to 20 l. The most westerly land having the appearance of small island bore W¼SW distant 7 to 8 l.,[1] the nearest 4 to 5 l., the easternmost from the topmasts E 5°S. Sounded from 40 to 50 f. as we plied for the land without finding bottom. At 3 a.m. I made for the land. Sounded from 3 to 4 at 45 f. without finding ground and from 4 to 5 and 60 f. without finding it either. At 7.30 we saw land from S¼SE to SSW very hazy with the horizon the same although the sky was quite clear. It is difficult to estimate the distance. At midday the easternmost land bore SE¼S 2°E, the opening of a bight like a port SSW 1°S distant 2 l., the easternmost point of the said port which is the nearest land S¼SW 2°W. From this port as far as W 3°N the land is level and not high along the coast, distant 4 to 5 l.[2] The most westerly land, having the appearance of islets bore W¼NW 5°W. As we approach the land, the above-mentioned opening appeared to me more and more like a port. I sent Monsieur Labé, my first officer, in the yawl with a small detachment of marines to go and see if there was enough water to allow a ship to enter. He left at 11.45. I continued to ply to windward under reduced sail off the port and to get closer to land. I gave him a signal which he has to make in case he finds a good harbour.

Courses ESE 3°25S 14′ or 4⅔ leagues. Lat. S 7°17′, diff. S 6′, Est. 7°23′, observed 7°21′. Long. E 151°54′, diff. E 13′, Est. E 152°07′.

Saturday 14th

I continued to stand inshore as long as I could yesterday afternoon, as much to give time to Mr Labé to make observations and to give me the agreed signal as to be ready to enter the opening of the port promptly if it was possible. For his part he had already entered and we could no longer see him. The E point of the entrance hid him from me when I was compelled, being too close inshore, to tack about for the open sea, but I just had time to be trimmed and to cover about 1′ towards the open sea when I sighted him with the signal of passage and anchorage. It was then almost 2 o'clock.[3] I immediately bore down

---

[1] The *St Jean-Baptiste*, after considerable tacking to the north of Manning Strait, was north of the group of islands which stretch north-west from Santa Isabel Island. The most westerly land described is probably small Suki Island and the various reefs which form its extremity.

[2] Doubtful reading due to erasures and interlinings. However, it is clear that the *St Jean-Baptiste* is standing north of Port Praslin, which is formed by deeply indented Gagi Island and several islands east of it, including Barola. The level land stretching to W 3°N is Bates Island and the most westerly land is tiny Suki.

[3] Marginal note: 'Entry into Port Praslin'.

to S$\frac{1}{4}$SW, making for a point a little ahead of the opening and continued thus until [I was] about $\frac{1}{2}$ l from land. Mr Labé joined me at the opening and came aboard to give me the remainder of the required information and, since he had just surveyed the place, I begged him to take over. At 2.30, with the W point of the island to larboard of the entrance bearing E$\frac{1}{4}$NE, we found bottom for the 1st time at 55 f., small coral. The wind then shifted SE and I was somewhat afraid that I might not reach the inner ground as I could see a squall forming above the land. We were already compelled to sail SSW close to the wind to keep to the channel between the two heads of the reef at the entrance. The remainder of the light breeze which the land squall was gradually forcing to die down nevertheless brought us inside to 24 f. where I dropped anchor because the breeze had died down completely and the tide then starting to ebb was causing us to drop astern. The ground was white sand. The W point of the larboard island of the bay bore ENE 3°N distant $\frac{1}{2}$ l., its reef extended to NE$\frac{1}{4}$E 3°E, the point of the starboard island bore NW about $\frac{3}{4}$ l., and its reef as far as NNW 2°N, the S point of the larboard island at the entrance S$\frac{1}{4}$SE 2°E 3$\frac{1}{4}$ l., the starboard one WSW 5°S ditto about $\frac{3}{4}$ l., the end of the harbour SSW 5°S about 3 to 4 l. approximately.[1] I had at first only anchored with a large kedge anchor, but we were forced to drop a large anchor because we were dropping astern although the land breeze was negligible.

While we were still outside and Mr Labé was in the pass, a canoe with only one man came up to the ship. He approached only to a safe distance from where he examined the ship. We gestured to him to come, showing him a small white flag which, according to history, is the one of peace among all these people. But he did not trust it and himself gestured with his hand for us to land, but he sighted our yawl and turned promptly towards it; he did not even take very long to get close to it. Mr Labé told us that, as he had tried to go towards him and catch up with him, he had fled and called as loudly as he could to another large [canoe] which was sheltering by a reef and was fleeing like himself. As soon as we had dropped anchor, 2 or 3 canoes came

[1] The larboard island is in reality a pair of small islands linked by a series of reefs, the starboard island is a peninsula attached to Gagi Island, and the back of the bay is formed by Barola Island. The dangers and the lack of a breeze led de Surville to drop anchor shortly after passing between the two heads. Of this locality the *Pacific Islands Pilot* has this to say: 'Port Praslin is a narrow channel lying between Marianne and de Surville islands on the east and Gagi on the west. On entering the vessel should close the reef on the eastern side and when past the inner entrance points alter course westward and anchor in the middle of the channel in depths of from 16 to 17 fathoms.' vol. I, 1946, p. 406.

up, one large, the other smaller, which circled around the ship without wanting to approach in spite of our invitations and the peace flag which I was still [waving]. One canoe from outside, which as soon as he was at the same distance as the others from the ship drew an arrow and his bow on which he placed the said arrow. He spoke to the others in a manner which showed us that he wanted them to attack us at once. I was in the corner of the stern gallery on his side. I gestured to him not to fire the arrow which he seemed to be holding in readiness for this purpose, showing him a small white flag, which at first seemed to calm him; nevertheless he bent his bow on two more consecutive occasions, still being undecided whether he should fire at us or not; to these gestures he added many words addressed to his comrades spoken in a loud and threatening tone which showed me that he wanted at least to instil fear into us, in which he was certainly not succeeding. I wanted to attract them by gentleness. I showed him a length of cotton cloth, making signs for him to come and fetch it. He did indeed come a little closer, but not much, and made a sign to the effect that I ought to throw it to him, which I did without hesitation, but it fell too close to the ship and they did not dare come to fetch it, so that it had time to become soaked and sink. He asked me for another; I threw one wrapped in a piece of wood. They picked up that one and one of them put it on his back. They then seemed to become our friends. They showed me the water and raising their half closed hands to their mouths and throwing their heads back they let me understand that there was some at the back of the harbour and that they would take me there, and they invited me by signs to go right away. I made them understand the sun was too low but that as soon as it reappeared on the morrow we would go with them. They understood me with no difficulty whatever and applauded, adding that they would take us there. During all these mimed conversations we had lowered all our boats, which they had watched carefully. Towards sunset left for the shore of the starboard island at the entrance, quite close to us, where we could see them and hear them without the assistance of a spyglass. They stayed there all night in a crowd. They lit fires there, and all night in the moonlight they talked and amused themselves by repeating everything we were saying on board. If anyone whistled, they did likewise, imitating the whistling they had heard; they also repeated perfectly a few sentences we were saying. In a word they were acting like monkeys, which we took to be an auspicious sign. This morning 4 or 5 canoes came from the bay, 2 of which with 35 or 40 people in. All the morning we hauled ourselves to get a little further in and get ourselves away from the reef by which we have been forced to anchor. Towards 11.30 this morning, the work being nearly finished, I made a sign to the canoe to come, which had promised on the day before to show us the watering place and which was there by the shore very close to us with all the others. It came at once and understood perfectly why I was calling it.

I have omitted to say that earlier and while we were moving the kedge anchor, all the canoes had gathered around us and some of the natives appearing to be persuaded by our friendly gestures had at first ventured to enter our boats which were alongside, then to climb halfway up the ladder, then onto the fore-and-aft gangway, and then on the quarter-deck and finally all over the ship where they seemed to be marvelling at everything. They proved to us during this time that they were thieves, for one of them stole the clothes of our people, which he came across and put in his boat, but we took them back at once without his raising any objection. As soon as we started hauling they all went back to the shore. I come back to the canoe to which I had signalled to come and show us the watering place and which had come up at once. It was waiting alongside us for two of our boats into which I was having barrels loaded and which I had well armed with soldiers and sailors, the former armed with muskets, the latter with swords. As soon as this was done, in order to encourage the native to serve us faithfully, I made him another present, of a piece of blue cloth which he appeared to receive with pleasure, and accordingly he repeated in sign language that he was going to show me the watering place. Mr Labé, my first officer, in whom I have, on good grounds, every confidence, as much for his caution and firmness as for his knowledge of correct behaviour in every kind of circumstance, left in command of these two boats at 11.30.

There were still a few canoes in the island at the right of the entrance and around the ship, but they left gradually and we now can see none.

Sunday 15th

As soon as I had had my lunch yesterday afternoon I went in the yawl intending to fish with the seine in a little sandy bay near the ship, but we could not find a landing place, the tide having risen as far as the trees. I looked in other places without being able to find a better access than this one. I finally reached a small corner where there was a little sand, but the coral was not far so that it was impossible to think of fishing. I landed with a few of our gentlemen who had accompanied me. The whole interior of the wood was nothing but a marsh. We were amusing ourselves shooting a few birds, when Mr Labé passed near us coming back with his two boats from the search for a watering place. He made me his report on the treason of these islanders who had gathered about 150 in number in various boats, one of which had 20 to 30 [people in it], the other 30 to 40. They had added trickery to the forces they were gathering. The chief of the canoe to whom I had given presents to show the watering place seemed angry that the others were coming to snatch from him the glory of showing where the water was and was gesturing to them to go away.[1] For their part, they were making signs to indicate that he was not showing the way to the good place. Then small arguments would start among them in which they seemed to agree that one place would be more suitable than another, so that they led Mr Labé to 2 or 3 places where there was no water or possibility of land. Finally they led him to one where they could land, but the water was not there: they made signs that one had to go up a little way. Mr Labé sent the sergeant with 2 or 3 marines to see where this water was. They brought back, I think, a couple of bucketfuls, and reported that one could not get water there. As soon as they had reached this place, nearly all the islanders had gathered on land and only a few had stayed in their boats. They were most anxious that our people should leave ours on the flat so as to go all looking for water and coconuts. They were making signs to our men to climb the trees. Some of them placed their hands on the bow of our boats and endeavoured by pulling them closer inshore to tie them up to the trees, which was not agreed to.[2]

Finally Mr Labé seeing that these people were only playing decided to leave them and return, intending to seek a watering place ourselves where we would have a chance of finding one, and consequently he ordered those who were on land to re-embark, especially the sergeant who having been affected by the sun on the way was feeling unwell

[1] This would seem to confirm the view that the visitors of the previous day had been won over, but lacked power or influence over the later comers. The gifts made on the previous day described by Labé in his Journal had made the peaceful intentions of the French as clear as circumstances made possible.
[2] This is not necessarily an indication that the Solomonese were endeavouring to beach the boats prior to an attack. Suspicious though this behaviour may seem, it could be explained by a desire to be helpful on the part of some of the more friendly islanders. Similarly the first stream to which the French had been directed did provide drinking water – that the islanders did not realise how inadequate the source was for the large casks is not necessarily evidence of bad faith.

and had twice fallen with his weapon. Mr Labé gave him his hand and was urging him to embark when suddenly the islanders, seeing they were not achieving their ends, decided to attack our people with lances and clubs made of extremely heavy wood. They did not try to use their arrows because they were too close and mixed up with our own people. As this attack was unexpected at this moment they had time to strike the first blows at some of our men. They drove a lance into the sergeant's back[1] and at the same time twice struck at Mr Labé who was standing just by him to get him to embark; he ran there the greatest risks, for the two blows struck him between the thighs and both pierced him; a small piece from one of the lances remained in one of the wounds, the other in his breeches. One of our sailors was struck across the arm, a soldier on the head with a club which cut his cap and his head to the bone. A sailor was also struck down and lost the sword he was holding which fell into the sea, although he was not seriously hurt.[2] All these blows were struck at the same time and our musket fire replied at once. Mr Labé who had not given up his weapon killed one himself on the spot and others fell as the result of the other shots. According to the general reports, thirty or even forty dead and wounded lay on this place. It was point blank range so that one shot could kill more than one. They promptly fled or re-embarked to get away. All their boats had been shattered by the shock of ours in the battle, except a few some natives had jumped into to escape as fast as they could row. All our men found themselves back in the boats without any loss whatever. Thank God. It is even possible that had it not been for the sunstroke of the sergeant taking up the attention of Mr Labé who was trying to get him to embark quickly, our losses would have been even less.

Mr Labé came back and joined me at the above-mentioned place. We returned to the ship together, where I forced him to stay to get his wounds attended to while I went with two of our boats to try to capture some islanders we could see on the shore of the island at the right of the entrance of the harbour. There were 4 or 5 altogether. As soon as they saw we were going towards them they quickly jumped into a canoe with their few belongings and tried to get away. We fired several shots at them which made one fall who reached the wood;[3]

[1]. Marginal note: 'where a piece remained which has since caused his death'.
[2] Marginal note: 'another was struck by a stone in one of our boats and Mr Labé was struck on the leg by a stone'.
[3] There is no evidence that this man was hit. He could have jumped or falled overboard out of fear.

the others continued, but at last as we kept firing fear seized them and they jumped ashore and reached the wood. We took their canoe as well as two other small ones they still had on the same shore. I looked through the wood to find them: but all that was a waterlogged marsh. To all appearances they had crossed it to go and hide further off. It did not really matter to me whether I found them or not; I was satisfied with frightening them off so that we could quietly get our water and firewood, and I went back to the ship. Soon after this a canoe appeared with two men from behind the island at the left of the entrance of the harbour. I was all the more anxious to catch them in that I wished to capture at least one. We used a stratagem for this. We sent two of our Malagasy[1] in the canoe which Mr Labé had brought back from his battle; we powdered their Kaffir hair as the people of this country do with lime and in this state they began to imitate the local people, circling the ship and making the same gestures we had seen them make. This did indeed succeed. The small canoe with the two natives approached the ship and began to examine her. Finally I saw they were going to leave without coming any closer and I ordered [our men] to fire. One was killed, the other jumped into the sea to reach land, but as I had had a boat bear off he was caught and brought to me. He is a youth of 14 or 15, dark like the people of Malabar, no darker; his hair is frizzy but not woolly; it is coloured red with the lime most of them use as powder; I think it is on account of vermin. We had a great deal of trouble to seize this young man, he dived whenever the boat got near. The small canoe where our Malagasy were was forced to go and help with the capture. Finally he was placed in the boat. When he arrived he kicked the officer in the stomach and knocked him over, he bit all those who tried to hold him. Finally he was tied. I had him placed in irons, because otherwise one could not be sure of him.

At about 1 a.m. two canoes came, one large and one small. The small one went to the shore of the island to the right of the entrance to the harbour, where had been the 4 or 5 men we chased yesterday evening, but having found neither canoe nor natives, it returned to the large one which was standing some distance from the ship. They then started to talk, and seeing that they were about to draw aside, since they were together, I ordered them to be fired on. There were 10 men in the large one and 2 in the small. The moonlight allowed us to see them. I do not know how many we could have killed or wounded, but they left and did not return.

[1] A native of Madagascar and presumably one of the ship's slaves.

At 12.30 a.m. I was forced to lower a bower anchor. We were dragging although there was almost no wind.

At 7 a.m. I ordered a long tow of 2 streamcables and two hawsers to bring us back to the channel. At 8.30 we had a northerly squall which gave us much rain and little wind.

At 10 o'clock I sent a detachment in our boats with some barrels and had our little native taken out of irons, who by signs promised us to show us where there was some water. I had him tied up with a good furling line passed over his shoulders, under his arms and around the body, well stitched and doubled everywhere, which made him cry a little. I took him with me and asked him by signs where the water was; he showed me where we had to disembark a little distance away. Mr Labé was with me in another boat (he had insisted on going with us in spite of his wounds). We landed with part of the detachment and left the remainder under an officer to guard the boats. The little native led us into the wood which is nothing but a marsh. We were keeping him on a leash. He made us travel like this for nearly a quarter of a league without straying far from the seashore. We were merely going round the island, which caused me to feel suspicious, for, I was saying, why did he make us leave our boats so far away since we were more or less following the sea? Moreover, as from time to time he would turn towards me and make a sign that we were simply going there to get something to drink, but that he would later go back to the ship to sleep, I thought he was trying to trick me and I was right, because we fortunately noticed that the rope holding him although three finger's breaths in width and made of new rope yarn was almost entirely cut through: he had skilfully picked up a shell without anyone noticing and was cleverly cutting the rope. We took the shell from him and watched him more closely and tied him up even better. I was almost tempted to take him back to the ship for fear of losing him, and to go looking ourselves along the entire shoreline for a place to obtain water, nevertheless as he made a sign to indicate that there was not much further to go we went on and finally one of our sailors noticed some water running down over a rock of soft stone. We decided to go no further and to dig a well there at the foot of this rock where we would get our water. The little native absolutely wanted to lead us a little further, but all his little tricks made us stick to what we had. We went to the sea shore by the shortest and most practicable [route] and I sent 2 men to fetch our boats which soon joined us. The tide had risen and they were able to reach the place where we were.

According to appearance the little native had not led them there at first because the tide was out, which is a fairly intelligent thing to do for a child of 15, for he was not deceiving us about the watering place: we found it a very short distance away from the one we had stopped at, but it gives less water. The natives had been there themselves, because we found quite recently arranged the leaves they had used to make the water run into their containers. The little native seeing us determined to stay there was wailing loudly, rolling on the sand into which he was thrusting his mouth and his face, in a word he was shouting so loudly and so continually that I got impatient. I took the end of his rope and I gave him a hard blow on the back, threatening him, to get him to be quiet and indeed he gradually quietened down. As soon as our boats had arrived I ordered an officer to take him back on board and put him back in irons, and we began to dig wells at the foot of our waterfall and to make a path on which to roll our barrels.

Monday 16th

We returned yesterday evening with 19 barrels of water we had filled during the day, which was not bad because we lacked tools to dig the wells, moreover we had to clear the path and put small trees in the middle to be able to roll the barrels, without which, since this is nothing but marshy holes full of water, it would have been impossible. All that meant a great deal of work, but when one is very thirsty one makes efforts and at 5 this morning we left again, Mr Labé and I, to get some more water.

Tuesday 17th

When we were at the watering place at 2 yesterday afternoon we heard a canon being fired on board and a moment later we saw a canoe coming from the neighbourhood of the ship. It passed opposite the place at which we were. When it was straight opposite I fired on it although [it was] rather far off, and I shouted to our surgeon who was by the water near our yawl to get in and follow it, which he did very diligently, and he would have caught up with them if his boat had not run aground, which enabled them to draw away. When he saw they were too far ahead he came back and landed in a small cover in the same island as ours about $\frac{1}{2}$ to $\frac{1}{4}$ league away. He found there a few small camping huts where the natives had been that very day or the day before; he found their nets on dry land and brought them to us. We returned to the ship in the evening with twenty barrels of water. Towards the late afternoon there was a heavy shower which caused much discomfort to our poor men whom I had sent down to the shore to breathe the land air.[1] When we were back on board the duty officer told me that during the morning he had brought the flag to half-mast to ask for a boat to inform us that he could see on the shore of the island to the right of the entrance of the harbour a dozen natives who, like the first, were making signs urging him to go to them, and to ask permission to fire on them (he could do so as I had explained this before leaving the ship; he wanted orders of a more positive nature); that at about midday a canoe had joined the said blacks, in which there were another 6; that he had then flown the flag half mast at the main mast to make it more visible, but we never noticed it; and that the shot he had fired was on the canoe we had also greeted with our musket fire; that the ball had passed very close; and that he had fired only to let us see that it was coming towards us. The weather had been fine all night and this morning. When the shot was fired on the canoe all the blacks who were on the shore of the above-mentioned island promptly fled. The ship had still dragged a little and they had lowered a second bower anchor.

Wednesday 18th

At 5.30 p.m. yesterday we returned with twenty barrels of water. The winds during the afternoon had veered right around the compass. At 4 this morning our sergeant died of his wound. The surgeon opened it and found in his back a piece of lance of areca palm more than 6 inches in length which was entirely hidden in the cavity and which had not been felt by the probe. On the day he was wounded we had to use pinchers to bring out this piece of areca which was jammed between the bones. We went back to the water at 4.30.

Thursday 19th

We returned at sunset yesterday having obtained 40 barrels of water and a little firewood during the day. We had been able to take advantage of two tides so that our boats had made two journeys. The winds had been easterly. This morning we went back at 3.30 a.m.

---

[1] This refers to the men suffering from scurvy, as land air was believed to be beneficial in such cases.

Friday 20th

At sunset yesterday we returned on board with 62 barrels of water having again been able to take advantage of two tides. In addition I had our wells cleared out a little, as much as our tools had allowed. The winds had been easterly all day. We went back again this morning at 3.30.

Saturday 21

Yesterday afternoon they sent us from the ship one Yondeva a Malagasy who had died of scurvy.[1] We came back at sunset with 49 barrels of water. All day yesterday the winds blew from SE to E. Fine weather. At midday it was dead calm and at 2 o'clock a light breeze came up from the SW. At 5 p.m. it veered E again. Our people all being very tired I decided to do no work whatever to let them rest. At 8 this morning we began work on raising all our anchors; we had 4 to do, namely one ordinary kedge anchor, one heavy ditto and two bower anchors. We began to weigh the heavy kedge, then in turn the bowers. We are at present working on the second one. There will only be the ordinary kedge anchor which I had cast by the stern and which we will ease off to the longboat. The conformation of this harbour forces me to do this on account of its bad holding ground and lack of space so that I can swing fairly promptly, because the pass is very narrow. I have also left all the other boats lowered, firstly because the longboat not being aboard, it is extremely awkward to haul the others in, but also because the entrance of the harbour being very narrow one can find a weak breeze or some kind of shift and then our boats assist you as required.

Sunday 22nd[2]

At one thirty yesterday afternoon, having nearly finished weighing our last heavy anchor, I cast off the careening warp astern because its anchor was starting to drag little by little although there was more than one cable out and the wind was blowing at only 3 knots, but as I have

[1] Yondeva may have been the slave's name, but it may be a corrupted form of Hova, a leading tribe in Madagascar.

[2] Marginal note: 'Departure from Port Praslin'. Prior to leaving the French carved a number of inscriptions on trees ashore; details of these are given by both Labé and Pottier de l'Horme. See Labé, *Journal*, entry of 20 October.

already said the ground is not good here. I left the longboat with 16 men and an officer and the yawl with arms to defend itself. I came out of the harbour and at first plied to windward E as close inshore as I could under the topsails. The sea was very smooth, the wind blowing straight from the land. But as with this shortened sail I kept on bearing off and did not see our boats coming back I veered back to land. Shortly after, we saw them coming out of the pass. When they were near I stood to sea with the wind in our topsails. We stayed thus until 9.45 last night stemming from E to ESE. Finally all our boats being aboard and our anchors catted and stowed I sailed as may be seen from the log-board.

Courses since then E¼NE4°N 33′ or 11 leagues.

I reckon that at 9 o'clock yesterday evening I was in approximately the same longitude as on Friday 13th of the same [month] when I was outside the harbour trying to enter. I am therefore taking my departure point from the same longitude. As for the latitude, I estimated myself yesterday at 9 o'clock to be 6′ further N than on the said day Friday 13th. I am accordingly deducting this from the latitude of that day, so:

Lat. S 7°15′, diff. N 9′, Est. S 7°06′, observed 7°17′, diff. S 11′. Long. E 152°07′, diff. E 32′, Est. E 152°39′.

As the time I have spent in this harbour has not ceased to cause me sorrow and exhaustion and our departure is keeping me busy, I am leaving a description to a quieter moment and after I have taken a little rest.

Monday 23rd

We had a dead calm from 2 to 8 p.m. yesterday. At 1 a.m. one of our blacks, named Sanganache,[1] died, and also at 5 o'clock, a sailor named Pierre Rondel.

At 10 this morning we saw a drifting catamaran[2] passing alongside. I lowered the small boat I had bought at Bashi and Mr Labé embarked in it. The catamaran we found was made of large banana trees fixed with pieces of wood and well tied together. I had it hauled aboard and as the sea water has not soaked into it and it is quite fresh our animals are eating it, even the pigs. At 11.30 the little boat was aboard and we continued on our way.

[1] This may be a corruption of Sakalava, one of the main tribes of Madagascar.
[2] A raft or float formed of tree trunks tied side by side. The word comes from the Tamil *Kattamaran*, tied tree.

Courses ESE1°E. Lat. S 7°17′, diff. S 11′, Est. S 7°28′, observed 7°28′. Long. E 152°39′, diff. E 28′, Est. E 153°07′.

Tuesday 24 October 1769

Yesterday at 4.30 p.m. we saw the land very distant bearing SSE to SSW. At sunset we could see it from the topmasts from SSE to SW, mountainous, especially the most easterly. At 5 this morning as we were again standing to land I sounded at half-hourly intervals at 50 or so fathoms without finding bottom. From 4 to 6 o'clock a shower with no wind, light rain; reduced sail as a precaution. At 6 o'clock tacked with the topsails and hauled the main tack. At 7 this morning we sighted land from S to SW¼S. High mountains towards the S. The western part seemed more level.

At 8 o'clock the southernmost land bore S¼SE, the westernmost W¼SW. At midday the easternmost, having the appearance of an island bears SE¼S1°S, the point which seems to belong to the more easterly mainland SE¼S4°S, the nearest [land] which stretches beyond some very high mountains SW distant 6 to 7 l., the most westerly is lost in a cloud W¼SW1°S.[1]

Courses SE¼S 22′ or 7⅔ leagues. Lat. S 7°28′, diff. S 18′, Est. S 7°46′, observed 7°42′, diff. N 4′. Long. E 153°07′, diff. E 12′, Est. E 153°19′.

Wednesday 25 October 1769

As we changed course at 1 yesterday afternoon, the easternmost land bore SE¼S2°S distant 6 to 7 leagues at least, the westernmost W¼SW. At 6 p.m. the easternmost point which looks like a detached island bore SSE 2°S distant 8 to 9 l., the westernmost land stretches out to SW¼W. At 9 p.m. furled the topgallants and at 9.30 hauled the main and fore topsails to midmast on account of gusts without rain. Furled the mizzen topsail. From midnight to 4 o'clock, standing in shore, sounded hourly without finding bottom at 55 f. From 4 to 6 sounded every ½ hour ditto. At 6.30 the sky became cloudy and the wind freshened. I had 2 reefs taken in the topsails to avoid having to work the ship during the showers and get our people wet. At 7 o'clock we had a fairly strong squall. We also had sight of the land, but not clearly on account of

---

[1] The *St Jean-Baptiste* had by then just passed north of Estrella Bay on the north coast of Santa Isabel. The easternmost land, an island, was possibly Fapuli Island with the eastern coast of Santa Isabel close by, the nearest land was the shore of Estrella Bay with Hakelake Island merged with it, and the most westerly point Cape Megapode.

the clouds. We saw it from S to WSW. At 9 during a break we saw the land stretching out to SE¼S. It is the same headland as we saw last night bearing SSE 2°S. At midday we could not see any land distinctly although we had come closer to it. We could only see a few mountains from S to SW¼W, but not clearly. What is certain is that we are a little further N and W than at midday yesterday.

Courses SE¼E1°E 9' or 3 leagues. Lat. S 7°42', diff. S 5', Est. 7°47', observed 7°44', diff. N 3'. Long. E 153°19', diff. E 8', Est. E 153°27'. I have noticed from the bearings that I had lost 7 to 8' W, consequently 8' lost and 8' by dead reckoning make 16, [so] amended Est. E 153°11.

Thursday 26th

At 1 p.m. yesterday we let out the topgallants. At 3.30 we furled them. At 4.30 furled the standing jib and stay sails. At 5 as the weather looked threatening, took in all reefs in the topsails. At 5.30 we can see the easternmost land having the appearance of a high cape with a lower headland to seaward of it with an opening, like an island; this latter bears S4½°E and the high cape S¼SW; the westerly land is very hazy, the most westerly we can see bearing SW¼S. Squall with light rain and wind. Furled the stay sail, main jib and mizzen topsail. Until midnight continuation of wind, squalls and light rain, with strong gusts from time to time. At 1 o'clock fitted a lazy guy to the mizzen. At 2 clewed up and furled the mainsail and immediately [after] the fore topsail. At 5 clewed up the main topsail. At 7 set the main and mizzen topsails, at 8 the main sail and mizzen stay sail. We were unable to set the fore topsail it is being mended, having been torn when we hauled it.

I have given overall the name of Arsacides Islands to the land we have discovered, because according to the Encyclopedia[1] several people

---

[1] The similarity between Surville's comments and the article in the *Grande Encyclopédie* makes it hard to doubt that he had a set on board. The article reads as follows: 'Several people claim that the word *assassin* comes from the Levant, where it originated from a certain prince of the Arsacides family, commonly known as *assassins*, who lived between Antioch and Damascus in a castle where he brought up a large number of young men to obey blindly all his orders. The Jew Benjamin, in his *Itinerary*, places these *assassins* close to Mount Lebanon and calls them in Hebrew style, derived from the Arabic, *il asasin*, which indicates that his name does not come from Arsacides, but from the Arabic *asis*, *insidiator*, a person in ambush. The above-mentioned *assassins* possessed eight or twelve cities around Tyre; they elected from among themselves a king they called *the old man of the mountain*. In 1213 they murdered Louis of Bavaria. They were Mohamedans but paid some tribute to the knight templars. The *assassins*' protectors were condemned by the Council of Lyons under Innocent IV in 1231. They were vanquished by the Tartars, who killed their old man of the mountain in 1257; after which the sect of the *assassins* disappeared.' *Encyclopédie*, vol. I, pp. 765–6. There are some inaccuracies in this article: the Assassins took their name from *hashishi*, a consumer of hashish – believed to be given to them to induce visions of

believe that the word assassin comes from the Levant where it originated from a certain prince of the *Arsacides* family, commonly called assassins. One Jew thinks that this word comes from the Arabic *asis*, insidiator, a person in ambush. (This is precisely what the natives of these islands did: they tried to lead us into an ambush to kill those of us who were there to fetch water, and seeing that they could not succeed fell upon our people regardless and killed one, or at least he died of his injuries, the sergeant; and wounded several, which they paid for by the death of thirty to 40 of theirs). The above-mentioned Assassins, according to a Jew, elected their own king, whom they called *the Old Man of the Mountain.* In 1213 they murdered Louis of Bavaria. See the article Assassins in the Encyclopedia, vol. I.

At midday we suddenly sighted an island, level, wooded and not very large. It seemed to be very far from the large mass of islands or continent we could see in the far distance consisting of high mountains in the south.[1]

Courses E1°20′S 57′ of 19 leagues. Lat. S 7°44′, diff. S 1′, Est. S 7°45′, observed 7°41′, diff. N 4′. Long. E 153°11′, diff. E 57′, Est. E 154°08′.

Friday 27th

We finished mending the fore topsail yesterday shortly after midday, it was hauled up at once, and at 2 o'clock we let out the topgallants, stay sails, mizzen, etc. At 2.30 we were N and S of *île Inattendue* distant about 4½ leagues. (I named this island thus because we certainly did not expect to see land again. The day before at sunset we had sighted a headland which seemed to be the easternmost cape.) One can see a very high mountain over its east point bearing S¼SE very distant from the said island which is extremely flat, especially its eastern point which gradually falls away to sea level; its western extremity is a little higher. It could be one league across from E to W.[2] At 6 p.m. the easternmost point of *Inattendue* Island bore SW¼S2°W, its westernmost point

paradise before they left on a mission; they belonged to a branch of the Ismaili sect of Shi'ite Muslims, founded by Hasan ibn al-Sabbah, the original Old Man of the Mountains, who established himself in 1090 in Alamut, a fortress near Kazvin; Alamut fell to the Mongols in 1256; Ludwig I Wittelsbach was assassinated in 1231, not 1213; the Council of Lyons was held in 1245.

[1] This, de Surville's Unexpected Island, is Ndai, first seen by Carteret and named by him Gower Island.

[2] Ndai is a small, low island, far to the north of the western extremity of Malaita, which Surville describes as a very high island bearing between S¼SW and S¼SE5°E. The high mountain seen over its eastern point is Malaita – Mt N. W. Alite rises to 2325 ft.

SW$\frac{1}{4}$W3°S by its centre appearing to be distant 5 to 6 l. Some more highland which I take to be a very high island bore, its westernmost point S$\frac{1}{4}$SW and its easternmost S$\frac{1}{4}$SE5°E; between this island and the small one one can see more high mountains further off than the latter, which from a high land I take to be an island. Between its point and these other more distant high mountains there seems to be an opening or bight.[1] At 11 furled the standing jib and the mizzen. We sounded every $\frac{1}{2}$ hours at 50 f. without finding bottom. At 6.30 a.m. the easternmost land forming a headland beyond which we see nothing more bore S$\frac{1}{4}$SE, the westernmost SW. We have been having squalls at intervals since yesterday, during which we occasionally reduced canvas more as a precaution than otherwise on account of our people who are all in a weak state, to avoid getting them wet by working the ship during the showers. At midday a low headland which marks the end of a very high island bore S$\frac{1}{4}$SW5°W.[2] The clouds do not allow us to see any beyond in the E and S but I thought I could glimpse some; but everything we are seeing at the moment is running S.

Courses ESE1°20'S 57' or 19 leagues. Lat. S 7°41', diff. S 23', Est. S 8°04', observed 8°22', diff. S 18'. Long. E 154°08', diff. E 52', Est. E 155°.

Saturday 28th

The point we could see yesterday at midday bearing S$\frac{1}{4}$SW5°W bears SW$\frac{1}{4}$W1°S at sunset. The western point is lost in the clouds, bearing W$\frac{1}{4}$SW, the eastern land ditto S. They are very high mountains very far off. At 11 p.m. clewed up the courses and furled the topgallants on account of the calm. At 12.30 a.m. hoisted the topsails. At 3 hauled aboard the main tack and the mizzen. At 5 this morning the weather overcast, very black, signs of heavy rain and of a wind change. The NW especially is overcast. At 7 clewed up the courses and hauled the main and fore topsails on account of the calm. At 8 trimmed the mizzen and the main and fore topsails, then again dead calm. At 11 trimmed again and at 11.30 hauled in the topsails. It rained almost continually from midnight to midday.

[1] Surville was now seeing Malaita Island. The first high island listed is its north coast, from Cape Astrolabe (the westernmost point) to Manaoba Island (the easternmost). The weather was squally and the distant high mountains referred to were probably a view of inland Malaita, rather than Guadalcanal, whose Mt Popomanasiu rises to more than 8000 ft.
[2] This is Cape Arsacides, the only relic of the name given by Surville to the Solomon Islands. It forms one extremity of the north-west coast of Malaita.

Courses E$\frac{1}{4}$SE5°S 25′ or 8$\frac{1}{3}$ leagues. Lat. S 8°22′, diff. S 7′, Est. S 8°29′. Long. E 155°, diff. E 24′, Est. E 155°24′.

I have reckoned 4′ of drift N for the intervals of calm. I have not allowed anything E because we also drifted W at times.

Sunday 29th

Sighted land at 3 o'clock from SSW to W distant 10 to 12 l.

Bearings when altering course: at 5 o'clock the most westerly land bearing W, the easternmost bearing S distant 10 l. approximately. This is very high land. An opening between two headlands bearing W$\frac{1}{4}$SW3°W, another ditto SW$\frac{1}{4}$W2°W.[1] At 1 a.m. we had fair weather, a light breeze and all sails out. At sunrise the opening we saw yesterday bearing W$\frac{1}{4}$SW3°W bears now W5°S and the one bearing SW$\frac{1}{4}$W2°W bears WSW2°S. The most westerly land is lost in the clouds, bearing W$\frac{1}{4}$NW3°N, the most easterly stretches out to S$\frac{1}{4}$SW. All the mountains on the beam are very high. From the top of the masts we can see 5 or 6 points rising like small islands stretching out as far as S$\frac{1}{4}$SE.[2] It could be that as we get nearer this will join and look like high mountains. A shower at midday prevents us from taking bearings.

Courses SSE5°15′E 24′ or 8 leagues. Lat. S 8°29′, diff. S 21′, Est. S 8°50′, observed 8°51′. Long E 155°24′, diff. E 11′, Est. E 155°35′.

Monday 30 October 1769

At 6 o'clock the southernmost land bore SSE distant 12 l., a headland by an opening S$\frac{1}{4}$SW, another ditto SSW about 7 l., the nearest land which consists of very high mountains WSW 4°S distant about 5 or 6 l., an opening W2°N, the one which at midday bore W3°S [and] the other which bore at midday W$\frac{1}{4}$NW bear now W$\frac{1}{4}$NW3°N distant about 7 l., the most N and W and NW$\frac{1}{4}$W3°W distant about 10 l. Had a sudden strong squall at 8 p.m. with heavy rain. We had furled all the small sails and brought the main and fore topsails upon the cap, then we clewed up the mizzen topsail and lee-clewed the mainsail. At 10 we hauled back the mainsail and the main and fore topsails. At 11 o'clock let out the mizzen topsail although the weather was still overcast with light rain. At 6 this morning we sighted an island well

[1] This is probably the opening formed by the south-east tip of Malaita, with Anuta Baita, a small island a short distance offshore, and Pyramid Island, off the northern tip of Maramasike Island.

[2] This is Surville's first sighting of the peaks of San Cristóbal Island.

off the coast. I named it [   ]. It bore SE¼S3°S distant 9 to 10 leagues.[1]
The most southerly land bore SSW ditto, an opening SW5°S distant
8 l., a high mountain which yesterday evening was the nearest land
bearing WSW4°S bears now W3°N, the most northerly land
W¼NW 2°N distant 12 l. At 8 o'clock the bearings remain the same,
they can scarcely change from such a distance, as we have hardly made
any headway. At midday the centre of [   ] Island bore SSE 6 to 7 l.,
the southernmost headland of the main coast bore SSW2½°W about
10 l. This headland falls away continually and very gradually from the
high mountains to sea level.[2] An opening in the main coast between
two small islands bore WSW3°S distant about 8 leagues, another ditto
W¼SW3°W 8 to 9 l., the most northerly point W¼NW4°N 12 to 15 l.
The opening lying to WSW seems to be formed by two steep headlands
which would seem to indicate that there is a good depth of water.

Courses ESE4°15′E 29½′ or 9⅚ leagues. Lat. S 8°51′, diff. S 9′, Est.
S 9°, observed 9°22′, diff. S 22′. Long. E 155°35′, diff. E 28′, Est.
E 156°03′.[3]

Tuesday 31 October 1769

At 5.45 clewed up the main sail, furled the royals, topgallants, stay
sails and mizzen topsail on account of a squall rising in the NW. At
6 p.m. the centre of *Contrariétés* Island[4] bore S¼SE2°S distant about 9
leagues, the southernmost point of the mainland SW¼S 12 to 13 l., the
southernmost opening SW¼S4°S, the 2nd ditto running N SW¼W, the
3rd WSW3°S, the most northerly land W¼SW about 15 leagues. We
cannot see the point clearly, it is lost in cloud. At 10 p.m. we kept the
mizzen and the main and fore topsails at half mast on account of squalls,
not wishing to make our people work the ship during the rain. At 11
hauled them back, let out the mizzen topsail and the stay sails. The
squalls passed without strength. At 6.30 this morning we clewed up
out two lower sails on account of calms. Sighted at sunrise *Contrariétés*
Island bearing S4°W, the southernmost land forming a point which

[1] This is Ulawa Island, north of San Cristóbal. The high mountain referred to was Mt
Kolovrat, 4275 ft. Ulawa was first discovered by Mendaña in 1568 and named La Treguada
or Truce Island 'because they attacked us after a broken truce.' See Jack-Hinton, *The
Discovery of the Solomon Islands*, p. 61.
[2] This would be Nialahau or Cape Zélée.
[3] The South Sub-Tropical Current which set westward at an average of 2 knots had
affected the *St Jean-Baptiste* which was now about 25 miles west of her estimated longitude.
[4] The name given to Ulawa by Surville on account of all the difficulties, unhelpful winds
and currents he had to contend with.

falls away gradually and can also be considered as low and level SW,[1] a high mountain near the most westerly point W¼NW4°W. At midday sighted the middle of the island bearing S5°E distant about 9 l., the southernmost point SW 3°S, the northernmost W¼NW2°W.

Courses SE4°S 12' or 4 leagues. Lat. S 9°22', diff. S 9', Est. 9°31', observed 9°20', diff. N 11'. Long. E 156°03', diff. E 8', Est. E 156°11'.

We have had almost nothing but calms. It is certain, from the position of *Contrariétés* Island, that I am further east than I was yesterday, a little more even, I think, than is shown by my dead reckoning, but I am somewhat more N than I was yesterday.

Wednesday 1 November 1769

At sunset yesterday the southernmost opening which bore SW¼W4°S yesterday bears SW2°S, the 2nd ditto running N which bore SW¼W bears by its centre SW5°S, and the 3rd which bore WSW3°S bears W¼SW2°W, *Contrariétés* Island bears S¼SE3°E, a large mountain close to the most W land W¼NW4°W, the southernmost point SW¼S3°S. The sky is overcast especially in the N. A light breeze from midnight to 4 o'clock. At sunrise the middle of *Contrariétés* Island bore SE¼S4°S distant 7 to 8 l., the southernmost point of the mainland SSW1°S distant about 8 l., the 1st opening SW5°W about 6 l., the 2nd running N WSW4°S, the above-mentioned large mountain near the W point W¼NW. At midday *Contrariétés* Island through its most E point bears SE¼S3°S distant about 9 l., the most northerly land WNW 12 l., the most southerly opening SE5°S, we cannot see the others. The most northerly and westerly land bears WNW.[2]

Courses SE 10' or 3⅓ leagues. Lat. S 9°20', diff. S 7', Est. 9°27', observed 9°29'. Long. E 156°11', diff. E 7', Est. E 156°18'.

This country here continues to appear attractive, and anyone in a position to examine it, and who had the time for it, as it should be done, would find here, I think, the finest country in the world and places of safety. We can see boats coming towards us from the mainland.

---

[1] This was Cape Zélée: the weather was too overcast at this stage for Surville to sight San Cristóbal, which would have been more southerly.

[2] Labé and Pottier point out that the horizon was hazy at midday and give no bearings. If Ulawa bore SE¼S from the *St Jean-Baptiste*, while bearing S5°E on the previous day, the ship must have been carried some distance south westward by the currents. The bearing SE5°S for the most southerly opening is an error for SW5°S – where lay the strait between Malaita and San Cristóbal, whereas all along the east stretched out the open sea.

Thursday 2 November 1769

The boats we could see coming from land arrived shortly after midday within normal speaking distance. They circled the ship. I hauled up our flag which is white[1] and is a sign of peace among these people. I joined to this another small one I held in my hand. I furthermore urged them to approach by making all kinds of friendly gestures. I showed them something I wanted to give them; they asked me by signs to throw it to them, which I did by tying to a piece of wood a length of red cloth and a knife; I also threw them an empty bottle. They picked everything up, but this did not make them come any closer. I made a sign that I wanted coconuts; they understood me and showed me there were some ashore and to come and fetch some. I made them understand I would not go, but to go and fetch me some. Shortly after they gave the signal to depart, possibly to meet my wishes, for towards sunset 2 of these boats were making every effort to reach us, but in vain: we were out of necessity standing to sea and as the wind had freshened a little they could not join us. All these boats were armed with lances and bows and with arrows. They are well-built kaffirs, of normal height. They are completely naked. Some parts of their faces are painted. Their boats seemed to me better built than those of Port Praslin. These men did not seem to me so handsome as those of Port Praslin; they seem also more evenly black. Their boats have slight differences, I find those here sharper.

At 6 p.m. *Contrariétés* Island bore SE$\frac{1}{4}$E2°E distant about 9 l., the southernmost land S5°W, an opening W$\frac{1}{4}$NW5°W about 6 l., a headland W$\frac{1}{4}$NW 4°N, the westernmost land WNW4°N lost in the clouds. At 8 p.m. strong gale in gusts. Furled the topgallants, stay sails and mizzen topsail. At 11 o'clock all that was let out again. At sunrise *Contrariétés* Island bore: its easternmost point E$\frac{1}{4}$SE1°S, distant 5 l., its southernmost point SE$\frac{1}{4}$S5°E 5 l., the headland of the mainland which bore S5°W last night now bears WSW4$\frac{1}{2}$°W. At 8 o'clock, the southernmost point of *Contrariétés* Island bears ESE, the easternmost SSE2$\frac{1}{2}$°S, the westernmost S$\frac{1}{4}$SW. At 8.30 we set a course for *Contrariétés* Island. My plan was to cast anchor there if possible, to find some refreshments, a few greens for our sick who are getting no better although they are fed good soup, and whose number grows daily. At 11.30 being near enough to the land and the ship dragging I took

---

[1] The French royal emblem was white with a pattern of fleurs de lys. Labé on the other hand refers simply to a white flag – a flag of truce.

advantage of this moment to change course and haul along the island at a distance of about 2 l. From 8 to midday a large number of boats from *Contrariétés* Island have been standing a certain distance from the ship. There are 4, 5 and 6 men in each. At midday the most southerly of the said island bears SE distant about 4 or 5 l., the most northerly in sight ENE4°N about 4 l., the nearest land which is almost the middle of the island about 2 l. The point of the main land which bore S¼SW5°W yesterday bears now W3°S distant 12 to 15 l. One can see land from the topmasts stretching from S¼SE to SW¼S.[1] We cannot yet know what it is, whether it is islands or a continuation of the coast; in any case if it is the latter, there is a large bight between this land and the point at W3°S 12 to 15 l. There is between them a void where we can see nothing.

Courses ESE4°E 25′ or 8⅓ leagues. Lat. S 9°29′, diff. S 8′, Est. 9°37′, observed 9°46′, diff. S 9′. Long. E 156°18′, diff. E 24′, Est. E 156°42′.[2] We are at the moment surrounded by local boats.

Friday 3 November 1769

While we had gone below to dine yesterday canoes which had surrounded us until then came up closer, enough for me to throw a loaf to one who came right up under the windows of the ward room to get it. The native in charge of it caught it in his hand and started eating it at once with a very good appetite. I threw an empty bottle to another canoe and a Flemish knife to a 3rd. These little presents emboldened them so that without any more delay several natives climbed on board. The chief himself climbed up with astonishing nimbleness; he climbed without bothering to go to up the ladder, he caught hold of the mizzen chains and climbed forthwith, like the best sailor I have ever seen, up to the mizzen top, from where he made numerous signs to his compatriots, examined how everything was placed there and came down to the poop where he started to dance, jump and make new signs to his companions. These gestures were most strange because he was making them with his penis (they were all completely naked and had a green leaf wrapped around the glans, after which the foreskin covered it up so that, as half the green leaf projected beyond it, it made like a small green tube hanging at the end of the penis: they all have a very long foreskin). After doing all these monkey

---

[1] This is the north coast of San Cristóbal from Cape Recherche east. The void referred to later is the strait which separates Malaita from San Cristóbal.
[2] Once more, the easting is far less than Surville estimated.

tricks on the poop, he went off to untie the halyard of the ensign I was flying and hauled it down. He wanted to undo it to take it away. Without showing any displeasure on this account we prevented him and hauled back the flag. He then came down on the quarter deck, where I was; I gestured to him to follow me to the quarter-deck cabin, which he did with no hesitation. He examined everything and would have carried most of it away if I had allowed him, but I merely gave him a Flemish knife and a little blue cloth. He then let me understand that he was the chief and as he could see I was one too he caressed me, letting me understand that we would be friends. He pointed out that he wore long hair similar to mine. There was one other who wore his similarly; nearly all the others had heavy kaffir-like heads, the size of a bushel. Some had very thick black hair, others had the tips reddened by the sun; I saw only one whose hair had been powdered with lime and consequently was red as in Port Praslin; this one had also a small peg through his nose, like those of the above-mentioned harbour, the others did not seem to me to have their noses pierced. They merely have like those of the above-mentioned harbour large holes in their ears where they hang bunches of aromatic leaves. They have bracelets like the former above the elbow made of a kind of hemp. They also have leaves with an excellent scent hung around the neck. The chief had numerous bead ornaments on his arms, even around his body as a belt, and a tuft of two feathers on his head, which he never allowed anyone to touch. For his part he was merely brown like an Indian, but nearly all the others were black. They were very ordinary in height, but well-built, their chest and shoulders broad and well thrown back. The chief's canoe was a masterpiece of polish, sculpture and inlay – or at least it was artistically inlaid with mother-of-pearl; there were small ornaments in the bow which I could not describe; inside were lances, arrows, and bows, and all the other canoes had their stocks of them, but I had given orders that they were not to be allowed to come aboard with arms. Each one tries to take what he comes across. One putting his arm through the half port of the pantry took a cheap flask, which he thought was a good one, and jumped overboard with it. This act which they noticed we disliked caused them all to depart.

At 2.30 we had a squall which led us to haul down the main and fore sails. At 3.30 plying for the land and beginning to be closer in I clewed up the courses and lowered the yawl to go ahead seeking an anchorage.[1] Mr Labé got into it with a detachment of 6 soldiers. The

---

[1] There is an adequate anchorage on the west coast of Ulawa, Suu Talahia; there is now a mission station nearby; but a better anchorage is found on the north coast in Suumoli Harbour.

yawl went on a course straight ahead of the ship and was taking soundings. Four canoes, seeing this little vessel in appearance more like theirs, came towards it, one especially fairly close where he took his bow and was readying it by placing an arrow in it. Mr Labé naturally did not wait for it to be shot; he fired at him; he was wounded with one other [shot] but without being knocked overboard. The yawl followed him for some time. Seeing this I fired solid shot at the canoes and [signalled] for the yawl to return and had it hauled in, giving up my plan to anchor since once again we were dealing with treacherous people.[1] Shortly after this some twenty canoes came to defy us and came although rather slowly towards the ship. I had 2 or 3 shots with grapeshot fired at the lot, which wounded a few and they all fled. I was sorry to leave this island. It appears to be charming, well-wooded, well cultivated; its shores seemed to us like quays covered with the finest greenery. What is certain [is that] all the aromatics these natives were adorned with prove that the island is full of them. I had asked them for coconuts, every valley of the island is full of them as we could easily see. Not one canoe had brought the slightest thing for barter.

At 6 p.m. *Contrariétés* Island bore: its most southerly point E¼SE 3°S distant 2 l., the northernmost point N 3°E distant about 6 l., the most southerly part of the mainland W¼NW 10 to 11 l. We can see more land separate from what I call the mainland to the S¼SE, it appears like two low islands.[2] At 11.15 sighted one of the said islands bearing SSE and S¼SE. At 11 o'clock altered course wind right aft. At 2.30 altered course head to wind and larboard tack. At 6 this morning the most northerly point of *Contrariétés* Island bore N 4°W, its most westerly N¼NW 2°W distant 9 to 10 l., the most southerly of the three islands (which I have named the Three Sisters[3] because they are all flat and level and are fairly similar, the southernmost is however twice as long as the others) S¼SE 4°E distant 5 or 6 l., the middle of the 2nd S 3°W 4 l., the 3rd also by its middle SSW 5°W 2½ l., the westernmost of the other land in sight, a little hazy, SW¼W 5°S 8 to 9 l. At 8 the most southerly point of the Three Sisters bore S 2°E, the middle of the 2nd

[1] However great was their need for fresh food, it is hard to see what else the French could do after their experience at Port Praslin. It might have been possible for trade to begin if the *St Jean-Baptiste* had merely brought to in the hope that the islanders might in time understand what the French wanted, but such a course was not entirely devoid of risks and would have taken time – besides which they were no indications that it would eventually have been successful.

[2] The Olau Malau group, which consists of three islands, named the Three Sisters by Surville, but first discovered in 1568 by Mendaña's expedition and named Las Tres Marías.

[3] The name given by Surville to the Olau Malau group remains in general use today. None rises above 250 ft. The southernmost, Malaupaina, is correctly described by Surville.

S¼SW 3°S, the middle of the 3rd SSW distant 4½ l, the most westerly point of *Contrariétés* Island NNW 2°N and its point which appears to us most northerly N¼NW 2°N; we no longer see the other land which at 6 o'clock bore SW¼W 5°S. Altered course at 8.30. Let out at 9.30 the 2nd reef which I had taken in this morning because the weather threatened to be squally, which did not eventuate: it merely turned into a fairly fresh but steady gale. We also set the stay sails and the standing jib. At 11.45 seeing that I had not gained enough to turn the Three Sisters I stood off to sea, wind astern.

At midday sighted the southernmost point of the 1st island bearing S and its westernmost bearing S¼SW 4°W distant 4 l., the southernmost point of the 2nd SW¼S 5°S, its westernmost point SW 2°S 2½ to 3 l., the southernmost point of the 3rd WSW 2½°S and its westernmost point W¼SW 1½°W.

Courses SSE 3°45'E 22½' or 7½ leagues. Lat. S 9°46', diff. S 20', Est. S 10°06', observed 10°09', diff. S 3'. Long. E 156°42', diff. E 10', Est. E 156°52'.

It seems to me that all the inhabitants of these settlements are constantly at war against each other, which removes entirely any confidence they might have in any stranger, because among them the greatest marks of friendship are merely means of deceiving, so they trust no one and attack as soon as they think they have the advantage.[1] I have not seen any smoke off the 3 Sisters. They are well-wooded and seem to have sandy bays on the eastern side, but that is the weather side. I do not think they are inhabited. My little native from Port Praslin, whom I have always treated well until now and who seems happy so far, did not seem to me to understand the people here. He seemed extremely surprised that they all went about naked; he joked with us about it. An inhabitant from here seeing that this child looked like him by the hair etc. invited him several times to go with him in his canoe and asked me for him; he out of prudence or for some other reason did not seem interested, quite the opposite, and when he saw they had attacked us he asked me eagerly for a bow and some arrows I had in my cabin, letting me understand that he would not miss his

---

[1] Head hunting was common and treachery frequent, e.g. '*Ranggi tila*, club dance.... This dance is specially for the purpose of deceiving an enemy and killing them. Men and women watched the dancers with great excitement and enjoyed the beauty of the movements, when suddenly a signal was given and the dancers broke out and killed the onlookers, clubbing the men, women and children mercilessly.' Bogesi, 'Santa Isabel, Solomon Islands', *Oceania*, vol. xviii, no. 3, pp. 229–30. It is apparent that Surville was by now obtaining information from Lova Saregua.

mark. Nevertheless he is sad at times and at every moment asks when I will return towards his father and his mother. He pronounces these two words[1] absolutely as we do without an accent or anything.

Saturday 4 November 1769

At 2 o'clock yesterday *Contrariétés* Island bore from us NW$\frac{1}{4}$N 3°N distant 12 or 13 l., the southernmost of 3 Sisters S$\frac{1}{4}$SW 2°W 9 to 10 l., the 2nd SSW 4°W 8 l., the 3rd SW 3°S 7 l. At 6 p.m. the southernmost of the 3 Sisters bore: its most southerly point SSW 2°W distant 4 to 5 l., its most northerly SW$\frac{1}{4}$W 2°S, the most southerly [point] of the 2nd island W$\frac{1}{4}$SW 5°S, its most northerly W, the 3rd, its most southerly W$\frac{1}{4}$NW 1°W, its most northerly WNW 2°W.

At 7.40 p.m. we were east and W of the southern point of the said most southerly island of the 3 Sisters. At 10 o'clock we suddenly sighted a fire on land at sea level, which caused me to change course. It bore S$\frac{1}{4}$SW. Then at 11.40 the weather became squally. I had the main and fore topsails hauled down and the mizzen topsail furled. Squalls rose from the E and ESE continually from midnight to 4 o'clock. At 2.30 [?] the main and fore topsails and set the mizzen topsail. At 4.30 I set course again for the S. At 5 o'clock we set the standing jib and staysails. At sunrise, the easternmost of the Three Sisters by its most S point bore S$\frac{1}{4}$SW 5°W distant 5 to 6 l. and its most W point bore SW$\frac{1}{4}$S4°W distant 4 to 5 l., the middle of the 2nd one SW$\frac{1}{4}$W 5°W 4$\frac{1}{2}$ l., the middle of the most westerly W 3°S 5$\frac{1}{2}$ l. approximately. At 7.25 we were E and W of the north point of the most easterly. At 8 its more southerly point bore WSW4°W 1$\frac{1}{2}$ to 2 l., its most northerly point WNW3°N 2$\frac{1}{2}$ l., the middle of the 2nd one NW$\frac{1}{4}$W2°N 3$\frac{1}{2}$ l., the middle of the 3rd one NW 6 to 7 l. At 8.10 east and W of the most N point of the most easterly island. At 8.45 the 3 islands are together by their opposite points, the southernmost of the 1st bearing W$\frac{1}{4}$NW3°N 3 to 4 l., the northernmost of the 3rd NNW 9 to 10 l. We can see some very high land stretching from WSW to SE$\frac{1}{4}$S. At 9.15 the Three Sisters are merged together bearing NW$\frac{1}{4}$N3°N distant 7 l. The most S of the other land which seems like a large cape SE3°S about 12 l. At midday the southernmost of the Three Sisters bears NNW distant 8 or 9 l. It still hides the other 2. The mostly southerly

---

[1] Surville's actual words are *papa* and *maman* which, being more correctly translated 'daddy' and 'mummy', add a touch of poignancy to the tragedy of this youthful captive.

of the other land bears SE 6 or 7 l. The most northerly we can see stretches to the NW¼W; it has the appearance of an other island rather high well to the landward of the 3 Sisters.[1]

Courses SE¼E 18' or 6 leagues. Lat. S 10°09', diff. S 10', Est. 10°19', observed 10°29', diff. S 10'. Long. E 156°52', diff. E. 15', Est. E 157°07'.

The difference I find in my altitude seems true to me judging by the bearings taken at the same time.

Continuation I was omitting: last night we could see land along a very hazy horizon and very tall mountains, as has been proved today. We could not be sure of it. All this indication of land towards the SSE. We saw nothing beyond the most S island of the Three Sisters; we had turned it by 8 o'clock. Suddenly we saw the fire I spoke about earlier; it seemed to me to be at sea level and very brilliant, the waves hid it from me from time to time. I considered that this could be a low island and promptly altered course.

Sunday 5th

All yesterday afternoon we tacked time and time again to try to gain fast in this gulf and we continued all night, with unstable breezes only, so that all we did was to fuss about, manoeuvre, and tear our sails through the flapping caused by the calms and the sea which was running high owing to a fairly strong current. Towards the end of the day I had for a short time a favourable wind with which to turn the S point of the entrance to the gulf, which I was of necessity ranging along fairly close.[2] Suddenly the wind dropped when I was halfway there, so that I found myself [?] stemming straight for the middle of the headland without the ship answering the helm. I nevertheless succeeded with a great deal of trouble in tacking wind astern and standing out to sea, but this operation was very time consuming and troublesome for anyone running for a coast he does not know in the midst of barbarians and who is already extremely close to it. The whole night was much the same thing, that is to say we could not get the ship to respond. Towards 4.30 a light breeze suddenly sprang up from the S which enabled us to stand to sea and make way.

At 6 this morning sighted the southernmost land bearing SE¼S5°E distant about 10 l., the headland we were trying to turn yesterday

---

[1] This was a distant view of Ulawa.
[2] Kahua Point, a prominent headland of the north coast of San Cristóbal.

evening SE$\frac{1}{4}$S4°S and the one which bore SSW 5°W yesterday bears S$\frac{1}{4}$SW 3°S 1$\frac{1}{2}$ to 2 l., the one which bore W$\frac{1}{4}$SW 3°W bears SW$\frac{1}{4}$S and the one bearing W3°S bears WSW. The northernmost land stretches out W. Gulf Island[1] bears W$\frac{1}{4}$NW2°W distant 7 or 8 l., the southernmost of the Three Sisters NW4°W 4 l., the middle one joined to the most southerly NW 2°W 5 l., the most northerly NW1°N 7 to 8 l., *Contrariétés* Island NNW2°N very distant. At 8 o'clock we can see something like islets stretching out SE[2] at the end of the point which we see as the most southerly, which bears SSE 5°E about 9 l. The nearest land which is a headland bears S$\frac{1}{4}$SW 3°S 4 l., the most westerly land through Gulf Island W 2°N 7 or 8 l., the southernmost of the 3 Sisters WNW 5°W 5 l., the middle one NW$\frac{1}{4}$W3°N 7 l., the most northerly NW$\frac{1}{4}$W 9 l., *Contrariétés* Island NNW 3°W. At midday the middle of the said island bears NW5°N, the most N of the Three Sisters W$\frac{1}{4}$NW, the most S W5°N, Gulf Island W$\frac{1}{4}$SW3°W, the most W [point] of the main land through Gulf Island, the nearest land which is the S point of the entrance to the gulf SSW, the most S point of the main land S$\frac{1}{4}$SE.

Courses NE$\frac{1}{4}$E1°45'E 18' or 6 leagues. Lat. S 10°29', diff. N 9', Est. S [10°] 20', observed 10°20'. Long. E 157°07', diff. E 16', Est. E 157°23'.

Yesterday during the afternoon a few canoes came to examine us and make signs for us to go to their settlements as they have done everywhere. These people here are kaffirs like those of the coast opposite *Contrariétés* Island. This morning, when we were already out to sea, 2 canoes came back, one with 1 man, the other with 4 with their weapons. One came forward a little; I threw him a bottle, and they went back after [illeg.].

Monday 6 November 1769

At 1 p.m. yesterday sighted the most S of the 3 Sisters bearing W1°N as far as the eye can reach. At 1.45 I could see a squall forming at sea; I altered course so as to be suitably trimmed and receive it profitably. As it turned out, we have had rain and wind all the afternoon. Squalls were forming all round us, but without wind. At 6 p.m. sighted the

[1] Ugi Island, a relatively low island off San Cristóbal. Surville adds in a marginal note: 'I have given it this name because it appears to stand alone in the middle of the gulf. It has about the shape of the 3 Sisters, but higher'.

[2] Surville's first sighting of Santa Ana and Santa Catalina at the eastern extremity of San Cristóbal, which he was to name Islands of Deliverance.

peak of *Contrariétés* Island at sea level bearing NW2°W; all the high country S of Three Sisters Gulf was hidden in cloud, only the SW¼S3°S part is visible and even then very hazy. At 5.30 we have sight of a small island from the topmasts, bearing SSE. From 6 to midnight we changed tack several times because the wind was shifting but with no strength whatever nor rain but for a few drops. At 6 this morning the islands we saw yesterday from the topmasts and which I have named Deliverance Islands[1] are together, the most E point of the one in sight bears S¼SE 7 to 8 l., its most W point S4°E, the cape that ends the main coast, which I have named Oriental Cape,[2] S¼SW2°S 10 or 12 l. This cape from a certain distance is attached to some very high land and looks like 7 or 8 islets; past the last one of these mountains, at least from this distance, a large headland which is the end of the most N land in sight bears W¼SW4°W. At 8 o'clock Deliverance Islands through the centre of the one in sight bears S5°W distant 7 l., it still hides the other. Oriental Cape bears SSW1°S 10 to 12 l. and more, the large headland which forms the most N land W. At 9.30 rain, squalls and wind. Clewed up the mainsail, furled the topgallants and hauled the main and fore topsails to half-mast. At 10.30 set it all again. At midday the most S of Deliverance Islands through its southernmost [point) bore SSW distant 9 to 10 l., through its northernmost which is by the southernmost point of the 2nd one SSW3°[W] 6 l. from the latter; the most northerly [point] of the same SW¼S. If I had not named these two Deliverance Islands I would have called them the 2 Brothers because they look alike. They are fairly level, elevated only at their S end but this elevation is gradual. Oriental Cape bears SW2°S distant 10 or 11 l., the most westerly land or the most northerly W5°N 15 l. and more.

Courses SE¼E1°S 28′ or 9⅓ leagues. Lat. S 10°20′, diff. S 16′, Est. 10°36′, observed 10°40′, diff. S 4′. Long. E 157°23′, diff. E 23′, Est. 157°46′.[3]

[1] Marginal note: 'I have named them thus because our men, the large majority of whom are sick, are suffering from always seeing the same land and meeting with vexations, for I would like to be in a position to examine things more closely. Their health does not allow me to stop here. I have given the name Oriental to the cape, because I believe it is the most easterly land of New Guinea.'

[2] Cape Oriental is now known as Cape Surville. Surville's description of it as having the appearance from a distance of 7 or 8 islets is correct: 'Cape Surville is the extremity of a peninsula extending about 9 miles eastward from the general line of the coast, and is dominated by a hill, 500 ft high, about one mile within it. A reef extends over one mile from the northern side of the peninsula, and about 6 cables south-eastward and southward from Cape Surville. Bulimatevera islet, 70 ft high and wooded, lies on the fringing reef on the northeastern side of the cape.' *Pacific Islands Pilot*, 1946, p. 301.

[3] Santa Ana is approximately 160°05 east of Paris. At midday, Surville was seven or eight miles further east than this, which an approximate error in his longitude of 2°30′ west.

Tuesday 7th

At 1 yesterday afternoon let out the studding sails, which we had not done for a long time. At 6 p.m. sighted the most W land bearing W¼NW2°W very distant, Oriental Cape SW¼W2°W 14 to 15 l., the most E point of the easternmost island of Deliverance SW¼W1½°W 7½ l., the westernmost of these SW5½°W 5 l., the middle of the easternmost Deliverance Island SW 12 l. At 6 a.m. sighted the most E Deliverance Island bearing WNW5°N 9 or 10 l., and the most W stretching out WNW 3°W. We can still see the tops of a few high mountains of the mainland WNW. At 9 o'clock the most easterly Deliverance island bore NW¼W 2°N. At 9 we can no longer see land.[1]

Courses SE¼S40'E 50' or 16⅔ leagues. Lat. S 10'40', diff. S 41', Est. S 11°21', observed 11°20'. Long. E 157°46', diff. E 28', Est. E 158°14'. The weather has been fine although a little cloudy all night.

Wednesday 8 November 1769

The weather has been almost continually fine since yesterday. At 5 this morning a few squalls blew up with no breeze. Since then the sky has clouded over. At 8 o'clock we had a little rain but not enough to make one take shelter and unaccompanied by wind: on the contrary it made it drop. From 9 to midday we saw numerous birds, these black sea-swallows I have always called wingbeaters because in fact these birds continually flap their wings.[2]

Courses SE¼E48'S 59' or 19⅔ leagues. Lat. S 11°20' diff. S 33', Est. S 11°53', observed 12°12', diff. S 19'. Long. E 158°14', diff. E 48', Est. E 159°02'.

Thursday 9th

We have had all sails out almost constantly since yesterday. The royals and the mizzen top-gallant alone were furled for a while.

Courses SSE3°15E 61' or 20⅓ leagues. Lat. S 12°12', diff. S 54', Est. 13°06', observed 13°19', diff. S 13'. Long. E 159°02', diff. E 26', Est. E 159°28'.

I could easily believe that we have passed not far from Taumago

---

[1] Marginal note: 'Left the Land of the Papuans'.

[2] The Pacific swallow (*Hirundo tahitica*) is widespread from the Solomons to Fiji. 'They can be told by their more deliberate wing beats, by their way of pressing the wings to the body in flight more often.' Mayr, *Birds of the Southwest Pacific*, p. 86.

Island,[1] from which according to our dead reckoning we were not far off, because we saw all day yesterday a large number of birds and who sat on the water as I have always seen them do when they are not far from land.

Friday 10th

The weather has been fine since yesterday. At 4 this morning the wind dropped and the sea swelled. The ship would not steer although the wind was favourable. At 10 o'clock a breeze rose from the NNW.

Courses SE⅓3°10′E 46′ or 15⅓ leagues. Lat. S 13°19′, diff. S 36′, Est. 13°55′, observed 13°56′. Long. E 159°28′, diff. E 28′, Est. E 159°56′.

Here we are in the latitude where Quiros discovered New Guinea[2] and we can see nothing, so that if what we have seen is a continuation of it they are of necessity further E or at least N and S. Possibly some other sighting will give us a better knowledge of the true position of the land we had discovered, because so far we cannot be sure whether we passed E or W of New Britain. Our difference would have to be considerable if we passed W of it and in that case the channel between it and New Guinea would be much wider than Dampier indicates, since we have seen no land to larboard.

Saturday 11th

At 4 yesterday afternoon the main topsail and main topgallant needing repair, we unbent them as we had to, and replaced them. At 5 o'clock everything was out. We have seen numerous birds today. When taking the altitude, I also heard a curlew. The sea has become pond-like. Maybe we are not far to leeward of some land.[3]

Courses S¼SE2°E 31′ or 11 leagues. Lat. S 13°56′, diff. S 30′, Est. S 14°26′, observed 14°22′, diff. N 4′. Long. E 159°56′, diff. E 7′, Est. E 160°03′.

[1] Taumako is the largest of the Duff Islands, discovered by Quiros in 1606 and rediscovered by Wilson in the *Duff* in 1797. Taumako, also known as Disappointment Island, lies in 9°57′ south, although shown on charts of the time as being in 10°20′. Surville did not sail close to it, or indeed close to the main Santa Cruz group which lay ahead between him and the Duff group – he was too far south and soon altered course for the south-west.
[2] Quiros did not discover New Guinea – it was known many years before him – but Surville is using New Guinea as a very broad term for the 'continent'. What he means is that he is approaching the latitude of Quiros' Tierra Austrialia del Espiritu Santo which was believed to form part of a large continental land mass.
[3] Surville was nowhere near any land – he was over 300 miles to the west of Espiritu Santo.

Sunday 12th

We saw large numbers of birds yesterday throughout the afternoon. I have still seen a fair number during the morning, but far fewer. I have only seen petrels and tropic birds which I had not seen yesterday. We have had fine weather always all sails out.

Courses S¼SW2°10′W 54′ or 18 leagues.[1] Lat. S 14°22′, diff. S 53′, Est. S 15°15′, observed 15°01′, diff. S 14′. Long. E 160°03′, diff. W 13′, Est. E 159°50′. The currents have been setting S for 2 days.

Monday 13th

As on the previous night there have been clouds rising in the N which have passed over us without causing a wind shift or giving anything. At 5 this morning we saw a large piece of wood go past. We have seen a quantity of birds, one flock of which consisted of velvet-sleeved boobies[2] like those of the Cape.

Courses S 3°W 84¼′ or 28½ leagues. Lat. S 15°01′, diff. S 1°24′, Est. S 16°25′, observed 16°29′, diff. S 4′. Long. E 159°50′, diff. W 2, 159°48′.

The sea is like a pond, which would make me think that we are not very far under the lee of Prince William Islands[3] or the shallows of Hamskerk,[4] because one could also think so from the great numbers and different species of birds we are seeing, some of whom come and get caught on board. There are also bonitos and large ears.[5]

[1] *The St Jean-Baptiste* was now sailing slightly west. On such a course, he was getting further from a chance landfall in the southern New Hebrides or New Caledonia.

[2] The description given is of a white bird with black-tipped wings: the red-footed booby (*Sula sula*) 'are either all white (partly buffy) with black wing-tips.... The subspecies *rubripes* Gould is widespread in the Indian Ocean and in the tropic Pacific'. Mayr, *Birds of the Southwest Pacific*, pp. 18–19.

[3] Prins Wyllem's Eylanden, discovered by Tasman in 1643, is Taveuni in the Fiji group. Taveuni is in 16°45′S and 180°E of Greenwich so that Surville is only grossly incorrect as far as the longitude of the island is concerned, but it was so incorrectly shown on the charts of the time that his error is understandable.

[4] Heemskerks Droochton is Nanuku Reef, discovered by Tasman. It is close to Taveuni and shown in its correct relationship to it on contemporary charts. On Vaugondy's *Carte Générale* of 1756 the 'Isles du Prince Guillaume' and 'Bas-fonds de Heemskerk' are shown to the south-west of the 'Isles de Salomon'.

[5] The tuna (*thunnus thynnus*) and possibly the longtailed tuna (*T. tonggol*).

Tuesday 14 November 1769

We have had very good weather. The sky has been cloudy at times but without squalls or rain. The sea is still so smooth and we continue seeing so many birds of all species that I cannot help thinking that there is some archipelago not very far to windward of us. Tasman found numerous islands from the 21st to the 17th degree.

Courses S3°48'W 73¾' [or 24½ leagues]. Lat. S 16°29', diff. S 1°14', Est. S 17°43', observed 17°32', diff. N 11'. Long. E 159°48', diff. W 5°, Est. E 159°43'.

Wednesday 15th

The weather was cloudy but fine yesterday afternoon, and the sea still like under the lee of a coast. We can see a large number of birds and fish. At 9 p.m. we had little rain. At 2.45 this a.m. the wind shifted to WSW during a squall. We just had time to alter the sails. We furled the topgallants, clewed up the mainsail and hauled the main and fore topsails to half mast. The wind blew enough to make 5 knots under this quantity of sails. There was thunder and fairly heavy rain. From 4 to 8 the weather was [?] with a light rain, and the winds changed constantly. This lasted more or less until midday as far as the unstable winds were concerned, but the sky had cleared. We saw a few more birds this morning but not many and almost no fish. The sea continues smooth.

Courses S1°30'E 73¼' or 24½ leagues. Lat. S 17°32', diff. S 1°13', Est. S 18°45', observed 18°34', diff. N 11'. Long. E 159°43', diff. E 2', Est. E 159°45'.

Thursday 16th

We have seen almost no birds compared with what we used to see. The fish have also disappeared; I think this is one of the reasons why we do not see so many birds. We see some [?]. The sea is not so smooth, a fairly heavy swell has come up from the S although the wind is not from that direction. The weather is dry.

Courses S¼SE4°25'S 31' or 10⅓ leagues. Lat. S 18°34', diff. S 31', Est. S 19°05', observed S19°19', diff. S 14'. Long. E 159°45', diff. E 3', Est. E 159°48'.

After midday yesterday, especially towards the evening we saw large numbers of butterflies of different colours. Where did they come from?

E or W. We had had a storm from the W the night before, but the winds were easterly when we saw them.

Friday 17th November 1769

From 4 p.m. yesterday until 6 there was a flat calm. At 6 o'clock a slight touch of wind lasting until 10 p.m. since which we have made a little headway. There is still a heavy swell coming from ahead. We see no fish and very few birds. We have been seeing for two days some jellyfish.

Courses SSW 3°45′S 22′ or 7⅓ leagues. Lat. S 19°19′, diff. S 21, Est. S 19°40′, observed 19°44′. Long. E 159°48′, diff. W 7′, Est. E 159°41′.

We are going very slowly and each day someone dies. I should like to come across some accessible island [where] we would surely get food even though it had to be obtained at the point of a gun. I mean fresh food and suitable to restore the blood to its proper equilibrium, because we are not short of good food but it has not got the quality of green vegetables and fresh meat.[1]

Saturday 18th

We have had continuous fair weather and all sails out. This morning we have seen more gannets than usual; they are those we call velvet sleeves.[2] At midday when we were taking the altitude we saw one of those shells called mother-of-pearl;[3] the fish was no doubt inside it, otherwise it would not have floated. A very strong tideway passed at 3 this a.m.[4]

Courses SSW 3°45′S 59′ or 19⅔ leagues. Lat. S 19°44′, diff. S 56′, Est. S 20°40′, observed 20°35′, diff. N 5′. Long. E 159°41′, Diff. W 20′, Est. E 159°21′.

Since the day before yesterday we noticed when reading the altitude a black patch in the sun. It seemed to us then that it was in the lower half of the disk, a little to the right. It is now in the upper half of the disk and still on the right. I have noticed for two days now that it rises considerably towards midday.

[1] Twenty nine men had died by this date.
[2] The red-footed booby, *Sula sula*.
[3] Surville is probably referring to the pearly Nautilus which is very common in these seas.
[4] The *St Jean-Baptiste* was in the neighbourhood of several dangers. She was sailing not far from Brampton Reefs and N.W. Bellona Reef well to the west of New Caledonia. There are breakers, some clusters of rocks and rip tides in this area.

Sunday 19 November 1769

We have still had fair weather, merely a heavy swell head on. At 9 o'clock we furled the royals because the wind was freshening a little. They were let out at daybreak. The westerly amplitude has varied greatly from the easterly; I am correcting it by 10°.

Courses S¼SW3°40′W 66′ or 22 leagues. Lat. S 20°35′, diff. S 1°04′, Est. S 21°39′, observed 21°34′, diff. N 5′. Long. E 159°21′, diff. W 18′, Est. E 159°03′.

We see neither birds nor fish. At 11 this p.m. a very strong tideway passed us. The sun spot has risen and is moving towards the left.

Monday 20th

The sea has turned very rough since sunset last night and is running from the S and the SE. The weather has been fair these 24 hours.

Courses SSE4°30′S 62′ or 20⅔ leagues.[1] Lat. S 21°34′, diff. S 59′, Est. S 22°33′, observed 22°53′, diff. S 20′. Long. E 159°03′, diff. E 22′, Est. E 159°25′. I saw a [?] this morning and at the stroke of midday a fairly considerable flight of birds. The sun spot is a little lower than yesterday and has moved towards the left of the sun.

Tuesday 21 November 1769

Our light wind left us at 9 last night. Since then we have had only a flat calm and it looks as though it will continue. We had the studding sails and everything out yesterday afternoon. The sun spot was well to the left when we were taking the altitude. We saw it go lower and appreciably towards the left.

Courses S5°E 22′ [or] 7⅓ leagues. Lat. S 22°53′, diff. S 22′, Est. S 23°15′, observed 23°15′. Long E 159°25′, diff. E 2′, Est. E 159°27′.

There is a great swell from the SE¼E and in addition these are cross-waves.

Wednesday 22nd

We have certainly been having very fine weather these last few days, but it is fine for those who are walking about on land and not for sailors.

---

[1] For a couple of days the *St Jean-Baptiste* will sail on a different course, slightly easterly instead of westerly, so that the course over a week or so amounts to almost due south.

It would not matter if the crew were in good health. The sun spot has risen again a great deal towards the top of the disk, but during the ½ hour we spent reading the altitude it comes down and moves appreciably towards the left. It is the same thing every day.

Course S¼SW 4°S 17′ or 5⅔ leagues. Lat. S 23°15′, diff. S 16′, Est. S 23°31′, observed 23°37′, diff. S 6′. Long. E 159°27′, diff. E 2′, Est. E 159°25′.

Today we saw some tropic birds like those [found] under the lee of the *Isle de France*[1] with a red beak and fire-coloured tail feathers.[2] They are also a little more yellowish than the ordinary ones, precisely like those of the *Isle de France.*

Thursday 23rd

Yesterday afternoon we had all kinds of sails out until 5.30 when we furled the studding sails because the wind was sharpening without becoming really sharp. All our people are dying or falling ill.

Courses S¼SW 5°12′W 78′ or 26 leagues. Lat. S 23°37′, diff. S 1°15′, Est. S 24°52′, observed 24°57′, diff. S 5′. Long. E 159°25′, diff. W 24′, Est. E 159°01′.

Sickness and death which appear indistinguishable among our crew have caused me to reflect seriously, to see if I could not find a solution more certain than that of following the course, planned from the start, which I am now keeping, and go, if I can, to New Zealand, and seek there a place of refuge where we can rest awhile. After considering the position, I believe that anything we could attempt elsewhere would be far less certain than this New Zealand suggestion, and that, anyhow, we have no alternative in the state in which we are, although according to the report of the travellers who have preceded us there, the natives of the country are ferocious and bloodthirsty,[3] but such obstacles are still easier to bear than scurvy, which suddenly attacks the chest, and chokes you in 2 or 3 spans of 24 hours.[4] Since men's lives is a delicate matter, I did not want to decide on my own without being supported by the approval of someone else competent in the matter. Consequently I called Mr Labé, my first officer, who is a man of experience and in whom I can and must place all my trust. Like me he knows the state of things. I outlined my line of reasoning on all this and told him (what

---

[1] Mauritius, in the Indian Ocean.   [2] *Phaeton rubricauda.*
[3] A reference to Maori attacks on Tasman's Men in Murderers' Bay (now called Golden Bay) at the entrance to Cook Strait.
[4] Pneumonia, consequent upon the debilitating effect of scurvy.

he could see as well as me) that the course I was keeping was to sight New Zealand, previously sighted by Tasman, and try to find there a place of refuge to rest our people, and at the same time asked him whether he could think of something quicker and more certain to put our troubles right. He was in full agreement with me, that it was the surest and quickest remedy at our disposal. We at once read together Tasman's Voyage[1] on this place about which he gives almost no details that would be of use to those who come after him. Apart from this, he speaks of it as an attractive country, well populated. One can therefore obtain help at gun point if not otherwise. It is indeed surprising that our crew find themselves in such a state.

Since Bengal they have always been coasting along, namely at Yanaon, Masulipatnam, Pondicherry, Malacca, Pulo Timon, Trengannu and Bashi. During all this time and long after leaving Bashi they have eaten nothing but fresh meat. They have never been cut down on water. We put in on purpose at Port Praslin to be comfortable, and in spite of that and the good food they have they die all at once.

Friday 24 November 1769

The weather has been very fine, but the wind is against us and we have a head sea.

Courses SW¼W 10'S 37' or 12⅓ leagues. Lat. S 24°57', diff. S 21', Est. S 25'18', observed 25°07', diff. N 11'. Long. E 159°01', diff. W 34', Est. E 158°27'.

The winds have been southerly and so the currents have been setting north. The sun spot is exactly on the edge on the disk at the left.

Saturday 25th

A squall blew up from the SE yesterday at 8 p.m., giving a little rain and wind. Furled the royals, topgallants and stay sails [and] the standing jib. Fine at midnight. From midnight until 4 squall after squall but not strong; it fell calm in between and the ship was very slack.

---

[1] The most recent edition of voyages giving an account in French of Tasman's expedition was the abbé Prévost's *Histoire générale des voyages* of 1753, reprinted in 1758; the account 'Voyage d'Abel Jansen Tasman' appears in volume 16, pp. 68–74. Charles de Brosses' *Histoire des navigations aux terres australes*, also likely to have been on board, was published in 1756; the account 'Abel Tasman en Australasie' appears in volume 1, pp. 456–63. Both authors drew on François Coréal's *Voyages de François Coréal aux Indes occidentales* of 1722 reissued in 1738 as *Recueil de voyages dans l'Amérique occidentale*. Unlikely to have been on board is Melchisédech Thévenot's *Relations de divers voyages curieux* of 1696, first issued as *Recueil de voyages de Mr Thévenot*, 1681, which contains the first French reference to Tasman.

Courses SW 2°45′W 62′ or 20⅔ leagues. Lat. S 25°07′, diff. S 40′, Est. S 25°47′, observed 25°37′, diff. N 10′. Long. E 158°27′, diff. W 52′, Est. E 157°35′.

We have seen a few birds, but not many. We have a great sea setting from the S and SSE. Our variation is considerable; I do not know whether it is because our compasses vary more than others did before; but Tasman did not notice as much variation as us, being further east.

Sunday 26 November 1769

The weather is still fair with a fairly fresh breeze. The sea has also almost completely moderated. We have seen at about the time of the reading large flights of wing-beaters. They were apparently following fish, because they have disappeared. I have never seen these birds very far from land.

Courses SW¼S 4°15′S 95′ or 31⅔ leagues. Lat. S 25°37′, diff. S 1°23′, Est. S 27°, observed 26°52′, diff. N 8′. Long. E 157°35′, diff. E 51′, Est. E 156°44′.

I do not find the air as cold as yesterday. Yesterday all our men put on shoes and stockings.

Monday 27th

We have had very fair weather yesterday afternoon, during the night and this morning. We have seen and heard a large number of wingbeaters, but since about 10 o'clock I have not seen any. We must be, or have passed, near some land. I have never seen this kind of bird stray far from it.[1]

Courses SSW 79′ or 26⅓ leagues. Lat. S 26°52′, diff. S 1°13′, Est. E 28°05′, observed 27°57′, diff. N 8′. Long. E 156°44′, diff. W 34′, Est. E 156°10′.

Monday 28th[2]

We have had fine weather and a fresh gale. The sea has been smooth until 10 this morning when it began to rise. At nightfall yesterday we furled the studding sails from below to be more prepared to manoeuvre in case of some sighting and also the royals.

---

[1] The nearest land was Australia, approximately where modern Brisbane stands, some 450 miles to the west.
[2] This should read Tuesday. De Surville will correct this error a week later.

Courses SSW1°15'S 103' or 34⅓ leagues. Lat. S 27°57', diff. S 1°36', Est. S 29°33', observed 29°25', diff. N 8'. Long. E 156°10', diff. W 42', Est. E 155°28'.

We have seen numerous birds this morning and in flights. I have also seen an albatross and a [?]. As early as yesterday evening [we saw] an albatross.

Tuesday 29th

At 6.30 yesterday evening furled the topgallants. At 7 took the second reef in the topsails. At 10 furled the mainsail. From 11 to midnight took in the 3rd reef and at once furled the main and fore topsails, and stayed under the foresail. The ship was labouring a great deal. We were making an inch of water an hour. Yesterday until dark we had seen [?].

Courses SSW4°15'S 143' or 47⅔ leagues. Lat. S 29°25', diff. S 2°16', Est. S 31°41', observed 30°54', diff. N 47'. Long. E 155°28', diff. W 51', Est. E 154°37'.

The ship has strained a great deal this morning when the wind dropped, trying to turn southerly.

Wednesday 30th

We continued on an easterly tack yesterday afternoon with fair weather, but the sea very high. By 3 o'clock the sea had moderated a great deal. In spite of that, as were hauling the wind on the larboard tack, we were falling off considerably. The weather kept on improving and the sea fell.

Courses SW¼S4°S 55' or 18⅓ leagues. Lat. S 30°54', diff. S 48', Est. S 31°42', observed 31°27', diff. N 15'. Long. E 154°37', diff. W 32', Est. E 154°05'.

I have seen numerous wingbeaters today, an albatross and some [?]. The weather is very fine and the sea smooth.

Thursday 1 December 1769

We have still had fine weather until 10 this morning, when it turned stormy, but in the distance. We had a few thunder claps and rain in the distance. All this did not quite reach us, but it nearly did. The wind dropped completely without shifting and the storm blew over completely, after which at about 10.45 a slight breeze came from the

SSE but not enough to allow us to steer. At 5 o'clock we had let out the studding sails and everything. At 7 seeing the storm which seemed to be blowing up we had clewed everything up for fear of a sudden wind change. At 8 the topgallants were hauled back seeing it was nothing.

Courses SSW 1°15′S 61¾′ or 20 l. 37′.[1] Lat. S 31°27′, diff. S 58′, Est. S 32°25′, observed 32°32′, diff. S 7′. Long. E 154°05′, diff. W 26′, Est. 153°39′.

We are still seeing large numbers of wingbeaters. I have also seen a gannet this morning and a few [?].

Friday 2nd

We had fairly good weather until midnight. From midnight to 4 o'clock rain, wind, lightning, thunder, fairly strong, and Saint-Elmo's fire[2] on the main vane. Everything was furled except the main and fore topsails and the fore sail. At 3 o'clock we had a sudden wind change. We stemmed for a time NNE to avoid getting the crew wet. The main and fore topsails were hauled up as soon as the strong rain had passed. We kept to the larboard tack.

Courses SSW 5°25′W 58′ or 19⅓ leagues. Lat. S 32°32′, diff. S 51′, Est. S 33°23′. Long. E 153°39′, diff. W 33′, Est. E 153°06′.

The thermometer stands at 19°,

Saturday 3rd

I had the main and fore topsails double reefed yesterday at 6 p.m. The weather did not seem to be promising a fine night. However there was no wind after midnight. I had two reefs let out at dawn. It was fine at sunrise and soon after light gusts and then squalls blew up. At 9 I had the reefs taken in again. The sky cleared completely towards 11 o'clock. There is a heavy swell from the S which is very tiring for us.

Courses SW ¼ W 2°30′S 35′ or 11⅔ leagues. Lat. S 33°23′, diff. S 21′, Est. S 33°44′, observed 33°30′, diff. S 14′. Long. E 153°06′, diff. W 34′, Est. 152°32′. We saw a great flock of birds during the morning.[3]

---

[1] An error for 20⅓ leagues.

[2] St Elmo's fire is a glow that accompanies a brushlike discharge of electricity appearing on the masts of ships during a storm. It was regarded by sailors as a visible sign of the guardianship of Sant'Ermo (St Erasmus), the patron saint of Mediterranean sailors.

[3] Marginal note: 'I have forgotten to state under Sunday afternoon that Mr Labé and I had agreed that with the wind continuing southerly, as long as we could not follow a northerly course we would run E, that if however we could stand W without falling N

Monday 4 December 1769

The sea is still running high from the S and SSW. We were yesterday under the 4 main sails and the mizzen topsail, [with] the 3 reefs in the main and fore topsails, on account of the weak state of the crew. I had one reef let out at 4 p.m. The sea had moderated a little. At 3 a.m. several of our men could smell land, but only intermittently and then nothing. At 5 a.m. we replaced our mizzen topsail which was all dilapidated. The sea seemed to me a little different at dawn. At 6 o'clock I saw a cuttle-bone pass alongside and we saw a considerable flock of birds but they did not follow us. I saw a few wingbeaters and a gannet. At 10 I saw another cuttle-bone and a piece of seaweed with large nodes. Immediately after the altitude I again saw a large bundle of seaweed similar to this morning's and I still find the sea different.

Courses ESE4°30'E 66' or 22 leagues.[1] Lat. S 33°30', diff. S 20', Est. 33°50', observed 33°36', diff. N 14'. Long. E 152°32', diff. E 1°15', Est. E 153°47'. The weather is extremely changeable. From fair to poor, from a cloudless sky to overcast.

Tuesday 5 December 1769

It was very fine yesterday afternoon. The sea was fairly smooth until 4 p.m. when it started to run high from the SSE. At 5 a.m. it rose considerably from the SSE although the winds had veered E and had continued to veer towards the N. This morning we saw a large number of jellyfish passing alongside for $\frac{1}{4}$ hour. Saw some albatrosses.

Courses SSE2°30'E 35' or 11$\frac{2}{3}$ leagues. Lat. S 33°36', diff. S 32', Est. 34°08', observed 34°07'. Long. E 153°47', diff. E 18', Est. E 154°05'.

Wednesday 6th

I had the last two reefs taken for the night in the topsails at 5 yesterday evening although the weather was still passably fair, and I was justified because a strong gale blew up at 3 a.m. Squally weather, little rain. At 5 o'clock furled the mainsail and the mizzen topsail for fear of a sudden wind change. The wind however did not shift beyond

we would change course again, that furthermore having reached a latitude where we could sight New Zealand which lies in 34°55' if we did not sight [it] we would go E [to seek] it'.

[1] Surville is now changing to a south-easterly course as he approaches the latitude of 35°S. When he does so, on the 7th, he starts on an easterly course to reach New Zealand, Tasman having reported coasting that country from approximately 42° to 34°30' south.

WNW. The sea is very high. There is a wave on the beam which is causing the ship to labour heavily. All we see is [?] and albatrosses.

Courses SE¼E 160° or 53⅓ leagues. Lat. S 34°07′, diff. S 1°29′, Est. S 35°36′, observed 35°54′, diff. S 18′. Long. E 154°05′, diff. E 2°42′, Est. E 156°47′.

Thursday 7 December 1769

Yesterday afternoon we were under the foresail and the topsails, all reefs taken. From 6 p.m. to midnight the sea was very high and there was a little rain at midnight in the W. At 1.30 the wind veered SW and the weather cleared at once. The sea then began to moderate a little. We let the reefs out at 4 o'clock.

Courses E 4°25′N 121′ or 40⅓ leagues. Lat. S 35°54′, diff. S 9′,[1] Est. S 35°45′, observed 35°51′, diff. S 6′. Long. E 156°47′, diff. E 2°28′, Est. E 159°15′.

We are seeing numerous albatrosses.

Friday 8th

We had very fine weather yesterday afternoon and the sea was smooth; before midnight there came such a swell, without there being any wind, that we were forced to reduce the topsails and topgallants a little on account of the waves. I saw this morning one of these fish that have a round spear at the end of their nose which is a little longer than an arm and the fish 9 or 10 feet approximately.[2] We have also seen floating this morning a number of small polyps and jellyfish.

Course E¼NE4°20′N 64′ or 21⅓ leagues. Lat. S 35°51′, diff. N 18′, Est. S 35°33′, observed 35°32′. Long. E 159°15′, diff. E 1°15′, Est. E 160°20′.[3] We are having a calm.

Saturday 9th

We had calm all yesterday afternoon until 7 p.m. when a breeze came from the N. This morning we had very fair weather and the sea had abated from about 4 o'clock so that I had hauled up what we have brought down yesterday of the topsails and topgallants and set the royals. It continued to freshen.

---

[1] A slip for N 9′.
[2] The spearfish *Tetrapturus*, similar to the swordfish *Xiphias gladius* but provided with a more rounded snout.
[3] The difference, on the distance travelled, would appear to be a slip for 1°05′.

Courses E4°30'N 62½' or 20⅚ leagues. Lat. S 35°32', diff. N 5', Est. S 35°27', observed 35°39', diff. S 12'. Long. E 160°20', diff. E 1°16', Est. E 161°36'. Yesterday when examing the hold we found a little damage caused by the recent weather. The ports abeam are letting the water in. I have had them masked.

Sunday 10th

The weather is very fine and the sea quite smooth. There were fog clouds covering the sky this morning, but the weather cleared early. There is a great deal of dew at night.

Courses E¼NE5°30'E 128' or 42⅔ leagues. Lat. S 35°39', diff. N 13', Est. S 35°44', diff. S 18'. Long. E 161°36', diff. E 2°36', Est. E 164°12'.

We have found a little damage in a bale of lampas,[1] but not extensive. We have washed the damp parts lightly with soft water and dried it. There are still 4 or 5 bales to examine.

Monday 11th

We have still had fine weather these 24 hours.

Courses E¼NE45'E 132' or 44 leagues. Lat. S 35°44', diff. N 24', Est. S 35°20', observed 35°32', diff. S 12'. Long. E 164°12', diff. E 2°40', Est. E 166°52'.

The weather is still very fair and the sea smooth.

Tuesday 12th

We have still had fine weather these 24 hours. There was fog this morning but it lifted very early and the sea was smooth. At 11.30 we suddenly sighted New Zealand from the NNW to the E. The horizon was very hazy which is why we were so long before seeing it, and did not see more because the two above-mentioned extremities are lost in fog. The land is very high and parts of it by the sea are sand dunes as in various parts of Africa towards the Cape of Good Hope. At midday the southernmost land bore E5°S and the northernmost stretched to NNW3°N, the nearest NNE5°E distant 7 or 8 l[eagues]; this part consists of sand dunes at the southern end of which is a bay but which seems barred by breakers.[2]

---

[1] Chinese silk.
[2] Surville was in sight of Hokianga Harbour, a deeply indented inlet, which has a bar at its mouth formed by Northwest Reef. North Head and the coast trending approximately

Courses E¼NE3°20′E 149′ or 49⅔ leagues. Lat. S 35°32′, diff. N 21′, Est. S 35°11′, observed 35°37′, diff. S 26′. Long. E 166°52′, diff. E 3°04′, Est. E 169°56′.

Wednesday 13th

Fine weather, all sails set except the topgallants. At sunset what bore at midday yesterday E 5°S bears SE¼E5°E distant about 9 l., the nearest land which consists of sand dunes NE distant about 2½ l., the most northerly in sight NNW3°W, a bay E5°N. This morning at first light we could not see the land because it was hazy. At 7.15 hauled down the main and fore topsails to half mast to alter course for fear of too great a jolt when laying back, since there was a fresh gale. At 7 o'clock the sand dunes bore NE¼E, the northernmost land, being high mountains, bore NNW, the southernmost land, being the same cape as yesterday evening E5°S. At midday the middle of the sand dunes bears ENE3°E distant about 6 or 7 l., the northernmost land we can see in the mist NNE 4°E.

Courses W¼NW2°30′N 21′ or 7 leagues. Lat. S 35°37′, diff. N 5′, Est. 35°32′, observed 35°27′, diff. N 5′. Long. E 169°56′, diff. W 24′, Est. E 169°32′.

The weather is beginning to be less fine.

Thursday 14th

I had reefs taken in yesterday afternoon at 3.30, because the weather did not look promising and was beginning to freshen with a rough sea. At 6 p.m. sighted the most S land bearing ESE3°E; the first sand dunes we had seen when we arrived bore E 5°N, distant about 4 l., the lowlying land is distant about 3 l. The coast continues to be dotted with sand dunes as far as N 5°W which is what we can see furthest N. At 9 p.m. furled the mainsail and at 10 furled the fore topsail. There was a hard gale until 8 this morning and it continued to increase with rain. At 11 this morning we sighted land during a bright interval. We are in about the same position as yesterday morning [at] 8. At 10 o'clock we hauled aboard the main tack but at 11 we furled it again.

Courses NW¼N4°N 7′ or 2⅓ leagues. Lat. S 35°27′, diff. N 6′, Est. S 35°21′. Long. E 169°32′, diff. E 4′, Est. E 169°36′.

north-west consist mainly of conspicuous sand hills. The northernmost land runs towards Reef Point, probably not visible because of hazy conditions. The bearings given for the southernmost land in sight corresponds to Kawerua where the hills rise to 472 ft.

Friday 15 December 1769

At 2 yesterday afternoon we hauled fore topsail sheet aft. At 3 we hauled aboard the main tack to try to bear up when plying for the land. At 5 the ship being too slack we set the mizzen topsail and clewed up the foresail to change it before the night which did not look promising. At 5.30 when we altered course for the open sea we sighted the most northerly land bearing NNW distant about 8 l., a mountain which has the appearance of a horse saddle NNE3°E, the nearest land distant about 5 l., the most southerly land bearing ESE distant 8 or 9 l. At 7 o'clock our foresail was changed and furled because the weather and the sea were very rough. I thought it advisable to stay under our 2 topsails,[1] because being near the land and likely to have to tack frequently, weak as we are, one can work the ship much more easily and quickly with this rig. From midnight to 2 o'clock there were several very strong squalls with rain, then the weather cleared and the wind became more even. At 5 this morning a bluff which was what we could see further S when we first sighted this land bears E¼NE distant 6 to 7 l., the most S land in sight ESE, this continuation of land from the bluff towards the S is level and low. The sand dunes we saw around our 1st landfall bear N¼NW, about 5 l., the most N land NW¼N all hazy. At 8 o'clock we could see nothing for our bearings. At midday the most S land which is the above-mentioned bluff bears SE¼E3°E distant 8 l., our first-sighted sand dunes ENE3°N 3½ l. approximately, the most N land in sight NW¼N3°N. The weather has been so bad since last night and the sea, which is driving us towards the land, so rough, the wind in addition bearing strong and straight for the coast preventing us from hauling it does not yet represent a [serious] danger because it can change from one moment to the next and the ship is strong on her beam ends, but there is enough to worry me.[2]

Courses SE¼S2°S 12' [or 4 leagues]. Lat. S 35°21', diff. S 10', Est. S 35°11', observed 35°32', diff. S 21'. Long. E 169°36', diff. E 7', Est. E 169°43'.

---

[1] Meaning the main and fore, the French having a different word for the mizzen.

[2] It was this storm which prevented Surville and Cook from meeting. Both were on a course that would inevitably have brought them within sight of each other, but Cook's *Endeavour* was blown out to sea while Surville continued to keep within sight of land.

Saturday 16th

We had a strong gale all the afternoon and evening yesterday. We were under the major sails and the mizzen topsail, everything double-reefed. In this way we resisted very strong rain and wind storms, but we had to beat up and turn Tasman's NW point.[1] At 5 o'clock we were clear of the W point[2] of a very large bay formed between this said point and Tasman's NW cape. At 6.30 during the bright interval we saw the mountains of NW cape or [some] adjacent to it in the above-mentioned bay. They bore NE$\frac{1}{4}$N. I then had all the reefs taken in the main and fore topsails for the night. At 7 finding the sea quite altered I sounded and we had a bottom of red sand like pulverised coral, 6 leagues from the W head of the bay, that is to say the one we were clear of at 5 o'clock. At 7.30 ditto. Since then we have sounded every hour without finding ground at 50 and 55 f. At 9 p.m. I had the two courses clewed up and kept the two topsails all reefs taken to avoid making too much headway and to see land again at daybreak, as I did not wish to hug it at night, not knowing it well enough for that. At 4.45 I set the foresail, having sighted the land under our lee. At 5.30 let a reef out in each topsail. The sea was still very rough, the ship was labouring heavily. At 5.45 we sighted Tasman's Kings Island[3] which bore from us NW5°W distant about 10 l. At sunrise Tasman's NW Cape bore NNE distant 7 or 8 l., it has 3 or 4 little islets adjacent to it and a small sugar loaf rock; the southernmost land stretched out to E$\frac{1}{4}$SE5°S, Kings Island WNW 3°N. At 11.30 Kings Islands bore W$\frac{1}{4}$NW2°W, Tasman's NW Cape S 3 leagues approximately, a point E5°S 6 to 7 l.,[4] a cape to which our officers were kind enough to give my name[5] E 5°N about 10 l. At midday Tasman's NW Cape, which is the most W land we can see, bears SW$\frac{1}{4}$S1°S distant 5 l., a headland E$\frac{1}{4}$SE3°S 6 or 7 l., Cape Surville E 7$\frac{1}{2}$ or 8 l., Kings Island in the distance W$\frac{1}{4}$NW3°W.

Courses N$\frac{1}{4}$NW20'W 64' or 21$\frac{1}{3}$ leagues. Lat. S 35°32', diff. N 1°03', Est. S 34°29', observed 34°22', diff. N 7'. Long. E 169°43', diff. W 15', Est. E 169°28'.

[1] Cape Maria Van Diemen, discovered by Tasman on 4 January 1643.
[2] Reef Point the south-eastern point of Ahipara Bay the coast of which opens out to the north into Ninety Mile Beach running to Cape Maria van Diemen.
[3] Three Kings Island – in fact a group of islands – discovered by Tasman and so named by him because he sighted it on the Feast of the Epiphany or Three Kings, on 6 January 1643.
[4] Hooper Point, the eastern head of Spirits Bay.
[5] Cape Surville is the northern extremity of North Cape. Known for many years as Kerr Point, it is now called Surville Cliffs.

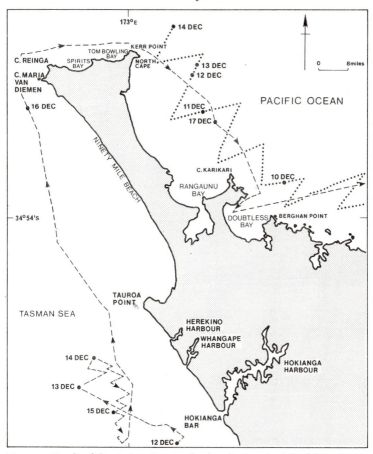

Map 3. Track of the *St Jean-Baptiste* (broken line) and of Cook's *Endeavour* (dotted line) off the northern coast of New Zealand

Sunday 17th

We had very fair weather yesterday afternoon and as soon as we had turned Tasman's NW cape the sea became very smooth. At 2.30 squalls blew from over the mountains, while we were hauling along close inshore, which caused us to bring the main and fore topsails to half mast. Cape Surville was then bearing SW distant ½ l. and the point it ends in further E in the sea, at the end of which there is a small breaker not far out[1] bore SE¼S2°E distant 1½ l. At 3.20 Tasman's NW

[1] The point is Cook's North Cape, and the breaker an islet known as Murimotu.

Cape and Cape Surville together bore WSW4°W and the point between the two capes, both together with Cape Surville, WNW 2½°W 7 to 8 l., the back of the bay SW 4°S; the N point of another bay further south S¼SW1°W distant 12 l. approximately; a mountain or island at the back of the S bay S¼SE2°E 15 l.; another islet SSE4°S at about the same distance; the easternmost land in the distance SE¼E2°S.[1] At sunset Cape Surville bore WNW 8 or 9 l., a point which forms the S head of a bay further north SW¼S4°S 9 or 10 l., the easternmost land stretched out to SE¼E2°S. Sounded every ½ hour from 8 o'clock to midnight at 40 f. without finding ground.

At 6 this morning Cape Surville bore WNW5°N distant 12 l., the back of the great bight forming a bay SW¼S3°W an entrance to another bay formed by islets SSE1°S 3 or 4 l., the most E land ESE, a small islet having the appearance of a ship under sail ESE 5°E. At 8 this morning Cape Surville bore WNW distant 12 l., the middle of the bay formed by islets SW¼S2°W, another bay also formed by islands S¼SE 3 l., the most E land SE¼E3°S.[2] At 8 o'clock several canoes came up which, after displaying some fear of coming closer, while showing us fish from a distance, nevertheless came closer little by little after much urging and through us showing them some cloth in exchange for which we obtained all their fish. At 10.30 they went back.

Courses SE1°S 33′ or 11 leagues. Lat. S 34°22′, diff. S 13′, Est. S 34°35′. Long. E 169°28′, diff. E 36′, Est. E 170°04′.

Monday 18 December 1769

The weather yesterday was very fine and continued thus until we anchored and later. At 2.30 p.m. the N point of an island situated between two bays or bights bore W¼NW distant about 4 l., the S point of this same island which seems to form the N point of what seems to be the most southerly bay SW¼W, a large bluff which seems to form the S point of this bay S¼SE distant 1⅓ l., another point SE¼E3°E 3½ l., a second point further east E¼SE4°E 12 to 15 l. At 3 o'clock as we altered course we sighted the point that bore W¼NW bearing NW¼W2°W 5 or 6 l., the one that bore SW¼W bearing W 5°S 3 l., a rock in the bay SW¼S 3°W 3½ l., the large bluff that bore S¼SE bearing SSE5°E 1 l.,

[1] Features may be identified as follows: the bay is Great Exhibition Bay leading down to Henderson Point; the northern point of the next bay 'further south' is probably Mt Camel; the other two islands mentioned are probably the heights of Karikari Peninsula; the easternmost land Cavalli Island or Cape Brett which rises to 1200 ft.

[2] At this point Surville was standing off roughly NNE of Doubtless Bay, also in view of Whangaroa Bay and of Cavalli Island 'having the appearance of a ship under sail'.

the point that bore SE$\frac{1}{4}$E 3°E bearing E$\frac{1}{4}$SE 5 leagues, the one that bore ESE4°E bearing E$\frac{1}{4}$SE3°S, the most easterly land one can see bearing E 10 to 12 l. At 6 p.m. changing course again sighted Cape Surville bearing NW$\frac{1}{4}$W1°W; the point that bore NW$\frac{1}{4}$W2°W at the last bearings bore W 2 l., the one that bore W bore SSE4°E 1$\frac{1}{2}$ l., the large bluff at SSE5°E bore SE$\frac{1}{4}$S3°E, the E$\frac{1}{4}$SE bore ESE3°S 4 l., the most easterly land E$\frac{1}{4}$SE2°S 12 to 15 l. Note: at several of the points one can see sugar loafs, that is to say rocks which have that shape. We sounded all the afternoon without finding bottom until 7 p.m. when we found 34 f. sand and mud, at 7.30 33$\frac{1}{2}$ f. rotted coral, at 7.50 30 f. small gravel, sand and mud, at 8.10 28 f. very fine sand, at 8.25 25 f. black and red gravel. At 9 o'clock clewed up the main sail, the foresail and the main topsail. At 9.15 hauled down the fore topsail, furled the jibs, etc. and anchored with a large kedge anchor and let out 80 f. cable. The bottom was 21 f. rotted coral.

From midnight to 4 o'clock, little SE to SSE breeze. From 5 this morning until 10.30 several canoes came from the land with a large quantity of fish, including the one where the chief was. I exchanged all their fish myself for cloth through the stern gallery by getting them to take away a basket where I placed a length of cloth which they took and then [they] filled the basket with fish. We did however bargain a little by gestures for a lesser or greater quantity. Several, after bartering their fish, came aboard; the chief himself climbed up and even came to the quarter deck cabin.[1] At 10.30 they had all left and gone back to land. Bearings of the anchorage are as follows:[2] the E point larboard as you enter E1°N distant $\frac{3}{4}$ l[eague], the W one starboard on entering N2°W $\frac{2}{3}$ l., another point on the same side W $\frac{3}{4}$ l., the [back] of the bay to which I have given the name of Lauriston[3] SSW 2$\frac{1}{2}$ to 3 l. This bay seems an attractive place. The first heights of the land near the sea appear a little arid except in the hills, where there are trees. Near the shore especially at the back of the bay one sees nothing but sand dunes, but the second mountains on the mainland side seem very well timbered and [with] fine trees.

[1] Pottier describes the meeting between the chief and Surville thus: 'When he arrived on the quarter deck he appeared astonished and shivered. We patted him a great deal and the Captain embraced him and led him to the quarter deck cabin, and gave him food and liquor. He made him a present of a jacket of heavy red cloth with green Bavarian lace and facings and red trousers. This man let the jacket be put on him for which he gave a dogskin cloak that covered him from the shoulders to his knees. He was taken to the great cabin where one of our gentlemen dressed him with a shirt under the jacket. This man returned to his canoe seemingly very pleased but when he was in it he decided to remove his new clothes.' *Journal*, p. 205.

[2] But see entry of 21 December in which de Surville states that the distances given are underestimated.

[3] It had already been named Doubtless Bay by James Cook.

Courses SE 5°30'S 14½' [or 4⅚ leagues] Lat. S 34°35', diff. S 11', Est. S 34°46'. Long. E 170°04', diff. W 10', Est. 169°54'.

Tuesday 19 December 1769

At 2 yesterday afternoon I had a boat lowered together with the small boat I bought at Bashi Island intending it to sound on the way to the land. I embarked a detachment of ten soldiers and gave a sword to each rower; they were 8. I acted as coxswain. I made straight for a small sandy bay, one point of which bears N2°W, the other W. To the left as you make for land is situated the home of the local natives on the peak of a fairly steep rocky hill. The depth increased to 25 f. at first when we left the ship, then it fell gradually to 12 f. within a musket shot of the little fortification. The ground was nearly always more or less large gravel and of different colours. At 15 f. it was sand and gravel and at the first 15 fathoms that one meets it is good holding ground, but after that it becomes foul until 12 f. where the lead sinks in although it is pure sand, so that this is an indication of shifting sand as at Port Praslin. As we approached we could see numbers of natives spread out along the shore and on the nearby heights, as well as in the little fort, waving some a loin cloth from right to left, others a branch, others a stick.[1] We did not know whether these signs were favourable or not. Finally we reached the shore, where there is a surf so that one is forced to weigh the grapnel offward and disembark on the sailors' shoulders. I disembarked in the small Bashi boat which can be pulled ashore right away, which is convenient; I had moreover had it manned by the natives of its country who are better at manoeuvring it. The chief was waiting for me on the shore. He received me graciously and offered me his nose; it is their way of kissing. I ordered part of the soldiers to land and the line officer who had accompanied me. I made signs asking the chief where there was water and he led me a short distance away to a little stream which comes down from the heights and loses itself in the sand of this bay. We sat down there and were soon surrounded by a number of local natives, some of whom were armed with great lances sharp at both ends, some had short ones, some had clubs made of whalebone, about four feet long, others had wooden ones; some had clubs also made of whalebone but only about a foot

[1] This ceremony of welcome, *powhiri*, occurs whenever strangers are to be received peacefully on a *marae* or tribal ground. The waving of branches is traditional, but Surville's term 'pagne', strictly loin cloth, cannot be taken to mean mats or skirts: it must refer to shoulder cloaks an end of which would be gathered over the forearm and waved to and fro.

[long]; some had them of the same length, [but] in stone. A cord was tied to these short clubs, which they wrap around their wrists so that one cannot snatch it away from them.[1] All these weapons present very little danger against our muskets, and there is nothing to fear with these people here although one has at first the trouble of having to be on one's guard because they are accustomed to deceit and treason among themselves. They stand close to you with marks of friendship and if you relax and they think they have time to flee after striking their blow, they will not fail to, and that is what happened to us at Port Praslin where the sergeant was mortally wounded with a blow in the back and Mr Labé received two from behind in the lower back which fortunately were light ones, but from which he might very well have not recovered if the one who gave them had been a little more skilful, a soldier had his headgear cut by a blow from a club and knocked to the ground, a sailor the same and another sailor had his arm pierced by a wooden lance; all that was done in a flash, and when one should have least expected it [;] they promptly fled and many were killed; but the first blows had nonetheless been struck.[2] We must at first be equally careful with these people here and be as much on our guard as if they warranted it and later, little by little, they begin to trust you when they see you wish them no harm, especially when they once know the superiority of your weapons which you must be careful to demonstrate and make [them] understand, after which you might have 10,000 around you not one would move, especially as soon as they see that you could kill them and do not do so; but you must not be surprised if at first these people here try to surprise you and kill you: they are accustomed to this with their neighbours.

They attack each other without cease, and kill and eat each other.

As soon as I had sat down near the watering place with the chief, he had dried fish brought to me and a few herbs which I took back on board. I stayed only the time needed to see what I would have to do for the morrow, and as the anchorage here seemed good I thought of bringing the ship in closer. I made signs to explain that at sunrise I would return to get water and cut some wood, and at the same time I pointed out to him a few trees which I planned to fell, to which he seemed to agree. He accompanied me back to the boat with all the

[1] The *taiaha* was strictly a long club, not really a spear; it was the pre-eminent weapon of the Maori warrior who usually used it to begin combat; one blow could kill or main an opponent. The shorter clubs or *patu* were made of stone, including the prized greenstone, wood or whalebone. The cord was usually tied to the wrist by means of a thong of dogskin.

[2] The repetition of this account reveals the impression the incident had made on the French and how their minds were consequently predisposed to suspicion.

crowd. I embarked and returned on board. This morning I landed with two boats, one manned like yesterday and carrying 10 empty barrels with axes and 6 wood cutters, the other carrying only sick cases. When I arrived they gave me the same ceremony as yesterday waving the loin cloth from right to left, a few palms and sticks, etc. It is apparently a kind of honour which they are accustomed to when welcoming one on landing. The chief welcomed me again, but more coolly it seemed to me. He made me sign to the effect that I should wait a little on the shore. I agreed to this and he went to discuss with various groups of local natives who had gathered on the neighbouring heights, after which he returned to me, offered me his nose, and we walked towards the watering place where I had the empty barrels brought. I also set my eight axe [men] to cutting wood, after which I waited some time before landing the sick because all the natives were coming imperceptibly closer with their weapons, coming down one after the other from the heights and surroundings us in a way to make us believe that they would be hoping for a favourable occasion. However, gradually, when they saw we were quietly getting our water and our wood and loading it, many of them went back. I then asked for the collation which I had brought and the chief ate, as well as some of the leaders which I allowed to share our meal, with a great deal of avidity, especially pork meat which was the basis of our collation. I then had the sick landed who walked about without wandering away.[1]

Wednesday 20th

At 1.30 yesterday afternoon I returned on board with 10 barrels of water, firewood and a few vegetables. Those we find here are excellent and have already done appreciable good to all our sick. There are two or 3 types of cress,[2] none of which is exactly similar to ours but quite as good. There is in addition a kind of wild celery[3] which tastes excellent in soup. This vegetable seems to be even more effective than

[1] There are two versions of the events of the 18th and 19th. Surville often wrote up two days together and on this occasion was not satisfied with his first account. There are few differences between the two. From the account he erased, we learn that the French dug a shallow well to get the water, that Surville, while noticing the fort or *pa* above him, was careful to avoid looking at it too much 'pretending not to bother much with what did not concern my needs, to avoid making these poor wretches suspicious', that the chief invited him to spend the night on land 'there on the grass', and that he seemed for a moment to want to return with him to the ship.

[2] J. C. Beaglehole in his edition of Banks' Journals puts forward the names of three identifiable varieties, *Lepidium oleraceum*, or Cook's scurvy grass, *Nasturtium palestre* and *Cardamine glacialis*. *The Endeavour Journal*, II, 8n.

[3] *Apium prostratum* and *Apium filifolium*, still found in northern Doubtless Bay.

the cress. All that grows wild and is found everywhere here; it even seems to me that the local natives do not eat it; they nevertheless offered us some, but it was only because they saw some of our people gathering it. I had endless trouble getting everybody back in the boats. The sea becomes rough near the coast at times, especially at flood tide, and at others it is smooth, and one can by dropping the grapnel offward and bringing up gently and carefully the boat's stern alongside a rock at the foot of the fortifications, jump on to it and disembark fairly quickly; but if the sea becomes even slightly rough it becomes impracticable, especially for sick men, and one could break up the boat. The fortifications are atop the small rocky hill I have mentioned before to the left of the small landing cove when you are making for the land. Above is a certain space on one level which leads to it from the surrounding heights, but they have cut this space with a ditch outside which they have placed a line of fairly high palissades but ill adjusted. There are on the top of the mount some kind of grassy ramparts inside which are situated the main huts, which does not prevent there being also others outside it especially by the landing where they reach almost halfway to the summit. There are also some scattered here and there a short distance away. The only crops are a few small potato fields,[1] but they are just starting to grow and have not yet formed their roots; in the meantime these people here live on dried fish and other [fish] which they cook in a hole at the bottom of which they have placed stones which become burning hot through a hot fire they light over them; they place their fish over them, cover it with leaves, then with soil and light another fire above. I know of no kind of receptacle they might use for cooking.

I landed again this morning with the same boats, the same number of armed men, the same number of barrels, but a few more sick. The chief again came as usual when I landed, but did not seem so affectionate. He again asked me to stop at the shore's edge, he carried out the ceremony as on the previous day; he went up to each group and then came to me to make sign that I was to go away. I at once indicated that I would not. Then taking me in his arms he urged me to wait a while and begging me to draw my sword he also asked me to give it to him for a moment and that he would bring it back. I gladly gave it to him. He took it by the handle and holding it upright he went back to each group. He returned and offered me his nose, making sign that I could advance to the watering place, which I did with the

---

[1] The kumara, *Ipomoea batatas.*

barrels, and I set the woodcutters to work and landed the sick.[1] I bought a little fish, but they did not want to bring very much of it as they had done before. At the watering place the chief again asked me for my sword, which he considered apparently as a certain pledge of my good faith. He went up to its foot with it and then brought it back to me. An old man seated near the watering place was haranguing me ceaselessly in a loud voice without making the slightest gesture that might make me understand what he was trying to say. He was annoying me because he never stopped and kept on staring at me and talking. I let him carry on. I had the lunch brought; we ate [with] the chief and some others he pointed out as belonging to him; I also gave some to the old orator and as the chief made signs that he was a dependent of his I tied a piece of red ribbon to his lance; from that moment he stopped talking and seemed happy.[2] I was forgetting to say that when I arrived I gave presents of cloth to the chief and of a red necklace with some red cloth. From what I can see these presents are being passed round only now.

Thursday 21st

I returned on board at 1.30 yesterday afternoon with the 10 barrels of water and some herbs. The small amount of land air breathed by our sick is doing them immense good. When I was on land yesterday three canoes came up to the ship with fish, but they were scarcely willing to barter it. All this was related to the coolness displayed towards us on land. At 3.30 p.m. yesterday I had the anchor raised to get closer to the small bay because we had too much trouble lightering from so far: we were 2 big leagues from land so that one can double the distances shown in the anchorage bearings. I tacked to try to come closer. The tide was against us, which prevented us from gaining ground as we should have done. The winds were westerly. We firstly had 24 f. coral and gravel, 22 f., 19 ditto. At 4 o'clock changed course to NW, the winds having shifted a little to the S. 23 f., 24 f. fine sand and gravel. At 5.30 veered to SW¼S; the winds had again shifted. At 6 o'clock 24 f. fine s[and]. We continued plying to windward by tacking, sounded from 24 f. to 18, s[and], gravel and coral. At 7.30 we dropped anchor and let out 40 f. of cable with a bower anchor.

---

[1] The chief had effectively asked Surville to show his peaceful intentions by giving by his *taiaha* or personal weapon, which was endowed with the same spiritual and personal value as the sword of a medieval knight.

[2] The elder was obviously a man of importance, probably a *tohunga*, a combination of priest and medicine man.

The village bore WNW distant 1 l., the nearest land N $\frac{1}{2}$ l., the easternmost [point] of the island or peninsula NE$\frac{1}{4}$N3°E, the south head of the bay ESE 3°S, the westernmost of the island or peninsula SW$\frac{1}{4}$W3°S. The winds stayed westerly and it was fairly fine. From midnight to 4 o'clock winds W$\frac{1}{4}$NW, from 4 to 5 winds WNW to WSW from where a squall came which caused us to drag a little as we had only a little cable out: as soon as we had let some out, it held. I did not land.

Friday 22nd

The winds have been blowing from SSW to SW during the whole 24 hours. Strong gale. Yesterday evening for fear of dragging during the night I let out 20 f. of cable, which made 100 f. [when] added to the 80 we had earlier. I also had the large anchor cockbilled. Several boats came up this morning but they brought only some green stuff[1] which I did not fail to buy, it is always a good specific for our men. At about 8 o'clock seeing the weather had moderated I heaved in. At 10.30 we had raised anchor. At 11 we were under way standing SSE; at midday we altered course to NNW.

Saturday 23rd

Yesterday afternoon plying NNW we sounded at 23, 19, and 18 f. shells and gravel. At 1 o'clock I clewed up the main topsail. Both yesterday and the day before we tacked only under the topsails, mizzen and jibs. At 1.30 we cast anchor in 18 f. same ground and at once let out 100 f. and more of cable to moor by the head. This operation was over at 2.30.

The SE point of the cove where we are to which I have given the name of Chevalier bore NE$\frac{1}{4}$E3°N distant $\frac{3}{4}$ l., the nearest land NNE distant 2 cable lengths,[2] the little bay with the watering place in Chevalier Cove SW$\frac{1}{4}$W $\frac{1}{4}$ l., the rocks furthest offshore of the S point of Chevalier bore SW3°S $\frac{3}{4}$ l., the deepest part of Lauriston Bay S$\frac{1}{4}$SW 4 l., a sugar loaf forming the larboard point as you enter E$\frac{1}{4}$SE 3 l., another ditto further off by another point E$\frac{1}{4}$SE2°E 6 l., the easternmost land where there appears a 3rd sugar loaf E 5°S. From 6 to midnight we had a light SSW breeze. From midnight to 3.30 calm.

---

[1] As well as the cress and celery which the Maoris noticed the French were looking for, they would have brought them their favourite *Puwha* greens, *sonchus oleraceus*.

[2] A cable's length is 120 fathoms or 720 feet.

It then began to freshen from the SW¼S. A boat came at 6 this morning, in which was the chief. Later 6 more came. The chief came on board. I showed him our guns and the cannon balls we put in them and tried to make him understand the effect, but as I did not succeed very well I offered to fire one on the seaward side, which he gladly agreed to. He began to watch attentively as well as those of his people who were with him on our quarter deck. We fired and they were all very frightened. He is the one who showed the least fear, because he did not stop watching carefully where the ball was to fall and when he saw it causing the water to spout up very high he gave a loud exclamation and spoke to his people. I then showed our pigs and gave him a young male and a young female trying to make him understand that if he kept them he would have many of them as a result of their mating. This seemed to please him greatly and he took them away with much satisfaction. They had brought large quantities of green stuff in their boats. I bought it all. They had no fish. At 6.30 I went ashore with the boats and the usual things. The chief came with me instead of going in his canoe. On the way he urged me to land at another cove than the usual one, telling me by signs that there was more fresh water there. It almost adjoins the other, it is separated from it only by the height on which is the fortification. For the latter you leave the said height on the right when you make for the land, and for the former you leave it on the left. I landed at this cove with him; it has indeed a much larger stream but the shore is pebbly; it would be impossible to roll the barrels, moreover when collecting the water one would be out of sight of the boats, and therefore in no position to be supported by them as in the 1st. I embarked with him and we made for the 1st cove where there was a large quantity of fish they had just seined; I think that was what they did not want me to see; as they share it among themselves and live on it I was harming them.[1] They finally sold me a fairly large quantity which I am sending at once to the ship. The winds have been SSW, light gale.[2]

[1] Surville shows here that he was aware of something that many other navigators did not realise – that the large-scale purchase of foodstuffs by a ship's crew could be a real threat to a native population living at a bare subsistence level. The French, however, were in no condition to go fishing themselves when they first arrived. Later Surville sought his own fishing area, which would not be in the way of the Maoris.

[2] Marginal note: 'The chief again asked me for my sword to walk about with it in front of the others, but this ceremony annoys me and I refused. He was slightly upset, but he had to put up with it.'

Sunday 24th

We have had fair weather and a good breeze from SW to WNW these 24 hours. At 2.30 p.m. I returned on board with all the sick, some fire wood and 10 barrels of water, [and] a little fish. In the morning several boats came up; the chief was with them, but they did not bring anything. The chief came on board with several others and he invited me to come down. At 6.30 this morning I landed with the usual preparations, the sick, etc. It is surprising how effective the air of this land and the cress and wild celery we find here has been. The very next day after they first had some they already felt better. As soon as I got to land I found some fairly good fish to buy which I sent at once to the ship by the Bashi boat and at 10 o'clock I sent the yawl loaded with wood, which came back immediately for the sick. Things went on as usual on land, but on these last two occasions ashore our people have been walking about quietly everywhere and the local natives no longer crowd around us. They are beginning to believe we mean them no harm; they are no longer on the alert.

Monday 25th

We have had fair weather and a good breeze from the WSW during these 24 hours. At 2 p.m. I went back on board as usual with 10 barrels of water, firewood, etc. Confidence having been established I made no difficulty about leaving the shore, this morning towards 11 having been there as usual, leaving our sick ashore with an officer and a few soldiers, on account of the water and the wood which clutter the boats, which is uncomfortable for our sick and sometimes causes them to get wet. As soon as I was on board I sent them back the longboat which brought them back to the ship at midday. I had gone ashore at 5 a.m.

Tuesday 26th

The winds were SE until midnight. Fresh breeze from midnight to midday ENE to N. Yesterday I had returned on board so early only because I wanted to go after dinner to visit the other end of the island in the bay. So at 3 yesterday afternoon I left with the longboat and the yawl, well armed, and the Bashi boat for landing. Mr Labé, my first officer, went with me. We took only the seine with us because we were going mainly to see if we could find some convenient place to obtain fish without the assistance of the local natives. Although there was not much wind [we had] trouble in reaching a sandy bay which is at the other end of the peninsula because from the cove where we are to that one the whole coast is lined with large rocks where the sea breaks. We had in addition the tide against us. We finally reached the cove at the end of the peninsula. We stopped there without rounding the point in order to throw the seine, the bottom being level and sandy. While Mr Labé was laying out the seine, I climbed with a few of our gentlemen to the top of a large bluff which forms the head of the peninsula. It was there that I discovered it was not an island and that on the other side of this bluff there were some very fine bays which could be very convenient for fishing.[1] I then decided to go there this morning instead of going to the usual cove. When we were at the top of the bluff, the natives, who had seen us, came at once, 3 or 4 of them, towards us, but as we had gone back as soon as we had had a quick look they caught up with us only in the bay where we were seining. We had caught nothing. The natives had brought us some green stuff; I gave them a little cloth, and we left because it was late; when we left they invited us to return. I did in fact go back this morning, having had another large boat lowered for the greater comfort of our sick, so as to be in a position to spend the day ashore, to seine and get the usual wood and water. We had very good weather on the way. I at once rounded the point and went to find the bay I had discovered yesterday from the top of the bluff. There is a minor chief here also who is the one who had brought me green stuff yesterday evening. He has also his houses built from the top of a little rocky hill which forms the head of this bay, and they come right down inside the bay. There are not so many people by far as in the other cove, but it is infinitely better as much for getting water which is more plentiful and runs freely 2 steps from a sandy shore when the barrels are not damaged as for the shelter. There are here 3 little coves one after the other which each have water and wood. There is a large round rock rising fairly high out of the water and isolated in the middle of the bay at the foot of which there is 4 f. of water. We threw the net in a few times and caught a few fish both to eat there and take on board. The pot was at once set up with a good quantity of greens in the fish soup. We and our men thus had an excellent meal. We also hunted a little, a few birds I cannot name, some like blackbirds in size, others the size of a hen.[2]

---

[1] Surville climbed Patia Point and gained a sight of the attractive beach of Patia. A monument commemorating the visit of the *St Jean-Baptiste* now stands on Patia hill.
[2] Possibly the *pukeko* or swamp hen. The 'blackbirds' could be *tuis*.

Since I have been here I have seen no four-footed game nor reptiles except for a few lizards.[1]

Wednesday 27th

It was very fine yesterday on and off and at other times we had strong squalls from the NE and ENE. I came back on board only at 8 p.m., having found the spot pleasant for our sick. I wanted to give them time. I brought back wood, fish and water as usual. I returned to the same bay this morning with the same equipment. We were not so fortunate this morning with the seine; we caught enough however for ourselves, but not for the ship. We hardly see any local natives here: as soon as we arrive they pack their belongings and go. A few stay who give us a great welcome. The winds have been NE to ENE, fairly fresh breeze.

Thursday 28th

The weather was very fine yesterday afternoon. There was just a fresh breeze from the ENE. I fished a few times with the seine in two different bays during the afternoon so as to bring a little fish on board if possible. We caught very little, but very good ones – plaice, gurnet and [?]. I went back to the ship much earlier than usual with my four boats taking away as usual water, wood, etc. We left the bay and outside found the wind much stronger, and it freshened continually as we progressed. The yawl and the longboat where I was were making headway although with a great deal of struggle; as for the other boat where were most of our sick with the small Bashi dinghy in tow [it] was dragging far behind. I promised a bottle of wine to my rowers if they arrived on board before the yawl which was a little ahead of us at that moment; this proved effective; we went ahead at once, in spite of which I did not reach the ship until 9 p.m. The yawl arrived soon after. I was well advised to go to the ship with these two boats as will be seen by what follows. As the wind was becoming still stronger, the other boat was forced to resign itself to the inevitable and return to the very bay we had left. The wind was still increasing. At 11 p.m. it blew from E¼NE. At 3 the ship dragged. We let out some cable and lowered the heavy anchor after the others had been [?]. Our

[1] There were effectively no quadrupeds apart from rats and one breed of dogs. The lizards referred to may have been a gecko, more probably a green gecko (*Naultinus elegans*) as most other types are nocturnal; or a skink. The common skink (*Leiolopisma zelandica*) is often found basking in the sun on or near stony beaches.

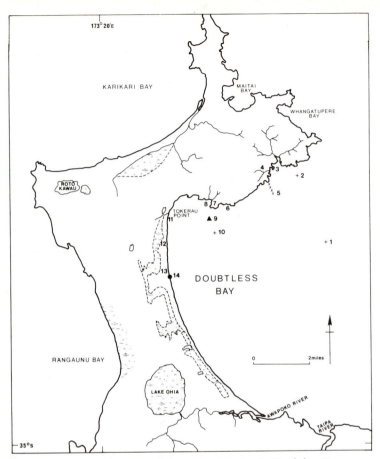

Map 4. Anchorages of the *St Jean-Baptiste* in Doubtless Bay

1. First anchorage of *St Jean-Baptiste*, 17 Dec. 1769.
2. Anchorage, 22 to 27 December.
3. Rangiaowhia Cove, where Surville landed 18 December.
4. Waitomotomo, visited by Surville, 23 December.
5. Reef which endangered the ship on 27–28 December.
6. Whatuwhiwhi, visited by Surville and Labé on Christmas Day.
7. Patia Point, visited on 30 December and now site of Surville Memorial.
8. Patia cove. Pottier's bivouac 27–28 December.
9. Tokanui, the large rock.
10, Anchorage, 28–31 December.
11. Parakerake, site of Ranginui's *pa* or village.
12. Beach where Ranginui was captured.
13. Waiotaraire, creek running parallel with the beach with several outflows.
14. Section of the beach where yawl was seen stranded on 31 December.

three anchors were working together. At 7.30 the starboard cable broke; we quickly let out some heavy cable, but as the ship was still dragging we were about to be wrecked on a large rock which was not even a ship's length away from us. The ship which had cast to starboard during the two previous driftings was casting to larboard. I was forced this time to brace round the head yards quickly; we had unfurled the foresail, it was on the brails. The ship fortunately responded, without which we would have been without resource. As soon as it began to cast I hauled up the fore staysail and hauled aft at once the mizzen, rather slackly, and as soon as the foresail had been filled I braced in and cast off the brails. The ship stood off at once and made way with great speed, which did not prevent our yawl which was astern from striking the same rock which represented a danger for us and breaking up, whereupon it sank soon after. When the ship fell off to leeward there was not more than twice the width of the ship between her and the rock. It is sheer. We cut only the main cable, we let the other go in the hope of dragging it and raising the other [anchor] which was buoyed. As soon as we were clear of all the rocks I clewed up and furled the foresail. I stayed under bare poles to give time for our last anchor to be secured which had not been done. The mizzen, which was very old, tore into shreds. Finally when everything was ready, the anchor secured and in position I altered course and stood for the bay where I had been the day before and which I have named Refuge; as I had sounded it I knew its approaches. The sea was extremely rough, the ship which I had to keep under bare poles rolled heavily, we were a little in disorder as a ship in port usually is, there were empty barrels on the quarter deck rolling back and forth at the risk of breaking legs [and] of knocking over and killing somebody; in the end I had them caught as best we could in the wind, and the few men I have left are fully engaged. They have moreover somewhat lost their heads; before carrying out my orders they stare as if they were a little lost, fear has seized them; in the end after much repetition and grumbling they carry them out. If the few men I have left were still behaving firmly and with their usual energy I would not have lost the yawl, but I refused to divert any of them from a work which was more essential for the ship's safety and preferred to let it sink, all the more so because I had to get someone to see to the longboat which is tied up to the larboard boom.

Friday 29th

Yesterday afternoon as I continued to stand for Refuge Cove I had the foresail unfurled and had it just half tallied to give the ship way and be able to reach the place I wanted. We had been sounding continually since we altered course and we found very gradually 9 to 6 f., fine sand. I finally clewed up and furled the foresail and cast anchor in 6 f. same ground. I at once paid out 120 f. of cable which was spliced then lowered our heavy kedge anchor with a very good stream cable and let out another twenty fathoms. The ship stemmed the wind at once and has not moved since, although from time to time as there is not much depth the sea breaks over our bow. In spite of that the ship is behaving marvellously well and does not pitch very much. As soon as we came to anchor [and] our men had taken a little food I hauled down the lower yards, unrigged and lowered the topgallants as well as their mast, in a word we tried to give the least possible hold to the wind. I had the remaining yards braced forward. I would have had the topmasts taken down, but not only was it too late and we could have done it only at night but our crew was too exhausted and we could not have done it in their condition and with a number of the few men who are fit being ashore with the other boat.

Someone might say: but why did you cut and let go your cables? Were you not trying to make sail and make way to reach the open sea during the bad weather? I certainly thought of it but gave up the idea at once as being impracticable. The sea was too rough, the waves were driving into the bay, I would have lost ground with each tack and would certainly have been unable to tack with a head wind, so that gradually the night would have fallen I would have been unable to choose a place of shelter and we would have been lost. The course taken with our only and last anchor[1] was as drastic but it was the sole one open to us. I took shelter as much as I could and it is very good holding ground and if our cable had snapped I think that the majority of our people would have been saved on this beach which is very level and firm sand. If I had thought myself able to make for the open sea, the men we had ashore would not have stopped me because I believed them to be safe with the local natives to whom we have shown nothing but kindness since we have been here, and this event proves it is always better to make one's way patiently and gently than through force and

[1] Marginal note: 'I am saying our sole anchor because the other one was only a kedge anchor.' One anchor had also been lost at Telok Juara, Malaya, on 25 July when a cable rubbed on rocks or coral and snapped.

violence which anyway always seems to me to be unfair towards people who are in their own home and have never thought of going to bother you in yours.

We had scarcely finished unrigging last night when the strength of the sea broke the tiller. We began without delay to put in a replacement which I had bought in Malacca. It no sooner was in place than it snapped. We had to remain in this situation because I was afraid it might break once more when we repaired it, and if the winds changed and we would have been in a position to use it, then only would I have had it fitted. I merely had the wedges watched for fear the rudder might strain its iron work, and I set up the small council room tiller. At midnight the winds veered NE and strong gusts with heavy rain blew up from time to time. At 4 this morning they shifted N. At 8 they were NW, but they had moderated considerably; moreover the sea has abated a great deal, as the wind was coming from the land. The boat that was ashore came back, emptying for this purpose its barrels and [leaving?] the fire wood which encumbered it. This boat contained 33 men, both sick and well. The people on shore had been friendly towards them and invited them to come and sleep in their huts, more evidence that the gentleness with which we treated them has been effective. From eight o'clock to midday, seeing I had all my people on board and that in case of an accident to our cable I could make for the open sea since the breeze was blowing from the land I had the lower yards set. I also had our carpenters making a new tiller out of two pieces but of good timber from the Islands[1] which will be better than the one from Malacca which is not what we expected. I had this timber from the Islands to make pullies with. Each of the two pieces is 15 foot long. I have had the scarf made 5 [ft] well bolted and woolded. I do not think this will snap and [if it did] we would be in a bad way because the Malacca tiller is not to be trusted and we have no other.

Saturday 30 December 1769

We spent yesterday afternoon hoisting in our boats, the one that had come back from the land as well as the longboat, and repairing our rudder, as well as tidying up the ship a little. I was hoisting in the boats because the wind, without being quite as violent, was still continuing to blow fairly hard. It did not shift during the night. It just moderated a little, as did the sea. This morning I lowered the boat which had been

---

[1] The French West Indies.

the least damaged, wishing to land with our ambulant sick, fish with the seine, and also see whether I could not take away a local native to try and obtain from him later what information I could about this country.[1] Mr Labé, my first officer, went with me. Meanwhile they bent a new mizzen and fitted the new tiller. The chief of this cove welcomed us in a most friendly manner. We climbed on a rise near one of their huts where they gathered 8 or 10 of them round us, including three young girls or women who danced in front of us for a long time, trying to attract us by all kinds of highly lascivious movements; two young men also joined them in their dance. Finally, bored with seeing always the same thing, because they did not desist, thinking apparently that we were simply difficult to arouse but that they would succeed in the end, we walked down after buying some fish from this little band; the 3 females followed us and finally, in a burst of excitement, one seized me around the waist and holding me tightly in her arms made the most lascivious movements against me. I freed myself and we got on with our work. The wind had risen considerably towards midday. I was forgetting to say that when I reached the shore the chief of the 1st cove where we used to be was present with the other at the reception and that I gave him a handsome cock and a hen which were the only ones we had left. I explained to him that through their mating they would produce many more, which seemed to please him greatly. I gave at the same time to the chief of this cove here some [?] some French peas and some wheat, explaining to him how they should be sown. The winds have remained throughout WSW and SW¼W.

Sunday 31st

The winds had risen yesterday towards midday as I have stated above, so that I was afraid for a moment that we would not be able to return. I think too that this wind was the reason for our seining without catching any fish. Finally the wind moderated a little towards the evening and became steady with no squalls. We embarked and arrived on board at 6.30 p.m. I hoisted in the boat which was making a lot of water. The wind blew in strong gusts from the SW to WSW until 4 this morning. At dawn we sighted our yawl stranded high and

---

[1] Having realised that, although his crew had not fully recovered, he could not remain any longer in New Zealand, Surville decided to repeat what he had done in the Solomons and obtain from a captive information which he could have gathered only through a prolonged stay.

dry on the shore at the back of the main bay, with several blacks inside looking at it. I at once lowered a boat. I took a detachment of 8 men, caulkers, carpenters, etc., and sped to its assistance. I was acting as coxswain and from the moment we left the ship I steered straight for the place where I had seen the yawl. One can see much better at a distance from above the ship than when one is in a boat: objects disappear from sight at sea level; however I was quite persuaded that I had kept the necessary straight course and was equally surprised to find when I reached the shore neither yawl nor blacks. I thought I had made a mistake and that it was further along this way or that; I searched in both directions with my people; we finally found a track which showed us that they had dragged it over the sand dunes which line the shore up to a little river on the other side of these same dunes. This river is full of reeds. They had either sunk it or hidden it there or perhaps taken it to nearby lakes to which this river seems to lead.[1] We were all very tired through having walked a long distance along the sand and in the dunes during our search. Fortunately on the way we had killed a large number of birds; we promptly put them in a cauldron with much wild celery. We had a heavenly meal. Afterwards until midday the wind blew from the SSW and SW$\frac{1}{4}$W, but the weather was fair. A few light gusts passed over, after which the sky remained clear and the breeze moderate.

Monday 1 January 1770

Yesterday after the excellent meal mentioned above, I wished to revenge myself for the theft which had just been committed under our very noses. I went towards the right hand corner of the bay where the houses are situated. We had not gone a third of a league when we saw large numbers of blacks moving about, some running up the heights, others running down, and groups of others sitting down on these same heights. Some of the bolder ones were not very far from us; one coming forward even gestured to me to come up, instead of which I stopped and myself gestured for him to come. He hesitated for a long time. In the end he made up his mind and came straight towards me,

---

[1] The meandering creek is known as Waiotaraire; it drains marshy lakes, Roto Ohia and the smaller Roto Potaka. Storms over the years have changed its exit into the bay. One French plan show a rivermouth about 3 miles south of the present creek mouth: this *Rivière dont l'entrée paroit belle* was the main rivermouth of Waiotaraire until about 1920 when a major flood changed it; traces of it are still visible. (Information provided by Mrs M. Stanton, of Kaitaia.)

unarmed. I reproached him for the theft of the yawl and at the same time told some of the sailors I had brought on purpose with ropes to take him prisoner, which they did.[1] I had him taken to the boat by these sailors and a soldier, then wanting to extend my revenge I turned towards two fine canoes which were close by loaded with fine nets and ready to go fishing. I had one launched and pushed as far as the boat and, placing all the nets in the other, because as they were only made of reeds[2] I could not have kept them, I set fire to it. I did the same with 5 or 6 lots of fishermen's huts which were along the above-mentioned river and which they had abandoned when we approached. There were even a few small stores of fern root which they use as food;[3] they were also set on fire. These people here are very agile: when I went towards them they suddenly appeared on the heights, and if I turned back they would follow me. As I was going back quietly, and setting everything on fire, I had one scare: a soldier noticed from the top of a dune some natives in line going towards our boat which was very distant. I was afraid they might take away our prisoner who was being guarded by just two sailors and one soldier. I ran very fast towards the boat and got very tired, because I would have been very sorry to lose my prey. By the time I reached the boat 5 or 6 natives had indeed appeared, who had been urged by our prisoner to defend him. They were brandishing their lances when the 1st soldier I had sent with another [joining him] later ran at them with bayonets fixed, which caused them to flee. We all embarked after setting fire to yet another little village near the boat, and we reached the ship at 4 o'clock. I had the boat and the canoe hoisted in without delay and seeing that each day the wind continued too strong for people who are down to their last cable and anchor, having furthermore what I wanted: a native and a local canoe, our crew having also partly recovered so as to withstand a short crossing, I gave order to raise anchor. At 9 p.m. we were under way with a fresh SW breeze and rain. We first found a depth of 7 f. very gradually rising to 15 f. At 10.45 p.m. the starboard point as you enter the bay bore N, this is where I am taking my point of departure from, and at once I set course for the NE¼N, with a SW breeze.

Courses NE53'E 65' or 21 leagues. Lat. of the point of last night's

[1] It seems clear that the expedition ashore had the dual purpose of recovering the lost yawl and of carrying out Surville's earlier expressed intention of capturing a Maori. The theft of the yawl angered the French and gives a semblance of rough justice to this action, but our knowledge that it was premeditated destroys it.

[2] These included the New Zealand flax, *Phormium tenax*.

[3] The food storehouse or *pataka* could be quite elaborate with rich carvings, but these being near the beach and undefended were probably much more basic.

bearing at 10.45 34°50′, diff. N 45′, Est. S 34°05′, observed 34°04′. Long. the same as when we anchored on arrival, wanting to keep to it as this land is shown [on charts] only on the basis of dead reckoning; Long. E 169°54′, diff. E 55′, Est. E 170°49′. We have again had squalls during the night.[1]

OBSERVATIONS on the country and at the same time on Port Praslin: In both places live barbarian people who are continually attacking their neighbours and kill and eat each other, on their own confession, according to what our two prisoners from these different places have led us to understand. In Port Praslin one is in a well enclosed harbour where there cannot be a heavy sea, but it is such bad holding ground that with two heavy anchors down and one small one our ship dragged with the slightest 3 knot breeze and we had to set to work and moor her again. Here the ground holds well. It is true that we dragged in Chevalier Cove with three anchors, but one failed and when we depended on the others we dragged; but we were stemming when we raised anchor. We sailed only because with the wind rising continually we could not remain with a rock astern on which if we had dragged by half the ship's length more we would have been lost with all the crew which would have been dashed to pieces on the rock. At Refuge Cove the ground is excellent as may be seen since we held on just one anchor, and certainly if I had had the lost anchors I would have stayed longer whatever the weather,[2] but I would have had to return to Chevalier Cove with the ship to try to save them, run again the greatest risks, strain the crew and wear them out without perhaps succeeding in fishing up these anchors with the few fit men we have left. [As for] sending the longboat, it is not capable of sweeping for a cable in 18 f. and of raising it with the anchor; in addition this boat

[1] Marginal note: 'I was forgetting to say that as soon as I was back on board I called the officers together to know what course we should adopt in our sorry situation. It was decided to go to Lima according to the minutes which were signed by all the officers and of which I have a copy'. Pottier gives a more detailed account of the meeting: 'At about 5 p.m. yesterday [31 December] our boat being back on board, Mr de Surville called all the officers together as well as the boatswain, for a meeting to discuss where we could go to seek some relief for our sad condition, after the loss of a third of our crew, 4 anchors, 4 cables, a boat, the rigging and furniture of the ship in a bad state. Finally we decided that, lacking all this, we could not remain at sea for 4 months at least, especially having lost 60 men, many others sick and the rest in a bad way, and moreover lacking food we have no other choice than to sail for the Spanish possessions, although this was forbidden by an article in Mr de Surville's instructions, which was read to us, and this Resolution was minuted; but nevertheless continuing our exploration as far as was possible.' *Journal*, p. 245. See also Labé.
[2] Here Surville gives the reason for his premature departure from New Zealand and his failure to explore it further.

once away from the ship is left without any resource, because with its anchor and cable, assuming it had been able to raise it, with the wind blowing from the back of the bay, it could never have returned on board. The sick and weak state of the crew has therefore prevented me from obtaining all the knowledge of the country I wanted. At Port Praslin it was because the anchors were not holding the ship and I was glad to take advantage of a favourable wind to get out of the harbour, and I was right to because it did not last and the very next day the wind was strong and unfavourable for anyone leaving the harbour. Port Praslin is dangerous because of the innumerable corals which surround the whole archipelago of islands that form it and which are dry at low tide. All the heights seemed very fertile and must be healthy, but the houses are apparently very distant because we did not see a single one and although the weapons of the inhabitants are quite inferior to ours it would be an undertaking for which one would have to be well armed and have a certain number of men because one has to enter thick woods far from the ship. I found at Port Praslin no vegetable one might give to the sick to restore the weight of the blood, and it is very difficult to get water where we did. We also encountered thunder showers which did us a lot of harm, but we had to have water.

At Lauriston Bay, water is easily obtainable in all the coves I visited. It is near the shore, runs freely and comes down from the heights, and one has simply to roll the barrels four steps along a very level beach. The air is healthy, the country is open and the soil seems very good. There are 3 or 4 different types of cress and a kind of wild celery whose effect on our sick was singularly prompt. There is no shortage of firewood and although the country is open approximately as it is at the Cape of Good Hope all the valleys and gullies are wooded and there are very large trees right up to the edge of the sea. In the district where we were I saw only two kinds, one we cut down, very hard, I do not know what to compare it to, we have none like it; it has bunches of red flowers;[1] the other is a tree they cultivate which has fruits the size of an acorn with a stone in the middle; I did not find it pleasant but they eat it; its top is well shaped, it looks rather like the Indian [?].[2] There are here numbers of beautiful good fish: [?], gurnards, plaice,

[1] The Pohutukawa, *Metrosideros excelsa*, is of a very hard and durable timber. It is very common in Doubtless Bay and its typical red flowers would be out at the time the French called, hence its common name, Christmas Tree.
[2] The karaka tree was cultivated by the Maoris. It is the *Corynocarpus laevigatus*. The fruit is poisonous, but prolonged cooking and washing produces an edible food which was much prized.

mackerels, larger than ours numerous [?] and what they call in India [?].

We could not seine in Port Praslin on account of the corals and we did not catch any fish on a line. Here we did both. I can express an opinion on the trees of this country only according to the types I saw in the distance where we were. The first line of hills which are close to the sea are, as I have already stated, bare except for the gullies, but the second line we could see in the S and SE is completely covered with fine trees. There the land must be very fertile. At Port Praslin I saw in the hands of the local natives a few roots similar to [?] and large bunches of almonds different from ours which they used as food. These almonds have a pleasant taste; I did find them however a little sticky to eat.[1]

In Lauriston Bay they eat dogs which they breed for this purpose and whose skins they use as furs. They eat much fish and the only bread they have, so far as I know for the present, is made of fern root which they cook for a moment, then each one has a bigh stone in front of him and a small wooden mallet, he beats the root, kneads it in his hand and eats it. I have tasted some; it is very unpleasant and is full of fibres harder than the hay our animals eat. I have seen their fields of potatoes, but they were just beginning to grow; the harvesting takes place later. The men here are of normal height like at Port Praslin, their legs are heavy and their disposition does not seem so good as at Port Praslin. Here they wear their hair long, pulled up and tied up over the top of their heads where they stick feathers. At Port Praslin some have large kaffir heads, others have long hair, many put lime on their hair, others do not, but they all have their hair shaved or plucked all round their heads to a width of about two fingers' breadth. Their ears are pierced to put ornaments through and the central cartilage of the nose is also pierced to put a bone or some flowers through and that without damaging either nostril. They also wear large shells hanging down over the middle of their foreheads, other have them on their chest and wear necklaces of human teeth or other ornaments on the upper part of their arms. Most wear a well ornamented hemp bracelet above the elbow. They seem very crafty and agile. Here they also have their ears pierced and wear human teeth there or those of another animal I do not know, or greenish transparent stones they have carefully polished into various shapes. They wear around their necks a small figure made of a stone of about the same quality which is fairly well worked. This figure looks

[1] The Ngali nut, *sp. Canarium.*

strange to me and seems to have a connection with some religion.[1] Some wear the tooth of a sea cow or no doubt of some fairly similar animal[2] because it is of well polished ivory, at the end of which are two eyes drawn in black. Nearly all of them rub oil and red paint in their hair. I have however seen one in yellow.

At Port Praslin they have bows, arrows tipped with human bones, wooden lances simply shaped into a point, others tipped with bone worked in such a way that it cannot be torn out of the flesh. They have clubs about 3 or 4 foot long, nearly all shaped like sabres very heavy at the base and wider than at the top, as sharp as it can be made on both sides, of very hard and heavy wood. The means they try to use are deceit, trickery and ambushes.

Those of Lauriston Bay have lances made of a very hard timber, also pointed at both ends; some are extremely long, others medium and small size. In some the timber is worked so as to resist being drawn out of the flesh.[3] Some are pointed red at the tip and decorated with a few hairs from a dog's tail with some feathers. They have large clubs, made of whale ribs, wide and thick in the lower part narrowing near the handle and rather bent like an S. They have others that are only about a foot long, very wide and thick near the base, with cutting edges on both sides, with a cord they pass around their waist so that one cannot snatch it from them; this type is of whale bone or highly polished stone rather like touchstone. They made signs telling me that it was with these little clubs that they finished off their enemies after first wounding them or knocking them over with their lances, and that with these same clubs they decapitated, cut up into pieces, opened their chest in the shape of a St. Andrew's cross and ate [them] at once; it even seems according to our prisoner that it is raw, because in his gestures he makes no interval between cutting and eating.

We know that in Port Praslin they eat men as our prisoner admitted, not his father, he told us, who does not follow this evil and abominable custom, but those who live quite close and with whom we had trouble; he would not tell us how this ceremony takes place saying he knows it exists but without having seen it because it is not practised among

---

[1] *The hei tiki*, the best known Maori ornament, worn by both men and women. The ear pendants are of greenstone or shark's tooth, and known as *kuru* and *kapeu*.

[2] Whalebone was commonly used because of its strong texture and because crisp designs could be carved in it, but shark teeth and bones of other animals including birds were also used.

[3] This would be unusual with the *taiaha*, a weapon very personal to its owner; Surville probably mistook the purpose of the elaborate carvings found on many of them.

his people. We have seen canoes holding forty and fifty men; they are of various types with ribs attached to cleats fixed in the side, the seams are filled with a very hard mastic[1] which does not soften under heat. There is some kind of carving at each end. I have also noticed a small figure on one, it may have some connection with their divinity because these people seemed to be praying by raising their hands to the sky, that is what the one was doing who seemed to be the chief who was in the middle of a large canoe accompanying Mr Labé, my first officer, to a so-called watering place they were going to show us. Mr Labé reported that this chief, who was standing in the middle of the large canoe giving orders to all the others, with pretty flowers in his nose, was from time to time raising his hands towards the sky and seemed to be invoking it; apparently he was asking the favour of making him succeed in the treason he was planning and of capturing us. He would no doubt have liked a taste of this white game.[2] Their canoes are rowed with paddles.

We also saw some very fine canoes in Lauriston Bay, the bottom being made of a tree which is hollowed out and then raised. There is a large carving at each end. There are no ribs as in those of Port Praslin and the side boards are sown rather like the [?] in the hold. The carvings are painted with orange oil; I do not know what they make this oil with, but one can suppose it is not fish because it has not a strong smell. I bought some for the lamp.[3]

The inhabitants of Port Praslin have [?] and wrap themselves in mats of fairly poor quality, at least those I saw. In Lauriston Bay they have dog skins as cloaks and another pelisse of the same animal round their middle tied with a wide plaited belt. Those who have no pelisse have coats made of reeds with long strands hanging down, that is to say they are as it were hairy. There is one as a cloak, the other round the waist. I have not seen any other clothing on women. They do not cover their breast and if one looks as if one wants to see the rest they show it in front of everybody. I have never seen anything so lewd as these women, but they are not appealing and I do not think anyone, even from the crew, had commerce with one, and this was certainly not the women's fault. I saw only one woman at Port Praslin and even then it was some distance away with the spy glass. She looked very ugly, her breast

[1] The mastic was usually made from the *Tita* nut.
[2] The use of a large canoe does suggest warlike intentions. Normally the captain would be at the stern, indistinguishable as far as the French were concerned; the man at the centre could be a priest, as the French surmise, but equally well be the battle chief.
[3] This was a vegetable oil extracted from the berries of the *Titoki*, *Alectryon excelsus*.

hanging down flat and completely naked in her canoe which she was alone manoeuvring. Port Praslin in spite of the marshy appearance of the place where we were and its poor holding qualities seemed to me a most suitable place for a settlement and where one would find a place of safety; from there one could make many discoveries in a country which seems admirable to me. *Contrariétés* Island, for instance, is charming. It is a real garden, within sight of the continent, full of spices since the people who came on board were covered with ornaments made of various types. Unfortunately I did not find the depth in the part I surveyed and our wretched state did not allow me to waste any time. These inhabitants who are completely naked as I have noted are the most lively and dexterous I have seen on my voyage. Their boats which are approximately of the [same] style as the others are finished off with carvings and polishing; some were inlaid with mother-of-pearl, Parisian inlay is not better worked.[1] They were the best equipped with lances and arrows I have seen. Lauriston Bay is very suitable for a small establishment from where one would discover numerous districts which are certainly very attractive and may well contain great riches.

I know of no iron tools in either of these places. They use axes and adzes of a sharp and polished stone which is not unlike touchstone. At Port Praslin the men paint their faces above the eyebrows, this design coming down in a point towards the base of the nose, then coming down along the temples reaches the cheek. It is mostly white.

In Lauriston Bay their faces are more or less elaborately decorated; some have up to $\frac{3}{4}$ of it done. It is pricked and coloured lead black so that it can never be erased. Their buttocks and legs are similarly decorated with various designs. I also saw some who had none. Women have the calf decorated, but not all of them, and the lower lip, [but] not the rest of the face. Like the men they put oily red paint on their hair.

The inhabitants of both places use approximately the same tools; these are axes and adzes of smooth stone, worked and cutting, of the touchstone variety, with handles of curved wood with a very tight[2] rope. At Port Praslin their hammers are made of the same stone. I have not seen any in Lauriston Bay. On the day I left Lauriston Bay I was to[3] visit and sound the mouth of a river which is at the back of the larboard

---

[1] The mother-of-pearl referred to is usually pieces of nautilus shells.

[2] Doubtful rendering, blotted passage.

[3] This marks the beginning of his third and final *cahier*. The title page reads 'Continuation of the Journal of the *St Jean-Baptiste* January 1770'.

side as you enter. It may be practicable for ships.[1] It is there that the attractive country is situated. It was too late, I could not go. At Lauriston Bay the fishing nets are only reeds. At Port Praslin they are well made and of some type of hemp with an elaborate thread. The fish hooks at Port Praslin are made of tortoise shell or mother of pearl, fairly well made. At Lauriston Bay they consist of a small piece of naturally-bent wood; they then work it and put on the small end a tooth of I know not what animal.[2] I cannot really understand how they catch fish with that.

We killed a small snake at Port Praslin and numerous salamanders. The lowlying parts of all these islands, which are marshy, are full of them and we saw a great many of them after it had rained. They come out of their holes to climb trees. In Lauriston Bay no one saw any reptiles, not quadrupeds except for dogs. We saw some wild ducks.[3] We did not kill any.

The local natives have no knowledge of arrows; at least we did not see any. It seems too that they have no slings, as travellers report about a few other peoples, so that these poor wretches are not very dangerous. But in both places they are thieves. At Port Praslin one cannot fish with the seine on account of the corals that line the shore everywhere; here there are fine sandy beaches. They have no knowledge of tobacco in these two countries, nor of any other drink than water, as far as I could see. At Port Praslin their beds are raised on feet at the four corners; in Lauriston Bay they all sleep, the whole family, on the ground in one hut in the middle of which there is a fire and no outlet for the smoke. They lead a wretched life in an excellent country through their lack of knowledge....

[1] A reference to the Taipa–Mangonui area. Mangonui in fact became an important port in the nineteenth century.
[2] Maori fish hooks were made of wood, bone, shell, stone or by combining some of these materials.   [3] Probably the Gray Duck, *Anas superciliosa*.

THE JOURNAL OF LABÉ

[Labé's Journal opens with various preliminaries relating to the manner in which he kept his log, measures used in Malaya and South America, his reluctance to join the expedition until persuaded by Chevalier, Surville and 'de Laissaière et Frères' (Delessert Brothers), a description and evaluation of the cargo, and the following expected itinerary: 'In the name of God and the Virgin Mary began the voyage from Bengal to Yanaon on the coast of Golconda, and to Masulipatnam and Pondicherry on the coast of Coromandel, to take in at these three places the balance of our cargo, and then sail for the Straits of Malacca and the China and Philippine seas, and proceed beyond to make discoveries in the north and the south, to New Guinea and New Zealand. After carrying out our search and our transactions, we will return to the Philippines, China and Batavia and back to Pondicherry...'*

These preliminaries, however, are more in the nature of additional material placed by the copyist at the beginning of the Journal, since reference is also made among them to Surville's death. The log proper begins after them, with the entry for 3 March 1769. The entry for 21 August has dealt with Labé's efforts to obtain water on Sabtang Island.]

Tuesday 22 [August 1769]

At 7 a.m. I went to Bashi Island with the captain and several of our gentlemen to see if there was any place where one could obtain water and buy a few provisions. We found only a few wells in the island. We went up to the village situated at the end of the island on the brow of a hill which forms [several] precipices. There we bought 17 pigs and 18 kids the latter cost 2 Flemish knives each and the pigs one piastre and one knife. These provisions were left in the village but the islanders faithfully carried them to our boats. The same day 3 of our sailors deserted, Le Timbre, Pierre Margue and Benier[1] by name, all three Bretons. We asked for the three men by making signs; seeing that they did not return, we went back to the ship where I was told by the officer

[1] Muster Roll nos. 57, 44 and 79.

164

on duty that up to 72 canoes had come alongside bringing their liquor, some yams, fishing lines etc., which our men bought in exchange for pieces of old blue linen pants. The crew had taken so much of this liquor during the day that there were all drunk when we arrived.

I must now talk of the islanders and their islands.[1] Goat Island is a small, fairly level island; its circumference is in the region of 2 leagues; it is not wooded but its plantations give it a slightly green appearance; it is a little more northerly than Bashi Island. There is a channel of about one short league dividing them. The sea breaks a great deal on it as it is surrounded by reefs. I think there is a pass between the two islands. People have assured me that there were numerous goats on the said island which gets its name from them. Bashi Island is well populated. There is a kind of town or village on the SW cape which is very steep and several walls around it made of stones piled on each other. The whole island is surrounded by a reef or bank. There are sand dunes along the shore on the side where we are anchored, then you find a rich black soil well tilled growing yams, sorghum, a kind of pea which is reddish when dry, much sugar cane from which they make a liquor they call Bashi, what we call frangourin; it is a rather pleasant drink; it is from this liquor that the island gets its name.[2] There are banana trees, a few coconut trees, cotton plants like those on the Coromandel coast, numbers of pigs and kids. The island is a little flat, very green on account of its plantations. Its circumference is in the region of 3 leagues. The islanders are very docile and good people. They are of the same colour as the Indians of Manila. They are not known to have any chief, they have no weapons, their jewellery consists, for the women, of glass beads of several colours which they wear on their legs, [they wear] a cloth made locally to hide their nudity, the men as well as the women have a woven cloak made of leaves, there are openings to pass their arms through, it looks like sheepskins. I saw only two or three people wearing earrings, others have pierced ears with a thread through them. These islanders have numerous small fishing canoes, but there is very little fish. I saw two large new boats, I think they go to Luçon Island during the good season. These poor people gave us a feast of their bashi, some pig and dried fish, and would not let our sailors carry the slightest thing, they themselves did a share of all our work. The women are not shy, [they] come to see you and talk to you. In a word all these islanders seem to be still living in a state of innocence.

---

[1] The modern names of the group are: Ibahos (Bashi), Sabtang (Monmouth), Batan (Grafton) and Dequey (Goat).

[2] Dampier thought it tasted not unlike English beer. It was a concoction of cane sugar and fruit.

Monmouth Island is only ¾ of a league from Bashi Island. We are at anchor between the two. This island is very high on our side, it is well populated, there are two villages on hill crests. This part does not produce much in the way of potatoes, canes etc., but the other part of the same island is well cultivated and produces the same things as Bashi Island; that part is not mountainous. They also have numerous canoes. Grafton Island which is directly behind Monmouth we cannot see and all these islands are approximately on the same parallel NE and SW. Monmouth and Grafton are larger than the others and very high. Grafton is one league distant from Monmouth Island, there is a channel between them as well as between Bashi Island. All the dangers are visible, you avoid them when you go through these channels.

I believe that the islanders are afraid of sudden attacks by neighbouring people, which is why they have entrenched themselves and built their town or village on crests of hills facing the sea and [built] stone walls around them. There are ladders in quite a number of places to climb up, otherwise it would be impossible. There is nothing to be got from these islands except foodstuffs, we bought some with blue and white cloth, a little iron, some knives, pearls of all colours of the type worn on the Guinea coast, they use them to adorn their legs and to make belts.

I am giving the map of the Bashi Islands drawn during our stay there.

I was forgetting to say that the islanders, I mean the men, wear their hair cut and shorn like the Recollects[1] and some have a tonsure. The women wear their hair long, hanging down, with a small cord around the forehead tied behind the head under the hair.

Note: The country produces gold. The islanders go panning at the foot of waterfalls in mountain gorges after heavy rain and get a great deal of gold. The soil in these gorges is yellowish red. These three islanders we carried off gave us this detail.

Departure from the Bashi Islands on our voyage of discovery

Wednesday 23 August 1769

At 6 a.m. the captain landed on Bashi Island in order to look for our deserters. He went to the village on the southernmost end of the island but was never able to make himself understood by the islanders to the effect that he was seeking the three sailors. They brought him 3 pigs, thinking that he was asking for them, and seeing him getting back into

---

[1] A branch of the Franciscan order, well known in France. The Augustinian Recollects, interestingly enough, had missionary stations in the Philippines.

the boats they brought the 3 pigs to the ship in their canoe, proof of the goodness of these islanders, but before the pigs were on board the captain gave me orders to arrest some of these poor people who had come on board to sell some potatoes. I had about 20 arrested and one of their boats. All the others fled, not knowing what this meant. We selected 3 out of these 20 people and let the others go free, who called their canoes which came to get them, they had stayed some distance from the ship to watch what was going on. We never succeeded in making them understand why we were keeping 3 of their comrades, at least judging by what they did a moment later, returning on board with pigs and kid in their canoe, offering all this to us to get their comrades back. We showed them by signs that we were keeping them on board to replace our 3 sailors who had deserted in their island. They went back very sad and took with them their pigs and their kid.

At midday, latitude observed N 20°22′.

Remained at anchor until 3 p.m. and, seeing that our 3 sailors were not coming back, sailed with a fresh westerly gale, the sea very swollen from the north, under the foresail and topsails. We are taking away the 3 islanders on board. We steered S to emerge and at 4 o'clock S$\frac{1}{4}$SE, at 4.30 E$\frac{1}{4}$SE. We had then the SE point of Monmouth Island bearing SE$\frac{1}{4}$S3°E. At 6 p.m. the same Babuyantes Island bore SE$\frac{1}{4}$S4°S the S head of Grafton Island WNW dist. 4 leagues, the northern one of the same island N 4$\frac{1}{2}$ l., the SW point of Monmouth Island NNW5°W dist. 8 or 9 leagues, the NE one N$\frac{1}{4}$NE3°N 9 or 10 l., a point which is approximately the middle of the island N. I am taking my point of departure from these said bearings which are, according to the midday reading, in latitude 20°N and in longitude 120°18′ east of Paris. Judging from Mr de Maurepas' chart[1] which does not agree with Mr D'Après', these Bashi Islands are placed too far north on Maurepas by 18′. His longitude although also based on Paris is also different from Mr D'Après' by 1°26′ too easterly. That is what is making me write this down in my log.

Among all these islands, starting from Luçon Island the sea is very rough, the ship strains considerably. Longitude from Paris [my point of] departure, according to Mr D'Après 118°52′.[2]

---

[1] Actually a chart drawn by J. N. Bellin for the *Neptune françois*, by order of the minister.
[2] An error of approximately 40′W which should be taken into account when reading Labé's subsequent estimated positions.

Thursday 24 August 1769

From 6 p.m. yesterday when I took my point of departure until today midday, strong gale, the sea very high, the ship straining considerably under the main and fore topsails and the foresail. At 6 o'clock it overblew, brought the topsails upon the cap and at 8 a.m. close reefed the main and fore topsails and furled the mizzen topsails, steered as shown in the board, the wind westerly. Course E¼SE, distance 34⅔ leagues. Lat. Est. N 19°39'. Long. Est. W 122°07'.

We obtained 14 pigs and 12 kids from the Bashi Islanders for Dutch knives, the pigs for one piastre and one knife each, the kids for one and two knives each, some pumpkins for pieces of cloth.

Note: I am mentioning here, owing to lack of space, an item of 19 August. As he already had some sick on board, our surgeon wanted some chickens to give them. There was a disagreement over this. The result was a strong reply that since they were needed for the sick this was quite acceptable but they would no longer be served at the officers' table. We expect this is one of our captain's jokes.

Friday 25th

Fair weather, fresh gale, the sea very high until 7 a.m. when it moderated, shook out the reefs and let out the topgallants.

Courses SE4°E, distance 38¼ leagues. Latitude N Est. 18°24', obs 18°34', diff. N 10'. Long. Est. 123°39'.

Saturday 26 August 1769

Fair weather, the sea fairly calm, the winds SSW, all sails high, topgallants and royals. Steered SE. Courses SE¼E5°15'S, distance 29⅔ leagues. Latitude N Est. 17°36', obs 17°36'. diff. 0'. Long. Est. 124°66'.

It seems that Mr Surville wants to keep to a southerly tack to cross the Line so as to make discoveries in that area. I am afraid that we may meet calms and that we shall suffer greatly through shortage of water and of other supplies which are already lacking. I was expecting him to ask me for my views on the course he is following, being partly in charge of the operations, jointly with him, but so far he has never given the slightest hint of anything, so if something unfortunate ensues, either through the shortage of food and water, or through death or sickness among the crew, I wash my hands of it. The shipowners will be unable to blame me for anything having never been consulted about the least thing.

Sunday 27th

Fair weather, all sails high, the sea sometimes swollen, I mean during periods of calm, steered SE until 6 p.m. when we sailed SE¼S, the winds SW. Courses SE 4°S, distance 19⅓ leagues. Lat. N Est. 16°52′, observed 16°50′, diff. 2′S. Long. [E. of] Paris based on Mr Maurepas 125°36′.

Monday 28 August 1769

The winds have prevailed as shown in the log. Steered SE¼S under various sails, the sea fairly swollen, carried out various manoeuvres. Courses SE¼S3½°E, distance 37 leagues. Lat. N Est. 15°21′, obs. 15°14′, diff. S 7′. Longitude Est. 126°46′.

Tuesday 29th

Fresh gale, squalls at times, the sea fairly rough, under various sails, steered SE¼S. Courses SE¼S4½°E, distance 38 leagues. Latitude Est. N 13°44′. Longitude Est. 127°59′.

Wednesday 30 August 1769

Stormy weather, sometimes squalls and continual rain, much thunder and lightning from 11 to midnight. Steered various courses, the winds south to westerly, under various sails as shown in the board. Course SE¼E4°S, distance 24½ leagues. Latitude Est. N 12°59′. Longitude 128°59′.

At midday, according to my reckoning Amorset Island[1] bears from me ESE3°S distant 93 leagues behind several small islands or islets 74 leagues [away and] an island which is the nearest bearing SSE5°S dist. 24 leagues.

---

[1] The unreliability of the charts Labé was using is shown by these and subsequent comments. The *St Jean-Baptiste* was sailing well to the north of the Palau group. Amorset was shown on French charts in the north-eastern Carolines.

Thursday 31st

Fair weather, smooth sea, light breeze, the winds varying from SW¼W to SSE, steered variously as shown in the margin, all sails out. Courses ESE 2°30′S, distance 16⅔ leagues. Latitude N Est. 12°38′, obs. 12°29′, diff. 9′S. Longitude Est. 129°45′. At midday, according to my reckoning, Amorset Island bears E¼SE4°S distant 75½ leagues behind several small islands along the same parallel, the nearest distant 58 leagues, another island the nearest to us bearing SSE dist. 15 leagues. They belong to the New Carolines or New Philippines archipelago.[1]

Friday 1 September 1769

Fair weather, smooth sea, almost calm, steered as shown in the board. Courses S¼SW. Distance 3½ leagues. Latitude N Est. 12°19′, obs. 12°12′, diff. S 7′. Longitude Est. 129°43′.

At midday, according to my reckoning following Mr de Maurepas' chart on the Paris meridian Amorset Island bears E¼SE distant 79 leagues and several other islands bearing SE and SW distant 17 and 9 leagues. [On] the chart I am using the New Carolines or New Philippines archipelago are very badly marked and on too small a scale, I mean all the islands that lie a little more northerly than the New Philippines which mark the beginning of the archipelago.

Saturday 2 September 1769

The winds blew from NNW to ENE, good breeze, smooth sea, under various sails, steering south. Courses S2°E, distance 31 leagues. Latitude Est. N 10°39′, obs. 10°26′, diff. S 13′. Longitude Est. 129°46′.

At midday according to my reckoning and Mr Maurepas' chart, Paris meridian, which is very poor for all this archipelago of the New Carolines or New Philippines and the other islands a little further north, I am south of the Amorset Islands and of the nearest, 20 leagues past them, which proves that they are badly placed in regard to their latitude and in every way, because if it had been even 25 or 30 minutes further

---

[1] 'New Philippines', a name that was intended to replace the more familiar 'Palaos', originated with Serrano (auther of 'Breve Noticia del Nuevo Descubrimiento de la Islas Pais o Palaos' of 1705) but survived for only a brief time. Burney, with tongue in check, remarks that Serrano's compliment to Philip V, newly crowned King of Spain, was 'paid at the expense of his predecessor and truth'. Hezel and del Valle, 'Early European Contact with the Western Carolines 1525–1750, *Journal of Pacific History*, VII (1972), 26.

north we would have sailed through them and at least 30′ south, but according to all appearances their correct latitude is 9° or 9°30′ north. Anyhow we are going to sight them and we will know exactly what their position is. Mr D'Après' chart shows them fairly well, but this said chart does not extend far enough east and becomes useless to me as it does not even reach the Marianas or Ladrones Islands.

Sunday 3 September 1769

Stormy weather, squally at times, rain and wind, carried out various manoeuvres as shown in the board and steered various courses, the winds NE to S variable. Courses S¼SW5°15′S, distance 13⅓ leagues. Latitude N Est. 9°46′, obs. 9°44′, diff. S 2′. Longitude Est. 129°42′.

At midday, according to my reckoning on Mr Maurepas' chart I am 33 leagues beyond the Amorset Islands by which I am south of [?]. The nearest island of the New Philippines bears from me S dist. 9 to 10 l.

And according to Mr D'Après' chart, which is the best one, the middle of Yap Island,[1] the westernmost of the New Carolines or New Philippines, bears E3°N, distant reportedly 79 leagues, and the northernmost island of the Paleu or Palos archipelago bears SE¼E3°S dist. 66 leagues.

Monday 4th

Stormy weather and squally [?] weather, little breeze, light rain, the sea smooth, steered various courses and altered course several times as shown in the board, under various sails, the winds south to SW. Courses SE¼E1°E, distance 12½ leagues. Latitude Est. N 9°24′. Longitude Est. following Mr Maurepas' chart 130°14′, according to Mr D'Après' chart 128°48′, Paris meridian [for] both maps. There is a difference of one degree between them. When I took my point of departure in the Bashi Islands, as may be seen on the 2 maps, Mr D'Après' is the good one and the other is worthless for the seas where we are at present.

At midday, according to my reckoning and Mr Maurepas's map, I am among the first islands of the New Philippines by a few leagues. And according to Mr D'Après' map the New Caroline, I mean Yap

---

[1] Taking into consideration Labé's erroneous longitude for the Batan Islands and making allowance for some easterly drifting, the *St Jean-Baptiste* was probably due west of Yap and north of Babelthuap, the northernmost of the Palau group, i.e. approximately 9°45′N and 134°E.

Island which is the most W of all bears E$\frac{1}{4}$NE2°E dist. 74 leagues, [and] the largest and the northernmost of the Paleu or Palos Islands SE$\frac{1}{4}$E dist. 68 leagues.

Tuesday 5 September 1769

Squally weather, rain and wind, the sea high, under various sails, steering close to the wind, the winds as shown in the board. Courses ESE1°E, distance 14$\frac{3}{4}$ leagues. Latitude Est. N 9°08'. Longitude Est. Paris meridian according to Mr Maurepas' chart 130°55', according to Mr D'Après' chart 129°29'.

At midday according to Mr Maurepas' chart, which is quite worthless, I am still among the islands of the New Philippines or New Carolines. And according to Mr D'Après' chart which is the better one, the most westerly of the New Philippines or Caroline Islands, I mean Yap, bears through its centre E$\frac{1}{4}$NE2°N distant 62 leagues, the largest and most northerly of the Paleu or Palos Island SE$\frac{1}{4}$E dist. 44 leagues. When it rains or when the sea is rough, water seeps into the ship through the seams above the store room up to the top and through the spirketings and then runs down into the hold and the ship loosens more and more.

Wednesday 6th

The winds prevailed from the SSW, tacked SE close hauled on the starboard tack, the main and fore topsails close-reefed, the weather overcast. Signs of fair weather at sunset. Clear sky at 9 o'clock. Shook out the reefs in the main and fore topsails and let out the topgallants. Since then light breeze, fair weather. Courses SE40'S, distance 27$\frac{1}{3}$ leagues. Latitude N. Est. 8°37', obs. 8°09', diff. S 28'. Longitude est. according to Mr de Maurepas' chart 131°53', on Mr D'Après' chart 130°27'.

At midday, according to my reckoning and Mr de Maurepas' chart, I am in the middle of the archipelago of the New Philippines or New Carolines. And according to Mr D'Après' chart, the northernmost point of the most northerly and largest of the Paleu or Palos Islands, bears ESE distant 17$\frac{2}{3}$ leagues; we have passed the archipelago of the New Carolines as well as Yap Island, being at present astern of us; Yap Island bears NE5°E dist. 53 leagues.

Thursday 7 September 1769

Almost calm, altered course several times, the wind as shown in the board, the weather fair, the sea smooth. Courses NW, distance ½ league. Latitude N Est. 8°10′, obs. 8°12′. diff. N 2′. Longitude Est. according to Mr Maurepas' chart 131°52′, according to Mr D'Après' chart 130°26′.

At midday, according to my reckoning and Mr Maurepas' chart, I am in the middle of the archipelago of the New Philippines or New Carolines. This map is utterly worthless.

And according to Mr D'Après' chart which is certainly the best that has appeared so far, the northernmost and the largest of the Paleu or Palos Islands bears ESE distant 18 leagues.

Friday 8th

Fair weather until 7 a.m., calm at times, then light breeze, steered as shown in the margin, all sails high. At 7 a.m. squally weather, heavy rain and wind change. Courses S1°20′W, distance 13 leagues. Latitude Est. N 7°33′. Longitude Est. according to Mr de Maurepas' chart 131°51′, according to Mr D'Après' chart 130°25′. At midday, according to my reckoning and Mr Maurepas' chart I am still among the islands of the New Philippines or Carolines. And on Mr D'Après' chart the largest and the most northerly of the Paleu or Palos Islands bears E¼NE, dist 15½ leagues and the nearest of the said islands ESE dist 13 leagues. We have as yet no land in sight. I think we are east of the said [islands].

At 11 a.m. saw two flights of small yellowish birds passing along the ships. There were 10 or 11 in each flock. They are no doubt land birds which have been blown to sea from a nearby island.

Saturday 9 September 1769

The weather prevailed as shown in the board, tacked south, the winds NW to WSW, all sails high. Courses S2°15′E, distance 19 leagues. Latitude N Est. 7°01′, obs. 6°36′, diff. S 25′. Longitude Est. according to Mr Maurepas' chart 131°53′, according to Mr D'Après' chart 130°27′.

At midday, according to my reckoning and Mr Maurepas' chart I have sailed beyond the islands of the New Philippines or New Carolines by 10 l. past the nearest which bears N¼NE. And according to Mr

D'Après' chart, the most southerly and westerly of the Paleu or Palos Islands bears SE¼S distant 13 leagues. We still have no land in sight.

But to all appearances Mr Surville does not want to visit them. Nevertheless water and food supplies are going down and we shall soon be among the calms, which will cause our crew to be laid up through a shortage of water because we will soon be compelled to cut down their ration of water.

I thought this business about chickens was a joke the day before we reached the Bashis, but I realize it is serious and that our captain is keeping the promise he made to our surgeon, for since that time not a single item of poultry has appeared on our table.

Sunday 10 September 1769

Until 6 p.m. crowded on sails; at sunset furled the same sails and from 9 to midnight clewed up the courses so as to sail under the minor sails all night for fear of finding ourselves caught among the Palos Islands, being very close to them according to our reckoning. Fair all night and at daybreak crowded on sail without sighting any island. Steered various courses and under various sails, the winds SW to WSW. Courses SE¼S15'S, distance 31½ leagues. Latitude Est. N the sun being at its zenith 5°17'. Longitude Est. according to Mr Maurepas' chart 132°45', according to Mr D'Après' chart 131°19'.

At midday, according to Mr Maurepas' chart, there are now no islands close to us, we have sailed past them all. We have New Guinea to the south of us very distant, I mean 115 leagues.

According to Mr D'Après' chart I will tonight have sailed into the channel of the St Andrew and Palos Islands.[1] St Andrew bears west distant 23 or 24 leagues and the most westerly and southerly of the Palos Island bears NW¼N dist. 17 leagues.

Monday 11 September 1769

Fair weather, smooth sea, all sails high. Courses ESE 2°S, distance 32 leagues. Latitude Est. N 4°37' the sun being almost at its zenith. Longitude Est. according to Mr de Maurepas' chart 134°13', according to Mr D'Après' chart 132°47'.

---

[1] St Andrews is Sonsorol south-west of the main Palau group, in 5°19'N and 132°13'E. Some adjustment is required, taking into account Labé's erroneous longitude for the Batan Islands and the ship's gradual easterly drift; it is more likely that the *St Jean-Baptiste* sailed east of the main Palau group.

Tuesday 12th

Fair weather, smooth sea, all sails high, steering ESE, the winds WNW. Courses SE¼S4°30'E, distance 32⅔ leagues. Latitude N Est. 4°09', obs. 3°20', diff. since my last observation S 49'. Longitude Est. according to Mr de Maurepas' chart 135°14', according to Mr D'Après' chart 133°48'.

No island is shown on Maurepas' map, I mean E and ESE from us, however I am continuing to use the said map which extends all across the east as far as the coast of Peru.

I am forced to leave Mr D'Après', being no longer able to use it, as it does not go beyond the 136th degree of Longitude.

Wednesday 13 September 1769

Fair weather, smooth sea, light breeze, overcast at times, signs of wind but disappearing without wind, easterly course, winds WNW, all sails high. Courses E 4°30'S, distance 28 leagues. Latitude N Est. 3°13'. Longitude Est. according to Mr Maurepas' chart 136°38' Paris meridian.

Thursday 14th

Light breeze, smooth sea, stormy at times, steering E, all sails high, the winds W. Courses E 3°46'S distance 26¼ leagues. Latitude Est. N 3°08'. Longitude Est. Paris meridian, according to Mr de Maurepas' chart 137°57'.

Friday 15 September 1769

Kept to an easterly course under various sails, the winds as shown in the board. Courses SE¼E4°50'E, distance 27 leagues. Latitude N Est. 3°03', obs. 2°29', diff. since my last observation S 34'. Longitude according to Mr de Maurepas' chart 139°08'.

Saturday 16th

Fair weather, smooth sea, sometimes all sails high as shown in the board, steering E, the winds WNW to WSW. Courses E3°45'S, distance 22 leagues. Latitude N Est. 2°25'. Longitude Est. according to Mr de Maurepas' chart 140°14'.

Sunday 17 September 1769

Easterly course, sometimes all sails out, fair weather, smooth sea, the winds as in the margin. Courses E$\frac{1}{4}$SE5°E, distance 20 leagues. Latitude Est. N 2°18′ Longitude Est. 141°14′.

Monday 18th

Fair weather, smooth sea, light breeze, followed various courses, the winds as shown in the board. Courses E$\frac{1}{4}$NE1°20′N, distance 10$\frac{1}{2}$ leagues. Latitude Est. N 2°25′. Longitude Est. 141°45′.

At midday the sun had reached our zenith, which means that I have not had a latitude by observation.

Tuesday 19 September 1769

Fair weather, smooth sea, light breeze, all sails high, steered ENE, the winds WSW. Courses E$\frac{1}{4}$SE1°S, distance 21 leagues. Latitude N Est. 2°43′, obs. 2°12′, diff. S 31′. Longitude Est. 142°47′. At midday, according to my reckoning, New Britain,[1] I mean its northern part, bears SE$\frac{1}{4}$S distant 112 leagues, Matthias Island[2] in the same point of the compass, distant 92 leagues, and the nearest part of New Guinea SW$\frac{1}{4}$S, dist. 46 leagues.

Wednesday 20th

Fair weather, smooth sea, all sails high, made E$\frac{1}{4}$NE, at 1 p.m. made E, the winds WSW. Courses E$\frac{1}{4}$SE14°15′E, distance 32$\frac{1}{2}$ leagues. Latitude N Est. 2°, obs. 1°55′, diff. S 5′. Longitude Est. 144°24′.

Thursday 21 September 1769

For midday yesterday until 5 p.m. stormy weather, signs of rain, experienced one squall without much wind. From 6 p.m. until midday today fair weather, smooth sea, all sails high, steering E$\frac{1}{4}$SE, the winds S to W. Courses ESE 3°30′E, distance 19$\frac{2}{3}$. Latitude Est. N 1°36′. Longitude 145°20′.

[1] Not New Britain but New Ireland and New Hanover, of whose existence as a separate island the French were still unaware, lay to the south-east. The correct longitude at this point would be approximately 146°30′ east of Greenwich.
[2] The St Matthias group consists of the small islands of Mussau, Emirau, and Tench, and lies to the north of Lavongai or New Hanover.

At midday, according to my reckoning, the north head of New Britain bears S¼SE dist. 83 leagues, Matthias Islands in the same point of the compass dist. 70 leagues.

Friday 22nd

Fair weather, smooth sea, light breeze, all sails high, studding sails and topgallants and royals, steering ESE until 8 a.m. when we set course for the SE¼E the winds WNW. Courses SE¼S1°E, distance 22 leagues. Latitude N Est. 1°14′, obs. 42′, diff. S 32′. Longitude Est. 145°57′.

The tree we have salvaged is of very light wood somewhat like a pine; cut it for firewood.[1] At midday, according to my reckoning, the north head of New Britain bears S4°E, distant 61 leagues, the middle of the Matthias Islands in the same point of the compass, dist. 50 leagues.

Saturday 23 September 1769

Fair weather, smooth sea, light breeze, all sails high, steered SE¼E the winds NW. Courses SE 5°E, distance 11½ leagues. Latitude N Est. 20′, obs. 14′, diff. S 6′. Longitude Est. 146°23′.

Here we are partly on the Equator and very little wind, almost calm. God knows when we shall wind enough to get us out of these regions. We have only enough water for 70 days, our men are beginning to suffer greatly from the heat and from thirst and several are affected by scurvy. I do not know what Mr Surville intends to do, since he has never spoken to me of these operations of discovery. I do not know what to think about him, whether it is ill-humour on his part. I reckon that within a month we will be reduced to the sailors' rations, as we have almost no fresh food left for the table. For a month now there has been no poultry on the table – it is pork with mashed vegetables, [?] and a little salt meat. Those who have wine drink some, those who have not drink water, the ship does not provide [wine] for the officers. Within a month we will have no extras, everything will be used up, our only resource will be a piece of salt beef at each meal.

[1] After sighting a quantity of tree trunks, branches and fruit floating alongside, the French had hauled up a tree trunk 15 ft long.

Sunday 24th

Almost calm, steered various courses, the winds as in the margin. Courses SE4°S, distance 6⅔ leagues. Latitude S 1′, observed 7′, diff. S 6′. Longitude Est. 146°36′. We crossed the equinoctial line during the night.[1] The calms and the great heat are making themselves felt terribly.

Monday 25 September 1769

Almost calm, smooth sea, fine weather, all sails high at times, then under the main and fore topsails as shown in the board. Courses SSE4°30′E, distance 1½ leagues. Latitude S Est. 11′, obs. 10′, diff. N1′. Longitude Est. 146°38′.

Tuesday 26th

Calm, the sea pondlike, unbearable heat, steered under various sails as shown in the margin. Courses SE4°45′E, distance 2½ leagues. Latitude S Est. 15′, obs. 14′, diff. N 1′. Longitude Est. 146°44′.

Here we now are in these famous calms. God knows when we will get out of them.

Our crew are suffering considerably from this great heat and have only their bottle of water to drink in 24 hours and if the calms continue we shall be forced to cut down their drink and ration of water. I am very much afraid that they may be affected by sickness, I mean scurvy, we already have several [cases] and a great part of the crew are complaining of stomach pains, first sign of scurvy. May God grant us soon the discovery of some land or islands to obtain water and make discoveries which are the purpose of our voyage. Mr Surville will get out of this as best he can; if I had taken any part in this and my opinion had been sought I would have been in favour of starting our discoveries in northern latitudes and sailing among the New Carolines and New Philippines when we should have certainly found quantities of food of all kinds at gunpoint.

Wednesday 27 September 1769

Until 10 a.m. calm, some hints of a light breeze at times as shown in the board. At 10 a squall, rain, not much wind, continuing to steer

---

[1] The *St Jean-Baptiste* crossed the line to the north of Tench Island.

SE¼E. Courses SE4°30′E, distance 6 leagues. Latitude Est. S 26′. Longitude Est. 146°58′.

Thursday 28th

Calm, a light breeze at times, carried out various manoeuvres as shown in the margin. Courses SE¼E5°15′E, distance 5 leagues. Latitude E Est. 33′, obs. 31′, diff. N 2′. Longitude Est. 147°13′.

At midday, according to my reckoning, the north head of New Britain bears SSW distant 40 leagues, at the same point of the compass Stormy Island[1] [is] distant 26 leagues.

Friday 29th September 1769

Almost calm, under various sails, sometimes everything clewed up, steered various courses as shown in the margin.[2] Courses SE¼E5°S, distance 2 leagues. Latitude S Est. 35′, obs. 26′, diff. N 9′. Longitude Est. 147°18′.

Saturday 30th

Stormy weather, squalls at times, rain and wind, carried out various manoeuvres as shown in the board. Courses ESE 2°S, distance 15⅓ leagues. Latitude S Est. 145′. Longitude Est. 148°.

At midday, according to my reckoning and Mr de Maurepas' chart Stormy Island, which lies off the north head of New Britain, bears SW¼W distant 35 leagues.

Sunday 1st October 1769

The winds prevailed from the south to SW, fresh breeze, steering ESE to SE under various sails as shown in the margin, the weather fairly fine, squally at times. Courses SE5°E, distance 33 leagues. Latitude Est. S 1°49′. Longitude 149°16′.

At midday, according to my reckoning and Mr de Maurepas' chart, the nearest of the islands lying to the NE of New Britain bears NNE

[1] Emirau, one of the St Matthias group, sighted by Dampier in 1699 and named by him Squally Island.
[2] What breeze there was was variable; to take advantage of it and make some headway the French steered E¼SE2°E, SW¼S, S, S¼SE and NE¼E.

distant 12 leagues, the northernmost point of St John's Island[1] bears SE¼S distant 47 leagues.

Monday 2 October 1769

Squally weather, rain and wind, the sky completely overcast, much thunder and lightning. At 4 p.m. close reefed the main and fore topsails and clewed up the mainsail and stayed thus as shown in the board, courses and winds as in the margin. Courses SE1°15′E, distance 24½ leagues. Latitude Est. S 2°40′. Longitude Est. 150°09′.

At midday, according to my reckoning and Mr de Maurepas' chart a small unnamed island bears S¼SW distant 9 leagues and the northernmost point of St John's Island S¼SE2°E distant 21 to 11 leagues.

Tuesday 3 October 1769

The weather, courses and winds as shown in the board, under various sails.

Courses SE3°45′E, distance 21⅓ leagues. Latitude S Est. 3°22′, obs. 2°40′, diff. N 42′. Longitude Est. 150°57′.

At midday, according to my reckoning and Mr de Maurepas' chart, St John's Island bears SSW, distant 20 leagues.

Wednesday 4th

Courses, winds and weather as shown in the board, with various manoeuvres and sails. Courses SE40′S, distance 18⅔ leagues. Latitude Est. S 3°20′. Longitude Est. 151°36′.

At midday, according to my reckoning and Mr de Maurepas' chart, St John's Island east of New Britain bears SW¼W dist. 20 leagues, the nearest islands or rocks of Ohong-java[2] SE¼S distant 10½ leagues.

---

[1] St John's Island is the Feni group, consisting of Ambitle, Babase and Balum, about 30 miles east of New Ireland's East Cape, in 4°5′S and 153°40′E. *St Jean-Baptiste*, however, had sailed past their longitude by this date.

[2] Ontong-Java, spelt Ohong Java and shown much too far west on the French charts, lies in 5°25′S and 159°30′W. It is a low-lying atoll group discovered by Tasman in 1643. At this point, the *St Jean-Baptiste* was in the neighbourhood of 156°W, far to the north of Bougainville Strait.

Thursday 5 October 1769

Weather and sails as shown in the board, steering SE until 6.30 a.m. when we stood SSE. The winds NW. Courses SE$\frac{1}{4}$S2°S, distance 27$\frac{3}{4}$ leagues. Latitude S Est. 4°31′, obs. 4°38′, diff. S 7′. Longitude 152°20′.

At midday, according to my reckoning and Mr Maurepas' chart, I find that I have sailed beyond the islands or rocks named Ohong-java. It bears NW$\frac{1}{4}$N, the nearest distant 8 leagues.

Friday 6th

Stormy weather, a fresh breeze at times and heavy rain, steering SSE to S under different sails as shown in the board. Courses S1°30′W, distance 23$\frac{2}{3}$ leagues. Latitude Est. S 5°49′, Longitude Est. 152°18′.

Saturday 7 October 1769

Carried out various manoeuvres and steered various courses as shown in the board. The winds easterly. At 5.30 a.m. sighted land partly covered with trees.[1] Tacked at 6 and stood off so as to round a kind of cape or island which consists of two mountains similar to the Two Brothers in the strait before one arrives at Malac and lined with lowlands on the eastern end. Sighted the middle of the two peaks or bluffs bearing SE$\frac{1}{4}$S dist. 7 or 8 leagues, the lowlands very distant SE, the land appears to be running W, very high, wooded. The mountain tops are hidden in clouds.

At 8 a.m. we can no longer see the SE lowlands, they [are] close to the point where the two bluffs are situated, the other lowlands to the south of them are visible, but slightly elevated. Our closest land which is the cape with the two bluffs and is surrounded with lowlands bears SSE 3°S distant about 9 leagues. The high land stretches as far as W 2°N where a low point may be seen. No opening is apparent as yet. We can [not] know for sure whether these are islands off New Guinea. When we get nearer we shall know more. From 8 until midday carried out manoeuvres as shown in the board.

Courses S$\frac{1}{4}$SE3°E, distance 13$\frac{1}{4}$ leagues. Latitude S Est. 6°28′, obs. 6°57′, diff. S 29′ since my last [observation]. Longitude Est. 152°28′.[2]

---

[1] The bad weather encountered on the 7th explains why the French had no inkling that land was near and were close enough to distinguish its main features by the time they first sighted it.

[2] Labé's longitude reveals an error of approximately 3°. Taura Peak is 155°08′ east of Paris. The Two Brothers referred to earlier are Pandang and Sulanama.

As we changed course at 10.30 a.m. sighted the island we are calling *Première Vue* Island on which there are two hills, the westernmost of which is shaped like two mamelons bore S¼SE5°S very distant. At midday the same island bore, I mean its easternmost point, S¼SE distant 6 leagues approximately. Some lowlands are becoming visible behind the island with small hillocks stretching as far as a high mountain which bears S5°W, from there quantities of high mountains as far as W¼SW. There are lowlands east of *Première Vue* Island but belonging to the mainland and running east. We are calling [it] *Première Vue* Island as it is the most remarkable of all those we can see. I am not altering my point of departure until we are quite certain where we are in our observed latitude of 6°57′ South. No voyager has been to this unknown region. I say also that this entire coast is lined with large and small islands, most looking as if they formed part of the mainland but one sees they are islands.[1]

Sunday 8 October 1769

Variable winds and rain, light breeze, steered various courses as shown in the board. Courses SE¼E3°S, distance 4¼ leagues. Latitude S Est. 7°05′, obs. 7°13′, diff. S 8′. Longitude Est. 152°38′.

Bearings for the 24 hours: at 2 p.m. sighted *Première Vue* Island, its most easterly point bearing SSE dist. 5 or 6 leagues, the low headland to the east of the island SSE2°E, the centre of another lowland looking like islands grouped together SE¼S1°E. At 6 p.m. the easternmost lowlands forming small islets SE¼S dist. 7 leagues, the mamelons of *Première Vue* Island SSE3°S, the high bluff forming the starboard entrance of the bay S 2°E; the land stretches on to WNW 5°W, high mountains. At sunrise the most easterly island S¼SE4°S, the high mountains at sunrise S 5°W, the most westerly land in full view W 5°N. At 8 *Première Vue* Island, its easternmost point SSE2°S, its other point S¼SE2°E. Some lowlands stretch on towards the east. At 11 a.m. the sea changed appearance, whitish. Sounded and found 27 f. coral, then 31 same ground and lost ground at once. At the first lead throw I sighted the most easterly lowlands bearing SE¼E, the eastern point of *Première Vue* Island SE 5°S dist. 3½ l., its most W point SE¼S2°E same distance, the 1st islet of the bay SSE5°E, 3¾ to 4 leagues, the 2nd islet SSE, the 3rd SSE 2°S, the 4th SSE 4°S, the high mountain on the

---

[1] For the identification of these various features, see the footnotes to Surville's *Journal* under the corresponding dates.

starboard side of the bay where the islets are S$\frac{1}{4}$SW3°S 2$\frac{1}{2}$ l., the land which seems the most westerly W in full view.

At 11.30 a.m. the sky a little clearer, saw land as far as WNW. At midday the easternmost lowlands bears ESE3°E dist. 7 leagues, *Première Vue* Island ESE4°S distant 2$\frac{1}{2}$ leagues, a rock over which the sea is breaking between *1ère Vue* Island and the first islet SE$\frac{1}{4}$S, the most W point of the bay S4°E, the nearest which is a high mountain SW$\frac{1}{4}$S3°S, 1$\frac{1}{2}$ l., the land which looks like the most westerly W$\frac{1}{4}$NW and WNW.

Note: *Première Vue* Island has two mountains. The eastern one is not very high and it is flat-topped. [In] the western part, the top of the mountain has the shape of two mamelons. The island is well wooded. It stands at the entrance of a bay. In the W part there are five islets which are a little further in the bay.[1] There are also several breakers. The starboard side of the bay consists of high mountains and there is a range of high mountains in the WNW and in the distance may be seen a headland. The eastern part of *Première Vue* Island consists of lowlands; when you see them from afar they look like islets in a group, but when you get to within 4 or 5 leagues of them you see that it is low-lying mainland. You can also see inside these lowlands a few high mountains. In the east you can also see from the topmast an island which seems isolated, but I think the lowlands run in this direction and that this island is not far from the mainland and this whole coast is covered with [trees?] and it seems that there are rivers looking like wide bays in several places, behind the islands among others and other breaks visible among the lowlands.[2]

Let us return to our landfall. I think we are the first to see this land, because if we had passed west of New Britain, which cannot be unless the distance between New Guinea and New Britain is much greater than is shown on all charts, and if we are east of it the error is even greater, since all the charts show the coast of New Guinea from New Britain to the cape or land of the Holy Spirit[3] running S$\frac{1}{4}$SE, which means a space of 140 leagues, and we are in latitude obs. 7°13′S and can see land bearing ESE and the coast seems to be tending in that direction, which may be verified by referring to our bearings. According to the famous voyager Dampierre who claims to have sailed between New Britain and New Guinea,[4] we cannot have sailed

---

[1] There are in fact six islands within Taura Bay but not all would be visible from the ship. At the same date Surville records seeing only four, as does Pottier.

[2] The island seen in the east from the topmast is Santa Isabel, across Manning Strait, or one of its westerly islands such as Gagi whose Mt Beaumont rises to 995 ft.

[3] Espiritu Santo, in the New Hebrides, so named by Quiros in 1606.

[4] William Dampier in 1700 'discovered the Strait that bears his name, between New Guinea and New Britain. It is clearly shown as 'Passage de Dampière' on French charts of the period.

through his strait without seeing land before getting to 5°S, and without any doubt we see none, and have seen none; from which I can safely conclude that we have sailed east of New Britain and that the coast of New Guinea, which is very little known, runs SE and ESE and that the land of the Holy Spirit may also be placed too far west; if we were west and sailed west of New Britain, New Guinea would have to be merely a land cut through by channels formed by islands and at a great distance for us to have reached 7°13′S and not seen land in the north, I mean off shore. I hope we shall do our best to discover the truth.[1]

Monday 9 October 1769

Carried out various manoeuvres and steered various courses, the winds as shown in the board. Courses E¼NE2°N, distance 5¾ leagues. Latitude S Est. 7°09′, obs. 7°10′. Longitude Est. 152°55′. Bearings for these 24 hours: at 5 p.m. after sounding and finding ground at 45 f. shells and pieces of coral, I sighted the eastern point of *Première Vue* Island, I mean we set down its bearings at ES¼E2°S distant 2½ to 3 leagues. At 6 p.m. they sighted the easternmost cape of *Première Vue* Island bearing SE¼E approximately 3½ l., the summit of the mountain at the starboard entrance to the bay S¼SE1°S, it is the land nearest to us; the land running WNW in the distance, the most easterly lowlands SE¼S5°E. At sunrise the middle of *Première Vue* Island bore S¼SE3°S dist. about 4½ leagues, the most easterly lowlands SE2°S dist. 7 or 8 leagues, an island very distant seen from the topmasts E, the high mountain forming the starboard entrance of the bay where there are several islets S¼SW5°W, the land which appears to us as the most westerly W¼NW4°W distant.

At 7 a.m. with the first light breeze, altered course wind astern. At 8 a.m. the middle of *Première Vue* Island bore S¼SE dist. ½ l., the most easterly lowlands SE; to continue the bearings: an island still further east ESE5°S, the high mountain on the starboard side of the bay S¼SW5°W, the most westerly land is no longer visible, it is hidden in haze. At midday the island which seems the most easterly bears ESE1°S, the easternmost lowlands SSE1°E distance 6 or 7 leagues, the middle of *Première Vue* Island SW¼S distant 5 leagues, the high mountain on

---

[1] This rather typical example of Labé's convoluted prose is nevertheless a careful analysis of the position. Their doubtful longitude, based on dead reckoning, combined with the lack of detail and the errors on the charts of the time, left all the officers uncertain of their actual position; but they all soon felt that it was impossible for the land in sight to be New Guinea (even though they still occasionally referred to it as 'the land of the Papuans') and that consequently it was a new discovery.

the starboard side of the bay where there are several islets between [it and] *Première Vue* Island SW, the most westerly land W5°N.

Note and instructions concerning *Première Vue* Island. When I left the ship I went in the yawl, which was well armed, to the most easterly point of the island. There is no ground there. Being at its easternmost point, I came back hauling along the sandy bay seeking somewhere to land. All along the island I found clusters of coral within a musket shot of the shore, where the sea breaks heavily. However I decided to land inside one headland where the sea did not seem to be breaking; but when I got near several heavy waves came up which nearly capsized me, at once realizing that I had ventured too far in I promptly stemmed the waves and was struck by a roller which nearly destroyed us; the boat was swamped. Fortunately I extricated myself from this danger and bailed the water out of the boat. This island is covered in forest [including] numerous areca trees[1] that were laden with fruit; they looked to me like lemons. On other trees there were like bunches of nuts hanging down a foot long and an inch wide [and] many other trees covered in white flowers.[2] I saw numbers of birds, parrots and other species we do have in Europe and two small birds the size of a blackbird [with] a black body and the head and neck white as snow.[3] I saw no sign of drinking water on the island, there is no stream. Over the coral clusters we could see clear of the water a beach of whitish sand mixed with stones. On the western side there are two small islets almost touching which are covered in trees, and further west and further in the bay there are four large islets also covered with trees and several breakers between the said islets. This island seemed distant some $2\frac{1}{2}$ to 3 leagues from the mainland, at least from what we take to be such. It also seems to be abounding with fish: I saw, while I was on the reefs or clusters, quantities of fish and of several kinds which were on the bottom. This island is uninhabited. I thought I saw some smoke at the back of the bay, but no habitations or boats.[4]

---

[1] *Areca catechu* or betel nut palm.
[2] Most of the north coast is covered with mangroves (*Rhizophora*) which were probably the trees Labé describes as having long bunches of nuts. The trees covered in white flowers are known locally as Karapolen.
[3] The Willy Wagtail (*Rhipidura leucophrys*) is black with a white abdomen and breast, with white spots on the side of the throat. It is very common on Wagina and in the lowlands of the Solomons generally. This, according to Fr Isa, the local resident priest, is the nearest local bird that could approach Labé's description.
[4] Labé possibly rowed as far as Haycock, a horseshoe-shaped islet, the eastern curve of which is known as Cape Labé, then westward along the northern reef. There are in fact, two streams on the island, the easternmost concealed by an offshore islet, the northernmost defended by an extension of the reef – the boat would have been swamped before Labé reached the second of these. As he rowed north to rejoin the ship he would have seen

Addition to the midday bearings: I was forgetting to say that while on a E¼NE course we left our *Première Vue* Island to starboard and hauled along several of the islets deep in the bay west of our island. We sighted some on the eastern side of *Première Vue* and we can see no more west of it and forming the bay with the island and the large mountain, I mean a few.

Tuesday 10 October 1769

Steered various courses and carried out various manoeuvres, the winds as shown in the table. Courses E3°30′N, distance 10⅔ leagues. Latitude S Est. 7°08′, obs. 7°06′, diff. N 2′. Longitude Est. 153°27′.

Bearings for the 24 hours: At 6 p.m. sighted the easternmost land in the distance, what I take to be the easternmost island or islet, bearing ESE4°E, a high mountain visible over the lowlands ESE1°E dist. 6 or 7 leagues; it could be an island near the lowlands. From this mountain or island as far as SSE [sighted] the back of the lowlands. There are gaps at intervals, which leads me to believe that there are some bays where there must be rivers, a kind of small islet which appears SE of a great bay, [and] the western point of another bay or gulf SSW distant about 5 leagues; near this bay 4 islets appear which are those we saw at first between *Première Vue* Island and the starboard head of the bay; we have now brought these round to between *Première Vue* Island and the mainland, I mean in the east; a great bluff inside the lowlands bears SW¼W2°S very distant, *Première Vue*, Island SW¼W2°W partly across the starboard mountain of *Première Vue*, the most westerly land in sight W 5°N, a very tall mountain. There are several islands along this coast which seem 3 leagues distant from the mainland.

At midnight saw a mountain or island bearing SE¼E4°E; at 4 a.m.

Tasman Islands off the western coast, which are close together ('almost touching'). The four other islands are those situated in Taura Bay. His estimate of 2½ to 3 leagues for the width of Hamilton Channel between Wagina and Rob Roy is excessive – the distance across is not more than 6 miles. The island was a bone of contention between the people of Choiseul and Santa Isabel and was probably not permanently settled in 1769, but today, as the result of the resettlement of Gilbertese Islanders, its population exceeds 1000.

According to Pottier, Labé went with the yawl and five soldiers 'firstly to a little cove N of the island but did not consider this a suitable place to land' and then rowed to the western side, but he was not with Labé and his comments are unreliable. He mentions however that 'as it got late, Mr de Surville was worried, not seeing the boat return, had two guns fired at regular intervals and two lights set up where they would be visible from the yawl which arrived at 7.30'. *Journal*, p. 109, Labé was therefore away for five or six hours.

the same land bore SE 5°E. At sunrise saw land stretching from ESE 4°S to S¼SE2°E having the appearance of separate islets and drowned trees. There are extensive lowlands in this interval, merely the islands or what we take for them appear high with some tall mountains inside the lowlands. The land that bore ESE4°E last night now bears S¼SE2°E. It has a very low point which stretches out WNW [and is] covered in trees, looking like little inundated islets. As you go south *Première Vue* Island with the large mountain on the starboard side of the first bay bear SW¼W3°W; the land which looks to us like the most westerly having the appearance, owing to the distance, of islands bears W¼SW4°W. At 8 a.m. the land stretches from SE2°E to SSE3°S, what bore S¼SE2°E at sunrise bears now S¼SE2°S, its tree-covered point which looked inundated is only visible to the south of the compass, the large mountain or bluff starboard of the bay of *Première Vue* Island, bears SW¼S4°W. At 9.30 sighted land as we altered course; the island that bore ESE4°E last night now bears S 5°E dist, 7 leagues, some lowlands having the appearance of several islets with drowned trees stretched from SE¼S to S¼SW1°W; from this point as far as SW¼W4°W where is situated the large mountain on the starboard side of the first bay, in that space we can see no sign of land except for a few islets on this side of the said cape. This is the great gulf we saw during the afternoon. At midday a line of islands or islets to all appearances and some high country from SE3°E to SSW1°S, among which is included the one which bore ESE4°E last night. It now bears S¼SE2°S distant about 5 to 5½ l. The starboard bluff at the entrance to the first bay and which is now the most westerly land in view bears WSW1°S distant 12 to 13 leagues.[1]

Note: All this coast appears lined with islands and islets covered with forests, [with] lowlands where the trees looked as if drowned. Inland a few high mountains may be seen. The western side is very high. I think too that there are many islands we are mistaking for a mainland. We can see large bays and harbours where ships could find shelter from all types of winds. There must also be rivers or fresh water streams. As our captain plans to go up close to land to get some wood and water and restore the health of our sick, I hope we may make some good discoveries that will enable us to continue our operations.

---

[1] The *St Jean-Baptiste* is now north of the western point of Santa Isabel and its adjacent islands which, with the Arnavons barely visible, stretch from the southeast to almost due south; Taura Peak is still visible to the WSW; Manning Strait can be clearly identified as 'the great gulf'; but other details cannot be distinguished. As Labé says in a marginal note 'we are still away from the land'.

Wednesday 11 October 1769

Carried out various manoeuvres, steered variously, the winds variable as shown in the board. Courses ESE5°15'S, distance 8 leagues. Latitude S Est. 7°17'. Longitude Est. 153°48'.

Bearings for the 24 hours: At 6 p.m. the mountains on the starboard side of *Première Vue* Bay bore W$\frac{1}{4}$SW2°S distance about 17 or 18 leagues, the lowlands that form islets having the appearance of drowned trees WSW3°W dist. 7 or 8 leagues, from there as far as the large mountain starboard of *Première Vue* Bay no land is visible; the nearest to us bears S$\frac{1}{4}$SW2°W dist. 3 to 3$\frac{1}{2}$ l., the point which seems the most easterly bears SE$\frac{1}{4}$E3°E. It is beginning to run ESE. The land is high. It seems that it is a mass of large and very high islands bordered by small islands and islets which [?] 3 leagues from the large ones; this is what gives us an impression of bays and large gulf. Until now we have seen neither smoke nor boats, no signs of fresh water streams or rivers; I cannot imagine, however, that such a large stretch of land is uninhabited.

All night we saw the land continuing to run ESE and at the same distance, steering E; what seemed to be the most easterly [land] bore SE$\frac{1}{4}$E. At 6 a.m. sighted some high land from SE$\frac{1}{4}$E3°S as far as WSW 3°W and some lowlands as far as SE$\frac{1}{4}$5°E. There are still small islands and islets. The nearest land bears from us S5°E distant 4 or 5 leagues. There seems to be an opening formed by islands and islets. All this land is covered in trees and numerous arecas. At 8 a.m. no bearings, the land hidden by haze. At midday the land hidden by haze; what seems the most westerly bears WSW3°W, the easternmost SE$\frac{1}{4}$E; all this land looks like a mass of large very high mountains lined by small islands and numerous islets; what is visible in the distance forms lowlands and also bays where I have no doubt there are good anchorages where ships would be sheltered, but one would have to know these good places. Nothing easier: we have four boats on board; [the method] would be to have two going along this coast investigating, to find a place of shelter for the ship and get water; we are in great need of some, there being only a 45 days' supply on board and sickness already making progress, with about 25 to 30 men affected by scurvy. We must absolutely restore our crew's health and fill our water casks and get firewood in these parts, if not we shall be wanting for all kinds of things and in less than a month will not have 20 men fit to work the ship. I hope God will take pity on us.

Thursday 12 October 1769

Carried out various manoeuvres and steered variously to make for the shore and find a suitable place to anchor with the ship and get water and firewood.

Courses SE¼E4°45′E, distance 3½ leagues. Latitude S Est. 7°22′, obs. 7°16′, diff. N 6′. Longitude 153°57′.

Bearings for the 24 hours and instructions: at 6 p.m. the land which seems to us most easterly bore SE¼E2°S dist. 7 leagues, the westernmost in sight SW¼W5°S 6 leagues, the nearest SW¼S5°S about 5 leagues. At sunrise the land which seemed most easterly SE¼S4°30′E, the westernmost SW¼S4½°S. At 8 a.m. sighted the westernmost land bearing SW, a kind of opening S¼SE2°E, the easternmost land SE1°E. At midday sighted the easternmost land bearing SE¼E2°E, the westernmost WSW4°S, the nearest forming bays, the easternmost SSE2°S, the westernmost S¼SW3°W distant about 5 leagues.

Until now the wind and the storms have not enabled us to hug the coast to look for anchorage and get water, and restore our sick whose number grows daily.

Until now the whole coast has given me the impression of being only a great number of large islands bordered by islets. This gives us the impression of great bays between the islets and the large island and edged with breakers. The whole coast has so far given no sounding depths. I hope we will soon find a good anchorage; we are in great need of it to recover from our weariness.

Friday 13th

Tacked several times standing off and on under different sails, winds and courses as in the board. Courses S¼SW5°W, distance 4¼ leagues. Latitude S Est. 7°28′, Obs. 7°21′, diff. N 7′. Longitude Est. 153°54′. Bearings for the 24 hours: at sunset saw the large bluff or high mountain at the starboard entrance of *Première Vue* bearing W¼SW3°W, distant at least 19 or 20 leagues, the easternmost land visible from the topmasts bearing E5°S, the nearest SW¼S dist. 4 to 4½ l. All this coast is lined with large and small islands, further inshore it seems to form a continent or else it is an island of a considerable size; we have been coasting along it for more than 30 leagues and we cannot see the end of it. This mainland that we can see above all these islands seems to be covered with fine forests but there seem to be no cleared areas, nor habitations, no boats along the coast. We have seen smoke only twice, yesterday afternoon. At daybreak, no land visible. At 7.30 a.m. saw land to the S¼SW and SSW very distant and hazy, at 8 S¼SE and SSW very distant. All the islands along the coast are of medium height, but the continent or large island we can see above them is very high. The sea shore seems bare [?] in places and we can see no sign of creeks or place where we could go and anchor with the ship. It is true that Mr Surville tacks widely; he ought to manoeuvre so as to find himself near land at daybreak; he could then send two boats to survey the coast and seek a good anchorage and a watering place to get water and firewood and restore the health of our sick whose number is considerable. At 11.30 Mr Surville sent me in the yawl with five soldiers to examine the coast and a wide opening where the sea was breaking heavily. At midday they sighted from the ship the easternmost land bearing E¼SE2°E, the opening of the bay SSW 1°S 2 leagues, the land nearest the ship which is the north point of an island forming the east coast of the bay S¼SW2°W, the westernmost point which is the head of the cayman W3°N 4 leagues, some islets further west forming the tail of the cayman W¼NW2°W; what we call the cayman is a group of islands and islets which appear all merged together and have the shape of a cayman. From the midday bearings it will be seen that we have made no headway since yesterday midday except a little to the south.

Continuation of Friday afternoon. When I left the ship I made for the eastern side of the entrance I was to explore. When I was almost on the bar or shore I coasted along in a westerly direction where I thought I could see an opening. I saw the sea breaking on all sides but when I was a little nearer I saw an opening half a cable length across where the sea did not break. I went to it but could find no ground. I passed between the two breakers and entered into a fine harbour where I found 25 to 18 fathoms of water, white and reddish sand. At 1.30 I sighted a small canoe coming in which had been close to the ship but had not felt it wise to go up to her. I rowed so as to bar its way. I started to get near it, the kaffir[1] in charge of it was tired, but I came up to a coral reef which forced me to leave him alone. At the same moment I sighted a large boat full of people and the small one was endeavouring to catch up with it, shouting loudly and his friends in the large boat replied to him. They were among islets in the eastern part of the harbour. I at once made for the ship and being within sight of her I signalled with a white flag as had been agreed with Mr Surville

---

[1] The French used this term frequently to refer to blacks or dark islanders.

in case I found a good anchorage, which I did therefore on my way back to the ship. The ship seeing me coming altered course towards me and steered S¼SW for the harbour entrance. I arrived at 2.15 and made a complete report to Mr Surville who requested me to take the ship into the said harbour, which I did at once. The pass is situated between two islands each with a large reef which advances into the pass on each side for a cable length, which means the pass is very narrow, its channel being at the most two-thirds of a cable length. Entered the small channel, steering SW¼S, keeping to the larboard side of the entrance, then rounding to SW. We found ground only when we were in the said pass, i.e. the larboard head of the pass bearing E¼NE distant ¾ cable length. We found a sandy bottom with rotted coral in 55 fathoms of water. The wind immediately shifted to SE which forced us to sail close hauled, that is SSW. At 3.30 a squall formed at the back of the harbour gave us a dead calm, forcing us to lower the large kedge anchor in 24 fathoms fine white sand inside the heads and the reef. As the ship was dragging, forced to lower a bower anchor and let out 30 fathoms of cable.

Bearings of the anchorage: the larboard entrance head ENE 3°N dist, ½ league, its reef continues as far as NE¼E3°E; the starboard entrance head NW, its reef continues as far as NNW2°W distant ½ cable's length from us; the back of the harbour SSW 5°S distant about 3 leagues; the points inside the two islets which form the entrance – the one bears WSW5°S and the other S¼SE2°E about ½ a league. As soon as we had anchored we saw 8 or 10 men on the starboard shore at the entrance and soon after several small boats came within pistol shot of the ship with from two to 8 men in each, one of whom began to take his bow and some arrows, aiming toward us. We tried to pacify him by showing him a small white flag at the end of a stick, signal of peace among all these savages according to the accounts of every voyager. He seemed to calm down; he still gave indications of wanting to shoot an arrow; Mr Surville showed him some blue cloth, then he calmed down and made a sign that we were to throw it in the sea, which we did, but it sank. We threw him a fathom length of white cloth tied up to a piece of wood which he took and used to cover his shoulders, seeming to be very pleased. He then gestured that he would show us a watering place, pointing to the back of the harbour with his hand and putting his hand to his mouth as if he was drinking water. We told him by signs that it was too late, but that tomorrow if he was willing to show us the watering place we would send some boats.

Consequently at 5 p.m. we lowered four boats. All these natives stayed at a distance, seemingly surprised to see us working. Towards evening the large boat I had seen when I entered with the small canoe in the harbour came to join all the small ones that were along our side. It seemed to me to hold 30 to 35 men armed with lances and arrows and a kind of shield two and $\frac{1}{2}$ feet long and 10 inches wide. When night had fallen all these boats went to the starboard island at the harbour entrance which is well wooded. They had a fire all night and replied word for word to what our sailors were saying: when someone whistled on board they whistled just like our own people and did monkey tricks. There were always during the night of Friday to Saturday some of their small boats roaming some distance from the ship. We could hear them talk, as well as those who were ashore. We are doing all we can to coax them, but it seems they are quite ferocious and that we shall have a great deal of trouble with all these islanders, I mean savages.[1] The islands are washed by the sea more than one cable's length among the trees.

Saturday 14 October 1769

At daybreak laid out a kedge anchor with four warps to haul ourselves a little further in and having worked up to the said warp lowered a bower anchor in 8 fathoms of water, fine white sand. I was forgetting to mention that when after I had laid out the warp, as I was returning to the ship, I was surrounded by five small local boats with 3 to 6 men in each. I signalled to them to come nearer and asked them where the water was. They continued to point to the back of the harbour, a distance of 3 leagues. One of the said boats came alongside the boat; I gave them two tobacco leaves which they took and placed in a little packet. When we got back on boat we made friendly signs to them. This reassured them.[2] They came nearer the vessel. We threw them a length of cloth and a bottle containing some arrack making sign that they should drink. They took all this and tasted the arrack without appearing to be satisfied with the said drink but very [pleased] with the bottle. These small presents having emboldened them a little,

---

[1] This correction is not to be taken in a pejorative sense. The term 'sauvages' is midway between the English 'natives' or 'tribesmen' and its literal equivalent 'savages'. The distinction Labé is making here is between people living on an offshore island and those living on a continent or mainland.

[2] The present of leaves, irrespective of their possible use, would have been interpreted by the Solomonese as a peace token – the waving of leaves or palms being a common sign of peaceful intention. Gifts of cloth and bottles would be received in the same spirit.

they came closer to the vessel and some climbed into our boats that were alongside and examined them attentively. One of them was bold enough to climb on board. We made him welcome. Following his example several climbed up. They were armed with clubs. They examined the ship carefully. We treated them very gently. Nevertheless we took care to have the soldiers under arms for fear of a surprise, as in addition to their clubs they also had lances, arrows and their bows, which had forced us to load all the firearms and the guns in order to fire at them at the slightest movement, without this seeming to have been got ready by us to inspire them with mistrust. I thought they were most impressed by the strength of our capstan when we were heaving on our warp. They are great thieves: two of our sailors had left their jackets in the longboat, the islanders or savages had taken them and placed them in their little boat; when our sailors saw this they went to get it back. They did not appear affected by this. In spite of all the marks of friendship we could think of with these people they retained an air of mistrust and anxiety and at the slightest movement on board the vessel they would run to their boats and those who were too far from them would throw themselves in the sea although we did all we could to reassure them. They again made us understand that if we wanted some drinking water they would show us the place where there was some. I do not know whether they have seen any other travellers or whether since they themselves have supplies of water in bamboos and coconuts they imagine that it was a need for this that led us into their bay.[1] Whatever the truth of the matter we always made signs in reply to the effect that we wanted some, to which they gestured to send our boats and that they would lead us to a watering place, continually pointing to the back of the harbour, although it was distant from us two and $\frac{1}{2}$ to three leagues.

At 11.30 a.m. our captain, Mr Surville, sent me with the two large boats manned by 17 sailors and 10 soldiers, including the sergeant and a corporal, all armed with their rifles and the former with swords. In one of the boats I had Mr Surville's nephew to command under my orders in case of need. I took seven or eight empty casks to fill at the

---

[1] Although no other Europeans entered this particular harbour and it is easy enough for a people accustomed to voyages of several weeks' duration to interpret a navigator's need of drinking water, the Spaniards had come very close to it in 1568. Jack-Hinton puts forward the hypothesis that the brigantine Mendaña had constructed for detailed exploration entered Popu Channel between Gagi and Barola Islands, only a few miles south of where the St Jean-Baptiste anchored (*The Search for the Solomon Islands*, p. 57). Whether any tradition of the earlier expedition remained among the local islanders is of course very doubtful.

first watering place we would find. The native to whom we had given lengths of cloth this morning came at first alone with us in his canoe and was showing me the back of the harbour. Shortly after, all the other islanders who were in various parts of the harbour left the shore and came towards us, numbering 12 or 15 canoes including the two large ones, all the said boats full of people all armed with lances, clubs and arrows with their bows. They seemed to me to be arguing with the small canoe that was showing me the way, but soon after this they kept quiet and led us firstly to the back of the harbour, a distance of $2\frac{1}{2}$ leagues and took us over coral shelves which forced me to make long detours to avoid striking them and [I] arrived at a small stream between two mountains where there was only three feet of water. I stayed at the outlet and made signs asking where the water was. They showed me the upper part of the stream and that I would find some there. I at once sent four soldiers and a corporal to investigate and stayed outside with the rest to keep these natives under control lest they attacked [the] five men I had sent. They soon came back and reported that they had advanced quite some distance into the forest and that there was no water but much marshy land more than three feet deep. I immediately came to a decision, suspecting some treason on the part of the islanders, and stood on my guard and got out of the trap which they had led me, and asked them peremptorily by gestures where I could find some good water. Then they argued among themselves and gestured to me to follow them. They rowed eastwards past a high mountain whose foot is lapped by the sea water for more than 2 musket shots but nevertheless tree-covered.[1] I decided to follow them. I left an archipelago of islands and islets to larboard. After about one and $\frac{1}{2}$ leagues all the canoes struck out ahead and went ashore in several places. I continued on my route. I could no longer see the ship, I was over 4 leagues away from it. This did not stop me from making for the shore and hauling close in. There was a large tree whose branches overhung the water; this is where I remained, holding a branch to prevent my boat from drifting athwart the shore. I had the other boat tied up behind mine. The shore was steep with 5 feet of water. When I arrived I saw a few of our natives.

[1] This would suggest that Labé made for Barola Island and landed on its northern peninsula, then rowed east past Mt Sears (914 ft), a distance of ten miles or so from the ship. The suggestion of islets to starboard and the mention of a 'forest' confirms that the ensuing affray took place on the northern shore of Barola Island. Labé's first attempt to obtain water may not have been the trap he calls it – the native they had befriended led the French to a stream, too shallow admittedly to fill their water casks, but probably adequate for small containers – the size of the barrels was quite outside the Solomonese's ordinary experience. It should be borne in mind that this account was written after the attack and is coloured by Labé's reaction to it.

They made signs telling me to enter the forest [and] that I would find water. They were expecting me to abandon the boats, but I took good care to do nothing of the kind. For the time being I sent the sergeant to investigate with 2 armed soldiers and 2 sailors with their swords to look for water. Meanwhile I kept the natives in check who were all staying on shore although with their weapons. Our people were a long time and in their absence the natives tried to take hold of the painter of my boat to bring it nearer land. I could see their evil design which made me stay on my guard and prepare to give them a good reception if they wanted to attack me. During this same time a strong storm blew up which gave a lot of rain causing me to feel anxious about our arms which I nevertheless protected from the rain. It lasted a good quarter of an hour.

Seeing this I called our men who had gone searching. They arrived exhausted, bringing two buckets full of rainwater which they had obtained from a kind of hole.

As I was getting our soldiers back in the boats, the sergeant fell in the water from weariness. I was in the bow of the boat, cursing at this man to get him to come out of the water. He was hardly in when I saw upwards of two hundred and fifty natives coming out of the forest, armed with areca wood lances 7 or 8 feet long, bamboo arrows tipped with very fine bone, others with very heavy wooden swords – they are a kind of club – and the others armed with stones, and many carried hand guards or shields to guard themselves from blows, [they] ran at us like tigers. My sergeant was mortally wounded with a lance thrust into his body, six inches of which remained in his back, one soldier was knocked down and fell in the water, he received several lance blows on his clothing, another a vicious club blow on the head which cut his hat and split his head open down to the bone, one sailor received a lance thrust in the shoulder four inches deep; for my part I received two lance thrusts on the right and the left of the parts below the groin, one of the points remained in the flesh at a depth of more than $1\frac{1}{2}$ inches, [and] I received several others in my clothes. All this was done in a flash. I replied with a volley of musketry which killed a large number.[1] In spite of this they were even more determined. The other boat I had got to tie up behind mine seeing one or two canoes rowing away as fast as they could made for them without my noticing it, which meant I was left alone fighting this multitude of savages. I would have been

---

[1] The number of dead, in excess of forty, shows that Labé was attacked by a considerable crowd and that the natives, unaware of the firearms, were close together along the shore.

overwhelmed if I had not noticed that their chief was standing some distance from the combatants and raising his hands to heaven and striking his chest and then raising his voice while looking towards his people, which must surely have encouraged them.[1] This made me decide to fire a musket towards him and kill him. At that moment I received a blow from a club on my left knee and saw the savages fleeing into the forest carrying away several dead and wounded on their shoulders. Seeing myself free and master of the battlefield, I left the shore and went towards our other boat and beckoned to them to come to where I was, which they did. I asked why they had left me; they said they had chased two canoes and killed 5 or 6 savages. I ordered them to come with me and went to the spot where the battle had taken place. I had a volley of musketry fired at the forest for fear the savages might be lying in ambush there. I then landed and found about 36 or 40 men lying dead on the spot. I took all their weapons and their fleet which I broke up except for a small canoe which I took to the ship. There were 15 or 20 coconut trees in this little bay laden with coconuts. All around this place one saw nothing but blood. In truth the affray had been very sharp. I had 5 wounded and several others were struck by stones. No one was wounded in the other boat. I was forgetting to mention that during this battle the savages were holding on to the boat and endeavouring to haul it ashore. I had almost no munitions left. I asked young Mr Surville whether he had much left,[2] he told me everything was used up, but I discovered that their powder had become wet during that heavy rain, which made me decide to return to the ship and not stay to take the coconuts from the 15 or 20 coconut trees. I merely towed one of the canoes behind my boat and some 30 arrows, some lances, clubs and other trashy items.

After breaking up some 15 of their canoes large and small I came back sounding as I had done on the way out. I have shown all the soundings on the chart of the said Port Praslin. And after covering about 2 leagues I caught sight of our ship and 1 hour later saw a dinghy ashore

[1] The Spanish had a similar experience: 'The General went towards one part of the village with most of our people...with determination of seizing food on account of our great need of it. And the Indians, seeing that we were determined, and that we were approaching the village from two sides, began to make a disturbance, and went to arms, making signs to us to re-embark. They held a meeting among themselves in a hollow...and I and they all saw one of the chiefs making exorcisms and incantations to the Devil'. From the 'Narrative of Gallego' in Hackney and Thomson, *The Discovery of the Solomon Islands*, p. 56.

[2] Thus indirectly we learn that the impetuous youth was the officer responsible for abandoning Labé and acting independently early in the affray. Possibly it was from this incident that relations worsened between them, becoming intolerable later in Peru.

within gunshot of the ship. I went to where it was. I landed, being in great pain from my wounds, and found the captain, Mr. Surville, who had gone hunting and had taken the seine to fish with but he had been unable to use it because the bottom was full of rocks and corals. I made a report to him on everything that had happened to me among these treacherous savages. He wasted no time. We placed the wounded in the dinghy to take them on board and dress their wounds. Mr Surville and I went to the ship in the large boats and the hunt was over. We took also with us the natives' small canoe; it was still full of blood.

When Captain Surville was on board he saw several canoes on the right-hand side of the port entrance and 5 or 6 savages on the shore. With no further need to treat traitors with consideration, after their treacherous behaviour towards me, he had the two large boats manned, refusing flatly to let me join him, telling me I was to get my wounds attended to – I was indeed in a bad way, my thighs and my legs were swollen and I was exhausted on account of my wounds. Consequently Mr Surville got into the boats with his nephew. The natives, seeing people were heading towards them, got back into their canoes and started to paddle quickly to pass over a reef on the starboard side of the port entrance, feeling quite confident that our boats could not pass there. We fired a number of musket shots at them, seeing which the natives jumped into the sea and made for the forest, abandoning their canoe. We looked for them there, but did not find them. One of our boats grounded on the reef, but freed itself. Mr Surville took the canoe abandoned by the natives, as well as two others stranded at the place which these 5 or 6 men had fled from. Among these natives there were two women. We found several implements made of shells in the canoes, some coconuts, some water in bamboos and in coconuts, some lime for sprinkling on their hair, several clubs, some bows, their paddles or oars and some almonds[1] the taste of which was excellent.

At 5.30 p.m. we saw a canoe with two men in it ahead of the ship. It was allowing itself to drift towards the ship, but seeing it was hesitating to come near us, we devised a stratagem which proved most effective in getting them to approach. We sent two of our Malagasy in the small canoe I had captured. They removed all their clothes and generously sprinkled their wooly hair with powder to imitate the lime that the savages put on; they then started to go round the ship copying all the gestures they had seen done the day before by all the natives

[1] The *Canarium Commune* or kanari: '...in the Solomon Islands the seeds of various species of *Canarium*, known as *Nali*, are important native foods'. Merrill, *Plant Life of the Pacific World*, p. 187.

who had been in canoes around the ship. The trick worked. The two natives came closer to the ship. We had taken the precaution of readying one of our boats and had tied [it] alongside ready to give it a chase. At that moment we noticed that the canoe with the two savages showed some mistrust and was going away towards the shore on the starboard side of the entrance. We fired at once at them and the boat bore off and made for them. One of the two savages was killed, the other, terrified at seeing his comrade killed, fell in the sea and disappeared, decided to jump into the water in order to reach the shore. The boat and our canoe barred his way. As he was about to be caught, he dived several times. We caught him after much trouble. He was biting like a dog and kicked to defend himself and try to escape. He was taken on board. He stayed for a long time stretched out on the deck shamming death without opening his eyes and giving no sign of life. He is a lad of 13 or 14 years of age. He is not very black, but he has frizzy hair. We are confident that, as he is young, he will quickly learn French; we will then be able to obtain from him a deal of information on their customs and usages, what the country produces, if they visit neighbouring countries or are at war with them, what they do, etc. Let us return to our little savage. He was not wounded, but for fear he had swallowed some sea water we told the surgeon to give him a potion to clear him. We then noticed that he was opening his eyes and was not sick. We shackled his feet and placed him in the care of one of our sailors for fear that he might escape by throwing himself into the sea. At nightfall he started to look at everyone and ate some biscuit given to him by the sailors. Mr Surville intends to take particular care of him, so as to take him to France and present him to our Navy Ministers as a rarity, being a native of New Guinea and an inhabitant of the famous port to which we have just given the name of our Navy Minister – I mean Port Praslin,[1] Arsacide Coast. I had forgotten to say that, when I was attacked at the back of the harbour, one of our sailors dropped his sword in the water and another, in the bow, upon being wounded also let the boat hook drop in the water, without my knowing about it. Consequently they were lost.

When we went in the harbour we were hopeful of making use of the natives, at least as far as food supplies and trade were concerned, assuming the country produced metals or spices, but we were deluding ourselves. The country seems to be very ill favoured, the people are

---

[1] César-Gabriel Choiseul, duc de Praslin (1712–1785), Minister of Marine from 1766. He was an able minister during a period marked by general inefficiency. Bougainville named nearby Choiseul Island after him.

barbarians, all we can see are mountains covered in trees with marshes along the low lying parts although these are full of large trees. At high tide the sea rises to cover the ground to a depth of one foot. All I can see so far is quantities of building timber. We must live in the hope that ultimately we will find a remedy for our troubles. If it is not at Port Praslin it will be elsewhere. At least we must hope so.

Note: The kaffirs of Port Praslin have very little in the way of beards. They are like the Malays, with this difference that these natives have them woolly like their hair, like all kaffirs

Sunday 15th

We sighted two canoes ahead of the ship at 1 a.m. They came to within musket shot. Since we can no longer doubt their bad faith and it is impossible to win them over by gentleness as they are barbaric people, we felt it wise to keep them away from the neighbourhood of the ship so that we could look for water.

Consequently, in order to drive them off by fear we fired several shots when they were within reach. They fled with loud yells. I think several of their people were killed. We saw in the moonlight ten men in one canoe and two in the other. Before that the smaller canoe had made a wide circle and had landed in the island at the starboard entrance of the harbour. I think it had gone to fetch the men we forced to jump into the water and abandon their canoe last night.

Shortly before we fired on these two canoes the vessel had dragged without the wind being very strong, which forced us to lower a bower anchor. At 5 a.m. laid out a kedge anchor to the SE with 4 warps. As the bottom is poor, consisting of white shifting sand, we will be able to reach the channel by warping out should the ship drag once more. At 8.30 a strong northerly squall, heavy rain, little wind, it lasted a ½ hour.

At 10 a.m. we readied the three boats. In one went the captain, Messrs St Paul and Monneron, in the other, Mr Charanton, a ship's officer, and I in the other although my wounds were causing me some pain. We also took on 16 well armed soldiers and the young islander we had captured the previous afternoon, well tied up with a rope passed over and under his shoulders, taking every precautions to prevent him from escaping. We asked him with gestures where water could be found. He showed us the ESE to SE area which is an island and made us understand that we would find water there. Consequently we left and landed in a sandy cove lined with corals. Mr Charanton stayed on to guard the boats with 8 soldiers, and the others with the captain, Messrs St Paul and Monneron and I followed the little native whom we held on a leash. The entire seaward part of this wood consists of nothing but marshes caused by the sea which comes in with each tide. In the end this young man made us walk nearly a mile without finding any water, showing us that we had to go further. He was taking us round a kind of hillock of rock and earth also covered in trees, but we could still see the shore through the trees and were only more than half a carbine shot away. We were beginning to despair of finding the water and thought this young man was deceiving us. However it was then that one of our men on our right shouted that he could see some running water. We went to it and indeed we found two small brooks falling from a small height into two small basins. [We] at once had the basins dug and enlarged and cleaned, and [I] went with two armed men to mark out a path to the shore and the shortest, which I did as best I could. Mr Surville and our gentlemen as well as the soldiers came by the path I had made to join me on the shore. As we had covered a great deal of ground when were were looking for water we found ourselves quite a distance from our boats which were on the opposite side facing the harbour while we were on the other side of the said island facing north. There is a sand and coral bank north from us partly covered with large trees, further off is a fairly deep channel between the bank and the island on the larboard side of the entrance to the harbour which is the southern part of the said island,[1] further east a pass opens out to the sea, but full of breakers, further on again, still in the east, numerous islands become visible, tree covered, and passes also giving onto the open sea, but breakers appear on every side.

Returning to our little native or islander. While we were waiting for our boats, he had found some shells and had found a way to cut through two-thirds of the rope that tied him although it was made of 9 or 10 yarn spun rope. We tied him up again and watched him more closely for fear he escaped. Seeing this, he made a great noise, biting the sand and rolling everywhere. The captain threatened him, which caused him to shout like a madman. We gave him a few blows of a rope's end to quieten him, but without success. In the end, our boats having arrived, we sent him back to the ship with Mr Charanton. I

---

[1] This is a rather confused explanation, but from it one can deduce that the French landed on a low peninsula belonging to one of the islands on the eastern side of Port Praslin from where they were able to view the channels, islets and reefs which stretch along the north of Barola Island.

think this young man was afraid of being eaten by us, giving every sign [of] taking us for cannibals, which leads me to believe that they are themselves and eat all the prisoners they take in their wars.[1] When this islander found himself back in the boat he became a little reassured and seeing our men eating some biscuit he asked for some and ate it. Back on board he was kept under good guard.

The source we found is about three hundred fathoms from the shore. We got back in our boats to return on board. The channel between the island and the bank dried out at low tide and at high tide there must be 7 or 8 feet of water which is the rise of the tide during the spring tides. Before going on board we began to level the path to roll the barrels, there being brambles in the hollow places and other parts [being] waterlogged or marshy. This will make a good path fairly easy for rolling the filled barrels and carrying the firewood which we need as much as we do water. The little channel will be the most troublesome as we can only go on board at high tide as there is insufficient water.

Monday 16 October 1769

It was fine throughout the night. We went ashore this morning with our three boats with 15 soldiers to back the workers, [and] Messrs Surville and S. Paul and two junior officers and I to hasten the work and lead the boats. As soon as I landed I had the path leading to the watering place finished by levelling it and cutting trees to make rollers. We filled 20 water casks. When we were in our boats a heavy shower came on which without a doubt did a great deal of harm to all our sick, Malagasy and lascars, who had nearly all become swollen in the night. I am very much afraid that several may die on us. At high tide, that is at 5 p.m., we left for the ship, arriving 20 m[inutes] later, and all we left ashore was the stone on which they beat their washing.[2] We bring the cauldron back and take it back to land every morning. Nothing noteworthy happened on land except what is mentioned above.

[1] Cannibalism existed in the Solomons, but its extent is arguable (as against head-hunting, which was widespread). The killing and eating of prisoners for revenge was, however, quite common – and this explains the boy's immediate anxiety. 'Some people do eat human flesh, not, however, as a staple food, but in some cases just for variety, and in some cases for revenge. A very brave man who has killed many people may one day be killed by somebody in an ambush; then his body would be cooked and eaten as a revenge for their hatred of him, or to gain his strength.' G. Bogesi, 'Santa Isabel, Solomon Islands', *Oceania*, v. xviii, no. 3, p. 224.

[2] 'They' refers to the sailors, as the next sentence makes clear. Smooth stones for use as washboards are still found in French villages today. See also entry of 21 October.

Report by Mr Charanton, duty officer on board during our absence, on what happened, namely at 10 a.m. sighted three islanders or natives or kaffirs, such as they are, in the bay west of the ship.[1] They held a small stick with on it a small red rag by way of flag and were making various signals which he could not understand. Shortly after they were joined by 8 of their friends who were also emerging from the woods. At 11 a.m. he saw one of their boats coming from the far end of the harbour and going along the starboard or western side of the entrance and it came to join the blacks who were on the shore. They talked together for a time, then the canoe left for the island where we were getting the water. When he saw this he fired a gun loaded with a ball as they were out of reach of grape-shot. He fired with a double charge to sink them if he could and to warn us. The shot went very close to their canoe, which made them paddle faster and go north of the bank that forms the other side of the channel where we were getting our water. We sent our jolly boat to cut them off, but they went faster than us. The boat was forced to return after firing several musket shots within a full range without hurting them. During the squall we were in ashore at 3.30 or 4 o'clock the ship dragged, forcing Mr Charanton to lower the bower anchor, which is the 4th down; however there had been almost no wind since we are in the harbour; this dragging is due to the poor quality of the ground which consists of fine white sand. The anchors have almost no hold although the sea is like a pond. In the place where we get the water there are numerous timber-trees and cabbage palms. We are cutting down quite a number to obtain the cabbage which we give our men.[2] The water although not plentiful is very good. Oysters may be found along the seashore and among the mangroves, which is a great delicacy for our men who eat them and take them on board for their comrades. The seine cannot be used on account of the coral, although [there is] a great deal of fish.

Tuesday 17 October 1769

† At 4 this morning Pierre-Francois de la Ville, known as Achille,[3] sergeant of our detachment, died of the lance thrust he suffered on the 14th in the affray I was involved in with the islanders, as was indicated

---

[1] A bay is formed by Gagi Island and the starboard island on the western side of Port Praslin, but it is barred by a large coral reef.

[2] 'The *úbud* or palm cabbage is the tender growing part of the palm within the terminal crown of leaves. That of most species of palms is an excellent food, eaten either raw or cooked.' Merrill, *Plant Life of the Pacific World*, p. 183.   [3] See Muster Roll No 166.

in the previous entries. He was a native of the parish of S. Sulpice[1] in
Paris, and about 38 or 40 years of age. Our surgeon opened the body
and found the tip of the lance, 6 inches long, which penetrated the
backbone [and] into the stomach; this tip, which had broken off level
with the bone was so deeply imbedded that it could not be extracted
with pincers, the bones had to be broken to get it out. In the morning
we left with three boats and 20 barrels to obtain water, which we filled
and loaded in our boats. At 3 p.m. I had the sergeant fetched to bury
him. When he was in the grave the detachment which was ashore fired
a volley into the grave. I had it well dug so that the natives would
not find it after we left.[2] We returned to the ship at 5.30 p.m. the same
people except for one officer. They take take it in turns to watch over
them,[3] Messrs de Lormes and Charanton each with a junior officer with
them namely Messrs Surville the nephew and Lorris. I am very much
afraid that we may lose a number of our sick, having no sweet things
to give them and the country has none and the land where we are is
a marsh. There are numerous lorises, cockatoos,[4] wood pigeons[5] and
other types of birds I do not know. We killed a few of them as well
as some [?] which we use to make broth for our scurvy cases. That
is all we can give them with a few hens that are still left on board.
To all appearances we shall lose a great number of men. Fair weather
throughout the night and day, the winds NE to E light breeze.

Wednesday 18th

Left at daybreak with a good number of empty casks in the three
boats. We filled 40 casks and [brought back] some firewood which I
had cut for the ship. The natives are not to be seen, they leave us alone,
they have not forgotten the saraband I gave them on the 14th. I think

---

[1] St Sulpice, originally a dependency of the Abbey of St Germain-des-Prés, is situated
on the left bank district or 'Latin Quarter' of Paris. The parish was a fairly wealthy one
at the time; the great parish church would have hardly been completed when de la Ville
was born.
[2] 'He was buried at the place where the path leading to the watering place begins. He
is buried at the foot of a tree on which is written Mr Achil IHS'. Pottier, *Journal*, p. 130.
[3] This is a reference to the sick, 'the same people' as those who went ashore the previous
day.
[4] The Cardinal Lory (*Eos cardinalis* Gray) and the Coconut Lory (*Trichoglossus
haematodus*) are widespread in the entire Solomons. Mayr in *Birds of the Southwest Pacific*,
pp. 230–4, lists as found in Santa Isabel the Duchess Lorikeet (*Vini margarethae* Tristam),
a subspecie of the Pigmy Parrot (*Micropsitta finschii*) the White Cockatoo (*Cacatua ducorpsi*
Bonaparte), the subspecies *solomonensis* Rothschild and Hartert of the King Parrot (*Larius
roratus*), and the Song Parrot (*Geoffroyus heteroclitus*).
[5] 'The Solomon Islands are very rich in pigeons. Not only are they very numerous in
individuals, but they represented by no fewer than 20 species.' Mayr, ibid., p. 221. About
half of these are found in lowlands or coastal mangrove swamps.

too that this part of the country is sparsely populated and also the lack of boats prevents them from making any attempts as they lost in this affray all their boats and three others which they had abandoned and Mr Surville captured. Fair weather night and day, light easterly.

Thursday 19th

The winds still E to SE. Fair weather, light breeze. We went at dawn with the three boats to get water. We filled 60 casks with our boats making several journeys. As there was insufficient water in the little channel between the sandbank and the island where we get water, we took the boats round the other side of the bank and at 5 p.m. they came to the island for their last load and we went back to the ship at high tide.

Today a lascar named Faquirra,[1] aged 24, died of scurvy and was buried. My wound [caused by] one of the lance thrusts is inflamed and most painful as is the club blow I received below the knees. I hope it will be nothing.

Friday 20th

The wind SE to E, light breeze. We left at 3 a.m. with three boats and went to the other side of the bank, there being no water in the small channel, rolled all our empty casks ashore, and at 5 o'clock loaded the three boats which took the water to the ship and returned with the empty casks and on the rising tide entered the little channel where they loaded once more. In all filled 58 casks during the day and much firewood, lengths of 30 to 40 feet to [?] and several tree trunks to make pulleys. It was all taken on. Today one of our Malagasy[2] died of scurvy, aged about 30. I had him buried ashore. Before we left, Mr Surville wrote on a tall tree above the watering place 'the year one thousand seven hundred and sixty nine the ship St Jean-Baptiste arrived in this port and took possession of it on 13 October in the name of His Majesty the King of France.'[3] On another tree at the same place 'Captain

---

[1] More correctly Fakira. This name suggests that he was a Moslem Indian.

[2] A native of Madagascar, presumably one of the ship's slaves. Surville gives his name as Yondeva.

[3] Louis XV, who died in 1774. Pottier de L'Horme in his *Journal*, p. 144, mentions that he too carved two inscriptions, in broadly similar terms to Surville's, and that the Chaplain attempted a more ambitious inscription, in Latin, which he was forced to leave unfinished through lack of time, saying 'Let those whom the Fates choose to send here dwell in the good fortune of a moment of victory, just as here on the 13th day [of October] in the year 1769 a ship called and overcame through fear these people discovered to be treacherous.'

Surville took possession of this port and named [it] Praslin in the King's name.' On another tree still in the same place is written carved in the bark of a tree 'Beware of the people of this place' and below near the watering place 'Le St Jean-Baptiste'. After writing this we all embarked and went aboard. The ferociousness of the local inhabitants did not allow us to go far from the ship for fear of a surprise attack by the kaffirs or islanders, which prevented us from drawing a plan of this harbour which is very fine. It is formed by a number of islands and islets which form as many channels. The affair of the 14th in which I was involved did not allow us to enter these channels in our boats unless we were to go in a group, but water was our sole purpose. We hastened to leave the harbour, seeing that it is poor holding ground and if a sudden squall were to blow up one would inevitably be driven on the reef and one be very embarrassed there. I have drawn a sketch of the said harbour which is in the drawing book, all the distances being approximate as I have been unable to measure even one shoal. We filled altogether 196 casks of water, which was enough to fill the empty barrels in our hold and approximately one longboat full of firewood and some hundred palm cabbages. That is all we have been able to obtain.

We named all the lands we discovered from *Première Vue* Island, which are in New Guinea,[1] until today, Arsacides Land or Islands, derived from the name of assassins which is what all the people of this country are, considering their attack and treason of the 14th instant, when I was in charge of the two boats, as may be seen in the entry of the 14th.

Description of the harbour where we are, named Port Praslin by Mr Surville, situated in New Guinea in 7°26' of southern latitude,[2] land unknown until now, no traveller having found himself in this latitude in the eastern sector. The sketch of the harbour and its entrance is in the book of sketches. You can see from a distance a tall mountain[3] and below it an opening which seems to have breakers on all sides, but as you approach you notice a pass; on the eastern side you can see an opening quite near but with broken water everywhere; further east again another pass where there seems to be a pass.[4] All that is made up by a quantity of islands and islets which are not very high and edged,

---

[1] Labé remained persuaded that this was an eastern extension of New Guinea.
[2] The latitude given is exact: the entrance to Port Praslin is just south of 7°25'.
[3] Mt Sears, on Barola Island, which rises to 914 ft.
[4] There are passes both east and west of the entrance, formed by Marianne and de Surville islands and Gagi. They are obstructed by reefs and lined by mangrove swamps.

so far as I could see, by coral reefs. Over all these islands one can see a very high land which appears to be 3 leagues further inside the harbour and at the back the highest mountain on the western side.[1] You can see quantities of fairly low islands having the appearance of lowlands, all of them covered in trees; 6 or 7 leagues further west a low land formed by islands which seem to hold together and have the shape of a cayman, which is why we have given it this name. You can also see across it, further inland, some tall mountains but not so high as those at the back of the harbour. Several islets formed by islands are also visible where surely good harbours could be found to shelter ships.[2]

Let us speak of Port Praslin. The entrance is very narrow, formed by two islands which have each a long reef that stretches forward and leaves only a channel of about $\frac{1}{2}$ a cable's length. You cannot find bottom until you are inside, the first depth is 55 fathoms, small coral, then as you continue on your way in, when you have passed the two reefs 30 fathoms, shortly after, keeping to the middle of the harbour until you can see the two channels on the inner side of the islands, you find 22 to 20 fathoms, fine white sand, the ground does not hold well, then on the starboard side you have 18 [to] 12 fathoms, same ground, but one is very close to the reefs that line the shore. You can see several rock clusters visible under 6 to 14 feet of water. At the back of the harbour there are also numbers of rocks that never become uncovered, but you can see broken water over them. A channel leads to the back. However when rounding the large larboard island further in it is a mass of innumerable islands all wooded and reef-lined, at least all those I saw. I am the only one to have gone to the back for about $2\frac{1}{2}$ leagues and after that 2 l. and turning this large island and then close to the high mountain, which is where I had the trouble with the islanders.

I have seen no cultivated land anywhere along the harbour, nor houses, nor native villages. It seems that they are poor people living merely on fish, shells and a few roots.[3] They have some coconuts and arecas in the woods. The lad we captured made us understand by signs that there were some boars. The people are kaffirs, their hair [is] woolly

[1] Barola and Gagi islands are separated to the south by Popu Channel which would be invisible from the ship. Mt Sears was south-south-west from the anchorage; further to the south-west is Mt Beaumont, 955 ft.

[2] This assumption would be correct were it not for the presence of numerous reefs and shoals. Bates Island is a low elongated island some distance to the west of Port Praslin, and it can give the impression of a cayman; the mountains referred to could then be identified with Molakobi Island, inland from Bates Is. which rises to 355 ft.

[3] Most of the low offshore islets are uninhabited and the lack of habitations was not a correct indication of the natives' standard of living.

[and] black, some wear their hair rather long, their body [is] the colour of the Malabar people, with fairly good features, but others are like the kaffirs, thick lips, flat nose, a good black colour, a fierce look and [I] think they are cannibals.[1] As ornaments they have bracelets of shells, whole shells on their necks, their ears pierced with a large hole, some flowers in it as well as through the cartilage of the nose, others have belts of human teeth cut in half, they let us understand that these were the teeth of prisoners captured in their wars. They are quite naked except for a kind of bark which they beat so as to render it supple, which does not conceal their nudity. They put lime on their hair which it turns red, and from a distance it looks like a little cap worn on the head. Their weapons consist of a lance of areca wood 8 or 9 feet long, clubs 4 feet long, arrows 40 or 44 inches long made of reeds, the point of which is a bone 4 inches long which looks like a human bone; they have a shield 40 inches long and 10 or 11 wide made of rushes, bark and stakes. Some put white on their foreheads like the Malabars. Their tools consist of axes made of shells firmly fixed in a piece of wood, shells used as knives, fishbones for sawing and making holes; the fishhooks are made of tortoise shell. The country supplies a kind of almond[2] which tastes very good, of which there are several species. Their canoes are very light, the large one I was involved with was 65 feet long, the smaller ones 15 to 25 feet, with small oars or paddles. It is surprising with the tools at their disposal that they can make boats, they must take a great deal of time on making them and their weapons. Their clubs are made of very hard and heavy timber, 5 or 6 feet long, the larger end is somewhat flattened and $2\frac{1}{2}$ inches wide, both edges are sharp. It is with one of these weapons that they wounded one of our soldiers – his hat was cut on his head. The tip of the arrows and lances is very sharp and the very tip blackened, I think they are slightly poisonous. The islander we captured made us understand by signs how they use their weapons. He seems to be very intelligent and very skilful with sign language. His temples are shaven, he showed us it was done with a stone similar to our flintstones. They also use stones to light fires, I think they use them to cut trees. The seams of their boats are caulked with a kind of pitch. I omitted to say that the country produces figs and bananas.

[1] The distinction between lighter skinned ('the Malabar people') and darker skinned islanders ('kaffirs') suggests the Polynesian elements which were predominant in Ontong Java to the north and commonly found in parts of Santa Isabel.

[2] The almond nut, *nali* or *ngali*, played an important role in the life of the native. George Bogesi (op. cit., p. 221) states that the seasons were reckoned according to the state of the *ngali*, *Gano* being the time when it is mature, *Volthola* the time when it bears no fruit. Extensive rejoicing marked the harvesting of the nuts.

Saturday 21 October 1769

Departure for Port Praslin, coast of New Guinea, to continue our discoveries. At 6 a.m. the captain went in the boat to the watering place with a detachment of twelve soldiers to fetch the stone of our *messattes* or laundry-men which had been left behind last night. Returned on board at 7.30. The winds SSW good breeze. We started to cast off at 8.30, having four anchors down, two bower anchors, and two kedge. At midday fresh breeze, having raised two anchors, we passed a spring[1] over the smallest kedge anchor, that is on the cablet, brought the longboat above it and passed it behind on the starboard side to cast to port and thread the channel which is very narrow. At 1.30 p.m. on Saturday, our third anchor being weighed, we paid out the cable to the longboat and the ship at once swung on the stern anchor. Set the mizzen and fore topsails and sailed down the channel. At two we were out of the harbour and clear of all dangers. Lowered the yawl and sent it to assist with the raising of the kedge anchor and tow the longboat. Mr Delhorme was put in charge of this expedition, to protect the crew in case the islanders should attack them. We made several tacks while waiting for our boats which came up at 5 p.m. with the kedge anchor and the cablet and spring. Mr Delhorme reported that he saw no canoes or natives. We were hove to at 4.30 while waiting for our two boats and during that time we fastened our anchors in position and [?] the ship. Remained hove to until 9.30 p.m. when we finished hoisting in our 4 boats, lying to NE to ENE; then filled the sails and made way as is shown in the board for Sunday.

At 6 p.m. I sighted the entrance of Port Praslin bearing SW¼S3°S dist. about 5 leagues, the westernmost land having the appearance of islands W2°S, the easternmost SE¼E4°S. The weather is thick and the east and west are hazy. The high mountain which is a little to starboard of the harbour, which we are naming Mount Contradiction on account of the differing opinions of our gentlemen,[2] on the 12th of this month bore from me SW¼S1½°S distant 3 leagues — it is the only landmark to find the entrance of Port Praslin. This same mountain was in the same point of the compass on the 13th when we went in and it is the only thing we can see since the weather is thick I am drawing it here.[3] It

---

[1] A rope which is put out from the stern or side of the ship and made fast to the cable.
[2] Mount Contradiction, which is Mt Beaumont on Gagi Is., symbolizes the varying theories advanced by the officers on the identity of the land they had discovered and arguments on the existence and suitability of what they were to call Port Praslin. See on this Surville's Journal, entries of 9 to 11 October.
[3] There is a small sketch at the foot of the page.

may be compared with the seventh sketch of the coast, dated the 12th. At 6 p.m. the high mountain seen to the south of the port in the 7th sketch is no longer visible. †A Malagasy aged 28 died of scurvy. Thrown overboard at 3 p.m.[1]

Sunday 22nd

The winds SE, courses since 9.45 p.m. when I took my point of departure based on my dead reckoning of the 13th of this month, E¼NE3°E, distance 10½ leagues.

Latitude based on my reckoning of the 13th of this month 7°16′, observed S 7°13′, diff. N 3′, Est. longitude based on my reckoning of midday on the 13th 154°25′. We have not seen land since last night, which leads me to think the coast is running SE.

We are continuing to call the whole mainland and its islands Land of the Arsacides, derived from the word assassin, on account of the ferocity of these barbarians.

Monday 23 October 1769

At 10 a.m. a catamaran passed alongside. Mr Surville at once lowered the small boat we obtained at Bashi Island. I got into it and went after the catamaran and was back on board at 11.45. It is a catamaran made of banana-tree trunks with wash boards on each side made of fig trees and pieces of timber tied up with ivy; it had a few benches on it shaped like chairs. I brought it all aboard. It was given to the pigs. I was forgetting to add that there were 2 black stones in it the size of a fist. I think the said catamaran was set adrift by the land breeze. At 11.50 filled all the sails and hoisted in the small boat.

Courses ESE4°E, distance 8⅔ leagues. Lat. Est. S 7°21′. Long. Est. E 154°50′.

† During the night one of our kaffirs from Madagascar, a ship's slave, died of scurvy.

† At 7 this morning Pierre Rondelle, from the parish of Pleurtius, department of Dinant, died of scurvy, aged 36. Said the prayers and threw him overboard.[2]

---

[1] This was the second to die in two days.
[2] See Muster Roll, No 33.

Tuesday 24th

Fair weather, smooth sea, light breeze. Courses South, distance 6¼ leagues. Lat. S Est. 7°40', obs. 7°45', diff. S 5'. Long Est. E 154°50'.

Sighted land at 4 p.m. from SSE to SSW, higher than what we have seen so far. At sunset sighted land from the topmasts bearing SSE to SW. According to the latitude I observed at midday yesterday the land is starting to run SE. At 7 a.m. sighted land from S to SW¼S, very high. At 8 what seemed the most easterly bore S¼SE, the most westerly W¼SW. At midday the easternmost having the appearance of an island bore SE¼S 1°S, the nearest land SW, what seemed the westernmost W¼SW 1°S.

The weather is now very overcast, one cannot estimate the distance accurately – I reckon myself to be 7 or 8 leagues from the nearest land.

We are continuing to call all these islands on the continent we are hauling along the Arsacides, derived from Assassins, considering the ferocity of people in this region which is part of New Guinea where no other ship or traveller has ever been before us.

Wednesday 25 October 1769

Bad weather, squalls, rain and wind and strong gusts. Tacked variously. The winds E to ESE. Courses W, distance 1 league. Lat. S Est. 7°45', obs. 7°45'. Long. Est. 154°47'.

Bearings for these 24 hours. At 6 p.m. sighted land having the appearance of an island bearing SSE2°S dist. 8 to 9 leagues, the westernmost land SW¼W. At 7 a.m. sighted land form S to WSW. At 9 o'clock saw what looked like an island last night, it bore SE¼S dist. about 9 leagues. According to the bearings we seem to have lost ground during the night. At midday overcast weather. We can see high land from the topmasts from S to SW¼W without being able to distinguish any details.

† Yesterday at 2 p.m. Francois Cagnard, a married man residing in Lorient,[1] died of scurvy after being sick for 2 months.

The dead men's belongings are inventorized and sold on the very day of their death.

[1] See Muster Roll, No 22.

Thursday 26th

During the night when we received a squall sailed as in the margin under various sails according to the strength of the wind. From 8 till midday fairly good weather, high seas. Courses E¼NE4°E, distance 19⅔ leagues. Lat. S Est. 7°46', obs. 7°38', diff. N 8'. Long. Est. 155°45'.

Bearings for the 24 hours. At 5.30 p.m. what seems to be most easterly bears S5°E, dist. 8 to 9 leagues, the most westerly, cloud covered, SW¼S. At dawn and at 8 no land. At midday discovered a small island flat [in] its eastern part and [it] may be 1½ leagues from E to W, at least 10 leagues from any land. We named it Unexpected Island.[1] We also saw some high land very distant in the south. The island bore SE¼S2°E, distant 7 leagues. Its shape is shown below.[2] According to the opinion of all our gentlemen, we are agreed that the whole continent we have seen is nothing but a mass of islands bordered with small ones which make up this part of New Guinea. Mr Surville has called all the continent or islands Arsacides Land on account of the ferocity of their inhabitants. The midday land, the high one still forms part of the mainland, it now trends SE¼E. I hope it will soon come to an end in the south. Our crew is becoming impatient at the sight of all this land and seem to be very worried; I do not know why; I presume it is because they see part of the crew attacked by scurvy and we find nothing in this country to relieve them.

Friday 27 October 1769

The winds N¼NW to NE, light breeze, stormy weather, steered as shown in the margin.

Courses SE3°E, distance 20⅔ leagues. Lat. S Est. 8°6', obs. 8°20', diff. S 14'. Long. Est. 156°31'.

Bearings for the 24 hours and comments. At 2 p.m. the flat island sighted yesterday afternoon bore S distant about 4½ leagues. This island has been called Unexpected Island. We can see a high mountain in the distance.[3] The furthest east bore S¼SE in the distance more than 15 leagues. At sunset the easternmost of Unexpected Island bears SW¼S2°S, its westernmost SW¼W2°S distant 5 leagues, a high land which I take for an island S¼SE5°E, its westernmost point S¼SW distant 12 to 15 leagues. No other land is visible. This land and these islands trend SE¼E

[1] Gower Island, discovered by Carteret in 1767, or Ndai.
[2] A sketch of Gower Island is drawn at the foot of the entry.
[3] This would be a view of Malaita.

and SE. At dawn saw another land which I take to be a large island, its easternmost bore S¼SE to S, its westernmost SW, very high land and all wooded.[1]

At midday the easternmost of this same land or large island bore S¼SW5°W, its westernmost is hidden in haze. It is the highest land we have seen. I think I am 16 or 18 leagues from it.

† During the night a black, a Malagasy, died of scurvy. Aged 28 to 30, a ship's slave. Thrown overboard two hours later.

Saturday 28th

Overcast and almost continual rain. Courses ESE, distance 5½ leagues. Lat. S Est. 8°26′. Long. Est. 156°46′.

Bearings for the 24 hours and comments. At sunset the point which bore S¼SW5°W at midday bears SW¼W1°S. The W side of this island is lost in clouds, one can see it only as far as W¼SW. The eastern most are visible only in the south. The horizon is so cloudy we can see no headlands.

† During the night Julian Hervé, a sailor from St Malo, district of Dinant, died of scurvy.[2] †In the morning two men died of scurvy, one a Moorish lascar and one a Malagasy, ship's slave.

As the whole crew is attacked by scurvy we brought out today some Portuguese wine from the cargo in the hold, 10 barrels, to give one ration of wine daily to the crew to try and restore them. It is to be feared that this illness will not allow us to continue our discoveries as far as we hoped, seeing that we can refresh our crew nowhere among people as barbaric as those of this country are according to our experience of the 14th instant.

Sunday 29 October 1769

Winds NE¼E to ESE. Courses SSE, distance 10⅔ leagues. Lat. S Est. 8°48′, obs. 8°56′, diff. S 8′. Long. Est. 156°58′.

Bearings for the 24 hours and comments. At 3 p.m. we saw land, very high, from SSW to W distant 12 leagues. At 5 the easternmost land bore S, 10 leagues, the westernmost W in the distance, a wide opening W¼SW3°W, another more southerly SW¼W3°W. I think there must be some very good harbours in these openings. At sunrise the

---

[1] This is the same island, Malaita, as seen on the previous day. In the centre of Malaita Mt Kolovrat rises to 4275 ft. [2] See Muster Roll, No 159.

opening we could see last night W¼SW3°W bears W 5°S and the other WSW2°S, what I can see furthest north W¼NW – there the land is lost in clouds – the furthest south or east S¼SW. All this land is prodigiously high. At 8 overcast weather, we could not see the land. At midday the most S land bore SSE3°S 12 to 15 l., a wide opening S¼SW2°S 8 or 9 leagues, another SSW3°S 7 leagues, one W 3°S, that is the one sighted this morning in WSW 2°S, what bore W5°S now bears W¼NW distant 7 leagues, the northernmost land NW¼W5°W in the distance. † This morning three men died, a tall Moorish Taudel and two Malagasy ship's slaves, all three from scurvy.

The coast, according to our route and the observed latitudes, is now running SSE.

Monday 30 October 1769

Courses SE5°E, distance 12 leagues. Lat. S Est. 9°1', obs. 9°19', diff. S 18'. Long. 157°26'.

Bearings for the 24 hours and comments. At 6 p.m. the southernmost land bore SSE dist. 12 to 15 leagues, another point where a bay or opening appears bears S¼SW, the nearest land which is very tall mountains WSW3°S 6 or 7 leagues, another opening W2°N is the one that bore W3°S at miday, another that bore W¼NW bears W¼NW3°N 7 leagues, the northernmost land NW¼W3°W 12 leagues. At 6 a.m. sighted an island out at sea which we are calling Contrariety Island[1] bearing SE¼S3°S distant 8 leagues, the southernmost land SSW3°S 9 or 10 leagues, an opening SW5°S 8 l., another formed by two islands W3°N, the northernmost land having the appearance of an island W¼NW2°N 12 to 15 leagues. At 8 a.m. same bearings as at 6. At midday Contrariety Island bore through its centre SSE 7 leagues, the southernmost land SSW2°W 9 leagues, the bay between two small islands WSW3°S 8 leagues, another W¼SW3°W 9 leagues, the northernmost land W¼NW4°N distant 12 to 15 leagues. The whole of this coast is very high. Several fine openings are visible. I have no doubt that there are some good harbours or straits opening out into the sea west of New Guinea. The entire coast along which we have sailed is very high and wooded with tall trees. The coast ends at present in the SSE and S¼SE. The island we named Contrariety is slightly elevated. Numerous trees appear along the shore and almost none in the centre of the island. Although distant it seems to be 3½ leagues across its widest part; we shall verify it when we are close to it.

---

[1] *Contrariété* is Ulawa, a medium-size island east of Malaita's southern cape.

We are in unhealthy latitudes. Very frequent calms, numerous storms, rain at night. The crew are in desperate straits. They are almost all sick and attacked by scurvy. We have no fresh food to give them to relieve them.

Tuesday 31 October 1769

Almost calm. Courses E$\frac{1}{4}$NE, distance 3$\frac{1}{2}$ leagues. Lat. S Est. 9°31', obs. 9°17', difference N 14'. Long. 157°36'.

† At 4 p.m. yesterday Faquier Mamot died, a Moor, chief sailmaker, aged about 60, a native of Pondicherry.[1]

Bearings for the 24 hours and comments. At 6 p.m. sighted the centre of Contrariety Island bearing S$\frac{1}{4}$SE 2°S distant 9 leagues, the most southerly land SW$\frac{1}{4}$S dist. 12 to 15 leagues, a kind of bay or opening furthest south SW$\frac{1}{4}$W 4°S, the second one further north SW$\frac{1}{4}$W, the 3rd ditto WSW 3°S, the northernmost land is lost in the clouds, it is visible only as far as W$\frac{1}{4}$SW. At 6 a.m. Contrariety Island bore S4°E distant 10 leagues, the southernmost land forming a headland bears SW, a low land, a tall mountain which is the northernmost land bears NW 4°W distant 15 to 18 leagues. At midday sighted Contrariety Island bearing S5°E distant about 9 leagues, the southernmost land bears SW 3°S distant 15 leagues the northernmost W$\frac{1}{4}$NW 2°W distant 18 leagues. All this land is very high. I still think that this land of New Guinea or Arsacides that we see is nothing but a mass of great islands bordered by other islands which form channels or passes inside which one can anchor, and possibly some straits which cross towards the west of New Guinea or Concord.[2] The whole coast is wooded, one can see fires at intervals, which proves there are numerous inhabitants, like Contrariety Island where one can see many fires. We named it thus through being set back by all the calms and rain storms, all this for several days. This island seems to be about 12 or 13 leagues from the mainland or mass of islands. We are continuing to call all this land Arsacides Islands. It is now running south.

Wednesday 1 November 1769

Fine weather, almost calm. Courses SE 3°S, distance 3$\frac{1}{4}$ leagues. Lat. S Est. 9°24', obs. 9°24'. Long. 157°42'.

[1] Or Fakira Mahmud.
[2] Eendracht Land, a name given in early Dutch charts to the west coast of Australia, after Dirck Hartog's ship *Eendracht* (meaning Concord) which sailed there in 1616.

Bearings for the 24 hours and comments. At sunset Contrariety Island bore S¼SE3°E distant 8 leagues, the southernmost of the other land which is the mainland or mass of islands SW¼S3°S very distant, the opening I saw last time to the SW¼S bears now WSW2°S, the 2nd trending north WSW 5°S, the 3rd W¼SW2°W, the northernmost land being a large peak-shaped mountain W¼NW in the distance.

At sunrise Contrariety Island bore SE¼S 4°S dist. 7 leagues, the southernmost of the other land SSW1°S dist. 8 l., the southernmost opening SW 5°W, the 2nd trending north WSW4°S. We no longer see the third. A large mountain which is the most northerly land W¼NW. At 11 a.m. we saw 3 small boats coming from the 1st opening and they came towards us. This coast seems to be well inhabited, more so that Port Praslin judging by the number of fires we can see all along the coast and many clearings that are plantations. At midday the land was hazy, which means there were no bearings.

† During the night Jean Filatre died of scurvy,[1] a sailor from Dinant district of St Malo, aged about 32.

Thursday 2 November 1769

Continuing light breeze, fair weather, smooth sea. At 1 p.m. yesterday the three canoes were within hailing distance of the ship. They are 8 in one and four in each of the others, making 16 in all 3. They are like the men of Port Praslin and their boats are a little more decorated. Their weapons are the same, arrows and lances. The islanders are also kaffirs [with] woolly hair and the same ornaments or bracelets. They are suspicious and were not prepared to come aboard. They came astern and showed us necklaces which looked like threaded teeth and a few corals cut in the shape of pearls. We displayed the flag as a sign of friendship as well as a little white flag at the end of a cane in the gallery. We threw them an empty bottle and a necklace of mock garnets tied to a piece of wood. They picked them up from the water without paying much attention to them. The young kaffir we caught in Port Praslin gestured to them to come aboard, but they were unwilling. He does not understand their language.

After staying 1½ hours looking at us, these three small boats decided to go to the mainland from which they had come.

Meanwhile we made several tacks to approach Contrariety Island. Several canoes came out from the said island at 8 a.m., turning around

[1] See Muster Roll, No. 36.

the ship but not coming close. Course S¼SE2°E, distance 8⅓ leagues. Lat S Est. 9°31′, obs. 9°44′, diff. S 13′. Long. Est. 157°48′.

Bearings for the 24 hours and comments or instructions. At 5 p.m. Contrariety Island bore SE¼E2°E dist. 9 leagues, the land that was the most southerly at midday S¼SW5°W 9 l., some other land appearing in the south S 5°W on the horizon, a headland W¼NW4°N, the northernmost land lost in the clouds WNW. At sunrise sighted the northernmost point of Contrariety Island bearing E¼SE1°S 5 leagues, its southernmost SE¼S5°E, the point that bore S¼SW5°W last night bears WSW4°W 9 leagues. At 8 a.m. the southernmost of Contrariety Island bears ESE, its northernmost NE¼E3°E, the point that bore WSW4°W this morning bears W distant 7 leagues, some high land on the horizon looking like a high island, bears, its southernmost part SSE5°S, its northernmost S¼SW. At midday the southernmost of Contrariety Island bears SE 5 l., its northernmost ENE4°N 3 to 4 l., the nearest part of the island, which is its middle, distant 2 leagues, the land which seems the most southerly SW¼S, it still looks to me like islands; the point that bore W at 8 o'clock bears W3°S 12 to 15 leagues. [This] is the last of the mainland, that bears SW¼S.[1]

Friday 3rd

Squally weather, rain and wind, altered course several times to approach Contrariety Island and three other islands we are discovering in the S¼SE so as to turn them.[2] The winds as shown in the margin. At midday yesterday some of the kaffirs from Contrariety Island who were following us in their canoes appeared under the gallery. We gave them a loaf and some other things. They ate the former with avidity, then they tried to climb aboard and seeing that they were coming without their weapons we let them come up, 12 to 15 of them. Their canoes were standing off. The younger islander we captured in Port Praslin certainly cannot understand their language and is very fearful of them, telling us by signs that he is afraid they may crack his head open, which forces him to remain within the shelter of the Captain's arms, whom he has asked for a bow and arrows to shoot at them, making us understand that he would kill several. Let us now return to the kaffirs who had climbed aboard. They are very strongly built,

[1] By the mainland, Labé means Malaita. The French could now see in the distance San Cristóbal, which they could only identify at this stage as islands.
[2] The Olau Malau group, consisting of Aliiti, Malaulalo and Malaupaina, which Surville was to name The Three Sisters.

5 to 5 foot 6 tall, a moderate height rather like those of Port Praslin, with woolly hair, reddened in some cases by the lime they put on it. They go about naked, not even covering the natural parts which all the various savages in the world cover up. They are great thieves, eager to see everything and take what they see without hiding themselves in the least. One of their chiefs who seemed to wield some authority over the others was the first one on board. He climbed at once to the mizzen top at an incredible speed and made some signs to his people. Then he came down. The Captain gave him a length of blue cloth and a knife. He picked up several things we took back from him; he did not appear embarrassed, but rather bold, covered with bracelets and necklaces around his neck, made of coral shaped like pearls, some mother-of-pearl shells 4 inches long, flat and quite attractive. He wore a small tuft of plants – I mean leaves – in his ears, smelling like cloves, and several other plants like basils and others with a scent like leaves of the European figtree. Their boats are better built than those of Port Praslin, provided like them with 12-foot lances, arrows and clubs. The chief and several others wear around the foreskin an orchid[1] leaf which projects 6 *lignes*[2] beyond the member in the shape of a small tube, touching it continually by which he speaks to his men.

At 2 o'clock one of them, having stolen a flask from the pantry and seeing we wanted to take it from him, jumped overboard with it and returned to his boat, showing his theft to his comrades. Those who were still on board spoke to those in the canoes and a moment later not one remained on board. Their canoes left us and went back to the shore, except for 4 that stayed between land and the vessel, watching our actions. I forgot to say that the chief is not a kaffir, his features are attractive, [he] is a handsome man, with hair like ours. At 2.30 we made for the land. At three o'clock took in the lower sails and lowered the jolly boat. At 3.45 Mr Surville sent me with a small detachment of five soldiers and a corporal to take soundings ahead of the ship and seek an anchorage in Contrariety Island. At 4.30 four canoes came up which tried to surround me. I noticed in time that one of the islanders, the nearest, was taking aim at me with his bow and was about to shoot an arrow. I fired at once at them, one was hit and several bullets struck the canoe. If the sea had not been choppy they would certainly have all been killed. While they were thus in disorder I tried to speed towards

---

[1] Doubtful rendering.
[2] A *ligne* was slightly more than one-twelfth of an inch. This suggests a protrusion of half to three-quarters of an inch.

them, but in vain; I stayed behind them, the ship fired two shots at them but without hitting them. She has also lowered the flag to half-mast, which did not prevent me from speeding towards them, but falling further behind I returned to the ship at 4.45. At 5 hoisted the boat in and put about. At 6 p.m. about 20 canoes gathered near, armed and challenging us as they came up. We fired four case shots at their feet. We did them no great harm, however one was killed whom we saw falling in the water. They did not wait for any more and sped towards their Contrariety Island. From that time, squalls, a little rain. Courses SE$\frac{1}{4}$S5°S, distance 11 leagues. Lat. S Est. 10°13′, obs. 10°09′, diff. N 4′. Long. Est. 158°04′. I was omitting to say that the man who seemed to be the chief seeing when he was on the poop the flag on the ensign staff hauled it down and I think he would have taken it and thrown it into the sea if we had not noticed it and had gone to get it from him and raised it without delay.

Bearings for the 24 hours and notes on the said land and islands. At 5.30 p.m. sighted the southernmost point of Contrariety Island bearing E$\frac{1}{4}$SE3°S [dist.] 2 l., the northernmost point N 3°E. At 6 the southernmost and westernmost part of the mainland bore W$\frac{1}{4}$NW 10 to 11 leagues, some islands appearing ahead of us S$\frac{1}{4}$SE. At 10.30 p.m. sighted an island fairly close to us bearing S$\frac{1}{4}$SE and SSE. At 11 changed course, being unable to weather it. At 2.30 a.m. tacked to run for the island. At 6 a.m. the northernmost part of Contrariety Island bore N4°W dist. 9 or 10 leagues. We sighted three islands,[1] last night's being one of them, and sighted the southernmost of the 3 bearing S$\frac{1}{4}$SE4°E distant 5 leagues, the middle of the 2nd S 3°W about 4 leagues, the third, the nearest to us, SSW dist. 2$\frac{1}{2}$ leagues. They seemed to be wooded with beaches along the shore. These three islands cover a length of about 4$\frac{1}{2}$ leagues, so that each is about one league long; however the most S and E is larger than the other two. They are fairly low, but high enough to be seen 8 leagues away. There is a good distance separating them and the entrance pass seems very fair. No shallows or breakers are visible. We named these three islands The Three Sisters on account of the resemblance, one of them, the southernmost being a little larger. The three seemed to me to run SE$\frac{1}{4}$E and NW$\frac{1}{4}$W. At the same moment a point of the main land bore SW$\frac{1}{4}$W5°S. At 8 a.m. the southernmost of The Three Sisters bore S2°E, the middle of the 2nd S$\frac{1}{4}$SW 3°S, middle of the 3rd SSW dist. 4$\frac{1}{2}$ l., the westernmost of Contrariety Island NNW 2°N, its northernmost N$\frac{1}{4}$NW2°N distant 9 l. The point that

[1] Already sighted on the 2nd, this is the Olau Malau group, or Three Sisters.

bore SW¼W5°S at 6 is no longer visible. At midday the southernmost of the three islands or Three Sisters bore S, its northernmost S¼SW dist. 4 l., the southernmost of the 2nd SW¼S5°S, its northernmost SW2°S 3 leagues, the southernmost of the 3rd WSW2½°S, its northernmost W¼SW1°W.

I omitted to say that Contrariety Island seems to be about 3½ leagues in length, well wooded, quite high,[1] the shore defended by high rocks in the shape of a breakwater, but a natural one, and above some plantations of coconut trees, but numbers of them in the slopes and in the valleys, and many areas of cleared land. This island is clear with no sign of breakers, but I could find no ground ½ league from the shore with a 45-fathom line. The south of the island is lowlying, the rest is very high. It may be seen from 12 or 13 leagues off.

Saturday 4 November 1769

Squally weather, light rain, strong squalls, changed courses several times on account of the islands we could not weather. Courses S¼SE3°S, distance 5 leagues. Lat. S Est. 10°24′, obs. (doubtful) 10°21′, diff. N 3′. Long. Est. 158°06′.

Bearings for the 24 hours and notes. At 2 p.m. Contrariety Island bore from us NW¼N3°N dist. about 11 to 12 leagues, the southernmost of the 3 Sisters S¼SW2°W dist. 8 to 9 leagues, the 2nd SSW4°W 6 to 7 leagues, the 3rd SW3°S 6 leagues.

At 6 p.m. the southernmost of the Three Sisters SSW 2°W 4 leagues, the southernmost point of the 2nd island W¼SW5°S 5 leagues, the southernmost point of the 3rd W¼NW1°W 5 or 6 leagues, its northernmost [point] WNW2°W. At 7 p.m. we were due east of the southernmost point of the most southerly of the 3 Sisters, a short distance away. At 10 p.m. saw a fire in the S¼SW very distant. Shortly after this we altered course on the starboard tack and ranged along to windward of the most southerly of the Three Sisters at a distance of about 2 l.; at 4.30 a.m. altered to the larboard tack. At sunrise the southernmost point of the most southerly and easterly of the Three Sisters [bore] S¼SW5°W and its easternmost point SW¼S4°W 4 leagues, the 2nd island SW¼W5°W 4 leagues, the 3rd which is the most westerly W3°S dist. about 5½ l.

At 7.25 we were due east of the northern point of the most southerly and easterly of the Three Sisters Islands. At 8 a.m. the southernmost

---

[1] Ulawa rises to 1200 ft.

of the most southerly and easterly of the 3 Sisters bore WSW4°W dist. $1\frac{1}{2}$ l., its northernmost point WNW2°N $2\frac{1}{4}$ l., the middle of the 2nd island NW$\frac{1}{4}$W3°N about $3\frac{1}{2}$ l., the centre of the 3rd island NW about 5 or 6 leagues; at 8.10 we were due east of the northern point of the most southerly and easterly of the Three Sisters. At 8.30 the three islands merged together by their adjoining headlands, the southernmost of the 1st bearing W$\frac{1}{4}$NW3°N and the northernmost of the 3rd NNW.

From 8 to 9 o'clock we see some very high land from WSW to SE$\frac{1}{4}$S at a distance of 8 leagues. At 9.30 the Three Sisters together bear NW$\frac{1}{4}$N3°N dist. about 6 leagues, always from the southernmost one; the other land bears SE3°S dist. about 8 leagues. At midday the most southerly of the Three Sisters bears NNW 8 leagues; it hides the other two islands. The most southerly headland of the high land ahead of us bears SE dist. 5 to 6 leagues, another land stretches out to the N$\frac{1}{4}$NW.[1]

Notes on the Three Sisters. From the southernmost to the large cape that bore SE at midday there is a distance of about 14 leagues. From this large cape the land trends WNW and NW as far as the eye can see. All this land is very high, covered in trees. One cannot find bottom quite close inshore; there are breakers only on the shore. One can see some fine sandy beaches within the shelter of this large cape.[2] There are signs that NW of this cape there is a gulf and [?] outside the Three Sisters and Contrariety Islands because when we were athwart the above mentioned 4 islands we could see no land. Athwart Contrariety we could see land to the west and WSW in the distance, then it was not seen again. From the large headland sighted at midday the coast trends NW and NW$\frac{1}{4}$W. It is the continent once more. We can see also a 4th island very low between this high land and the most southerly of the Three Sisters;[3] it seemed to be distant 4 to 5 miles. I was forgetting to say that at 11 a.m. three small canoes came to within a short distance from the ship with 4 men with their lances in each. They had come from the high land, a little to the north of the large headland where the beach is splendid. They gestured, pointing to the shore. They are kaffirs with woolly hair and go about quite naked, their parts even are not concealed. They are of average height, 5 to 5 ft 6 inches high. Their country looks charming, we can smell aromatic odours. It is a pity that such a fine country should be inhabited by such barbaric

[1] A distant view of Ulawa.
[2] Labé is referring to Wanoni Bay within the shelter of Kahua Point. The coast then trends in a north-westerly direction as far as Cape Recherche. The gulf to which he refers is the strait separating Malaita from San Cristóbal.
[3] Ugi Island off San Cristóbal.

people, which means we cannot obtain anything in the way of food and to relieve our men who are almost all sick of the scurvy.

† This morning one of our Malagasy kaffirs, a ship's slave, aged 25 to 26, died of scurvy.

Sunday 5 November 1769

Almost constantly squalls, rain and wind, and calms in between. We were followed by several canoes during the afternoon, which then went back to the shore. They would not come aboard. We tacked to weather the large headland, but without success, the sea being very heavy and the winds contrary as is shown in the board. This headland seems to mark the end of the gulf. It is the one that bore SE at midday. At 5.30 p.m. being on the larboard tack a squall blew up from NNE to NE¼N which could have made us turn the cape but it suddenly fell dead calm; the sea was preventing us from making headway and was bearing us towards the land from which we were only a mile away. We sounded several times with 60 fathoms of cable without finding bottom. As the ship could not tack with a head wind we tacked wind astern and waited a long time before we could switch tacks owing to the calms and the high seas. All this brought us a little nearer to land but thanks to a light NE¼E and NE breeze, stemming north to NW on the starboard tack, and to the current which was bearing us towards the SE [?], at 6 p.m. the headland which seems the most easterly bore SE1°E about 1 league, the point of a small bay formed by the headland[1] SSW5°W ½ league, another which with the SSW 5°W point forms a fairly pleasant bay W¼SW3°W,[2] another point W 3°S 6 to 7 leagues. The most westerly in sight bears W5°N, the southernmost point of an island that has been named Three Sisters Gulf Island[3] W¼N4°N 7 to 8 leagues, its northernmost [point] WNW2°N, the Three Sisters together NW5°N 8 to 9 l. At midnight, having sighted one of the Three Sisters ahead of us we altered course to E¼SE and continued until 3.30 when the winds veered south. At once steered E¼NE. At 5 the winds shifting back to ESE steered NE close-hauled to avoid the land and get out of the bay where we were too embayed. At 6 a.m. saw more land stretching to SE¼S5°E distant about 10 leagues;[4] the cape by which we were last night

---

[1] The most easterly headland is Mahua Point which with Kahua forms a small V-shaped bay.
[2] This is the western extremity of Wanoni Bay, with Tawaro Point just behind it.
[3] Ugi Island.
[4] This was the eastern extremity of the north coast of San Cristóbal.

bore SE$\frac{1}{4}$S4°S, the point that bore SSW5°W now bears S$\frac{1}{4}$SW3°S about 2 leagues, the one that bore W$\frac{1}{4}$SW3°W bears SW$\frac{1}{4}$S, the one that bore W3°S bears WSW, the northernmost land in sight W, Gulf Island W$\frac{1}{4}$NW2°W 8 l., the most southerly of the Three Sisters NW4°W 5 leagues, the middle one joining with the most southerly in NW2°W 5 to 6 leagues; the most northerly is detached from the other two NW1°N 7 to 8 l. Contrariety Island NNW2°N in the distance. At 8 o'clock we sighted from the topmasts some land bearing SE having the appearance of islands, but this belongs to the continent and continues as far as SSE which is the most southerly land. At midday Contrariety Island bears NNW3°W, the northernmost of the Three Sisters W$\frac{1}{4}$NW, the southernmost W 5°N, Gulf Island W$\frac{1}{4}$SW5°W with behind it the most westerly land we can see, the nearest land which is our point or headland of last night SSW, the southernmost land S$\frac{1}{4}$SE. We are sighting some land further E which I take to be one or 2 islands: they can be seen from the topmasts.

Courses NNE 5°E, distance 2$\frac{3}{4}$ leagues. Lat. S Est. 10°14′, obs. 10°24′, diff. S 10′. Long Est. 158°10′.

† Two men have died of scurvy these 24 hours: one of our Malagasy kaffirs, a ship's slave, and a lascar, both aged 25 to 30.

All the continent we see is high and wooded. At 10.30 this morning two canoes came from the land, I mean the large headland or point, with 4 kaffirs, one man only in one, 3 in the other with lances. They came quite close to the ship. We threw them some empty bottles which they accepted. We gestured to them to come aboard. They did not consider it wise to do so. If they had I think we would have taken them prisoners and kept them on board to work. They are scoundrels and robbers and murderers and one must not observe the niceties with them because these people think of nothing but to catch you unawares so as to tear you into pieces by treachery.

Monday 6 November 1769

Stormy weather, squally at times, rain and wind. Courses SE$\frac{1}{4}$E2°30′E, distance 9 leagues. Lat. S Est. 10°38′, obs. S 10°39′, diff. S 1′. Long Est. 158°34′.[1] From Oriental Cape,[2] the coast appears to trend south.

Bearings and comments for the 24 hours. At 1 p.m. sighted the

---

[1] Labé's longitude is erroneous by approximately 1°37′ west.
[2] Cape Surville, the easternmost extremity of San Cristóbal.

southernmost of the Three Sisters bearing W 1°N very distant, having
the appearance of drowned trees. At 3 altered course starboard tack,
at 5 altered course larboard tack. At 6 p.m. sighted Contrariety Island
bearing NW 2°W, all the high country south of Three Sisters Gulf is
covered in cloud, only the SW¼S 3°S is visible and even then quite hazy.
At 5.30 p.m. we saw a kind of island from the topmasts, bearing SSE
and SE¼S very distant. We lost sight of it immediately. At sunrise the
easternmost point of Deliverance Island bore S¼SE 7 l., the southernmost
point S 4°E, Oriental Cape S¼SW 2°S 10 to 11 leagues, a point being
the northernmost land W¼SW4°W. At 8 a.m. the middle of Deliverance
Island bore S5°W 7 leagues, Oriental Cape SSW1°S 4 leagues, a point
which is the northernmost land West. At 9 o'clock we sighted another
island to the SW of Deliverance Island,[1] which is why we have called
them Deliverance Islands. At midday the southern point of the
southernmost of the Deliverance Islands bore SSW 9 to 10 leagues and
its northern point across the southern point of the first one SSW3°W
6 l., its northernmost SW¼S, Oriental Cape SW2°S dist. 12 Leagues,
the westernmost or northernmost land stretching out in W5°N. Note:
Oriental Cape trends towards the SE¼E of the large headland that marks
the way out of Three Sisters Gulf. The former is a jagged headland
that looks like a group of small islands and rather low. The 2 Deliverance
Islands are not very high, they have the shape of a hurdy gurdy.[2] They
are some 3 or 4 leagues distant from each other and 5 to 7 leagues from
Oriental Cape. They are wooded. We gave the name Oriental Cape
as we could not see any land further east than the two Deliverance
Islands, [named] in the hope that the fine weather will take us out of
these parts.[3]

Tuesday 7th

Weather quite fair, smooth sea, good breeze at times. Several squalls
blew up with neither breeze nor rain. The winds W until 8 p.m. when
they veered east. Hauled aboard the courses close hauled, larboard tack.
Courses SE¼S 5°15'S, distance 14¾ leagues. Lat. S Est. 11°18', obs. 11°18'.
Long. Est. 158°56'.
† The chief gunner, Nicolas Solimant, a native of Lorient, aged about
30, died of scurvy at 8 p.m.[4]

[1] Labé's sighting of Santa Catalina.
[2] The stringed instrument. Although both islands are rather circular, taken together
they have broadly the appearance of a violin.
[3] Marginal note: †During the night a lascar died of scurvy, aged between 22 and 23.
He is from Bengal.   [4] See Muster Roll No. 158.

Bearings for the 24 hours. At 6 p.m. sighted the westernmost land bearing W¼NW 2°W very distant, Oriental Cape, a low foreland, SW¼W 2°W 14 to 15 l. One cannot see the mainland any further. The westernmost and northernmost point of Deliverance Island bears SW¼W 1½°W. It is almost joined to Oriental Cape. Distance of the island 9 leagues. The southernmost point of the same island bears SW 5½°W 6 to 7 leagues, the small Deliverance Island farther S and W than the other bears SW 12 leagues. Each seems to be 2½ to 3 leagues in length, being the same upturned hurdy-gurdy shape. They are well wooded. At 6 a.m. sighted the westernmost Deliverance Island WNW 3°W dist. 12 l. and the other, more easterly island WNW 5°N in the distance. We can still see some high mountains belonging to the mainland bearing WNW. At 8 a.m. the westernmost Deliverance Island bears NW¼W 2°N very distant, looking like drowned trees. At midday no more land and none appearing south of Oriental Cape. It must trend S¼SW and SSW.

Wednesday 8 November 1769

Winds NE, good breeze. Courses SE¼S 3°E, distance 19½ leagues. Lat. S Est. 12°05′, obs. 12°12′, diff. S 12′. Long. Est. 159°32′.

We no longer see any land. At midday we are due west of the most northerly land of New Guinea that the famous traveller Quiros discovered[1] and in this latitude of 12°12′ he left the land and made for the open sea to continue on his route to California on the coast of Mexico and took about 80 days to get there. Being away from the land he kept to a NE course. Let us return to the 12°12′ Quiros Land, from this point as far as the land of *Première Vue* Island which we discovered, no traveller before us had seen them. We named them Arsacides Land, on account of the savageness of its inhabitants, as is recorded on the 14 to 31 October last. Large numbers of the crew are attacked by scurvy and very discouraged by the sight of their friends dying of the same illness. There remains only 15 poultry on board and no other provisions to relieve them. For our table we have a few pigs left, nothing more.

---

[1] Labé is referring to Espiritu Santo in the New Hebrides which Pedro Fernandez de Quiros discovered on 3 May 1606. The latitude, however, is 15° south, so that Labé was wrong in his estimate that the *St Jean-Baptiste* had reached the latitude of Quiros' landfall. The reference to New Guinea reflects a fairly wide ignorance and definite uncertainty about the western section of New Guinea, which leads both him and Surville into using it as a general term for land and islands in this part of the Pacific. Labé is correct when he says that Quiros sailed to California from this latitude: he sailed on 13 June and sighted the Californian coast on 23 September, 102 days later.

I do not know what course Mr Surville is intending to keep to. He does not mention it to me.

Thursday 9th

Fair weather, smooth sea, good breeze at times, the winds NE to ENE, larboard tack. Courses SSE4°E, distance 20¼ leagues. Lat. S Est. 13°06', obs. 13°18', diff. S 12'. Long. Est. 159°59'.

† At 4 a.m. a lascar died of scurvy, aged about 17, a native of Bengal.

Observations on the land of New Guinea that we have discovered and coasted, and named Arsacides Islands as indicated in my log: Some of our gentlemen claim that we have sailed W of New Britain, which cannot be, and without doubt we sailed east of it, because if we had sailed W between it and New Guinea the celebrated traveller Dampierre[1] would have been grossly mistaken in respect both of his latitudes and of the distance between New Guinea and New Britain because if we had passed between them the distance from one land and the other would be more than 55 l. which is unbelievable. We sometimes were more than 20 leagues off the New Guinea coast and never saw any land to larboard. Mr Dampierre shows a channel of 25 leagues edged with islands on both sides 8 and 10 leagues off shore. Impossible to pass through the said channel without seeing the islands that line New Guinea, which confirms that we passed east of New Britain and made New Guinea in a latitude which no one had reached from 6°57' to 11°18'. We hauled along the coast for a long time sailing E and then ESE and SE to S. No voyager has sailed along this part of the coast. The maps show it too far west, it extends by more than 100 l. further east.[2] In truth it is drawn in accordance with simple conjectures, it is thought that it ought to extend from the land discovered by Quiros in 15°S which ought to extend north and south as far as Dampierre Strait but we have proved the contrary by experience.[3]

---

[1] William Dampier. Dampier Strait, the channel referred to by Labé separates New Britain from the north-easternmost point of New Guinea.

[2] This makes it quite clear that at this stage, Labé, in common with most of his fellow officers, considered that the *St Jean-Baptiste* had sailed along the coast of New Guinea and that, consequently, New Guinea was a far more extensive 'continent' than was believed.

[3] Uncertainty about the Solomon Islands and lack of detail about Espiritu Santo gave rise to the theory that a great continent or archipelago extended for the distance mentioned by Labé. Quiros himself tended to exaggerate the importance of his discovery, but Torres' voyage had already shown that Espiritu Santo could not be part of New Guinea – since he had sailed south-west. There was, however a large unexplored area east of New Guinea, which could be filled by a land mass. It was Bougainville who disproved the continental theory by sailing around the Louisiades archipelago and through the Solomon Islands.

Friday 10 November 1769

Courses SE¼S3°20′ E, distance 15 leagues. Lat. S Est. 13°54′, obs. 13°57′, diff. S 3′. Long. Est. 160°27′.

† At 8 p.m. last night Mr Errigouillient, a volunteer[1] born in Pondicherry, aged 27, died of scurvy.

We can see no more land. The Captain, Mr Surville, has this morning set a course for SSE. I do not know what he intends doing, he tells me nothing. I think he wishes to reach the latitude of the Horn Islands[2] to try to reach them. I have set the caulkers at work on the seams astern of the mainmast, later they will do the same operation on the larboard side and then forward on both sides. Each time the ship rolls the oakum and rope strands that are in the seams and above the chains all come out so that one can see daylight through them. We are forced to have this part caulked frequently.

Saturday 11th

Fair weather, smooth sea, light breeze, all sails high, the winds variable. Courses SE, distance 10¼ leagues. Lat. S Est. 14°27′, obs. 14°20′, diff. N 7′. Long. Est. 160°33′.

† At 10 p.m. the cassobe of the lascars, a native of Bengal, of Moorish nationality,[3] aged 42, died of scurvy.

Sunday 12 November 1769

The winds ESE, good breeze, fair weather, smooth sea, all sails high, steering close-hauled on the larboard tack. Courses S¼SW3°W, distance 14 leagues. Lat. S Est. 15°12′, obs. 15°01′, diff. N 11′. Long. Est. 160°23′.

Sickness is making great progress day by day among the crew. It is scurvy. Many are dying and great part of the rest of the crew are all sick of the said disease and we have no fresh food to give them to relieve them. If this continues as appears likely, God knows what will become of us. God's will be done. I have had no hand in this. Mr de Surville will answer for anything that may happen.

---

[1] A volunteer (*volontaire*) was a youth from a good family who was being trained as a naval officer. See Muster Roll No. 190.

[2] The Horne or Hoorn Islands consist of Alofi and Futuna, discovered in 19 May 1616 by Schouten and Le Maire. Although the French were not far from their latitude, they were still a great distance away: the position of Horne Islands is 14°15′ south and 178°05′ west of Greenwich (179°35′ east of Paris).

[3] i.e. a Moslem. The *kasap*, a Malay term, was used to refer to a general handyman who looked after the ship's provisions and was frequently put in charge of the ship's lanterns.

Monday 13 November 1769

Fair weather, smooth sea, good breeze, all sails high, steered close-hauled on the larboard tack, the winds E¼SE. Courses S5°W, distance 28 leagues. Lat. S Est. 16°25', obs. 16°29', diff. S 4'. Long. Est. 160°29'.

† At 7 p.m. a Malagasy kaffir, a ship's slave, aged about 32 died of scurvy.

† At 7 a.m. George Lorieus, sailor, born in Hennebon, aged about 20, died of scurvy.[1]

This sickness is becoming worse day by day and our men are struck down by it – I mean those who are fit, who are in a minority. No fresh food left, neither hens nor sheep to relieve them: none are left on board, neither for the sick nor for the officers.

My wound of the 14 October has healed, but callosities remains, the size of hazelnuts, which neither plasters nor ointments have been able to dissolve. I do not know whether I will suffer from them later.

I visit the sick daily. I suffer to see the poor wretches in such a deplorable condition. I deprive myself of many little delicacies I took in at Pondicherry for my own use. I give them [these] as the ship has nothing – I mean by that, sugar, syrup, lime juice, [?] tea, coffee, jam, wine. I distribute them to alleviate their pain.

Tuesday 14 November 1769

Fair weather, smooth sea, good breeze, all sails high, close-hauled, larboard tack. Courses S¼SW 5½°S, distance 21 leagues. Lat. S Est. 17°43', obs. 17°32', diff. N 11'. Long. Est. 160°10'.

Wednesday 15th

Variable winds, steered S¼SE. Courses S1½°W, distance 24⅓ leagues. Lat. S Est. 18°45', obs. 18°41', diff. N 4'. Long. Est. 160°08'.

† At 3 p.m. Michel Esonne, from the Paris diocese, a soldier in the detachment we took on at Pondicherry, died of scurvy, aged about 35.[2]

---

[1] See Muster Roll No. 94.
[2] The Muster Roll gives his name as Dessaunin, see No. 177.

Thursday 16 November 1769

Light breeze, calms at times. Courses S¼SE4°35'S, distance 9¾ leagues. Lat. S Est. 19°10', obs. 19°18', diff. S 8'. Long. Est. 160°11'.

† At 5 p.m. a Malagasy kaffir, a ship's slave, aged about 24, died of scurvy.

† At 7 a.m. a lascar aged 17 or 18, a native of Bengal, died of scurvy.

Friday 17th

Fair weather, light breeze, calms at times, the winds E to SE, steered close-hauled on the larboard tack. Courses S2°W, distance 8 leagues. Lat. S Est. 19°42', Obs. 19°41', diff. N 1'. Long. Est. 160°10'.

† At 2.30 a.m. a kaffir from Mozambique, a ship's slave, aged about 17, died of scurvy.

Saturday 18 November 1769

Steered south, larboard tack, light breeze, all sails high. Courses SSW4°W, distance 19⅓ leagues. Lat. S Est. 20°36', obs. 20°34', diff. N 2'. Long. Est. 159°51'.

The entire crew is attacked by scurvy. Those who are not swollen by it are affected in the chest. We need a good rest to set them right.

Sunday 19th

The winds SE to E¼NE, good breeze, all sails high, steering close-hauled on the larboard tack. Courses S¼SW2°30'W, distance 22 leagues. Lat. S Est. 21°38', obs. 21°34', diff. N 4'. Long. Est. 159°35'.

† At 6.15 a.m. Jean-Jacques Navet, a sailor, a native of Hennebon, aged about 20, died of scurvy.[1]

Monday 20 November 1769

Fair weather, good breeze, all sails high. At 9 o'clock a heavy sea rose coming from the south which strains the ship. Courses S¼SE3°E, distance 26½ leagues. Lat. S Est. 22°33', obs. 22°51', diff. 18'. Long. Est. 159°55'.

[1] See Muster Roll No. 77.

Tuesday 21st

Light breeze until 7 p.m., then calm; the winds NW to SSW. Courses S¼SE5°30′S, distance 7 leagues. Lat. S Est. 23°12′, obs. 23°14′, diff. S 2′. Long. Est. 159°57′. Increasingly scurvy is making considerable progress among the crew. Everyone is affected in the chest and the limbs are swollen, with continual vomiting. I can see we have not reached the end of our misfortunes, being short of everything, having no refreshments to give our sick. May God grant us the favour of finding among our discoveries some good islands where we could get supplies and restore our sailors and other men. I would be glad indeed to be able to land in New Zealand or at least in Easter Island[1] or other places where the people or islanders might welcome unhappy travellers.

Wednesday 22 November 1769

Almost calm, fair weather, heavy seas from the east and ESE, steered S¼SE and S, the winds SW to NW¼W. Courses S3°30′W, distance 5⅔ leagues. Lat. S Est. 23°31′, obs. 23°42′, diff. S 11′. Long. Est. 159°56′.

† At 6 a.m. François Alin, caulker, aged about 45, married, of Dinard, parish Ste Nogatte, district of Dinant, died of scurvy. We have only 2 caulkers left, of whom one is sick.[2]

Thursday 23rd

Fair weather, smooth sea, all sails high, steered south until 7 p.m. when we altered course to S¼SW. The winds NW¼W. Courses S¼SW4°45′W, distance 26 leagues. Lat. S Est. 24°57′, obs. 24°55′, diff. N 2′. Long. Est. 159°33′.

† At 10 p.m. a Malagasy kaffir, a ship's slave, aged about 24, died of scurvy.

† At 3 a.m. a Malagasy kaffir, a ship's slave, aged about 24, died of scurvy.

† At [blank] 30 a.m. a Malagasy kaffir, a ship's slave, aged about 25, died of scurvy.

† At 7.30 [a.m.] a lascar seaman, born in Bengal, aged about 26, died of scurvy.

[1] The *St Jean-Baptiste* was of course much nearer to New Zealand than to Easter Island, but in the latitudes which the French had now reached there are no other islands. Labé's 'at least' refers to the lesser size and correspondingly fewer opportunities of Easter Island.
[2] See Muster Roll No. 28.

Friday 24 November 1769

Fair weather, good breeze, fairly smooth sea, all sails high, the winds SSE. Courses SW¼W2°45′W, distance 12⅔ leagues. Lat. S Est. 25°14′, obs. 25°05′, diff. N 9′. Long. Est. 158°58′.

† At 10.45 a Mozambique kaffir, a ship's slave, aged about 32, died of scurvy.

The Captain, Mr Surville, consulted me today and told me of our situation, namely many dead and the rest of the crew sick and part of them affected in the stomach – I mean by scurvy – and all of them in no condition to undertake a lengthy crossing. He has therefore decided to continue our exploration and to sail for New Zealand, which Tasman discovered, as being the land nearest to us, to refresh our crew and restore them to enable them to continue our discoveries. He asked me my opinion and I agreed with him that it was the only course we could follow and that I would have done the same if I had been in his place. If one has to die it is better to seek food at gunpoint among these barbaric people[1] than to perish at sea for lack of men, being unable to last more than 24 days.

Saturday 25th

The winds SSE to E. Fair weather until midnight, then squalls, heavy seas. Courses SW¼W2°15′W, distance 19¼ leagues. Lat. S Est. 25°49′, obs. 25°35′, diff. N 14′. Long. Est. 158°04′.

Sunday 26 November 1769

Fresh gale, heavy seas, all sails high, steered close-hauled, larboard tack, the winds SE to E¼SE. Courses SW¼W2°W, distance 31½ leagues. Lat. S Est. 26°52′, obs. 26°53′, diff. S 1′. Long. Est. 157°02′.

Now the weather has turned cooler, scurvy is not making serious progress, our sailors are feeling a little better.

Monday 27th

Fair weather, the sea fairly smooth, all sails high, steering S¼SW. Courses SSW1°30′W, distance 26⅓ leagues. Lat. S Est. 28°05′, obs. 27°55′, diff. N 10′. Long. Est. 156°26′.

[1] The only information Europeans had about the New Zealand Maoris came from Tasman, who had been attacked without warning while off the coast of the South Island in Murderers' Bay, now Golden Bay.

Tuesday 28 November 1769

Light breeze, fair weather, smooth sea, all sails high. The winds started to freshen at midnight, fresh gale, all sails high, the sea rather heavy, steering S¼SW, the winds northerly. Courses SSW1°15'S, distance 34 leagues. Lat. S Est. 29°31', obs. 29°28', diff. N 3'. Long. Est. 155°44'.

† At 5 a.m. a Mozambique kaffir, a ship's slave, died of scurvy, aged about 26.

† At 9 a sailor named Manoun or Mamile Klause from Disteldrof[1] in Germany, died of scurvy, aged about 25.

Wednesday 29th

Strong gale, the sea very heavy. Courses SW¼S4°30'S, distance 32¾ leagues. Lat. S Est. 31°42', obs. 30°54', diff. N 48'. Long. Est. 154°48'.

† At 11.30 [p.m.] Nicolas Bengal Topat, the chaplain's servant, a native of Bengal, died of scurvy.

† At 9.30 a.m. Pierre Charles Deslandre, known as Nanoix, from Brest, diocese of St Paul de Lion, a soldier from the detachment taken on at Pondicherry, died of scurvy.[2]

Thursday 30th 1769

Fair weather. Courses SW3°15'S, distance 15¼ leagues. Lat. S Est. 31°39', obs. 31°28', diff. N 11'. Long. Est. 154°13'.

† At 8 p.m. a Moorish lascar, a native of Bengal, aged about 24, died of scurvy.

† At 2 a.m. a Moorish lascar, a native of Bengal, aged about 20, died of scurvy.

† At 5 a.m. one Mouton taken on for [?], a native of Pondicherry, aged about 40, died of scurvy.[3]

Friday 1 December 1769

Fair weather, good breeze, smooth sea, steering S¼SW, the winds NNE. Courses SSW1°S, 21⅔ l. Lat. S Est. 32°26', obs. 32°34', diff. S 8'. Long. Est. 153°47'.

---

[1] See Muster Roll No. 70.   [2] See Muster Roll No. 171.
[3] Not an ordinary lascar. Listed separately in Muster Roll, see No. 194.

Scurvy continues and is working increasing havoc among the crew who are becoming more and more desperate when they see no one becoming cured of this sickness. They are losing courage. I do not know what will become of us.

Saturday 2 December 1769

Courses SW$\frac{1}{4}$S1°45′S, distance 19$\frac{1}{4}$ leagues. Lat. S Est. 33°23′. Long. Est. 153°11′.

† At 3 p.m. a Mozambique kaffir, a ship's slave, aged about 30, died of scurvy.

† At 8 a.m. a Moorish lascar, a native of Bengal, aged about 22, died of scurvy.

Sunday 3rd

Squally weather, light rain at times, very high seas. Courses WSW3°W, distance 11 leagues. Lat. S Est. 33°34′, obs. 33°31′, diff. N 3′. Long. Est. 152°33′.

Monday 4 December 1769

Courses E$\frac{1}{4}$SE1°40′E, distance 21$\frac{3}{4}$ leagues. Lat. S Est. 33°42′, obs. 33°35′, diff. N 7′. Long. Est. 153°51′.

At 3 a.m. we smelt a scent of meadow, like dry hay and for more than 3 hours. It came from the south to SSW. This is an indication of the neighbourhood of land, either New Zealand or New Holland.[1] I expect that the Captain will soon begin easting and running down the latitude of New Zealand. Then after we have easted the distance between New Holland and New Zealand if we meet nothing we will know for certain that what we could smell this morning came from New Zealand; on the contrary, if we sight New Zealand then that scent would have come from New Holland and not far away.

[1] Estimating the position of the St Jean-Baptiste on this day compared with Labé's estimated longitude on 12 March when the French sighted New Zealand, the expedition was not more than 200 miles from the coast of New South Wales – probably far less. The wind at the time was blowing from SSW. Any land odour could only have come from Australia. At this point, Surville could have sailed SW and reached the neighbourhood of Botany Bay, but three factors militated against this: the coastline and its resources were not known and would not be until Cook reached it in 1770, the prevailing westerly winds were likely to delay him considerably (although they had been shifting to easterly at times), and his uncertain longitude meant, as the rest of Labé's entry shows, that he had no idea of his true position.

The birds, cuttlefish, red grained polyps and Flemish caps denote the proximity of land, with the great numbers of birds named velvet sleeves[1] which never stray more than 20 to 25 leagues from land, there are many like them at the Cape of Good Hope. They are all like gannets except that the tip of their wings is black or brown and the rest white.

Tuesday 5th

Fair weather. Courses SSE4°30'E, distance $11\frac{2}{3}$ leagues. Lat. S Est. 34°06', obs. 34°07', diff. S 1'. Long. Est. 154°10'.

At midday Mr Surville after consulting me stood SE. If we are W of New Zealand we will sight it. We expect to reach the latitude of 35 degrees to then bear away east. If by chance we are in the east we will continue along the same parallel until we find an unknown land.[2]

Wednesday 6 December 1769

Strong gale, rough sea, the ship straining considerably through the rolling, working the pumps every 2 hours,[3] steering SE to east rounding so as to reach the latitude of 35 to 36 degrees to sight New Zealand where we hope to put in. At 5 p.m. as it was overblowing took in all reefs in the main and fore topsails and kept the foresails and main and fore topsails.

The winds N to WNW. Courses SE$\frac{1}{4}$E5°30'S, distance $56\frac{2}{3}$ leagues. Lat. S Est. 35°35', obs. 35°54', diff. S 19'. Long. Est. 156°52'.

Scurvy is making greater inroads on the remains of our crew. All are attacked. God knows what will become of us. Scarcely any fresh food for them except for a little pork. At the officers' table we are down to thick soup, occasionally the giblets of pigs killed for the sick, we get them at the table. We are fortunate indeed that our sows have given us several litters; if it were not for that we would have no fresh food for our sick. Nothing was taken in for the officers' table, neither any [?] nor ham, tongues, and no butter, nor cheese. We are reduced to the deepest penury.

---

[1] The red-footed booby, *Sula sula*.

[2] So far the area east of New Zealand and south of the thirtieth parallel was completely unknown up to approximately ninety degrees west. Labé's considerable uncertainty about his position relative to New Zealand is explained by contemporary charts, such as Vaugondy's of 1768 which shows New Zealand as being almost 15° west of the latitude of Prins Wyllem's Islands, near which the French believed they had been on 13 November.

[3] In his log board Labé notes that the ship was making one inch of water an hour.

Thursday 7th

Courses E1°45′N, distance 39⅔ leagues. Lat. S Est. 35°38′, obs. 35°51′, diff. S 13′. Long. Est. 159°18′.

This morning going on my rounds in the hold I noticed that a great deal of merchandise was damp and all the bags of rice and wheat. We are working at making good everything by drying it all. This damage is due to the ship not being strengthed and when she rolls all the seams open up everywhere which means that water enters the hold, especially all along the water way or spirkettings. It is true that the stowage was very lightly done in such a ship. They should have put at least 8 inches of [?] on the hatchways of the ship and the standing ends and the bulwarks[1] so that the water could run off along the gutters. I have nothing to reproach myself with over the said stowage having come on board in Bengal only the day before the departure of the ship; consequently I found the ship loaded, but very badly. I do not know whom to put this down to except to those who were in charge of the operation.

Friday 8 December 1769

Fair weather, heavy seas which strains the ship. Courses E¼NE5°N, distance 20½ leagues. Lat. S Est. 35°34′, obs. 35°33′, diff. N 1′. Long. Est. 160°31′.

We have taken out of the hold what I found to be damp, about twenty bales, 200 sacs of wheat and rice, lentils [?]. We have been drying it all and will line the sides of the ship, I mean in the hold to prevent things becoming wet, at least to some extent.

At midday, according to my reckoning, the southernmost of Coningen Island[2] bears from me NE¼E distant 23 to 24 leagues, [and] the nearest part of New Zealand ESE distance 38 leagues.

Saturday 9th

Courses E 3°S, distance 21 leagues. Lat. S Est. 35°36′, obs. 35°40′, diff. S 4′. Long. Est. 161°48′.

---

[1] Doubtful rendering owing to poor legibility.
[2] This is the Dutch name of Three Kings Islands ('Drie Kooningken Eijlanden', as they appear on the Vingboons map). However, in the chart in Tasman's journal the main island of the group, Great Island, is called 'T'Eijlandt Drie Coningken.' See A. Sharp, *The Voyages of Abel Janszoon Tasman*, p. 138 n. As is clear from the next entry Labé regards Great Island as a separate entity from the rest of the group.

† At 10 a.m. Francois Couzin, a Portuguese, helmsman, born in Pondicherry, aged about 17, died of scurvy.[1]

Today we finished drying the bales of merchandise, rice, wheat that had become wet in the hold.

At midday, according to my reckoning, Three Kings Islands[2] and the middle of Coningen Islands bears from me N¼NE2°N distant 20 leagues, the nearest land of New Zealand E 2°S dist. 13½ leagues, the northernmost land of New Zealand NE4°N, dist. 36 leagues.

Sunday 10 December 1769

Courses E5°N, distance 42½ leagues. Lat. S Est. 35°29', obs. 35°42', diff. S 13'. Long. Est. 164°25'.

Scurvy continues to ravage the rest of the crew. I am very much afraid that, owing to an insufficiency of men, we may not be able to complete our planned discoveries which are the basis of our voyage.

At midday, according to my reckoning, I find myself 29 leagues inside New Zealand. When we have sailed another hundred to one hundred and fifty miles east without sighting New Zealand we will have to assume that the currents have borne us far to the east. If on the other hand we do sight it there will be a great difference west [in my reckoning], which I can scarce imagine as all the travellers who have sailed the seas from the equinoctial line to 30 deg. of latitude south report that the currents bear strongly to the east. Anyhow a few days of fair winds will put our minds at rest about the currents.[3]

† At 5 a.m. a Moorish lascar, born in Bengal, aged about 20, died of scurvy.

Monday 11th

Fair weather, smooth sea, fresh gale, all sails high, steering ENE, the winds NNW. Courses E¼NE50'E, distance 44¼ leagues. Lat. S Est. 35°18', obs. 35°35', diff. S 17'. Long. Est. 167°05'.

---

[1] See Muster Roll No. 197.

[2] Three Kings is a group of four islands with small offshore islets situated in 35°50'S and 172°10'E, approximately 30 miles to the north-west of New Zealand. They had been discovered by Abel Tasman on 4 January 1643, who named them thus in honour of the forthcoming feast of the Epiphany or Twelfth Night. As the remainder of the entry shows, Labé believed the islands to be south-west of Cape Maria van Diemen. The plural form for Coningen in this entry is in all likelihood a copyist's error.

[3] Labé's perplexity was due to the outline of New Zealand as reported by Tasman being shown some 8° too far west. Vaugondy's chart of 1768 shows 'C. Cipige' (Clippige Hoeck or Cape Foulwind) as being 180° east of Tenerife, instead of 188°08'. See Sharp, *The Voyages of Abel Janszoon Tasman*, p. 118n.

† At midday a Mozambique kaffir, a ship's slave, aged about 27, died of scurvy.

† At 7.45 a.m. Moutoy, a Christian Malabar from Pondicherry, aged about 40, died of scurvy, taken on as servant to Mr St Paul, the Captain commanding the detachment of infantry which we took on at Pondicherry.[1]

At midday, according to my reckoning, in latitude 35°35′ south I am 74 leagues inside New Zealand.

Tuesday 12 December 1769

Fair weather, smooth sea, all sails high, fresh gale, the winds NW¼N. Courses E1°S, distance 50 leagues. Lat. S Est. 35°17′, obs. 35°37′, diff. S 20′. Long. Est. 170°09′.

Saw New Zealand at 11.15 this morning, saw the land of New Zealand, very high, from NNW to E, very distant.

At midday sighted New Zealand from E5°S to NNW3°N, the nearest land consisting of sand dunes with some scrub on them bears NNE5°E distant 7 to 8 leagues. This is the lowest land, the remainder consists of very high mountains seeming black with trees on them.[2]

According to my landfall I find I have difference of 134 leagues west since my departure from the Bashi Islands.[3] Nevertheless I will continue with the same longitude until I reach a place where the longitude is known, this part not being known as only one traveller, named Tasman, has seen it, who carried out no observation of any kind or even set foot on land.[4] The smell of land of the 14th instant denoted the approaches of New Holland, the distance we covered from then until we sighted New Zealand corresponding to the distance separating those two lands.

[1] See Muster Roll No. 195.
[2] The French were in sight of Hokianga Harbour, a deeply indented inlet with a bar at the entrance and prominent sandhills in the north. The northernmost land could have been Reef Point.
[3] In fact, through a series of compensating errors, Labé's longitude was only some 40′ wrong. His position at midday was in the neighbourhood of 170°50′ east of Paris, an error of approximately 20 leagues.
[4] It is correct that Tasman, having lost four men in Golden Bay on 19 December 1642, six days after sighting New Zealand, did not set foot on land. He did carry out a number of observations. His longitude reckonings however were, like the French's, subject to the errors that result from dead reckoning.

Wednesday 13th

NW winds, fresh gale, fairly smooth sea, under different sails, standing off and on so as to reach the north point of New Zealand and find a harbour or roads where we could anchor to restore our crew attacked by scurvy.

Courses W5°30′S distance 6 leagues. Lat. S Est. 35°39′, obs. 35°28′, diff. N 11′. Long. Est. 169°47′.

Bearings for the 24 hours. At sunset sighted what bore E 5°S at midday bearing SE¼E5°E 9 leagues, the nearest sandy mountains NE dist. 2½ to three leagues, the northernmost NNW3°W, a bay E5°N. At dawn, hazy weather which means we could not see the land. At 8 a.m. sighted the same sand dunes of last night bearing NE¼E, the northernmost land NNW, high mountains, the southernmost which is last night's cape E 5°S very distant. At midday the middle of the sand dunes ENE3°E [which] are this morning's, distant 7 to 8 leagues, the northernmost land hazy NNE4°E, the truncated mountain which was this morning the most easterly is no longer visible. Note: this same mountain is very easy to recognize as it forms a steep cape with a small bluff. From the said cape to the sand dunes is formed a bay. The dunes are the lowest by the high mountains where it seems there is scrub on the shore. The appearance is rather similar to the Cape of Good Hope with high mountains inland. The coast looks safe to me.

Thursday 14 December 1769

Strong gale, the sea very rough, signs of whole gale, stood off and on under different sails, the winds NW. Courses SSE4°S, distance 1 league. Lat. S Est. 35°31′. Long. Est. 169°48′.

† At 2.30 a.m. Julian Cadet, sailor caulker, aged about 24, born in the parish of Pleurtuis, diocese of St Malo, district of Dinard, died of scurvy. We have only one caulker left, who is also a carpenter.[1]

† At 6 a.m. a Malagasy kaffir, a ship's slave, aged about 30, died of scurvy. Bearings for the 24 hours. At 6 p.m. sighted the southernmost land bearing ESE3°E very hazy, the first sand dunes we saw bear E5°N 4 leagues, a high mountain inland shaped like a horse saddle NE¼N3°N, distance of the nearest land which appears to be the lowest 3 leagues; the coastline continues full of sand dunes from one point to the next with in parts small scrub and dark patches as far as N5°W which seems

---

[1] See Muster Roll No. 51.

to be the northernmost land in sight. The other mountains look black and wooded. Several are on the coast and others further inland. At dawn the weather very stormy and foggy which means that we cannot see the land. At 11 during a break sighted the land which is the same as yesterday morning, and same bearings, which shows us that far from making headway we have lost ground. No reef or danger is visible off this coast. The sea breaks at times [but] only on the shore. We have not yet sounded, I think however that we would have found bottom 2 or 3 leagues from the coast when we altered course to stand to sea, the sea having changed considerable to a greenish colour, as at the entrance to a river and port.

Friday 15th

The gale sudden on us, the sea very rough, the wind laying us on our side unable to straighten up, stood off and on until 6 a.m. when the winds veered SW and shortly after SSW. We changed course on the larboard tack and crowded sail to weather the coast but the sea is so high that we keep falling back, which creates a dangerous situation. However it seems that the coast is no longer trending NNW which gives rise to the hope that we will soon be clear. The bad weather continues until midday; courses SW, distance $\frac{1}{2}$ league. Lat. S Est. 35°43′, obs. 35°32′, diff. N 11′. Long. Est. 169°47′.

† At 6 p.m. Le Cam, assistant gunner, aged about 27, a native of Lorient in Brittany, died of scurvy.[1]

Bearings for the 24 hours. At 5.30 p.m. the northernmost land bore NNW dist. 7 to 8 leagues, the mountain that resembles a horse's saddle NNE3°E distant from the shore 4 to $4\frac{1}{2}$ l., the southernmost land ESE 7 to 8 l. At 5 a.m. a mountain that was the most southerly we saw when we first sighted land bears E$\frac{1}{4}$NE dist. 6 to 7 leagues, the southernmost land hazy in the distance ESE, the first sand dunes N$\frac{1}{4}$NW dist. 5 leagues, the northernmost land NW$\frac{1}{4}$N hazy. At midday the southernmost land which is the mountain with a small bluff on it SE$\frac{1}{4}$E3°E dist. 8 l. During the morning, being close to the Cape, we saw some low land still trending towards the sea. The sand dunes, the first we saw, bear now ENE3°N at $3\frac{1}{2}$ leagues. A little to the north of one of them appears an opening which looks like a rivermouth.[2]

---

[1] See Muster Roll No. 157.
[2] Probably Whangape, a tidal inlet. The Herekino River or False Hokianga, a few miles further north, is less likely to have been seen from the *St Jean-Baptiste*'s position.

The northernmost land bears NW¼N3°N. All the coast is partly lined with dunes, the hinter land consists of high mountains covered in trees. On the sand partly some [scrub ?].

Saturday 16 December 1769

From midday yesterday until 5 p.m. very dangerous weather, the winds and sea driving us towards the coast, finally forced to sail [?] in the heavy squalls to bear off. We were clear by 5.30 which means that from then until midday we carried out various manoeuvres, the winds SW¼S to S fresh gale, the seas still high. In the morning we were 2 l. from the shore. Courses N¼NW3°N 22 leagues. Lat. Est. S 34°27′, obs. 34°22′, diff. N 5′. Long. Est. 159°36′.

Bearings for the 24 hours. At 5 p.m. we were clear of the land of the W point which forms the bay with the NW Cape of Tasman.[1] At 6 p.m. the northernmost point NE¼E3°E 6 to 7 l., another in the distance which I take to be NW Cape N¼NW5°W about 12 l. It has off its point 2 small islets visible from the topmasts.[2] At 5.30 a.m. saw an island NW5°W in the distance;[3] at sunrise the northernmost land forming a cape NNE 6 or 7 l., the southernmost E in the distance. At 7.30 a.m. we were due E of the NW cape of Tasman, the southernmost land bore E¼SE5°S, the largest of Kings' Islands WNW3°N. At 11.30 Kings' Islands the largest again, bearing W¼NW2°N at least ½ league, Tasman's NW Cape S about 2½ l., a headland trending east E5°S 4 l.,[4] a truncated headland we can see as we are weathering round, we have named it Cape Surville after the captain,[5] bears E5°N dist. 5 l. At midday Tasman's NW cape which is the most S and W land in sight bears SW¼S1°S 3½ l., another headland with a sandy beach within it E¼SE3°S 3 l., Cape Surville which is the most easterly land E dist. 3½ to 4 l., Kings' Islands, the largest W¼NW 3°W in the distance, we can no longer see the others.

Notes: Tasman's NW cape is fairly high lined with sand dunes; the higher land looks as if burnt in the gullies, there are some scattered

[1] Cape Maria van Diemen, discovered and so named by Tasman on 4 January 1643.
[2] There is one small island off this cape, Motu Orao.
[3] A sighting of Great Island, the largest of Three Kings Islands.
[4] Hooper Point, the easternmost head of Spirits Bay, the sandy beach referred to in the midday bearings.
[5] Cape Surville was known for many years as Kerr Point; it is the north-west head of North Cape. The whole northern headland is now known as Surville Cliffs. The other headland referred to is Hooper Point; Labé, following Tasman, does not differentiate between Cape Maria van Diemen and Cape Reinga.

trees in the hollows. There is a $\frac{1}{2}$ league spit of sand advancing offshore in S4°W [?] from us, almost attached to this spit is an islet like a pointed steeple.[1] From NW Cape the land trends ENE. You can see Cape Surville which is very high at a distance of approximately 8 leagues from NW Cape. Along this there are sandbanks and mountains seeming burnt, you can see in the hills some trees here and there. There are several bays from one cape to the next but with the WNW winds one is sheltered. There is a large bay as shown in the bearings of yesterday evening but we sailed past it at night. Nothing can be said about it. We saw 4 Kings Islands, one large, one medium-sized and two small.[2] The large one is quite high. They are about 17 leagues from NW Cape by our reckoning. It seems that all along this coast there is a depth of 40 to 50 fathoms as we found yesterday evening quite some distance from the shore. The sea still rough. As we are very weak we are taking few depths to avoid exhaustion.

Sunday 17th

Courses SE$\frac{1}{4}$4°E, distance 13 l. Lat. S Est. 34°41′, obs. S 34°44′, diff. S 3′. Long. Est. 170°17′.

† At 10 p.m. Meaugé, a sailor aged 24, born in St Malo, died of scurvy.[3]

Bearings for these 24 hours. At 2.30 yesterday afternoon Cape Surville bore SW $\frac{1}{2}$ league, the point ending the said cape further east having almost the shape of a peninsula[4] on which we saw two huts or tombs bears SE$\frac{1}{4}$S. There is a small breaker off the point close inshore. The land distant 1$\frac{1}{2}$ l. At 3.20 NW Cape with Cape Surville bore WSW4°W, a headland between the two capes WSW2°W. Sounded, found no bottom 40 to 30 fathoms but the sea is quite different, I am sure from the colour of the sea that there is a bottom at 50 or 60 f. To save time we are not altering sail [?]. At 6 p.m. Cape Surville WNW2°W dist. 5 l., the back of a wide bay with small [?] S, the northern point of another bay further south S$\frac{1}{4}$SW1°W dist. 8 l., a mountain or island at the back of the said bay S$\frac{1}{4}$SE2°S very distant, another island SSE4°S, land appearing furthest E in SE$\frac{1}{4}$E2°S. At sunset Cape Surville WNW 6$\frac{1}{2}$ leagues, a point forming the S of a bay

---

[1] Motu Orao.
[2] North-East Island and West Island are small. South-West Island can qualify for the description of 'medium-sized'. Great Island is by far the largest. There are also a number of islets and uncovered rocks. [3] See Muster Roll No. 58.
[4] Cook's North Cape, with the islet of Murimotu.

SW¼S4°S dist. about 7 l., the easternmost land SE¼E2°E.[1] Sounded until 6 a.m. 30 to 40 f. no bottom. At 6 a.m. Cape Surville bore WNW5°N dist. 9½ l approximately, the back of the great bight lined with islets SW¼S3°W, an entrance to a bay lined with large islands SSE1°S dist. 3 l. This seems to make a harbour inland, the most easterly ESE, a small islet looking like drowned trees ESE5°E. At 8 a.m. Cape Surville WNW dist. 11 l., the middle of the bight SW¼W4°W, another bay formed by two large islands S¼SE 3 l., it is the same as at 6 a.m. It seems we are to anchor in it. The easternmost land SE¼E3°S. The sea is still muddy.

At midday sighted Cape Surville WNW in the distance, another mountain WSW3°S, the entrance of the bight or bay where we want to anchor formed by several islands S¼SW5°W 2½ l., the easternmost land SE¼E distant [?], a kind of island in the distance ESE4°S. At 8.30 a boat paddled by 8 men came up and remains under the gallery; they gave us fish for a length of white cloth and a knife. At 9 another 4 boats arrived, 3 of which brought quantities of fish they gave in exchange for blue and white cloth. The crew both white and black have eaten well, excellent fish. [Follow semi-legible comments on the dangers surrounding North Cape.] Until midday we hauled along a coast lined with islands; there is a great bay within, the sea much changed, no bottom with 30 or 40 f. of cable. This coast is low with some high dunes with trees in the gullies. The 5 boats that came alongside are 28 to 30 feet long, they haul [?] larboard or starboard. On the boats they have sculptures and carvings, they have 10 robust men 5½ to 5⅔ feet tall, [with] long hair, wearing dog skins and [?]. They put red on their hair; their boats had 4 lances not more. They look like poor people, but thieves like the people of New Guinea.[2]

Monday 18 December 1769

From midday yesterday until 9.30 p.m. Sunday when we dropped anchor in a bay of New Zealand to which Mr Surville gave the name of Loriston [Lauriston] Bay, name of Mr Law, Governor of Pondicherry on the Coromandel coast, tacked about several times to enter the said bay as shown in the margin, without finding bottom until 7.30 p.m.

[1] The *St Jean-Baptiste* at this stage was in sight of Mt Camel to the SW and Rangaunu Bay to the south. The easternmost land could be Cavalli Island or possibly Cape Brett which rises to 1200 ft, approximately 70 miles away – Cape Brett is the 'kind of island' mentioned in the midday bearings.
[2] The bulk of these comments are crowded into a small space and only partly legible.

when we had 34 f. sand and mud. We were at that time inside the second point at the starboard entrance where I end my course. I will take up my same longitude when I leave athwart the same point. At the same hour, my courses were SW3°S, distance 14½ leagues. Lat. S Est. 34°54′, Long. Est. E 170°06′.[1]

Bearings from yesterday midday until 9.30 p.m. when we dropped anchor in Lauriston Bay in New Zealand: at 2.15 the point of an island situated between two bays bears W¼NW 4 leagues, the point of another bay SW¼W; there are several islands or islets between those two. The starboard head of the bay we want to enter bears S¼SE 1⅔ leagues, the other point to larboard SE¼E3°E 3½ leagues. This is about the opening of the bay. From seaward these two points seem to form two islands, they are not [islands] they are the mainland. Another point further east ESE2°E 5 to 6 leagues, the easternmost land E¼SE4°E in the distance. At 3 p.m. altered course being to larboard of the bay. Here are the bearings: the point that bore W¼NW at 2.15 bears NW¼W2°W 5 to 6 leagues, the other one that bore SW¼W bears W5°S 3 leagues, a rock in the bay SW¼S2°W 3½ l., it is close to land. The large cape that bore S¼SE bears SSE5°E dist. 1 league, the point that bore SE¼E3°E bears E¼SE about 5 leagues, the one that bore ESE2°E bears E¼SE 3°S, the easternmost land E 10 to 11 leagues. At 6 o'clock last evening as we changed course to bear up the bay sighted Cape Surville in the distance bearing NW¼W1°W. The land which at the last bearings bore NW¼W2°W bears W 2 leagues, what bore W at 3 o'clock we brought to at 6 p.m. when we tacked to SSE4°E dist. 1½ league. The large cape or bluff that bore SSE5°E bears SE¼S4°E, the other one that bore E¼SE bears ESE3°S 4 leagues, the easternmost land E to E¼SE2°S in the distance. There are numbers of isolated rocks forming pyramids all along the coast but close inshore. We are bearing off the starboard point of the bay and are weathering the headlands. At 7.30 p.m. we were within shelter of the second island where we found 34 fathoms sand and mud. As the winds did not allow us to reach the inside of the bay on the starboard side we were forced to bear off and anchor at 9.15 p.m.

Bearings of the anchorage of Lauriston Bay: the larboard point as you enter bears E1°S three short leagues, there are almost touching two small rocks including one sugarloaf; the starboard points as you enter which is however the second point bears N4°W 1⅔ leagues; another point on the same side W3°S one and ⅔ leagues; the back of the bay

[1] Marginal comment: It is very cold.

SSW $3\frac{1}{4}$ l. Note: As we bore towards the bay at 6 p.m. we hugged the starboard coast, it is very high [and] bare with scrub in places, sand in others. We left on our starboard a kind of rock with huts on them; there are two sandy coves at the foot where the natives put away or ground their canoes. As you sail round a large cape you find a bay that could hold several ships but they would be exposed to the NE to E winds. Between these places is a point which is the first of the bay. There is a reef about one hundred *toises* from land. You can see the waves breaking over it. The first point also has some small breakers inshore, the second one closer in has the same. No other dangers are visible. The entire bay is safe. The bottom is fine sand, sand and mud, small black gravel, rotted coral, and the lack of dangers is apparent. The inside of the bay is sandy along the shore with bare country 2 or 3 l. away; further inside the dunes wooded mountains are visible. [On] the larboard side as you enter, further inland, the land is higher, and less sandy and has trees in the hills.[1]

This morning 8 or 10 of the natives' large canoes came up to the ship, each with 4 to 10 men. They came to trade fish in quantity for pieces of blue and white cloth. We had enough fish to feed four hundred men. They had in their boats 3 or 4 women who came on board with the men. As weapons they have a small number, 3 or 4 lances, some clubs made of black stone and others in a kind of ivory 13 inches long having the shape of a small shovel. They also have a kind of wooden swords decorated with gold.[2] I did not see any arrows. They paint their faces and buttocks like the kaffirs of New Guinea and put red on their hair which they arrange partly as do [?] women in India. Their dress consists of a few mats they tie around the waist, others have dog skins sewn together, others have only a kind of large skirt with plaits 6 inches long. For ornaments they hang a greenish glasslike stone round their necks, representing the face of a devil,[3] I cannot describe it correctly. Others wear earrings made of the same stone, 3 or 4 inches long and $\frac{3}{4}$ wide, thin and pear shaped but flat. Others wear pieces of dog skin [tied] to their ears. A few have a bird skin underneath to cover their

---

[1] See entry of 20th which states these bearings are unsatisfactory.

[2] The common Maori lance or spear was the *tao*, six to ten feet in length; more ornate and personal was the *taiaha*. The clubs were *patu*. Not ivory but bone, usually whalebone, was used in manufacture. The blackstone club was called *patu onewa*. The 'golden' sword was in all likelihood a club or lance decorated with yellowish grasses, as gold as a colour was not known to the Maori.

[3] The *tiki* or *heitiki* carved in New Zealand greenstone could easily bring to mind a medieval devil. It is a stylised crosslegged figure with a large head held to one side. A widely held theory claims that it represents a human embryo. The greenstone ear pendant was known as the *kuru*.

nakedness, others do not hide it. They have no modesty and are great thieves, but they do not appear to be dangerous. Their features are not ferocious like those of Port Praslin nor those of Contrariety Island.

I had forgotten to say that these people wear tufts of white feathers on their heads and others black ones; some wear them across the forehead.[1] They all have pierced ears. The designs on their faces and buttocks are the colour of gunpowder. The designs are [?] and elaborate. They also put this colour on their lips, some red mixed with oil on their hair[2] and sometimes on the body; the women do likewise. I have seen some of their canoes 50 feet in length; up to 24 men come out in them with pikes and lances and [?].

At 1 p.m. I lowered our second boat with 8 sailors [and] 10 soldiers with their weapons. The captain and Mr Charenton, second lieutenant, with him also got in to look for water. They went NW to the shore and found 21½ f. [to] 25 and then 17 f. [to] 9 fathoms close inshore, rotted coral, yellow gravel, red and white rotted coral, brown sand and coral up to the sandy cove where there is a settlement on a steep hill on the left side of the cove but close to the shore. When the boat was almost ashore the chief came to welcome it. He is a man some 45 to 50 years to age, dressed like the others. The said chief seemed terrified at the sight of muskets. They made him understand that we only used it against bad people, which reassured him. He made our gentlemen sit above the sandy cove, but did not invite them to the dwellings. A large number of people, men, women and children then came to look at our men. The chief spoke to them, they went away and came back soon after with bunches of greens or wild celery and cress;[3] the country produces quantities of them; and gave them to the Captain. I think it will do a great deal of good to our scurvy cases. They have numbers of long haired domesticated dogs. The country looks fairly well cultivated with greens, etc. At 6 p.m. the second boat came back with greens. They had found a small soft water stream in the sandy cove coming down from the hills and some trees near the shore and quite easy to obtain.[4] This little stream bears from us NW distant one league, right of the settlement that is on a small steep bluff. As the second boat

---

[1] The hair was usually drawn well back in a topnot, known as the *tikitiki*, into which the feathers of various birds were fixed, those of the *huia* being especially prized.

[2] The red colouring used was derived from the red ochre mud or *kokowai* which was then mixed with oil obtained from the livers of sharks or from vegetable oil extracted from tree berries.

[3] The two words are *silkyre* and *brelton*, which are meaningless. They presumably represent what the copyist could make out of Labé's writing and erratic spelling of *céleri* and *cresson*.   [4] Labé is presumably referring to firewood.

looked overloaded when it came back I hauled it in and lowered the longboat at 8 p.m. These people so far seem to be good people, poor, wretched, ill-clothed, living only on fish and greens. Their fish is very good. They have water fowl and many others. There are quantities of teals or small wild ducks.[1] Throughout the afternoon there was a strong westerly breeze, the weather was overcast. I forgot to say that they have in the sandy cove some large seines or fishing nets to bring ashore.

For the last two days the remainder of our crew has been attacked by scurvy. Only 7 or 8 men are fit. I hope that this call will restore them by staying a whole month and putting them ashore. If not we would be in a nasty situation.

We expected also to find in this country wealth in the form of gold or silver, but our hopes were vain. When our crew has recovered we will continue our search in the east. We may be more fortunate in finding islands rich in metals in exchange for our goods and to make up for the time we have lost so far and the hardships caused by lack of food and sickness. Well, God is merciful, He does not abandon his children.

Tuesday 19 December 1769

Good SW to W breeze throughout the night but we have only the [?] of the wind. The sea is still smooth, being sheltered.

† At 4 this morning a Malagasy kaffir died of scurvy, a ship's slave aged about 25. None is left, all the others are dead.

The Captain, Mr Surville left in the long boat at 5 a.m. to go to yesterday's cove and get water and wood and to set up a tent for the sick. I placed ten empty barrels in the boat [with] 8 oarsmen [and] 6 sailors to cut the wood and 14 sailors chosen from the least sick to breathe the land air. All the others who are staying on board cannot stand, which is why they are staying on board, as we have been unable so far to set up a tent ashore for fear of giving umbrage to our islanders. From 5.30 until 9 this morning 5 or 6 large canoes came up to the ship, without weapons, with 12 to 20 men in each, to barter [fish] for cloth or bottles. For a yard of heavy Bengal cloth we obtained 4 or 5 large fish about 20 inches long shaped like a bonito[2] and for the same amount of cloth we obtain 40 to 60 [?] and similarly with the other fish that

---

[1] Teals include the Black Teal, *Anas novae zealandiae*, the Brown Teal, *Anas castanea chlorotis*, and the Grey Teal, *Anas gibberifrons gracilis*.

[2] Possibly a small Butterfly Fish (*Gasterochisma melampus*) which belongs to the Umbridae family as does the bonito, but probably a trevalli (*Caranx lutescens*) common in the area, silver bluish as is the bonito and usually 10 to 20″ long.

are delicious. There are also clams, shells and mussels.[1] Strong **W** breeze until midday but also we have a kedge anchor and 80 fathoms of light cable. It is such good holding ground that we are not dragging at all. It is true that the sea is smooth. Mr Surville arrived back at 1 p.m. with the longboat and everybody, the sick and the others; he is bringing back the ten barrels full of good water and a dozen billets of firewood. Mr Surville told me that the skins we took to be goat skins are the skins of a long haired domestic dog. They wanted to sell him some, making signs to indicate they were good to eat. We can see small plantations of potatotes[2] and other rather similar roots. Mr Surville also reports that in addition to the little stream there is a small river in the cove on the starboard side but quite near but surrounded by rocks although at high tide a boat can enter into it but could only go out again at high tide because of the rocks. That is all these gentlemen could see since they remained throughout in the cove to protect our workers against a surprise attack. The islanders do not trust us yet, which is why they do not want us to go into their homes or even beyond the cove. This morning there was a loud dispute between several of these natives who seemed to be chiefs or kings of several villages. A large number of these natives had gathered armed with clubs, lances and wooden swords, but one of these chiefs, who seems to be a good man, tried to appease them and succeeded by doing as follows: he asked Mr Surville for his naked sword, then into the village to various groups of islanders, spoke to them, showed them the sword. We presumed he was telling them we were peaceful men who wished no harm, with the proof in his hand since we trusted him with one of our weapons. It seems that his speech quietened them gradually as they made no further commotion. Their women also came to amuse our men and our sailors, making extremely lewd gestures at them to urge them to enter the bush with them; the men also made signs to go. We took good care not to wander away from the group for fear that this might be to draw us into a trap as at the Island of the Fair Nation,[3] where

---

[1] A common and prized shell is the *pipi* or *Amphidesma australe*; the mussels would be *Mytilus canaliculus*.   [2] Sweet potatoes or kumaras, *Ipomoea batatas*.

[3] Labé is referring to Gente Hermosa, discovered by Quiros in 1606, which is probably Rakahanga in the northern Cooks. The 'Isle de la belle nation' is shown on Vaugondy's map of 1756 to which Labé would have access. His comment, however, is based on a misunderstanding. The islanders appear to have attacked the Spanish with little provocation and continued until subdued by force; thereafter they were relatively peaceful and the episode of the 'lady, graceful and sprightly' followed, resulting in 'the great loss of six souls' – those of the sailors who met her and found that 'the lady did not prove to be prudish in going with them' and so emerged with safe bodies but imperilled immortal souls. See Markham, *The Voyages of Pedro Fernandez de Quiros*, pp. 214–15.

the women played a similar trick on the crew of a traveller who had several of them killed through being too trustful in going to a rendezvous.

I therefore said that we trusted only the chief of the watering place who was the first to come on board when we were more than 3 leagues from the bay. When he came aboard we gave him a singlet and trousers of red cloth and a shirt. He at once gave the Captain a dog skin cloak in exchange.[1] Since that moment and with the good treatment he has received the chief seems to trust us, in a word see how his preventing the disturbance this morning proves it, and when the boat left the cove for the ship he embarked in the said canoe to come with Mr Surville, but the islanders, men and women, seeing him leave started to weep and shout like the devil; then he told the Captain not to row any further, the local men at once launched one of their canoes and came to get him from the boat. We know not what to think of all these farces. The boat went to the ship. We will see tomorrow how things turn out.

I was forgetting to say that the country has neither pigs, hens nor goats. The said chief asked for an empty barrel and an axe, [which] we will bring him tomorrow morning. Strong W breeze until 8 p.m. I bought today for Mr Surville two clubs which seemed to be made of bone but less heavy and a kind of devil or one of their idols of a kind of green stone.[2] The lot cost a six-foot length of red cloth. Mr Surville gave me one of the said clubs and a dogskin cloak. I have also 2 fishing hooks [?] and an earring of that green stone 3 inches long [and as] thick as a pipe stem.

I was forgetting to say that natives of Lauriston Bay have no iron or other metals. They use a green stone axe and shells for knives, all as at Port Praslin. They also have a weapon which is a lance 10 to 12 feet long made of very heavy wood, there is a green stone axe 6 inches long at one end with a club at the other end.[3] They know what slaves are, for they offered to sell some to the Captain and even to the soldiers in exchange for pieces of red cloth; however we were unwilling to take them for fear [?],[4] and the only game this country produces is teals and sea birds. The tide rises here by about 7 feet, the currents run SSW and SSE although they are not strong.

[1] The dogskin cloak was a *Kahu kuri*. The Maori dog or cur (*kuri*) was probably brought by migrating Polynesians from Tahiti. It became extinct in the 1860s.
[2] The *hei tiki* carved of greenstone.
[3] The lance is the *taiaha*. The greenstone axe is the ceremonial adze, *toki-poutangata*, consisting of a stone blade tied to a covered wooden handle with a heavy ornamented head.
[4] Slaves were enemies captured in war or the offspring of women similarly taken prisoner.

Wednesday 20th

From 8 p.m. yesterday until this morning strong SW to W breeze, fairly fine weather, smooth sea. At 5 a.m. the Captain left in the longboat to get water in the sandy cove, as before with 8 oarsmen, 6 sailors to fetch firewood, 4 of our scurvy cases who are able to walk to breathe the land air, and 13 soldiers armed with their muskets to protect the workers and others. The boat took away 10 empty barrels and one to be given to the chief as a gift together with an axe which he had requested from our Captain. We gave him yesterday a [?] which he had asked for. We refuse him nothing. It is true that he is a good man who seems to be very fond of us. Mr Surville took ashore for presents and barter some red cloth and blue and white linen in order to tame them and coax them and to avoid any disagreement with these islanders. It is not that we are afraid of them, for ten armed men would be enough to drive them out of their homes, but then where would we find what we need once we have driven these people away? This is why we humour them [that] and humaneness and nothing else. I forgot to say that this morning I lowered the yawl which took our sick to the watering cove.

At 7 this morning three small canoes laden with fish came up under the ship's gallery. I was able to buy only five fish from them. They went away towards the SE part of the bay[1] without agreeing to sell any more. At 1 p.m. today Mr Surville came aboard with the two boats and all the men who had gone ashore with him, sailors, soldiers, sick, and ten barrels of water and a little firewood. They had much more difficulty landing today than on previous days. The chief seeing the boats ready to land in the cove came to tell the Captain to return to the ship. We gestured that we needed water, wood, etc. He then went to hold a parley with other chiefs and after a half hour made a sign saying we could land remaining in the same place, I mean on the beach close to the stream of fresh water, and no further. Unwilling to break with these people, we do what they ask. However 10 men would be more than enough to drive them off although they numbered today more than two hundred men gathered on the hill armed with lances and stone clubs. After the discussions they dispersed and left our people alone to get the water and the wood and a great quantity of greens such as wild celery, large cress and a type of water cress. Our sick and others eat quantities of it raw and cooked in soup and in their stews.

[1] Making for the heavily populated Mangonui–Oruru part of Doubtless Bay.

It does them a power of good. I have no doubt that this will restore all our men. We also buy lamp oil, it does not smell bad, I think it is made with seeds.[1] We again gave presents to the chief; in spite of that I fear that we will have to make war in order to be safe and capture their entrenchments along the shore on a ridge. If that happens we will put our sick there to restore their health, the entire crew being attacked by scurvy to a greater or lesser extent. The presents we made to the chief today consist of an empty barrel, an axe, some linen cloth, a small length of red cloth. Only the women are pleased to see us, for they are continually provoking our officers and the sailors and soldiers, making gestures that are not made even in brothels, going so far as to lift up the bird skin that covers their nakedness and showing them all they have. The country produces no fruit, at least none can be seen. Strong breeze. Weighted anchor at 3.30 p.m. to get nearer the sandy cove where we get the water. Steered S¼SW sounding at 24 f. coral and gravel, 22, 19 f. At 4.30 made for the beach steering NW close-hauled larboard tack, then sounded 23 and 24 f. fine sand and gravel. At 5.45 tacked SW¼S and found 24 f. fine sand. The winds W and W¼NW. Continued to sound 24 to 18 f. Altered courses at 6.45 bearing for the cove where we get the water. Since weighing anchor tacked as shown above in the said bay until 7.30 p.m. when we were forced to drop anchor in 18 f. of water fine sandy bottom. It is night which forced us to drop a bower anchor and let out 40 f. of cable. Bearings of the anchorage: the sandy cove where we get the water of the palissaded hill bears WNW dist. 1 league, the nearest land which is a large mountain with its brow on the shore N ½ league, a headland further off the same side NE¼N3°E, 1 short league, the southernmost point of the bay ESE 3°S.

† At 8 p.m. the man called Sans Regret or Mathieu Pupier from Lyon, a soldier from the detachment on board, died of scurvy, aged about 42.[2]

Bearings of the first anchorage in Lauriston Bay Monday 18 December 1769, at 9.30 p.m., the bearings shown for the said 18th are unsatisfactory; the one that follows is correct, cancelling the first, namely the starboard point of the bay as you come in which is the only one visible although it is the second one bears N4°W 1⅔ l., the watering place in the sandy cove below the islanders' habitation on a steep bluff

[1] Oil was extracted from the berries of the *Titoki* (*Alectryon excelsus*), less frequently from those of the *Tutu* (*Coriaria arborea*). The reference to lamp oil is to the use the French had in mind, as oil was not used for lighting purposes by the Maoris.
[2] See No. 188.

bears NW2°W 1⅔ l., the headland with small islets or reefs slightly off shore bears W3°S 1⅔ l., the bottom of the bay in this part WSW 5°W 3¼ league, the middle of the bay SSW2°W about 3¼ leagues, a house at the back of the bay on a steep hillock near the shore S2°E 3¼ l.

[In] the SE there seems to be a river by a truncated headland which seems to be detached. It bears SE dist. 3½ l.[1] The larboard point as you enter the bay bears E1°S 3½ l. Another headland is visible in the distance behind the first. There are close by two small isolated rocks between this said point and the SE.

We can see close inshore two small rocks where the sea breaks.

Thursday 21st

Strong W to WSW gales from 8 last night to 4 a.m. At 7 a.m. a succession of squalls. As the ship dragged we had to let out up to 80 f. of cable, then the ship held. For the rest of the day rain wind and strong gusts. At 6 p.m. the wind increased, hoisted in the yawl and [?] until 8 p.m. The canoes did not appear today.

Friday 22nd

Strong gale and squally weather from 8 last night until today 5 a.m. when the weather improved. At the same time several canoes came up, but with no fish; they brought a little cress which they gave to the Captain. The chief who seems to favour us was in one of the canoes with some other kind of chief from another village. We made them presents of linen cloth, blankets etc, so as to coax them.[2] Then we made signs indicating we were going ashore to get water and wood; we also told them we were too far off and were going to bring the ship nearer the cove. They returned to land apparently satisfied. At 6 a.m. set the cable to the capstan and hove with a strong SW wind until 11.30 a.m. when we got under sail and stood SE and SSE under the topsails and the jibs, finding 18 [to] 20 f. fine sand and rotted coral, small gravel. At 12.45 stood for the watering place finding 20 [to] 18 f. shells and gravel until 1.45 when we lowered a bower anchor in 18 f., rotted shells and black gravel. Paid out all the cable up to the bit. Then we lowered the other bower anchor to moor by the head and hove on the SW

---

[1] Mangonui harbour.
[2] Pottier is more specific: 'The captain gave the new chief a jacket similar to the one given to the other and a green woollen blanket he coveted.'

cable. We have a length of 65 f. of cable left and about 50 f. of the one we are using. We are moored SW¼S and NE¼N.

Bearings of the anchorage: The NE point which marks the starboard entrance of the bay which is the second one, the first being hidden, bears NE 5°E dist. half a league, the land nearest to us NNE two or three cable lengths, the mouth of the small river with small rocks NW5½°W one third of a league, the sandy cove where we get our water at the foot of a small hill when the native village is situated bears WNW a good third of a league, a broken headland with a large reef offshore bears SW4°W dist. 1 league, the seaward point of the reef SW. Lauriston Bay seems to sweep in a curve from this point which is WNW. To begin with the natives made the boat go to the other side of their village in a rocky cove when one finds more water than in this sandy cove, but the boats have difficulty in approaching, which caused us to go to the first cove. I do not know why they wanted us to change watering places. Continuation: the middle of Lauriston Bay which consists of low and sandy land bears S¼SW dist. 2¾ l. All the parts of the bay which consist of bare country where I think there is a river SE 3¼ leagues. High mountains are visible far inland covered with trees; I think it is from there they get the timber for their canoes which are made of one piece, although some are 55 to 60 feet long; this requires fine trees. According to the bearings the larboard point of the bay as you enter with two small rocks almost touching, a large one and a small one, bears E¼SE2°S 4 leagues; another cape with a sugar loaf close by bears E¼SE3°E 7 leagues; other land in the distance E 4°S very distant. Fair weather, light breeze until 8 p.m. the winds SW.

Saturday 23rd

From 8 last night until this morning fair weather, devilishly cold, the winds SSW to SW. At 4 this morning we readied the longboat and lowered the yawl and readied at once to go to land. At 5 o'clock 6 canoes came up bringing much cress and other [food?]. The chief who seems full of good will towards us came in one of the canoes and again gestured for us to go ashore to get water. He was curious to know what a gun was. We showed him and assured him that all we put in it was what struck and to show him its effect we fired a canon ball out at sea which caused him to fall down in fear on the main deck.[1]

---

[1] Labé is allowing his prejudices to show. Surville states that the chief watched carefully where the cannon ball fell, and Pottier comments that he looked ecstatic.

All the canoes that were alongside fled back to land. Shortly after the longboat and the yawl left for the water cove which we are calling Chevalier Cove,[1] with the Captain and 14 rowers, 12 soldiers and the sick cases who could walk armed with swords as were the rowers, the soldiers with their muskets. The chief who had stayed on board after the shot went back in the longboat with three other natives who had stayed on board. The small boat we obtained at Bashi Island is used to land our men off our boats.

At 9.30 this morning Mr Surville sent back the small boat with some fish for the crew, which I distributed at once and sent it back to load our people. It is manned by the 3 islanders we took from Bashi Island, who are very docile men. The winds have prevailed SW to WSW from 8 to midday, good breeze, fair weather.

The yawl came back at 1 p.m. with the sick. The land air and the boiled cress is doing them good. I reckon that if we can land and set up a tent for a fortnight they will all recover. This morning I had all the guns loaded with balls and another with grapeshot, ready to fire at the natives if they do the least harm to our people ashore and at the slightest signal from our boats. It was agreed that if they saw the slightest evidence of harm on the part of the natives they would haul up a flag. At 2.30 this afternoon Mr Surville arrived in the longboat with the rest of the men and brought back ten barrels of water, a little wood and a little vegetable cress. When our boat reached the shore saw a great deal of fish; namely mackerel[2] and [?] which the natives had taken in a large and very long net; it is this fish which the Captain sent this morning to the ship. They made no difficulty today over letting our people land, they even gave quantities of fish to the sailors and soldiers. They were not so much in groups as formerly and allowed our sailors to go up in the valley to within a musket shot without saying anything. A few women appeared, immodest as usual, and a few men without weapons and they questioned our men by signs to know what we did with the prisoners we took and whether we ate them. We make them understand that we bury them. They told us that in their country when they have prisoners they cut their heads off, showed them to the people, then opened out their stomachs and ate them; I conclude from this they are cannibals.

Good SW breeze until 8 p.m. The chief suggested to Mr Surville

[1] Rangiawhia Cove is one of several small bays along this deeply indented and precipitous coast.
[2] The Horse Mackerel, *Trachurus novae-zelandicae*, and the Southern Mackerel, *Pneumatophorus colias*.

to go to windward of the bay where is situated a large sandy cove with a kind of steep rock in the middle with a village on it, it is a cove we did not see upon entering which we left to starboard, a very bad place for ships as it is exposed to the winds from NW to SE. Accordingly this suggestion was not accepted. Mr Surville is too considerate towards them. They do not deserve it. They are scoundrels and great thieves. If I had been in charge I would have been blunt with them and would have set up camp on the hill on the starboard side of the watering cove and would have driven them all off in order to put our sick there and restore our health. Ten men would be more than sufficient to hold the said haven, but Mr Surville does not want to break with them, consequently we cannot discover what is in the interior of the country. The chief who comes aboard is importunate, he wants everything he sees. Sometimes we give it to him or else one has trouble in refusing. [This is] nonsense on the Captain's part. At 5 p.m. our NE [?] broke off and floated away, sent off the yawl at once to recover it, which was done. Nothing noteworthy until 8 p.m.

Sunday 24th

From 8 p.m. yesterday fair weather, light SW to WSW breeze all night. In the morning overcast sky, signs of rain. At 4.30 this morning several canoes came up but without fish. The chief of the village was in one of them and climbed on board. Seeing that the muskets were being prepared to go ashore he made the Captain understand that we were not to go ashore with them. It seems that this frightens them, but we still go well armed for fear of a surprise attack. There were two women in the canoes that came up, they came on board, they are very ugly but this does not prevent them from making gestures as usual very lewd. Once more the chief asked for what he saw in the quarter deck cabin but we gave him nothing.

At 5.30 this morning the longboat, the yawl and the small Bashi boat, with 18 sailors each with a sword, 12 soldiers with their muskets and 18 ambulant sick; I also gave them a sword each. The boat is taking ten casks for water and some axes to cut firewood. At 9.30 Mr Surville sent back the small Bashi boat with fish for the crew. I sent it back at once. I have obtained from the islanders some stone axes and some dog skins they use to cover themselves, some clubs which I think are made with whalebone and other trash of this kind.[1] At 11.30 this

[1] Trash from the trading point of view: Labé is thinking of the commercial aims of the voyage contrasted with the poverty of the natives he has met.

morning a canoe came up under the stern gallery. The clerk, Mr Monneron, was fishing. These people are such thiefs that they cut his line and sped away at once. I was about to fire muskets at them, but for fear of alarming our men who were ashore I held back. The cress we are eating as a salad and in the soup has caused a revolution on four officers including myself who were very exhausted, but it passed after an hour.[1] It is a vegetable that sends the blood pulsing through the veins but it does good. At midday the yawl came back with firewood, unloaded and sent it back. At 1.15 all our boats came back with all our men and ten barrels of water. They had no trouble today with the natives as far as landing was concerned. In addition our gentlemen and our sailors were able to walk inland. They met very few natives on their way, however they remained on their guard for fear of a surprise attack, but it seems that our firearms intimidate these people. We showed them and even fired several shots and made them understand that when they fired men were killed [and] moreover that it was thunder. They believed it and consider us more than men and no longer go near our weapons. Mr St Paul being ashore near one of the chiefs happened to raise his musket inadvertently, the chief fled at once, no doubt for fear of being shot at. The women alone go near our sailors. It would seem from their signs that they would be delighted to have dealings with our sailors. The chief of the district is still favourable towards us. Mr Surville's knife having been stolen, he got angry and the said chief did so well that he found the thief and brought back the knife. Fair weather throughout the afternoon until 8 p.m.; partly cloudy, light breeze, smooth sea. At 4 o'clock several canoes crossed the bay; some have large shells they use as trumpets.[2]

Monday 25 December 1769

Christmas Day.[3] From 8 last night until midnight fair weather, slightly overcast, light breeze. † At 1 this morning one of the Mapias,[4] natives of Bashi Island, one of the 3 taken as replacements for our 3 deserters, died of scurvy. He was 22 years of age. For the rest of the

[1] The sudden intake of fresh food and vitamins – the use of the greens as salad would have preserved their full vitamin content – would affect men suffering from malnutrition. There is nothing harmful or poisonous in the greens themselves.
[2] The *putara* or shell trumpet, sometimes fitted with a wooden mouthpiece, was fairly common in northern New Zealand. The shells used were the New Zealand Triton, *Charonia capax euclioides*, the *Struthiolaria papulosa* and the *S. vermis*.
[3] This is the only reference to the Christian festival. There is no mention of any religious service; see Appendix C.
[4] *Mapia* being the word most frequently recognised by the French as meaning 'good', the Bashi Islanders became known as Mapias; see also below the reference to the Mapia boat.

night light breeze. In the morning sent the 3 boats to the watering place under the Captain with ten empty casks for water. They were manned by 18 sailors, 12 soldiers, and some sick who can walk; the others are on board in a serious condition, Mr Surville does not take them ashore; I consider them as dead men since they cannot get better on board. I do not know why the Captain keeps them on board, however I told him it was advisable to take them ashore setting up one or two tents, he replied that it would cause their loss. I offered to stay ashore with a guard of 15 to 20 men to protect them from the natives and a surprise attack, but all to no avail. What is going to happen? Our sick will not be able to recover and we will have unpleasantness of seeing them die on board and will be in serious difficulties to run the ship. And then the Captain will reproach himself all his life for the deaths of poor wretches whom we could have saved if we had acted differently. As for me I am not responsible, I pointed out everything that can happen later. At 9 this morning the small Mapia boat, I mean the one from the Bashi Islands came back. It brought a sackful of vegetable and no fish. I am surprised Mr Surville does not use the seine, seeing the country is rich in good fish. Sent back the Mapia boat to land. No native canoes came on board. Two left Chevalier Cove this morning and crossed the bay. At 11.30 our two boats arrived. They left the sick ashore [and] an officer and four soldiers to guard them. The longboat brought back ten barrels of water, [and] the yawl laden with firewood and sand. As soon as the longboat was unloaded I sent it back to the shore to fetch the sick and the others who had stayed ashore. They arrived at 1 p.m. We unbent the mainsail and mizzen top, a new sail, and bent other well mended sails.

At 2 p.m. our men left in the two boats manned by soldiers, the sailors with swords, to go seining in a cove to the left of the watering place.[1] This spot turned out to be full of rocks awash, which caused them to follow the starboard side of the bay going towards the cape where there is a bank or reef stretching out to within a musketshot of the shore. The Captain passed by at a good distance and I through the middle where the sea was breaking, nevertheless there was not more than 3 feet of water. Not finding a clear area to seine all this part being full of rocks awash and clear of the water, we were forced to go in, I mean to the other side of the cape which bears SW 4°W. We found

---

[1] The boats followed the coast west of the watering creek or Brodie's creek, along a series of rock strewn inlets and around the reef on which the *St Jean-Baptiste* was almost lost on 27–28 December to Whakaroro, a cove to the east of Patia Point; this cove lies behind a headland, hardly a cape, to the SW of the ship's anchorage.

there a fine sandy bay east of the point, with some rocks, but you can throw the seine 3 times without fear of meeting rocks. We seined there and caught no fish, this was because the wind was blowing straight into the bay. I found quantities of wild celery which is a good vegetable. The Captain climbed up on the hill of the cape and saw on the other side a large sweep of a very fine sandy bay, and higher up a village. In a word this seemed to form a magnificent port. After examining this carefully he came down and soon after 6 or 7 natives came on the beach where we were, they brought cress and made us understand there was a great deal of fish in the port on the other side of the headland. Mr Surville expects to go tomorrow with three boats. He will get water and wood, etc., very easily while ashore in the small cove. At 7 p.m. we left this large cove and reached the ship at 8.15 p.m. with sail and oars. The wind SSW to SSE, light breeze. I was forgetting to say that this morning our boats went to fetch water and firewood from Chevalier or Watering Cove and the natives said nothing to them, consequently our gentlemen and our sick went walking in the plain[1] and on the hills, they met no one who said anything to them. They saw fields of potatoes,[2] but they are still too small. Our firearms inspire terror in the natives, which means they no longer dare [blank].

Tuesday 26 December 1769

Since 8 p.m. last night fair weather, almost calm, the winds SSE to ESE. At 4 this morning I had our second boat lowered and manned, as well as the large one and the yawl and the small Mapia. Messrs Surville, Charenton, Lorry, the clerk, also embarked with 28 sailors and petty officers, 12 soldiers and all the ambulant sick, all armed with muskets or swords. The boats are taking ten casks for water, axes to cut firewood, and the seine for fishing. At 5 this morning they left with a SE breeze and sailed for the port we discovered yesterday afternoon on the other side of the point which is at the turning of the bay, still to starboard and on the other side of the place where we seined yesterday evening. The winds remained ENE to North, almost calm. From 4 to 5 this evening two small canoes came up to the ship, they had neither fish nor vegetables. I let them climb aboard. They left at 5 for the watering cove and their little village. At 8 p.m. our boats returned with all our people, sick, soldiers and sailors; 10 barrels of

---

[1] In fact an area of low-lying ground surrounded by an amphitheatre of sloping hills.
[2] Kumaras, *Ipomoea batatas*.

water, some firewood, a large quantity of fish caught with our seine, some cress and a kind of celery which was bartered from the natives for a little cloth. According to the report of the Captain and of our officers the place where they went on the other side of the bay by SW Cape is a magnificent place. It is in the WSW. It forms a wide bay with fine sandy beaches, sandy bottom with 10 to 12 feet of water; almost inshore is a rock with 5 or 6 f. of water on the off side and 3 or four fathoms on the land side, still sandy bottom. We have named this place Refuge Port or Bay.[1] It forms a cul-de-sac closed by a sand spit about a league wide, from above the hill you see a kind of [?] and on the other side is the sea where there is a large opening which is the same one we saw when we came from Cape Surville. There are several islands or islets at the entrance, it must make a fine bay, however it is not equal to Lauriston Bay, as it is exposed to the N to NW wind, the most dangerous. Mr Charenton has sounded all this bay. I am drawing the plan. The starboard entrance of Lauriston Bay which we believed to be islands is not, but is a peninsula.

The natives are very welcoming, much more than those of Chevalier Cove where we have always obtained our water, consequently we have given it up in favour of Refuge Cove although it is more than $2\frac{1}{2}$ leagues from where we are anchored. The water is very good, easy to get as is firewood, weeds, cress and the kind of wild celery, [and] quantities of fish caught in the net. The local chief was the first to lead our Captain up the palissaded mountain which they use as an entrenchment when they are attacked by the other natives from the landside, according to what he told our Captain: when they come and attack me I withdraw to the mountain with my people, where it is very difficult to climb, and I defend myself with long lances and many stones which I drop on them and when I have killed some I run at once to take them and cut them into pieces and then eat them, which does prove they are cannibals and that they kill their prisoners to eat them. The people of Refuge Cove are affable, but our firearms intimidate them, they have seen our gentlemen bringing down birds in flight [which] surprised them considerably and [they] must take us for demigods and not men. We gave two small pigs, a male and a female, and a cock and two hens to the watering cove chief.

[1] The bay sweeps west from Patia Point, climbed by Surville the previous day. A monument commemorating the *St Jean-Baptiste* now stands on the hill.

Wednesday 27th

Light breeze since 8 p.m. last night the winds E to NE throughout the night. At 5 this morning sent our three boats to Refuge Cove with several officers, 24 sailors, 12 soldiers and 20 ambulant sick, all armed with muskets or swords for fear of a surprise attack. They took ten empty barrels in the boats, axes to chop firewood and our seine to catch fish. The day was continually overcast, the winds ENE, the sea breaking and somewhat rough. No canoes came out today; they have not brought us any fish for several days although I see them fishing continually and catching quantities of fish, I don't know why, it seems it is due to the nets these islanders use. Our 3 boats came back[1] from Refuge Cove at 9 p.m. The longboat brought seven barrels of water, some firewood and some vegetables such as cress and a kind of celery. At 9.30 the yawl also came back, bringing only the seine – the fish stayed in the second boat. It is overblowing, I fear it will not be able to make the ship. The winds ENE, strong gale, signs of heavy squalls; all the sick are in it with 4 soldiers and its crew, making in all 35 men with firewood and 3 water casks. Strengthened the main cable bitt. According to the officers' report the natives of Refuge Cove abandoned two huts and retired inland for fear of being harmed, and are subject to attacks by other people in the island.

I saw yesterday in the cove where I fished a small orchard with a yellowish red fruit the size of a large olive which has a long stone like an olive's. This fruit is edible, I have seen quantities of it in our American islands which is also eaten [there]. This fruit is the only one we have seen.[2] We have shot game: a type of blackbird,[3] curlew.[4] There are also some parrakeets,[5] [?], turtle doves[6] and sea birds.

Thursday 28th December 1769

Since our two boats arrived last night strong gale, rough sea, the winds ENE. At 3 this morning overblew, the ship dragging, we lowered the main anchor, the two others we were moored to being

---

[1] Literally translated, but what Labé means is that they were seen making their way back. [2] The berry of the *karaka* tree, *Corynocarpus laevigatus*.
[3] There was no native blackbird. Labé is probably referring to the tui, *Prosthemadera novaeseelandiae*. [4] The long-billed curlew, *Numenius madagascariensis*.
[5] Two types of parakeets would have been found in the area, the Red-crowned Parakeet or Kakariki, *Cyanoramphus novaezelandiae*, and the Yellow-crowned Parakeet, *Cyanoramphus auriceps*.
[6] Probably the New Zealand pigeon, the *kereru* (*Hemiphago novaseelandiae*).

(?), let out 30 fathoms of heavy cable for the strain and also 3 hawsers. The weather overcast with light rain. At dawn we saw no sign of our 2nd boat, I am afraid it may have suffered some accident as it is very poor and overloaded with men, firewood, etc. I expect the officer, Mr de l'orme seeing he was making no headway, will have decided to return to Refuge Cove or Port where he will be protected from the prevailing winds; if not I think they are lost.

At 8 this a.m. the NW cable snapped, strong ENE gusts, the sea very rough, the ship dragging 2 anchors. At 9 a.m. being within a musket shot of the breakers we decided albeit a little late to let out our two cables and sail under the foresail, fore staysail and mizzen, being a mere two longboat's lengths from the breakers of an islet close inshore. The sea breaks over us and drives us towards the coast. To make things worse the ship remained for quite a time without responding to the rudder and we could see death in front of us, seeing the rocks alongside the ship close enough to make our hair stand on end. However we were fortunate enough to bear off, the ship having gone ahead a little, God preserved us from a great danger and worked a miracle in our favour. Having the breakers quite close we have to cover more than half a league ranging along the reefs of SW Cape always within musketshot. At last having turned the reef we made for Refuge Cove or Port to anchor there, with gale force winds, the sea breaking over the ship which strains her considerably with the heavy rolling, the gunnel in during all this time. We lowered a heavy anchor and clinched a brand new cable, the only anchor and cable we had left with the large kedge anchor which has a 7 inch cable securely clinched, and another small one of seven hundred with a 7 inch cable, a sad situation being able to depend only on our large anchor. Before we reached Refuge Cove, lost our yawl which was swamped and sank and cut its tow-rope on the rocks. Being athwart Refuge Cove, the islet within two musket shots, we anchored at 12.30 today withour main anchor in $6\frac{1}{2}$ f. fine sandy bottom and let out 130 f. of cable; also lowered our kedge anchor and let out 80 f. of cablet. The seas mountainous, covering the ship from one end to the other, the ship straining and making water at two inches per hour. When at anchor we sighted our 2nd boat at anchor in Refuge Cove, it is sheltered from the prevailing ENE winds, but I am afraid some of our poor sick may die being exposed to the rain and weather. All the afternoon continuing squalls and rain. Unbent the topgallant yards and hauled in the lower yards. Having too few men we could not haul in the topsail yards. We are forced to freshen our cable and cablet every two hours and to remain in this critical position until 8 p.m. with our crew terror-stricken. I have only 10 or 12 men able to help me, the others are more dead than alive. Bearings of the anchorage. Being assailed by the ENE wind, hauled ourselves on 130 f. of cable into Lauriston Bay. The point of the SW cape and a reef off it by the starboard head as you enter bears NE3°E dist. 2 short leagues, the point of Refuge Cove or Port where our 2nd boat is N3°E dist. ¾ league, the rock or islet off the cove NNW4°N ½ league, the W point of the same cove NNW5°W. The weather overcast so that we cannot see the SE part of the bay nor the larboard side and headland as you enter the said Lauriston Bay. The 1st cove, Chevalier, where we obtained our water, was named Chevalier by our officers. [In] Refuge Cove a ship of 300 tons could take shelter without being afraid of high seas. A rock or islet can be seen inside by 3½ f. of water. Good shore and a very pleasant place.

Friday 29 December 1769

ENE gusts continued from last night until 4 a.m., the sea very rough breaking over the ship, constant light rain, forced to pump every 2 hours. At 6 this a.m. the tiller of the helm broke because of the rolling. At once wedged the rudder head and set to work to make a new one. It is the second one broken in the gale. At the same hour the wind shifted to NNW to NW which means that the sea moderated a little, but we are still rolling heavily as the swell is on our beam. At 7 this a.m. the 2nd boat took advantage of a lull to come to us with the men, sick and others. Several are in a bad way, I mean the scurvy cases, having spent two days in the rain and wind. Hoisted the boat in at once, they [had] emptied the 3 casks and thrown the firewood in the sea to lighten it. The longboat was also being towed by the ship, we have just hoisted it in. When we weighed anchor the grapnel of the said boat which was in it was thrown overboard through the rolling as we sailed. I thought that this time we would have lost the boat, but fortunately it was only damaged.

Here is the report of our officers who were ashore in the 2nd boat during the worst of the gale. The natives seeing us in the greatest danger consoled our gentlemen making them understand that they would give them some land to cultivate; they treated them very well and brought them some cooked fish, almost the only food they use and wanted them at all cost to stay in their huts; our gentlemen were not prepared to for fear the sailors might have dispersed and also for fear of a surprise attack, not trusting too far the promises of the natives. I was forgetting to say that at 6 this a.m. we lost our large kedge anchor, its cablet having snapped 20 fathoms from the ship.

† This morning one of our boatswain's mates named Julien Sicot from Dinan and Cartin, department of St Malo, aged about 30, died of scurvy.[1] Thrown overboard 2 h. later. Squally weather all day with rain from the NW then the WNW and W. The sea moderated completely, the wind coming from the back of the bay we have only the remainder of it and are partly out of danger with the W winds. If our cable should snap we can leave the bay without fear. Worked on the tiller of the helm all day, the spare one having snapped after being put into position.

† This morning a Moorish lascar, native of Bengal, age 30 or 31, died of scurvy this evening. Squally weather continuing until 8 p.m.

Saturday 30th

From 8 p.m. yesterday until this a.m. strong W to SW gale with only the remainder of the wind, smooth sea. At 5 this a.m. while the weather cleared lowered the longboat and with 10 sailors, 8 soldiers and 12 sick, Mr Surville and I went to Refuge Cove or Port. We went to their habitation on the crest of the hill where they retire when they are attacked by their enemies, which consists of precipices, impossible to oust them from there if one has no firearms. The said natives, headed by their chief, brought us some dried and cooked fish whereupon we gave them a few ells of blue cloth in exchange and some wheat and green peas as seeds showing them that they should be sown. We had squalls and winds all day but were sheltered by a small clump of trees where we prepared a meal for the sick, the sailors and the soldiers and ourselves. Returned near their habitation in the afternoon; we were brought more dried and cooked fish. Three young women came up who danced for over an hour some very lascivious and immodest dances, even more so than the Spanish dance called the Mosquito Bag.

At 5.30 p.m. we re-embarked and reached the ship at 7 very tired and wet with sea water. Hoisted the boat in at once. † Another Malabar, born in Pondicherry, aged about 29 died of scurvy. Continuing squalls, rain and wind until 8 p.m.

[1] Muster Roll No. 18.

Sunday 31 December 1769

From 8 p.m. yesterday squally weather, rain and wind, all night.
† At 1 this a.m. my Topar servant named Jonon [?] born in Pondicherry, aged about 30, died of scurvy.[1]

At 5 this a.m. sighted our yawl or small boat which we had lost during the gale, washed up ahead of us in the SW¼W distant ⅔ league, with a number of natives hauling it towards the sand dunes. I warned Mr Surville at once who told me to lower the longboat, which I did immediately, manned by 8 soldiers, 16 sailors, 3 caulkers carpenters with planks, nails, pitch, etc. to mend it and bring it back. The Captain and several of our gentlemen got in and left at once. The said boat was not half way to the land when I saw firstly a quantity of natives struggling to haul the said yawl and soon after I saw it no more. They had got it over the sand dunes. All day squally weather. At 2 this p.m. saw all our people, Captain and others in a group setting fire to villages where there are numerous huts[2] and also to two canoes and launched one which was sent towards our longboat. The huts and canoes set on fire were in the NW to SW¼W quite close to the shore. At 5 this p.m. the Captain and all our people returned in the longboat. This is what happened to them. The Captain on his way to the shore sounded from the ship to the shore found 6 and 5½ f. at about ⅔ of the distance from ship to shore, sandy bottom, then a very level bottom until he disembarked and even did it with difficulty. Once ashore he looked for the yawl without success; he did find tracks which he followed, it brought him to 3 or 4 ship's lengths where there is a small deep river but very narrow. This river is lined by great reeds and has several branches, two leading to the bay[3] in the NW and others that end in large lakes inland. The water is brackish at the mouth and very fresh further up. I think the natives took away our yawl into the lake I have just mentioned or hid it in the great reeds lining the river. Mr Surville, seeing the perfidiousness and the dishonesty of the natives, great thieves, having sought the yawl in vain, had decided so as to get it back to arrest one of the natives who might come to him. All the people seeing our men armed fled, only one came to meet our gentlemen, holding a green bough in his hand as a symbol of friendship with all these people.

[1] No. 100 in the muster roll, Jean de Rozario, who is shown as dying on 30 December 1769. The relatively large number of deaths occurring at the end of this month can be ascribed to the storm that battered Doubtless Bay at this time.

[2] This was not a formally laid out *pa*, but a collection of storage huts along the beach.

[3] The Waiotaraire Creek.

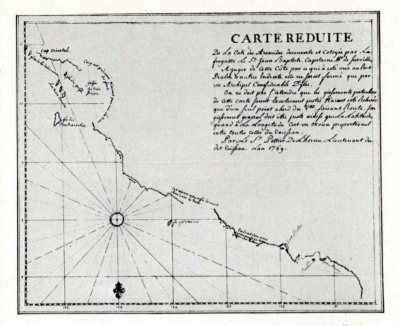

Plate 6. Chart of part of the Solomon Islands coast, by Pottier de l'Horme

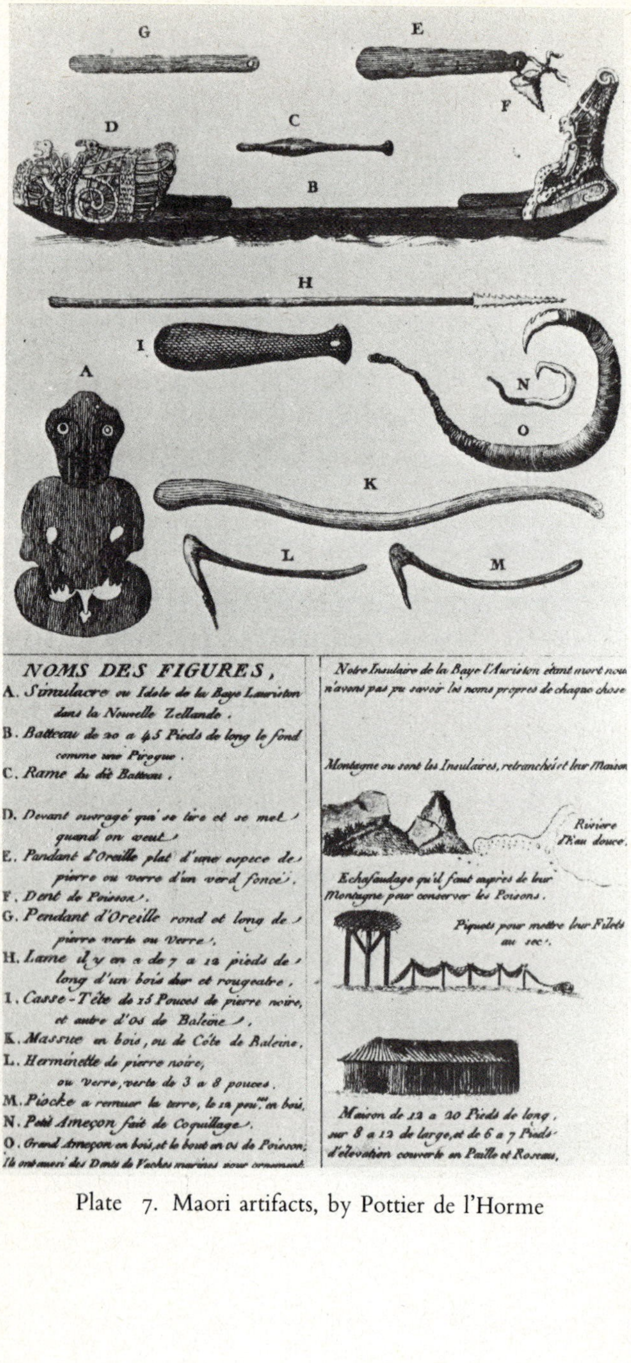

Plate 7. Maori artifacts, by Pottier de l'Horme

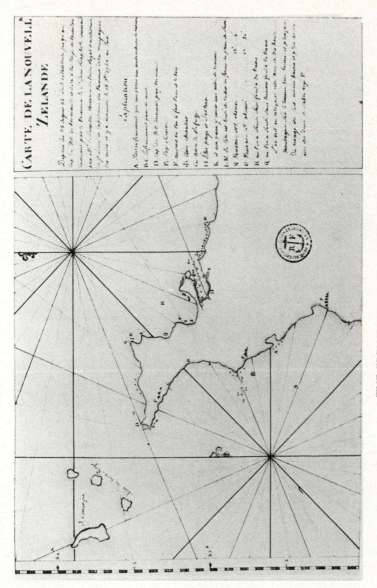

THE FRENCH MAP OF NORTHLAND

Plate 8. Chart of northern New Zealand, by Labé

Plate 9. *St Jean-Baptiste*'s anchor recovered from Doubtless Bay

Plate 10. Plaque on Surville monument, Patia Head, New Zealand

Mr Surville had him arrested, tied him up and taken to the boat under strong guard, then had some thirty small huts burnt in several small villages from the NW to SW¼W by the sand dunes close to the shore. He also burnt two large canoes and several very large nets. He took a canoe that was 35 feet long from stem to stern. The natives seeing their houses, canoes, nets, etc. on fire gathered about sixty [of them] armed with lances, clubs, but they never dared to approach until our men had gone back to the boat, then the poor wretches gathered around the huts which were still on fire but it was too late, the fire even reached the heather as far as the mountains at the back of Refuge Cove and did not go out until 8 this evening.

The native Mr Surville captured and led to the ship is a man of about 35 years of age, strong and wiry, 5 foot 2 in. tall, square built and crimped [hair?] like the kaffirs of the Guinea coast, long hair tied in a knot, a body the colour of the people from the Coromandel coast; this dress consists of a kind of dogskin cloak which covers his body, his nudity is not covered with cloth. This poor man looks very gentle and quiet. He is the one who invited the gentlemen in our boat to sleep in his hut, and who had brought them fish, etc. I had him put in irons and manacles for fear he might escape by swimming away. To my mind Mr Surville was wrong in not carrying away a dozen natives, they would have been useful on board for working the lower sails, as we have already lost 60 men from the crew in addition to 40 who are still sick. With the small number we have left we are not in a position to complete our work being short of men, food, rigging, etc. This New Zealand where we hoped to do marvels resulted in no trade, the islanders being poor and wretched, knowing no metals and having no goods of any worth, for all food [they] have only fish and fern roots[1] and in season a few potatoes. I have seen several small plantations twelve to 20 square feet in size. It is true that these people are lazy and do nothing but fish; the country is fairly poor, full of heather and ferns and reeds; [they] do not use pots to cook their food, everything is cooked, fish etc., in embers, they also make holes in the ground, put in them greens which they cover with leaves then with a little soil and light a fire over it and when that seems cooked to them they take it out and eat it, it is a little tough [?]. To preserve their dry fish and other food cooked and dried in the sun they have in front of their huts some stands [?], above is a small platform on which is their fish covered with sticks or reeds etc. Several of the natives have a thick beard, others

---

[1] Aruhe, the rhizome of the New Zealand bracken fern, *Pteridium aquilinum*.

very little like the Malays. At 5 this p.m. I had the longboat hoisted in as well as our small Bashi boat and the canoe captured today and rigged the capstan to leave. Mr de Surville had just decided to, it not being safe in such a windy bay, having only one anchor lowered with its cable [which] saved us in the gale, but we can no longer depend on it, it is closely examined now; it must have been good and good holding ground for us not to have been wrecked. God did a miracle in our favour and made it possible for us to see our homeland again, we owe Him thanks indeed. I am even surprised that Mr Surville did not decide earlier to leave this Lauriston Bay, having been constantly in danger, having lost four anchors and 4 cables in the gale, which we are forced to leave behind for fear of more bad weather if we were to stay a few days more working to get them back. It is not even then too safe, gusts and rain are still continuous, the wind SW, the sea fairly smooth. Departure from Lauriston Bay in New Zealand situated in 34°43′ S, I mean its headlands.

Sunday 31 December. At 7 p.m. set the topsails half mast up, eased off and at 9.30 weighed anchor from Refuge Cove and made sail at once, the winds SW, squally weather and steered to leave the bay weathering E from SSE to NE¼N. Sounded from the time we sailed from 7 to 15 f. of water, sand and pebbles, depth increasing gradually. At 10.45 p.m. the headland where I had ended my reckoning when I came in bears N dist. 1 league. I take up from there my same latitude and easterly longitude as I had when I came in: latitude of the entrance to the bay 34°53′, Est. longitude E 170°06′. Courses since the bearings of 10.45 this p.m. [blank].

Our native who is on board seems very sad, he often sighs and weeps. However he has a good appetite and eats and drinks all he is given. The Captain takes good care of him, makes him sleep on a [?] in the quarter deck cabin as well as the young kaffir taken in Port Praslin; that one is accustomed to our habits and does not think about his homeland, he begins to speak French, that lad is mischievous and has a lot of good sense. As far as the three Mapias taken in the Bashi Islands are concerned we have lost one through scurvy; they are quiet people who live a simple natural life, the two still on board we don't hear say a word and [they] don't speak a word of French, they are treated like the sailors – I mean as regards food, they do not work.

At 6 p.m. Captain Surville gathered us all the officers together as well as the boatswain in the quarter deck cabin to discuss our present state and hold a council in consequence. He read us an article of his instructions which forbids him to call at any Spanish settlements in America and asked our advice; in reply we described the state of the vessel with neither anchors nor cables, save one, no food or rigging, 62 men dead, the remainder ill of the scurvy, the ship in a poor condition, therefore unable to return by either Manila or China where a ship needs to be well provided with cables and anchors, since according to all the reports of travellers in all the places on the way to these two countries there are savage people and coasts with neither shallow anchorages nor shelter. In addition our crossing would take one hundred to one hundred and ten days, owing to the calms and contrary winds one finds in the said sea. To attempt this journey would be to risk [the strictures] of religion by sacrificing the remaining debris of our unhappy crew which to all intents and purposes would perish at sea as we would ourselves. To obviate such an inevitable disaster, we all agreed to call at South America as being the place we could reach the soonest, since we find ourselves in seas where winds prevail continuously from the SW to W, and, by keeping to the 33rd parallel we should not take more than three months to get there. It is the only course left to us, although a forbidden one, but being allied to the Spanish crown and knowing that nation for its feelings of humanity, we have great hope from the gentlemen who rule there and in that way we shall be able to restore the health of our crew, repair our vessel and obtain supplies of cable and anchor, food, sailors, etc., in order to leave promptly to continue our search for new discoveries and return to Pondicherry. In consequence, we drew up a statement which we all signed before sailing from Lauriston Bay. We are at present going to sail E.

Monday 1 January 1770

Since 10.45 last night until today midday, fresh gale, angry sea, squally weather, under the topsails and foresail, steering NE¼N to bear off from New Zealand. Courses NE, distance 21⅔ leagues. Lat. S Est. 34°07′, obs. 34°04′, diff. 3′N. Long. Est. E 171°02′. This morning saw New Zealand in the distance from S to S¼SW.

Our native from Lauriston Bay seems to have become resigned, he no longer seems sad, laughs with everyone, drinks and eats well and sleeps well, he eats a great deal. From time to time he is afraid that we will open his stomach and then eat him, that is what these natives do to people they make prisoner in their country, being subject to attacks from peoples who come from the middle of New Zealand, which explains why those from Lauriston Bay live in fortified areas in steep rocky ridges at the edge of the sea and are out of reach of their enemies.[1] I can speak of it, having seen and climbed on the said rocks. They eat each other and are good cannibals, but these people did not strike us as enterprising, if they had dared I am sure they would have seized some of our men and would have killed them; I think our firearms kept them quiet, having seen us shoot and seen the effect of the muskets.

[1] In fact, inter-tribal warfare was widespread in New Zealand and most villages were built on sites which provided natural protection and were defended by an intricate system of palisades and ditches.

APPENDIX A

THE DEATH OF SURVILLE

The following extract from Labé's Journal relates the circumstances surrounding the Captain's death and Labé's reaction to it, and the problems which the first officer encountered in bringing the ship to anchor in Callao and in dealing with the Spanish authorities.

Sunday 8 April

At 7 p.m. lowered a kedge anchor in 40 f. of water green ooze, and let out 112 f. of cable.

Courses SW¼S, distance 50 thousands of a league.

Bearings of the 7 p.m. anchorage taken this morning at dawn. What I take to be the Morre Solard[1] NW dist. about 10 l., a small long island [taken] for St Laurent Island[2] bearing NW¼W 3°N dist. 12 l., the larboard headland as you enter in the bay when we are at anchor bears NW¼N4°W dist. 3 l. It is a large cape overhanging the sea with a small rock like an upset canoe at the foot of it. The chain of mountains which ends in the plain of the bay bears N¼NW 1½ l. There is a kind of fortress in ruins on the ridge of this mountain, in the middle of a fine savanna or plain is seen a church on a low rise bearing NNE4°N 1½ l., it is not far from the shore. We can see numbers of houses around and numerous groves in the northern part, which I take to be orchards, the rest of the plain seems arid and dry. A large headland barring the entrance to the bay to starboard bears NE dist. 1 league, a flat island named Dazia Island[3] SE 3½ l, it is covered with bird droppings which makes it seem white. Between these two bearings we can see some capes and inside them some small bays with several small rocks or islets, sanctuaries for birds, this whole coast being full of different types. The entire coast is lined with ranges of mountains of different heights, those further

---

[1] Morro Solar rises to 925 ft near Punta La Chira.
[2] San Lorenzo, the large island off Callao.
[3] The small Isla de Asia, to the south of Chilca.

inland being visible from more than 20 l. on a fine clear day, which is fairly rare judging by the almost constant fog [we saw] on these high mountains. At 10 this a.m. the Captain, Mr Surville, sent me in our small boat to take some letters in the bay for the Viceroy of Lima. I went as far as the bar, but seeing it was impossible to land without endangering the boat and the sailors on the bar which was very high I decided to return to the ship where I gave the letters back to Mr Surville. I was back at twelve.

Description of what I was able to see of note: the shore is a sandy beach, the sea breaks more than three cable lengths offshore and rises and falls considerably. Chilca is at the foot of mountains and surrounded on all sides. The gentle slope which comes down to the sea may have a cultivable extent of 3 to 4 l.

Monday 9th

At anchor in the same Chila bay or cove.

At 1.15 yesterday afternoon the Captain went ashore to obtain food for our crew; for the rest he gave me instructions, should he not return, to sail for Callao roadstead. At 6 p.m. I saw his small boat being hauled up on the beach; I reckoned he would be spending the night ashore and that he would come aboard in the morning. I waited for him until 9.30 when, not seeing him return nor even his boat on the beach, I thought he might have been arrested by the coastguards, which led me to sail this a.m. at 9.30 with a S¼SE breeze for Callao roadstead where I expect to find our Captain. Courses N¼NW Est., NW¼N amended, distance Est. 1⅔ l., amended 3 l.[1] Lat. S Est. 12°41', obs. 12°34'.

Bearings at midday. What I take to be St Laurent Island bears NW4°N, the middle of Morro Solard NW¼N1°N dist. 9 or 10 l., a small islet by the shore NNW4°N, the land nearest to us forming a large cape NE¼E2°E dist. 3 l. The middle of Chilca bay or cove bears E¼NE2°E 4 l., that is where we were at anchor, Dazia Island being the southernmost land SE5°E in the distance. This entire coast consists of a range of mountains, very arid and rising gradually inland out of sight. I do not know what to think of our captain, I am even afraid he may have met with some accident when he crossed the bar with his small boat. I was watching with a glass when he reached the bar, I saw the boat in extreme danger and then saw no more of it for a long time

[1] The distance is first estimated by dead reckoning, then corrected according to the bearings.

and then further N by two musket shots. I shall be uneasy until I have news because it seems apparent that the boat was swamped or capsized on the bar. I am very much afraid he may be drowned. I hope I shall know for certain tomorrow once I have anchored off Callao.

† At 3 a.m. Pierre Lorey, a sailor, born in Lorient, department of Port Louis, died of scurvy, aged about 20.[1]

Monday 10 April 1770

From midday yesterday until midday today when we were athwart the Galley Point[2] of St Laurent Island and $2\frac{1}{2}$ l. from Callao roadstead, steering $W\frac{1}{4}NW$ to $NW\frac{1}{4}W$, light breeze, all sails high, studding sails and topgallants until 7 p.m. when we furled the studding sails and topgallants and hauled in the mainsail. At 8 o'clock being athwart the pass of Callao Island and St Laurent Island, I mean the opening, where one can see nothing but breakers and small rocks or islets, then to remain overnight at a certain distance I decided to stand off and on all night under the foresail and main and fore topsails so that I might be near the north point of St Laurent at dawn. At daybreak I bore up $N\frac{1}{4}NE$ and N edging away from the said point of St Laurent Island and clear of the small islets or rocks on the seaward side of the island. At 10.30 we were athwart Galley Point dist. $\frac{1}{2}$ a league as is shown in the bearings. We then see the ships in Callao roadstead. At 11.30 the longboat of the ship *Aurora* came alongside with sailors under command of their captain Don Joseph Beaxocul and shortly after, the longboat of the ship *Hercules* with sailors and their captain Don Juan Yxezboxocta and of the *Diamond* with captain Don Sutro Lloxes, all three Spanish vessels which are to sail at dawn for Cadiz to be paid off. The crews of the three ships started manoeuvring to get to the anchorage. The effect of the land rendered the sailors we had left incapable of work and the Spaniards' arrival was timely.

Bearings of the 24 hours. Yesterday at 6 p.m. the highest part of St Laurent Island bore from me $NW5°N$, distance about $5\frac{1}{2}$ l., the islets or rocks off St Laurent Island $NW2°N$ and the furthest out to sea NW, the nearest land which is Morro Solard NNE 3 leagues. At 8 p.m. St Laurent Island, which seems most northerly, ENE. At 11 p.m. the said

[1] Muster Roll No. 85.
[2] 'The worst punishment was being relegated to St Lawrence Island off Callao, a place of exile for blacks and mulatoes who were sentenced for some crime to quarry stones for public buildings. This penalty was compared to being sent to the galleys in Europe, as a result the western point of the island was known as the galley'. J. Descola, *La vie quotidienne au Pérou au temps des Espagnols*, p. 32.

island bore N2°W. At 4 a.m. a point which seemed the northerly one N$\frac{1}{4}$NE. At 6 a.m. a headland a little more westerly than the northern one bore N$\frac{1}{4}$NE5°N, Callao Island NE4°N about 2 l., the Pierced Stone NE$\frac{1}{4}$E1°E, one of the islets off Callao and St Laurent island NNE, the middle of Morro Salard ENE1°E very hazy, one of the points of St Laurent Island which I took at 8 o'clock to be one of the most northerly bore N$\frac{1}{4}$NE5°E dist. 2 short leagues, another point of the said island NE 1 league, the middle of Callao Island E$\frac{1}{4}$NE4°N 2 to 2$\frac{1}{2}$ l., the middle of the islet E5°N 1$\frac{1}{3}$ l., the end of the breaker of this same island E1$\frac{1}{2}$°N, the southernmost land very hazy.

† At 10.30 this a.m. the man named Victor, slave belonging to Mr Dulucq, ship's surgeon, died of scurvy.[1]

At 10.30 Galley Point bore E$\frac{1}{4}$NE distance half a league; when taking this bearing we sighted Callao roadstead when numerous ships were visible. That is my last bearing. I am steering and manoeuvring to reach the anchorage, it is some 2 leagues. The effect of land is having a cruel influence on the remnants of our crew and renders them incapable of working.

Continuation of Tuesday 10 April from after midday until we anchored; I mean when the three longboats of the Spanish ships came alongside with their captain[s] and many of their sailors, I asked these three gentlemen to provide help to work the ship, being forced to ply windward by tacking to reach the anchorage with none of our crew fit to work. These gentlemen at once allocated their sailors for the work and as we tacked in the bay during the afternoon several boats came up with food sent by the Royal Officer[2] by order of the Viceroy. In one of these boats came a Lieutenant-Colonel named Demetrius Egam,[3] sent by the Viceroy in Lima with 25 soldiers and an officer to see that nothing was taken off or sold. He showed his written instructions from the Viceroy enjoining him to allow no goods to be unshipped, not even new clothes for our own use. This Mr Demetrius Egam is to stay on board for as long as we are undergoing repairs or, if we unload our cargo, until we have finished discharging and the Royal Officers and the major of the guards. If we unload the cargo it will be stored in

---

[1] Muster Roll No. 203.

[2] *Ofizial real.* There were four such in Lima, one of whom was entrusted with the supervision of Callao.

[3] Egam, sometimes spelt Egan, is Labé's rendering of Hagan or Higgins. It is likely that Labé's *bête noire* was a relative – uncle or cousin – of Bernardo O'Higgins (1776–1842), the 'Liberator' of Chile. Bernardo's father, Ambrosio customarily signed himself 'Higgins'. The dates of the latter's career do not place him in Lima in 1770; however a number of his relatives had come to South America in the eighteenth century.

Callao fort. This Mr Egam is to receive 12 piastres a day for his wages. I do not know who will pay, whether it is the king, but I am very much afraid that we may be responsible for this expense, as well as the Ohidor[1] or counsellor of the royal *audiencia* at Lima who is also the commissioner named to supervise matters relating to our ship, he is called Don Manuel de Gorenne. Let us now go back to our manoeuvre. Continued to tack, having a coastal pilot from Callao, a quite useless thing. Finally at 8.30 p.m. lowered our large anchor, the only one we had left, with a little kedge anchor, in 8 f. of water, olive-coloured ooze, and moored by the head with the kedge anchor the longboat from the *Hercules* with a cablet, both lent. We are too far S and too far from the shore and very distant from where the other ships are anchored, but these are the orders of the Viceroy, Don Manuel Amat.[2] I blew the whistle to forbid our men to infringe the Viceroy's orders which are that anyone caught selling the slightest thing will be punished and sent to the Baldives[3] for 10 years.

Bearings of our anchorage in the port of Callao. The anchorage of the European ships and of the local ones [is] further N and nearer the shore. The flagmast of the fortress of Callao $E\frac{1}{4}SE3°E$ half a league, the pierced stone $SE\frac{1}{4}S3°S$, the middle of Morro Solard $SE\frac{1}{4}E5°S$, the tongue of land of Callao which forms the port[4] SSW 3°W, Callao Island $S\frac{1}{4}SW4°S$ about $1\frac{3}{4}$ l., the south point of St Laurent Island SSW4°S, Galley Point on the same island $W\frac{1}{4}NW$ $2\frac{1}{2}$ l., the northernmost land in the distance NNW4°W.

Continuation of Tuesday 10 April from midday until we dropped anchor in Callao roads.

At 11.30 this a.m., being by the point of St Laurent Island, a small fisherman's canoe came alongside. I asked him what news there was ashore. Here is the reply: your captain died on Chilca bar with 2 sailors with him, the 3rd, who had the letters for the Viceroy, escaped but with great difficulty although he had thrown himself into the sea with the parcel in a small bottle before the boat capsized. This news gave me great concern about Mr Surville's fate, yet I did not want to believe any of it, but unfortunately when the 1st longboat came alongside with the captain of the ship *Lorolles* called Don Joseph de Berrocal, I drew

---

[1] The *oidores*, four in number, were magistrates, members of the *audiencia* or superior tribunal.

[2] Don Manuel Amat y Juniet, thirty-first viceroy, who held office from 1761 to 1776.

[3] The penal colony at Valdivia, Chile. Frezier writes in *A Voyage to the South Sea*: 'That this Port may not want Men, the Whites of Peru and Chili, condemn'd to Banishment for any Crime, are sent thither, so that it is in the Nature of a Galley', p. 45.

[4] La Punta.

him aside in the gallery and asked him whether he had news of Mr Surville; he confirmed what the man in the small canoe had told me, furthermore that our Topas Joachim Joseph, a helmsman who had charge of the bottle where the letters were, had been taken from Chilca to Lima where he was held in the guardhouse of the Viceroy's palace and that they had seen him. This bad news drove me to distraction, I was so dumbfounded by this blow that I did not know where I was. I have lost a true friend. The expedition may lose through this, as the deceased has never confided in me what he hoped to do. I am now quite embarrassed, being unable to go through the papers to see whether there is an item which speaks of our commission or other [documents] that might cause us to be impounded by the Spaniards. I am watched by commissioner Egam; on the other hand I am afraid the Viceroy may send orders for all the papers to be seized, both the ship's and the deceased's, and all those of the officers, and that some part of the plan of our voyage may be found. Now I am in command. I am the *bête noire* of part of the officers, some are capable of doing me a bad turn, the chaplain in particular who is a very bad character.

† Mr Surville, Captain, drowned on Chilca shore, Sunday 8 April.

† Louis Rigousselle, sailor, born in Lorient, aged 18 to 20, drowned in Chilca.[1]

† Julien Fleury, sailor, born in St Malo, aged 20 to 21, dd. in Chilca....[2]

---

[1] See Muster Roll No. 81.   [2] See Muster Roll No. 63.

APPENDIX B

The holograph Muster Roll is held in the Archives of the Port of Lorient, under the reference 2P 45, 1, 10.

The basic information it provides consists of the individual's name, his father's name, the town or village he came from, the ship he had served in prior to joining the expedition, his rank or trade where applicable, and his monthly pay expressed in *livres*. Changes in rank or rates of pay, desertions or deaths are also recorded in a number of cases.

The original roll plus the closing roll of 1773 forms the basis of the following list, but additional information has been added (except in the case of the officers, who are referred to in the Introduction) whenever it has been possible to find it, either from comments in the Journals or in naval or other records. Strictly, every sailor was required to register, whether he served in the royal or the merchant navy, in order to be available for call-up in time of war; many of the naval registers have survived to this day and represent valuable sources of information about the coastal population of France and the careers of serving men; however, there are inevitably many gaps, due to carelessness, clerical omissions, unreported deaths or disappearances and to the sheer magnitude of the task of maintaining such records over long periods of time.

The original Muster Roll is not numbered: numbers have been added to simplify references in the text of the Journals.

Included in the Muster Roll are several sailors who signed on, but did not report in time and were left behind. These have been included, but have not been given a number.

Very little information is available about the marines (*fusiliers*) unless they earn a special mention through death, desertion or promotion. Many of their names were *noms de guerre* – names which soldiers adopted when they signed on; a change of identity which cut them off from civilian life, either as a symbolic break with their non-military past or to avoid being pursued into the army for some misdemeanour, a practice now only acceptable in the Foreign Legion. Their standard rate of pay was 14 *livres*.

The closing roll contains five names previously omitted, three of them stowaways. Additional names will be found at the end of our list: these include the five natives kidnapped during the voyage and several slaves or lascars who are referred to in the Journals. The slaves are not listed as a group but the deaths of sixteen Malagasy slaves are recorded up to 19 December 1769 on which day the last of them died, and of five slaves from Mozambique up to 11 December; in addition Victor (203) and Hyacinthe (204) died in April 1770, and two (207, 208) were sold in Lima. This gives us a total of twenty-five.

The unnamed Indonesian who deserted at Pulau Tioman (210) and the chaplain's servant (211) may be part of the group of lascars who are reported to have all died by the end of November 1769, but in that case numbers 205 and 206 who died after that date must have been omitted from the official roll. However, if we assume that servants were not normally referred to as lascars, then Antoine (209) and Nicolas (211) are also omissions.

A total of 232 men are therefore mentioned as having taken part in the expedition. Of these 38 were left in Pondicherry or died before leaving that port. Of the remaining 194 a total of 29 deserted, mostly in Peru, and 103 died.

Deaths are shown by an asterisk and desertions by a small *d* against the man's number.

The Muster Roll abbreviation, *St Jean-Bte*, is retained in this Appendix.

Department of Bengal
Year 1769

The *St Jean-Baptiste*
privately owned vessel

MUSTER ROLL of the privately owned ship, the *St Jean-Baptiste*, of approximately six hundred tons, carrying thirty-six guns with a crew of one hundred and seventy-two men, both blacks and whites, sailing from Chandernagore, Bengal River, for Manila and China, namely:

SENIOR OFFICERS

★1 François de SURVILLE, from Port-Louis, Captain, previously in the *St Jean-Bte*, 240 *livres*, died, drowned at Chilca, coast of Peru, 8 April 1770.

2 Guillaume LABÉ, from Saint-Malo, first officer, previously in *La Concorde*, 160 *livres*,[1] captain at 240 *livres* from 9 April 1770.

3 Jean POTTIER, from Lorme,[2] second officer, previously in the *St Charles*, 120 *livres*, first officer at 160 *livres* from 9 April 1770.

d4 Hughes-Jean-Marie de SURVILLE, from Nantes, first ensign, previously in the *St Jean-Bte*, 95 *livres*, deserted during the night of 9 to 10 September 1771, arrested in Lima 6 October 1771, deserted a 2nd time during the night of 4 to 5 January 1772 being under arrest on board.

5 Hibon de VILLEMONT, from Bourbon, second ensign, previously in the *St Charles*, 80 *livres*, signed off at Pondicherry 1 May 1769.

6 Amable LORRY, from Nantes, *volontaire*, later ensign, previously in the *St Jean-Bte*, 80 *livres*.

7 Pierre-Antoine MONNERON, from Annonay in Vivarais, clerk, ditto, 80 *livres*, sent to France 26 October 1770 to obtain the release of the ship arrested in Lima, returned with an order from the King of Spain releasing the ship 28 August 1772.

d8 Rev. Father Paul-Antoine Léonard de VILLEFLEX [*sic*], Dominican, from Périgueux, chaplain, previously in the *Marquis de Castries*, 80 *livres*, deserted in Lima on 9 to 10 September 1771, brought back on board 6 October ditto, deserted a 2nd time during the night of 4 to 5 January 1772 being under arrest on board.

9 Pierre DULUCQ, From Ste Boisse in Bearn, diocese of Dax, surgeon, previously in the *St Jean-Bte*, 80 *livres*.

— (See also Nos. 71, 164 and 189).

PETTY OFFICERS

10 François CHAUX, son of François, born in 1737 in Dinan, boatswain, sailed from Lorient in the *St Jean-Bte*, (in 1767), 66

---

[1] In his journal, Labé quotes his pay at 82 rupees a month, plus 100 rupees for his wife.
[2] De Lorme was part of Pottier's surname; the *de* misled the clerk.

livres, paid off 30 May 1769 in Pondicherry. Killed in India in 1772.

11 Olivier DOUCET, son of François, from Vannes, boatswain's mate, previously in the *St Charles*, 45 *livres*.

12 Nicolas LAFFICHE, son of Jacques, born in 1773 in Dinan, master gunner, previously in the *St Jean-Bte*, 50 *livres*, paid off 30 May 1769 in Pondicherry. Died at sea in 1774.

d13 Joseph GRASLE, (or Le Grasle), son of Hervé, from Ploeumeur, second gunner, later appointed master gunner, previously in the *St Charles*, 40 *livres*, deserted in Peru 8 March 1773.

— Yves Costiou, son of Sébastien, from Lorient, master carpenter, previously in the *St Charles*, 39 *livres*, stayed ashore.

14 Julien CHENOT (or Chesnot), son of Etienne, from Nantes, master caulker and pulley maker, previously in the *St Jean-Bte*, 42 *livres*.

15 Alain CASTEL, son of Bernard, from St Servan but born in Morlaix in 1730, 2nd caulker and carpenter, embarked on *St Jean-Bte*, 9 May 1767, 42 *livres*; reported present at the 1773 call-up.

16 Augustin LE MOEL, son of Louis, Lorient, master sailmaker, b. approx. 1715, married to Louise Prudhomme. Sailed in November 1750 for China in the *Montaran*, a French India Co. vessel; back in October 1754, he sailed again for China, in the *Pondichéry*; taken prisoner on 23 December 1756 by the English ship *Dover*, taken to Kinsale, Ireland, and held prisoner in Britain until 1757; sailed on 7 March 1758 for India in the *Comte d'Argenson*, returned 15 February 1763 in the *Berryer*; sailed for India as master sailmaker at 36 *livres* in the *Praslin* on 22 April 1764; joined the *St Jean-Bte*, at 42 *livres*, but paid off in Pondicherry on 30 May 1769.

17 François DESMIAUX, s. of François, b. approx 1740 in St Coulomb, sailed from Lorient in the *St Jean-Bte*, on 9 May 1767, 30 *livres*, common allowance,[1] appointed second-class petty officer at 36 *livres*, per month 2 April 1773. He returned to India in the *Duc de Fitzjames* in 1774 and died in China 7 October of that year.

*18 Julien SICCOT, son of René, from Corseul, common allowance, 28 *livres*, previously in the *St Jean-Bte*, died of scurvy in Doubtless Bay 29 December 1769, aged about 30.

[1] The *ration simple* was the standard allowance of the common sailor.

WARRANT OFFICERS

*d*19 Joseph VERNES, son of Clément, from Sablé, parish of Chevèmes en Chablais, armourer, previously in the *St Jean-Bte*, 28 *livres*, deserted in Peru 26 or 28 March 1773.

20 Louis FILLIE, son of Louis, from Chantenay, Nantes, master cooper, previously in the *St Jean-Bte*, 30 *livres*.

★21 Francois NEVEU, son of Jean, born approx. 1729 in Paramé, sailed to Martinique in the *Vigilant* in 1764–67, joined the *St Jean-Bte* in Lorient on 9 March 1767; cooper and chief steward, 30 *livres*, died at sea 31 March 1769.

SAILORS

★22 François CAGNARD, son of Jean, born in Plougouvert near Lorient; married, 24 *livres*; died at sea 24 October 1769 of scurvy 'after being sick for two months'.

23 François HELLECQ, son of Robert, from Auray, 24 *livres*.

24 Jean DELAHAYE, son of Michel, from Rennes, baker, 21 *livres*.

★25 Pierre LESCARMUR, son of Alexis, from Pleurtuit, 28 *livres*; 'an extreme case of scurvy on arrival at Lauriston Bay'; still sick on departure, but cured by 26 February 1770. Died of scurvy in Peru 29 July 1770.

26 Julien LE BIGOT, son of Jean, from Pleurtuit, 28 *livres*.

★27 Jean TANQUERAY, son of Jacques, born in Trigavoux approx. 1751; 30 *livres*; died in Peru 7 April 1773.

★28 François ALLAIN (or Alain), son of Julien, born in St Enogat 1724, caulker, married, 28 *livres*; died at sea 22 November 1769, of scurvy.

29 Nicholas-Thomas BOURGES, from St Enogat, 28 *livres*.

30 François CHEMINOUX, son of Pierre, from St Meloir, 28 *livres*.

31 Jean VIGOR, son of Giles, from Arromanches, 26 *livres*; paid off in Pondicherry 30 May 1769.

★32 Julien FOUQUET, son of Jean, born in Chateauneuf (or Pleudieu, according to Labé) in approx. 1732; 26 *livres*; died of scurvy in Peru 21 April 1770.

★33 Pierre RONDEL, son of Jean, born in Pleurtuit, department of Dinan in 1733; 26 *livres*; died at sea of scurvy 23 October 1769.

34 François HERVE, son of Pierre, from St Servan, 25 *livres*; paid off in Pondicherry 30 May 1769, is believed to have sailed home

in September 1770 in *La Tourterelle* and eventually settled in Martinique.

★35 Jean CRESTE, son of Louis, born in Miniac-Morvan approx. 1741, sailor and helmsman, 24 *livres*; died in Peru of consumption 14 May 1771. Labé gives his birthplace as the 'environs of St Malo'.

★36 Jean FILASTRE, son of Jean, born in Dinan 1735, joined the *St Jean-Bte*, at 16 *livres* on 25 May 1767, raised to 21 *livres* for the expedition; died off Ulawa of scurvy 1 November 1769.

★37 Pierre BUSSON, son of Pierre, born in La Rivière-en-Pleurtuit approx. 1735, 'acting butcher', 20 *livres*, died of scurvy in Peru 9 July 1770.

38 Pierre RAFFRAY, son of Jean, from St Meloir, 17 *livres*.

39 Bertrand MESLE, son of Bertrand, born in St Coulomb approx. 1740, 22 *livres*; recorded as being in the *Duc de Fitzjames* in China seas in 1774, paid off in Lorient 1775.

★40 Jacques GIRARD, son of Jacques, born at St Coulomb approx. 1751, 18 *livres*, died at sea 7 April 1773 'day of our departure from the coast of Peru'.

*d*41 Jacques MONNOT, son of Pierre, from Lorient, previously in the *Petit Choiseul*, 27 livres, deserted in Peru 24 August 1772.

★42 François BAYARD, son of Nicolas, born in Dinan approx. 1745, previously in the *Petit Choiseul*, 21 *livres*; died in Peru 4 May 1770.

*d*43 Jean GAUDEL, son of Henry, from Quimper, previously in the *Petit Choiseul*, 26 *livres*; deserted in Peru 12 September 1771.

*d*44 Pierre MARC, son of Gabriel, from Brest, previously in the *Petit Choiseul*, 25 *livres*; deserted in the Bashi Islands 22 August 1769.

— Jean-Baptiste Desfournier, son of Michel, from Brest, previously in the *Petit Choiseul*, 25 *livres*, stayed ashore.

45 Guillaume GIRARD, son of Quintin, born in Lorient, cook, previously in the *Petit Choiseul*, 24 *livres*.

— Jean-Michel La Coste, son of Hervé, from Lorient, previously in the *St Charles*, 18 *livres*, stayed ashore.

*d*46 Joseph BERCOT, son of Pierre, parish of Carnoet, 26 *livres*, deserted in Peru 12 September 1771.

47 Pierre HALBON, son of Nicolas, from St Malo, 22 *livres*.

*d*48 Marc LE COMTE, son of Pierre, from St Brieuc (or from Cap Fréhel, 30 miles further east, according to Labé), 24 *livres*; deserted in Peru 12 September 1771.

— Jean-Michel Le Borgne, son of René, from Chateauneuf, 20 *livres*, stayed ashore.

49 Jean-Louis DANIEL, son of Louis, from Vannes, 20 *livres*.

*50 Vincent MAUCARD, son of Jean, born in Pleudihen approx. 1750, previously in the *St Charles*, 17 *livres*, died in Peru 17 July 1770. Labé however gives the name as Julien Moquart, born in Lorient.

— François Jaffray, son of Yves, from Riantec, 22 *livres*, stayed ashore.

*51 Julien CADET, son of Julien, born in Pleurtuit approx. 1745, caulker, 20 *livres*, died at sea of scurvy 14 December 1769.

*52 François RICHARD, son of Noël, born in Pleurtuit (or St Malo, according to Labé), approx. 1749, 21 *livres*, died of scurvy in Peru 14 April 1770.

53 Julien LEPINE, son of Oliver, from Paramé, 19 *livres*, paid off in Pondicherry 30 May 1769.

54 François LAURENS, son of Joseph, from Plestin, 21 *livres*.

55 Jacques THOMAS, son of Jacques, from Paramé, 21 *livres*.

56 Pierre BOISSELOT, son of Pierre, from Nantes, 28 *livres*, paid off in Pondicherry 30 May 1769.

d57 François LE TIMBRE, son of Giles, from St Malo, 19 *livres*, deserted at Bashi Island 22 August 1769.

*58 Jean MAUGER, son of Vincent, born in St Malo in 1745, 19 *livres*, died at sea of scurvy 16 December 1769.

59 Jacques GOMAIN, son of Jean, from St Servan, 28 *livres*.

60 Bernard RUAULT, son of Jean, from Pleurtuit, 20 *livres*, paid off in Pondicherry 30 May 1769.

61 Jean MOINET, son of Pierre, from Pleurtuit, 20 *livres*, paid off in Pondicherry 30 May 1769.

62 Joseph CROSLARD, son of Charles, born in St Coulomb in 1747, 19 *livres*, raised to 22 *livres* from 16 January 1769; reported in China in the *Maréchal de Broglie* in 1774, in Lorient in June 1775 and at Cadiz in the *Félicité* in 1775.

*63 Julien FLEURY, son of Jean, born in St Malo approx. 1750, 22 *livres*; died by drowning at Chilca, coast of Peru 8 April 1770.

*64 André GALLERY, son of Jean, born in St Servan 1746 approx., 22 *livres*, died in Peru 3 July 1772.

65 François CLEQUIN, son of Pierre, from St Coulomb, 22 *livres*.

66 François BREDEL, son of Jean, from St Jouan, 17 *livres*, paid off in Pondicherry 30 May 1769.

67 Thomas CORTHIEU, son of Pierre, from St Malo, carpenter, 18 *livres*, paid off in Pondicherry 30 May 1769.

68 Henry HEZY, son of Guillaume, born in Dinan 1743, previously in the *St Charles*, 24 *livres*; reported sailing to the Guinea coast in the *Prince de Conty* in 1774, and back in France in 1775.

d69 Pierre BENECHE (or Bénaches), from Montauban, previously in foreign service,[1] 24 *livres*, deserted in Peru 23 January 1771.

*70 Manus KALUS (possibly Klaus Manus or Mann), from Distelbord, Prussia, Germany, age about 25, previously in foreign service, 27.10 *livres*, died at sea of scurvy 28 November 1769.

— Christian Doff, from Colberg, previously in foreign service, 27.20 *livres*, stayed ashore.

— Rombaud. from [blank] in Holland, previously in foreign service, stayed ashore.

— Louis Leneuf, son of Jean, from Vannes, previously in the *Petit Choiseul*, 18 *livres*, left at the Chandernagore hospital.

71 François AVICE, son of Guillaume, born in Cancale in 1749, resident in Mauritius, sailed in the *Marie* from Bayonne to Miquelon in 1764, second ensign in the *Hardy* 1765–68, served in the *St Charles*, then joined the *St Jean-Bte*, as *volontaire* at 21 *livres*, appointed 2nd ensign at 80 *livres*, on 5 January 1772; reported sailing as ensign in the *Ville de Lorient* bound for India in February 1774.

— Dominique Canet, from Provence, previously in foreign service, 24 *livres*, stayed ashore.

d72 Joseph RALIGUE, son of Yves, from Lorient, previously in the *Ajax*, 18 *livres*, deserted in Peru 28 March 1773.

73 Jean-Chrétien COLONIA, son of Joseph, from Paris, quarter-gunner on common allowance, previously in the *Ajax*, 24 *livres*, paid off in Pondicherry 15 May 1769.

74 John STILE from [blank], previously in foreign service, 27.10 *livres*, paid off in Pondicherry 30 May 1769.

NOVICES

75 Joachim GOPLE, son of Jean, from Montcontour, 18 *livres*.

d76 Jean CHAUX, son of Barthélémy, born in Dinan approx. 1748, sailed from Lorient in *St Jean-Bte*, at 10 *livres*, raised to 16 *livres*, for the expedition; helped Labé and Monneron burn

---

[1] Indicates that he was serving in a foreign ship.

incriminating documents 11 April 1770; deserted in Peru 20 November 1771; recorded on registers as 'married in Lima'.

— Yves Gouvelle, son of Michel, from Quimperlé, previously in the *Petit Choiseul*, 16 *livres*, left at the Chandernagore hospital.

*77 Jean NAVET, son of Jean, born in Hennebond approx. 1749, previously in the *Petit Choiseul*, 14 *livres*, died at sea 19 November 1769.

*78 Julien LE MANTEC, son of Mathieu, from Ploermel (or Lorient, according to Labé), previously in the *Petit Choiseul*, 16 *livres*, died at Bellavista hospital, Peru, 17 April 1770.

d79 Bertrand-Louis BESNIER, son of Pierre, from Rennes, previously in the *Petit Choiseul*, 14 *livres*, deserted at Bashi Island 22 August 1769.

80 Vincent L'ECUYER, son of Guillaume, from Lousiné (or Locminé) previously in the *Petit Choiseul*, 16 *livres*.

— Pierre Evano, son of Guillaume, from the same town [as L'Ecuyer], previously in the *Petit Choiseul*, stayed ashore.

*81 Louis RIGOUSSEL (or Rigouselle), son of Charles, from Guédel (Lorient, according to Labé), previously in the *Petit Choiseul*, 16 *livres*, died from drowning at Chilca on the coast of Peru 8 April 1770, aged 18 or 20.

d82 Louis ROUSSEL, son of Julien, from Dinan, previously in the *Petit Choiseul*, 13 *livres*, deserted in Peru 23 January 1773.

83 Gilles ROBIN, son of Gilles, from Erquy, previously in the *St Charles*, 16 *livres*, increased to 19 from 16 November 1769.

*84 François TANGUY, son of Joseph, born in Port-Louis in 1749, previously in the *St Charles*, 16 *livres*, died on the coast of Peru 7 September 1771.

*85 Pierre LOREY, son of Joseph, from Lorient, previously in the *St Charles*, 16 *livres*, died at sea of scurvy near the coast of Peru 9 April 1770.

86 Julien POULAIN, son of Julien, born in Rennes in 1716, baker, previously in the *St Charles*, 16 *livres*, appointed chief steward at 30 *livres*, from 1 April 1769 on account of the death of Louis Neveu (see No. 21) who was paid at 30 *livres*. He is reported as having died in 1773.

d87 Jean-Marie JAFFRAY (or Joffroy), son of Jean, from Quimper (Labé states Lorient), previously in the *Petit Choiseul*, 14 *livres*, deserted at Callao 14 November 1772 (Labé gives the 24th).

88 Alain FRAVAL, son of Oliver, born in Lorient approx. 1749,

sailed to China in the *Berryer* 1765, returned to France 1767 and sailed for India in December in the *Penthièvre*, left behind sick at Mauritius June 1768, signed on the *Petit Choiseul*, then the *St Jean-Bte*, at 12 *livres*. Subsequently dismissed from the service as a 'ne'er-do-well'.

89 Jean-Baptiste COLLIN, son of Jean-Baptiste, from St Malo, 12 *livres*.

★90 Jean-Baptiste GEFFLOT, son of René, born in St Malo approx. 1753, 12 *livres*, died in Peru 28 October 1770.

★91 Guillaume GROSSET, son of Guillaume, born in St Servan approx. 1751, 12 *livres*, died of scurvy at sea 6 April 1770.

92 François HUET, son of Pierre, from St Meloir, 13 *livres*, increased to 15 from 15 January 1770.

93 Jean GAULTIER, son of Jacques, from Paramé, 13 *livres*, sailed for France with Monneron 26 October 1770.

★94 Jean-Georges LORIEUX, son of Jean-François, born in Vannes (or Hennebond, according to the closing roll) approx. 1749; died of scurvy at sea 13 November 1769.

★95 Dominique TREHUIDIC (or Trévidic), son of Vincent, born in Vannes in approx. 1752, 13 *livres*, died of scurvy in Peru 25 July 1770.

96 Julien RIVET, son of Michel, from Doulon, diocese of Moulins, 16 *livres*.

SERVANTS

d97 Pierre MASSELIN (or Marcellin), son of François, from Rennes, chief steward, 41 *livres*; deserted in Peru 17 January 1772; is reported as having sailed in the Spanish vessel *Septentrion*.

98 SALMY, black, cook, 18 *livres*.

d99 Joseph QUIVEL, son of Guillaume, from Plohinec (or Lorient, according to Labé), M. de Surville's servant, 15 *livres*, deserted in Lima 25 March 1773.

★100 Jean de ROZARIO, first officer's servant, 17.10 *livres*, died in Doubtless Bay 30 (or 1 a.m. on 31st) December 1769.

BOYS

— Joseph QUIVEL, promoted to Captain's servant. See No. 99 above.

101 François LEROY, son of Guillaume, from Chateauneuf, previously in the *Marquis de Castries*, 12 *livres*.

INDIAN WARRANT OFFICERS AND SAILORS

102 One Sarangue (*Serang*, the Malayan term for chief lascar or boatswain's mate). He is not recorded as forming part of the crew in the closing roll and may have died at sea.

★103 One senior Taudel [?], died at sea 29 October 1769.

— Two young ditto; did not embark.

★104 One Cassap (*Kasap*, deck supervisor and lamp attendant), died at sea 10 November 1769.

— One ditto; did not embark.

★105– Fifty-five Indian sailors. Only 47 embarked. Paid off 22
51 lascars 9 May 1769. Three died in October, the others in November. All the lascars died.

NAMES OF PEOPLE OMITTED FROM THE MUSTER ROLL

d152 Antoine TERRADEC (or Terrade), son of Antoine, from Rochefort, surgeon's first mate, previously in the *Pénélope*, 45 *livres*, deserted in Peru 25 July 1770.

153 Nicolas CHENAIK, from Luxemburg, previously in foreign service, 25 *livres*, paid off 30 May 1769.

154 Dominique DECRUZ (or Decrux), cook's mate, 12.10 *livres*.

ADDITIONAL COMPLEMENT TAKEN ON AT PONDICHERRY

155 Jean-Claude ARVOINE, son of Alain, from Quimperlé, previously in the *Pénélope*, 24 *livres*, granted 30 *livres* on account of circumstances, this increase being applicable to all the sailors who had come from Europe in the said ship.

156 René JAFFRAY, son of René, from Zinzacque [Saint Jacques?], previously in the *Actionnaire*, 20 *livres* increased to 30 *livres* for the same reason as above.

★157 Allain LE CAM, son of Jean, born in Chateauneuf-du-Faou approx. 1742, gunner's mate, previously in the *Actionnaire*, 26 *livres*, died at sea 14 December 1769 of scurvy.

★158 Nicolas SOLIMAN, son of Nicolas, born in Lorient approx. 1739, master gunner, previously in the *Petit Choiseul*, 50 *livres*, died at sea 6 November 1769. His father, also a master gunner, had sailed on a number of occasions to India and China.

*159   Julien HERVE, son of Jacques, from Plétou, district of Dinan, previously in the *Brisson*, 20 *livres*, died at sea of scurvy 27 October 1769.

d160   Joseph LE PAPE, son of Joseph, from Concarneau (or Lorient, according to Labé), previously in the *Pénélope*, sailmaker, 20 *livres*, deserted in Peru 5 April 1773.

*161   Peter (Pieter?) MARQUIS, born in Brussels approx. 1732, master sailmaker, previously in the *Lauriston*, 50 *livres*, died at sea of scurvy 22 March 1770.

162   André BEAUDIN, gunner's mate, from Pondicherry, 26 *livres*.

163   Jacques ROBERT, son of Jean, from Quimper, previously in the *Actionnaire*, 24 *livres*, increased to 30 *livres* in view of the circumstances, this increase having been granted to all the sailors who had come to Europe in the said ship.

164   Jean-René LE MIRE, son of Adrien, born in Brest in 1743, boatswain at 72 *livres*, appointed second ensign at 80 *livres*, from 8 April 1773. He had sailed twice in the *Les Six Corps* as Leading Seaman, went to China in the *Beaumont* in 1765, was back in France in July 1766, sailed in the *Adour* for the French India Co. in March 1767, after which he embarked in the *St Jean-Bte*, where he remained until her return to France. He sailed to India in April 1775 in the private vessel the *Boynes* at 45 *livres*. He had his home in Port-Louis.

DETACHMENT TAKEN ON IN PONDICHERRY
28 May 1769

165   Jean de ST PAUL, captain, officer commanding the detachment, 160 *livres*. He may be the Captain de St Paul who sailed with a detachment of troops raised by the French India Co. from Lorient on 2 February 1762 in the *Berryer*, arriving in Mauritius on 14 June 1762, and that same Lieutenant-Colonel de St Paul, from the Pondicherry Regiment who sailed with his two sons in the *Superbe* for the Mascareignes on 15 April 1783.

*166   ACHILLE, whose real name was Pierre-François de la Ville, born in Paris, parish of St Sulpice, approx. 1730. Sergeant at 25 *livres*, died in Port Praslin, Solomon Islands on 17 October 1769 as a result of wounds suffered on 14th.

167   BAGUETTE, drummer, 14.14 *livres.*

d168   ROBERT, real name Renardel, fife player, 14.14 *livres,* deserted in Peru 13 May 1773.

169   FESSARD, corporal, 16.4 *livres.*

170   BARON, corporal, 16.4 *livres,* transferred 1 April 1773 to the *Ste Barbe.*

★171   LA NOIX, real name Pierre-Charles Deslandres, born in Brest, diocese of St Pol de Léon, fusilier, 14.14 *livres,* died at sea of scurvy 29 November 1769.

d172   DIVERTISSANT, born in Orleans, fusilier, deserted in Peru 23 January 1771.

173   TOURNAY, fusilier.

(d)174   FORCEVILLE, fusilier, deserted in Peru 17 August 1771, returned to the ship 20 March 1773.

d175   LAFLEUR, of Italian nationality, fusilier, deserted in Peru 20 October 1770.

176   TOURELLE (or Tournelle), fusilier.

★177   Michel DESSAUNIN, born in Paris approx. 1734, fusilier, died at sea 14 November 1769.

178   DUTILLEUL, fusilier.

(d)179   GOUJUS (or Gouges), fusilier, deserted in Peru November 1771 but subsequently returned to the ship.

180   LEMPRIER, fusilier.

★181   LA DORADE, real name Marquet, born in Toulouse approx. 1734, fusilier, died at sea 21 March 1770.

★182   BONOUVRIER, born in Burgundy approx. 1732, fusilier, died in Peru 12 April 1770 of scurvy.

d183   François LAMBERT, from Lyons, fusilier, deserted in Peru 13 March 1773 (or 26 March, according to Labé).

184   FOUDEUX, fusilier.

★185   LA PORTE, born in Paris approx. 1730, fusilier, died in Peru 11 April 1770.

186   DOMPART, fusilier, appointed armourer at 28 *livres* per month 1 April 1773.

d187   GALLANT, from Bierne, fusilier, deserted 24 August 1772.

★188   SANSREGRET, real name Mathieu Pupier, born in Lyons 1727, fusilier, died in Doubtless Bay 20 December 1769.

ADDITIONS TO THE MUSTER ROLL

*d*189 René CHARENTON (or Charanton), son of Jean, born in Lorient approx. 1730, sailed in April 1749 in the *Auguste* for the French India Co. for Pondicherry as *pilote*; back in January 1752; sailed for Senegal in the corvette *Le Cerf*, French India Co.; back in November; returned in the *Cybèle* in May 1753; a further voyage to Senegal in the *Petit Chasseur* on 30 November 1753. Sailed in 1755 in the frigate *Danaë* for Pondicherry, returning in the *Lys* in February 1757; sailed again to Pondicherry in March 1758 in the *Baleine*, taken prisoner in 1760 while serving in the *Hermione* and spent two years in England: sailed for India in the *Praslin* 22 April 1764; joined the *St Jean-Bte* as 2nd lieutenant at 120 *livres*, deserted in Peru 5 April 1773.

★190 Martin HERIGOYEN, born in Pondicherry approx. 1742, listed as passenger, but probably 'volontaire', died at sea of scurvy 9 November 1769.

*d*191 Henry MALLORE, Dutch deserter taken on board by order of Mr Law, deserted in Peru 4 October 1772.

192 Gabriel LE ROUX, from St Malo, stowaway, previously in the *Villerault*, 13 livres.

ADDITIONS TO THE CLOSING ROLL

★193 Ignatio ROZARIO, black, from Pondicherry, cook, 24 *livres*, died at sea 28 March 1770.

★194 MOUTON, Malabar Indian, 21. 12 *livres*, age 40, died at sea 30 November 1770 of scurvy.

STOWAWAYS

★195 Chavel MONTOUX, Malabar Indian, Christian, from Pondicherry, age about 40, Mr de St Paul's servant, no wages recorded, died 11 December 1769.

*d*196 Joachim JOSEPH, Portuguese, from Pondicherry, helmsman, 24 *livres*; swam ashore with de Surville's message to the Viceroy, Chilca, 8 April 1770; deserted in Peru 1 July 1770.

★197 François COZIER, Portuguese born in Pondicherry approx. 1752, helmsman, 24 *livres*, died at sea of scurvy 9 December 1769.

LATER ADDITIONS

*198 —, Bashi Islander, died in New Zealand, 25 December 1769.

*199 —, Bashi Islander, died at sea, 20 February 1770.

200 —, Bashi Islander.

201 Lova SAREGUA (possibly Love from Serenge, Gagi Island, Solomons), captured at Port Praslin, sent to France with Monneron, sailing from Callao 26 October 1770.

*202 RANGINUI, Maori chief, captured in Doubtless Bay, died at sea 24 March 1770.

OTHERS

*203 VICTOR, Dulucq's slave, died 10 April 1770.

*204 HYACINTHE, Monneron's slave, aged about 11, died in Peru 11 April 1770.

*205 Mamouth CASSEM, real name probably Mahmud Qāsim, born in Pondicherry approx. 1755, died in Peru 14 April 1770.

*206 NASRIN, Bengali, aged 16 or 17, died in Peru 14 April 1770.

207 —, Lory's slave, sold in Lima 1771.

208 —, Le Mire's slave, sold in Lima 1771.

d209 ANTOINE, Charenton's servant, from Pondicherry, deserted in Peru (possibly with the connivance of his master) 28 March 1773.

d210 (?) —, unnamed Indonesian born in Batavia, helmsman, deserted at Pulo Tioman, 24 July 1769.

*211 NICOLAS, Bengali, chaplain's servant, died at sea of scurvy 29 November 1769.

*212 YONDEVA, Malagasy slave, killed at Port Praslin, Solomons, 20 October 1769.

*213 SANGANACHE, Malagasy slave, died at sea 22 October 1769.

*214– —, unnamed Malagasy slaves, died between 23 October and
27 19 December 1769.

*228– —, unnamed Mozambique slaves, died between 17 November
32 and 11 December 1769.

APPENDIX C

VILLEFEIX AND THE PROBLEM OF THE FIRST MASS

The *St Jean-Baptiste*'s chaplain was Paul-Antoine Léonard de Ville-feix, a priest belonging to the Dominican order. He was born in or near Etouars, in Périgord, in 1728; he belonged to a good family and had at least two brothers: one, Léonard de Lestang, was parish priest of Etouars from 1755; another Jean Léonard de Clagour signed Antoine's death certificate in 1780.

A mention occurs of him as an *étudiant non prêtre* in 1752-4, which was presumably his period as a novice and deacon; his ordination would have followed soon after, as we find him intervening on behalf of his brother in 1756: 'This year of 1756, I received patent letters from Rome from the general of the Order of St Dominic; it is my brother, Father Villefeix, who received this commission so that it is canonically instituted.' (Registre de la paroisse d'Etouars). The grant referred to the setting up of a confraternity of the Holy Rosary.

From 2 October 1760 until at least 1766, Fr. Villefeix was registered as a student of advanced theology at the Convent of St Jacques in Paris. He is recorded as passing the required examination in February 1765, and a year later was given a lectureship, the appointment to date from 1770. At this point, he disappears completely from the college books and there is no trace of him until 1768 when he is recorded as having sailed for India in the *Marquis de Castries*. We can assume that he wished to spend a few years in the East before settling down to a life of teaching and pastoral duties. Whether the reason for this was the lure of adventure or missionary zeal remains an open question – the answer is probably a mixture of both.

We know that the Surville family was noted of its piety. Elizabeth de Surville founded a religious community at Saint-Lô; the home of the Survilles in Port-Louis frequently provided hospitality to missionaries on their way to the Orient – the Bishop of Halicarnassus called Madame de Surville 'the Missionaries' mother'.[1] We know that

[1] From a letter quoted in Buffet, 'Voyage à la découverte du port-louisien Surville', p. 90.

Jean-François was in France in 1766 and sailed from Port-Louis in June 1767, and it is possible he met Villefeix there, and that this meeting resulted in the priest's decision to serve in the colonies. It is easy to imagine Surville urging him to join the expedition to the Pacific, to discover new countries and begin his missionary work – to which would be added the likelihood of some financial gain. Such prospects would override the attraction of a lectureship at St Jacques. Villefeix's enthusiasm as a missionary is not particularly in evidence, although admittedly the opportunities were scarce: nowhere did the *St Jean-Baptiste* spend more than a few days. In addition, most of what we know of him comes from Labé, who disliked him. On one occasion, Villefeix makes a present of half a bottle of brandy to some native; in New Zealand he somewhat imprudently wanders among native huts. On the other hand, he appears to have carried out with due diligence his duties as a chaplain, ministering to the sick and the dying.

On 20 September 1771, while the ship was held at Callao, he deserted with the late Captain's nephew. This episode supports the theory of a friendship between the chaplain and the family; it also gives a less favourable image of Villefeix, as the motive for the escapade was a desire to prospect for gold:

> The two fugitives were caught on 7 October and brought back under escort to Lima...It was learnt that these gentlemen planned to go and work by a river 200 leagues from where they were arrested, in a gold mine, having sent mules ahead of them with their belongings and several gold mining implements, such as picks, shovels, and iron probes made on board by the ship's blacksmiths.'[1]

They apparently had friends ashore because during the night of 4 to 5 January 1772 they disappeared once more and 'it appeared that a canoe has come alongside the ship during the night to make their escape possible, as we found a rope hanging from a main cabin porthole'. This time, they were not caught, and the chaplain's few belongings were auctioned. Villefeix, however, returned to France and to his religious duties, for the death is recorded at Etouars in 1780 of 'Antoine Leonard, sieur de Villefeix, priest, aged 52'.[2]

The character of the chaplain is significant in connection with the

---

[1] Report in Archives de la Marine, Lorient, 2 P 71 VI, No. 4.

[2] Archives de la Dordogne, loc. cit. An unsuccessful plea by the agents of Delessert, the Chandernagore bankers, to be granted 1804 *livres*, unpaid arrears held by the Navy, towards repayment of a loan made to Villefeix, indicates that, at the date the appeal was made, 16 April 1775, the chaplain had not reappeared in France (notes and misc. corresp. appended to muster roll).

problem of the first religious service to be held in New Zealand. The generally recognised 'first' is the Rev. Marsden's Christmas Day 1814 service held in the Bay of Islands. However, the French spent three Sundays plus Christmas Day in New Zealand. A priest is required to say Mass daily: could we assume that the chaplain failed to say Mass at the very least on a Sunday or indeed on Christmas Day, especially with a crew mostly composed of Bretons – who are renowned for their piety – commanded by a man whose family had close links with the Church; and furthermore a crew in such straits that a number of sailors were on the point of death?

Such omissions would only be credible if Father Villefeix had been a priest with little or no vocation who had entered the Church in accordance with a family tradition or to gain the benefit of an ecclesiastical living. But the Léonard family had already one son in the Church – Léonard de Lestang – and there is no record of Fr. Villefeix being granted any living, other than the promise of the teaching post in Paris. The eighteenth century *abbé de cour* often had no real vocation, but Villefeix had spent six years studying theology at St Jacques – so that we cannot doubt that his vocation and his interest in religious matters were genuine. Had Fr. Villefeix been ill, the likelihood of a Mass being said would diminish, but he was in good health, strolled ashore and visited a Maori settlement.

On the other hand, Labé refers to him as a 'fort mauvais sujet' and mentions his reluctance to come back to the ship to carry out his functions when the vessel was in Lima – but Labé and the chaplain disliked each other, and Labé was not a man to mince his words. The chaplain's desertion does not improve matters, but again we must bear in mind that the ship was totally immobilised in Lima for three years: the extent of the boredom this situation created can be left to the imagination. The telling argument is surely that a priest does not need to be a canonisable saint to carry out such a basic function as holding a Christmas Day service.

There is, of course, no record of this in any of the Journals; but nor is there of many other routine matters. In the account of La Pérouse's voyage, filling three large volumes, the chaplain, Father Receveur, is mentioned a dozen times, but on each occasion the reference is to his accomplishments as an amateur naturalist, not to his religious duties which, like those of the officers, were taken for granted. A Mass said ashore would have probably earned a mention in one of the Journals: one on board would not – but the chaplain's neglect of his duties on

Christmas Day would surely have resulted in an adverse comment by the outspoken Labé.

Although firm evidence is lacking, we can reasonably assume that New Zealand's first Christian service was held in Doubtless Bay, probably on Sunday 24 December 1769 and certainly on the 25th, and in all likelihood on board ship.

APPENDIX D

Scurvy is a disease caused by inadequate diet, causing a deficiency of Vitamin C. It often affected sailors on long voyages, troops in the field, prisoners and those besieged in walled cities. It was accordingly blamed on bad or insufficient food, damp, cold and sea air. Malaise, weakness and lassitude are early symptoms, but those would be no cause for surprise in the harsh conditions of shipboard life. Perifollicular haemorrages usually follow, but here again such a minor disorder would hardly warrant notice. A later stage brings ecchymoses on various parts of the skin where friction or irritation occurs – joints, thighs, the back of the calf – but the first really serious indication is a swelling and inflammation of the gums. These become spongy, and bleeding occurs, with infection and necrosis of the tissue. Teeth loosen and can fall out, and the sailor, by now hospitalised to the extent the facilities on board permit, reaches a state of moral and physical weakness, which the unpleasant odour his mouth gives out does nothing to alleviate. Anaemia is common, with a loss of blood into the skin and deeper tissues. Vomiting and diarrhoea can occur, cuts or wounds do not heal, joints become stiff and painful, the spreading subcutaneous haemorrages break down to form putrid ulcers, and haemorrhages in the muscles and around the joints cause tenderness, swellings and pain on movement – which the rolling of the ship inevitably accentuates. Death occurs as a result of prostration, weakness, heart failure or superadded infection. Labé's and Surville's observations suggest that most of the men were suffering from scurvy: the smell and their cries of pain as the ship rolled and their arms and legs became increasingly tender is evidence of this. The disease was about to disappear from the high seas, as its cause had by then been determined and only the spread of this knowledge and its acceptance by captains and navy officials were needed to banish it.

A change of diet, fresh vegetables and fruit, especially citrus fruits, would have prevented scurvy; but Surville and Labé, as can be seen from their journals, still believed in the beneficial effects of 'land air' to counteract the pernicious effects of prolonged exposure to sea air. It is for this reason, for instance, that a party of sick was landed at Doubtless Bay, New Zealand, there to endure the additional discomforts of camping ashore with the minimum of facilities and in bad weather. Yet the dietary basis of the disease had been suspected for some time. The French naval surgeon Dellon had suggested this to his colleagues as early as 1685 in his *Relation d'un voyage aux Indes orientales*, but it was James Lind, a Royal Navy surgeon, who carried out the first controlled investigation of scurvy in the *Salisbury* in 1747. His conclusions were that citrus fruit – oranges and lemons – effected a prompt recovery in even severe cases; but his views took years to gain general acceptance.

The crew of the *St Jean-Baptiste* suffered because they sailed at a time when the real cause of the disease and the simple cure were suspected by only a few. Had Surville sighted Cook's *Endeavour* on the New Zealand coast, he would have met one of these few knowledgeable and enlightened men and many French lives could have been saved. The French noticed the prompt effect of wild celery and other herbs fed in soup or stew to the men in Doubtless Bay, but they lacked the knowledge or insight to draw the simple conclusion – although, it must be added, even if they had, they would have had few of the required facilities to take advantage of this newly gained knowledge on the long journey that still faced them.

BIBLIOGRAPHY

MANUSCRIPT SOURCES

(a) *Main documents*

Abbreviations:
A.M.   Archives de la Marine, Paris.
A.N.C.   Archives Nationales, Section Colonies, Paris.
A.N.M.   Archives Nationales, Section Marine, Paris.
B.N.   Bibiothèque Nationale, Paris.

Labé, Guillaume, Journal de navigation. A.N.M. 4JJ 143: 22.

Lacombe, Juan (translator), Diario de la navegacion que hazo el navio Frances nombrado el San Juan Baptista su Capt. Mr Surville, cavallero del orden real y militar de Sn Luis...tranucido en lingua Castellana. Translation made in Lima of Surville's Journal (A.N.M. 4JJ 143: 24); A.N.M. B4 316.

Monneron, Pierre, Extrait du Journal de Guillaume L'abé [sic] premier Lieutenant sur le Vaisseau le St Jean Baptiste, commandé par de Surville, parti de Pondichéry en 1768 [sic] pour les Terres Australes, A.N.M. 4JJ 143: 23.

Extrait du journal d'un voïage fait sur le Vau. Le St. Jean-baptiste commandé par M. de Surville, ch. de l'ordre Roïal et Militaire de St Louis, Capn. des Vaux de la Compagnie des Indes, 4 October 1771 A.N.M. 4JJ 143: 23 Cote M35 (presumably Monneron's summary of Surville's Journal).

Journal du Voyage fait sur le vaisseau le St Jean-Baptiste commandé par M. de Surville. [another abbreviated account] A.N.M. B4 316; also B.N. N.A.F. 9436: 1–87; and Service Hydrographique de la Marine B 5708.

Pottier de l'Horme, Jean, Journal du Sr Pottier de l'Horme, lieutenant du Vau. le St Jean-Baptiste, A.N.M. 4JJ 143: 25.

Role de l'équipage du Vaisseau particulier Le Saint Jean-Baptiste, Archives du Port de Lorient, 2P 45, 1, 10.

Surville, Jean-François-Marie de, Extrait du journal du voyage fait par le St Jean-Baptiste, commdt Mr de Surville, de Bengal à Ceilan et côte Coromandel, contre mousson, (1768), A.N.M. 4JJ 108 No. 161.

Dossier personnel, A.N.M. C7 314.

Journal du vaisseau le St Jean-Baptiste A.N.M. 4JJ 143: 24 1–3.

(b) Sundry documents

Archives Nationales, Colonies: Sundry Correspondence: Jean-Baptiste Chevalier C2 99 243: 55.

Report by de Boynes to duc d'Aiguillon B140 fo. 316; instruction to P. Monneron and G. Labé 25 November 1771, B 140 fo. 25.

Letter from de Boynes to duc d'Aiguillon concerning protest by Spanish about kidnapping of three Bashi islanders, B140 fo. 163.

Archives Nationales, Marine: Sundry maps and Correspondence B4 316; C4: 26.

Archives de la Marine, Brest: Registres de la Marine, records of officers, men and sick, districts of St Malo and Dinan, A. M. Brest, PC4 50–6, 58, 101–6, 108; PC6 109 28–9, 32; PF1 89.

Registre des ordonnances et règlements, I-L: 46 No. 8.

Archives de la Marine, Lorient, Port Registers 1P 64–5, 137–8, 140, 144, 146, 157, 161, 183, 187–8, 190–1, 215–16, 258; 2P 39–40, 45, 71 VI: 4 and VII: 194.

Procès-verbal de la désertion de Hughes Surville... et du P. Paul-Antoine de Villefeyx. [includes inventory of belongings] 2P 71 VI No. 4.

Archives de la Dordogne, Registre de la paroisse, Etouars, Series E Suppl. 895 GG3.

Archives d'Ille-et-Vilaine, C 4143 records of Mme de Surville 1789.

Archives du Morbihan, B3042 Inventory of Surville property.

Bibliothèque Nationale, Paris: Sundry correspondence and reports, under Nouvelles Acquisitions Françaises 9438: 84; also Correspondence of Law de Lauriston NAF 9365.

Turnbull Library, Wellington: Bourgeois et Gallois Appel [Appeal for the judicial liquidation of the syndicate to Admiralty Tribunal in Vannes] 14 August 1779, Misc. MS W14.

PRINTED SOURCES

AMAN, JACQUES *Les Officiers bleus dans la marine française au XVIIIe siècle.* Geneva, 1976.

AMHERST OF HACKNEY and THOMSON, BASIL (eds). *The Discovery of the Solomon Islands by Alvaro de Mendaña in 1568*, 2 vols. London, 1901.

AUSTIN, H. C. M. *Sea Fights and Corsairs of the Indian Ocean: being the naval history of Mauritius from 1715 to 1810.* Port-Louis, 1935.

BEAGLEHOLE, J. C. *The Discovery of New Zealand.* Wellington, 1939.

The Life of Captain James Cook. London, 1974.

The Exploration of the Pacific. London, 1934, third ed. 1966.

(ed.). *The Endeavour Journal of Joseph Banks, 1768–1771.* 2 vols. Sydney, 1962.

The Journals of Captain James Cook, 3 vols. Cambridge, 1955–69.

BELLIN, J. N. *L'Hydrographie françoise ou Recueil des cartes dressées au Dépost des Plans de la Marine pour le service des vaisseaux du Roy*. Paris, 1756.

Le Petit Atlas maritime, recueil des cartes et plans des quatre parties du monde. 5 vols. Paris, 1764.

Remarques sur la carte réduite des îles Philippines. Paris, 1752.

Remarques sur la presqu'île de l'Inde. Paris, 1766.

BÉRIOT, A. *Grands voiliers autour du monde: les voyages scientifiques 1760–1850.* Paris, 1962.

BOGESI, G. 'Santa Isabel, Solomon Islands', *Oceania*, v, 18, no. 3 (1948), pp. 208–32.

BONNASSIEUX, L. J. P. M. *Les Grandes Compagnies de commerce; études pour servir à l'histoire de la civilisation.* Paris, 1892.

BORAH, W. *Early Colonial Trade and Navigation between Mexico and Peru.* Berkeley, 1954.

BOUCHARY, J. *Les Manieurs d'argent à Paris à la fin du XVIIIe siècle.* Paris, 1943.

BOUGAINVILLE, L. A. DE. *Voyage autour du monde par la frégate du Roi la Boudeuse et la flûte l'Etoile en 1766…1769.* Paris, 1771. (Second edition in 2 vols. including an account of Cook's first voyage, 1772.)

BOURDE DE LA ROGERIE, M. *Les Bretons aux îles de France et de Bourbon.* Rennes, 1934.

BROSSARD, M. R. DE. *Moana, océan cruel.* Paris, 1966.

BROSSES, CHARLES DE. *Histoire des navigations aux terres australes*, 2 vols. Paris, 1756.

BROWN, J. MACMILLAN. *The Riddle of the Pacific.* London, 1924.

BUACHE, PHILIPPE. 'Eclaircissements géographiques sur la nouvelle Bretagne et sur les côtes septentionales de la nouvelle Guinée', in *Mémoires de l'Académie Royale des Sciences.* Paris, 1789, 128–47.

'Extrait d'un Mémoire sur l'existence et la position des îles de Salomon, présenté à l'Académie Royale des Sciences le 9 Janvier 1782', in Fleurieu, *Découvertes des François*, pp. 297–309.

BUCK, P. H. *Explorers of the Pacific.* Honolulu, 1953.

BUFFET, H. F. *La Ville et la citadelle du Port-Louis.* Rennes, 1962.

'Voyage à la découverte du port-louisien Surville', *Mémoires de la Société d'histoire et d'archéologie de Bretagne*, xxx, (1950), 87–114.

BURNEY, J. *A Chronological History of the Discoveries in the South Sea or Pacific Ocean*, 5 vols. London, 1803–7.

CALLANDER, J. *Terra Australis Incognita, or Voyages to the Terra Australis or Southern hemisphere during the sixteenth, seventeenth and eighteenth centuries.* 5 vols. London, 1766–68.

CARRINGTON, H. *The Discovery of Tahiti* [see Robertson, G.].

CASADO, R. C. and EMBID, F. P. *Memoria de Gobierno del Virrey Amat 1761–1776.* Seville, 1947.

CHAILLY-BERT, J. *Les Compagnies de colonisation sous l'Ancien Régime.* Paris, 1898.

CHARPENTIER, F. *Relation de l'establissement de la compagnie françoise pour le commerce des Indes orientales.* Paris, 1666.

COLLINGRIDGE, G. *Pacifika* Sydney, n.d.

CORDIER, H. 'Les Voyages de Pierre Poivre 1748–1757', *Revue de l'histoire des colonies françaises,* VI (1918), 5–88.

COREAL, FRANÇOIS. *Recueil de voyages dans l'Amérique méridionale.* Amsterdam, 1738.

Voyages de François Coréal aux Indes orientales, 3 vols. Amsterdam, 1722.

Recueil de voyages dans l'Amérique méridionale. Amsterdam, 1738.

CORNEY, B. G. (ed.). *The Quest and Occupation of Tahiti by Emissaries of Spain during the years 1772–76.* 3 vols. London, 1913–18.

The Voyage of Captain Don Felipe Gonzales...to Easter Island in 1770–1. Cambridge, 1908.

CROZET, J. *Nouveau Voyage à la mer du sud* [see Rochon, A. M.]

DAHLGREN, E. W. 'L'expédition de Martinez et la fin du commerce français dans la Mer du Sud', *Revue d'histoire des colonies françaises* (1913), 257–332.

Les Relations commerciales et maritimes entre la France et les côtes de l'Océan Pacifique (commencement du XVIIIe siècle). Paris. 1909.

'Voyages français à destination de la Mer du Sud avant Bougainville (1695–1749)', *Nouvelles Archives des missions scientifiques,* XIV (1907), 423–568.

DALRYMPLE, A. *A Letter from Mr Dalrymple to Dr Hawkesworth, occasioned by some groundless and illiberal imputations in his Account of the late Voyages to the South.* London, 1773.

An Account of the Discoveries made in the South Pacifick Ocean previous to 1764. London, 1767.

An Historical Collection of the Several Voyages and Discoveries in the South Pacific Ocean. 2 vols. London, 1770.

Considerations on M. Buache's Memoir concerning New Britain and the North Coast of New Guinea. London, 1790.

DAMPIER, WILLIAM. *A New Voyage Round the World.* London, 1697, new ed. 1703.

D'APRES DE MANNEVILLETTE, J. B. N. *Le Neptune Oriental, ou Routier général des côtes des Indes orientales et de la Chine.* Paris, 1745.

DERMIGNY, L. *La Chine et l'Occident: le commerce à Canton au XVIIIe siècle (1713–1833).* 3 vols. Paris, 1964.

DESCOLA, J., *La Vie quotidienne au Pérou au temps des Espagnols.* Paris. 1962.

DUNMORE, J. 'A French account of Port Praslin, Solomon Islands, in 1769', *Journal of Pacific History,* IX, (1974), 172–82.

'Découvertes des ancres de Surville', *Journal de la Société des Océanistes,* XXX, 44 (1974), 241–2.

French Explorers in the Pacific. 2 vols. Oxford, 1965–1969.

'French visitors to Trengganu in the eighteenth century', *Journal of the Royal Asiatic Society, Malaysian branch,* XLVI, (1973), 145–59.

'Holy Mass was the first Christian service in New Zealand', in *Marist Messenger*, XXXVII, 5, (1967), 6–7.

'Le Père de Villefeix et la première messe en Nouvelle-Zélande', in *Journal de la Société des Océanistes*, XXV, (1969), 305–6.

The Fateful Voyage of the St Jean Baptiste. Christchurch, 1969.

FAIVRE, J. P. *L'Expansion Française dans le Pacifique de 1800 à 1842*. Paris, 1953.

FESCHE, C. F. P. *La Nouvelle Cythère (Tahiti), journal de navigation inédit* (ed. J. Dorsenne). Paris, 1929.

FEUILLET, L. *Journal des observations physiques, mathématiques et botaniques faites par l'ordre du Roy sur les côtes orientales de l'Amérique méridionale & dans les Indes occidentales, depuis l'année 1707 jusques en 1712*. 3 vols. Paris, 1714–25.

FIGUEROA, C. S. de. *Hechos de Don Garcia Hurtado de Mendoza cuarto Marques de Cañete*. Madrid, 1613.

FLEURIEU, C. P. C. de. *Découvertes des François en 1768 et 1769 dans le Sud-Est de la Nouvelle-Guinée et reconnaissance postérieure des mêmes terres par des navigateurs anglois qui leur ont imposé de nouveaux noms*. Paris, 1790. English transl. London, 1791.

FORREST, T. *A Voyage to New Guinea and the Moluccas...in the Tartar...during the years 1774, 1775 and 1776*. London, 1779.

FORSTER, GEORG. 'Des Französischen Schiffkapitäns J. F. de Surville's Reise in das Südmeer', *Magazin von Merkwürdigen Neuen Reisebeschreibungen*. XVIII, (1793).

Franska Capitainems och Riddarens Jean-François de Survilles Upptäcks-Resa. Nykoping, 1795.

FREZIER, A. F. *Relation du voyage de la Mer du Sud aux côtes du Chily et du Pérou, fait pendant les années 1712, 1713, et 1714*. Paris, 1716. English transl. London, 1717.

GAUTIER, J. M. 'Apogée et déclin du mirage tahitien en Angleterre et en France (1766–1802)', *Journal de la Société des Océanistes*, no. 6 (Dec. 1951), pp. 270–3.

GAZEL, A. *French Navigators and the Early History of New Zealand*. Wellington, 1946.

GUPPY, H. B. *The Solomon Islands and their Natives*. London. 1887.

HAMILTON, ALEXANDER. *A New Account of the East Indies*. Edinburgh, 1727, rept. London, 1930.

HARGREAVES, R. P. *French Explorers' Maps of New Zealand*. Map Collectors' Circle. London, 1966.

HARLOW, V. T. *The Founding of the Second British Empire*, I, Discovery and revolution. London, 1952.

HEZEL, F. X. and DEL VALLE, MARIA-THERESA. 'Early European Contact with the Western Carolines', *Journal of Pacific History*, V, (1972), 26–44.

HYDE, H. MONTGOMERY. *John Law*. London, 1948.

HYDROGRAPHIC DEPARTMENT, BRITISH ADMIRALTY. *Pacific Islands Pilot*, 3 vols and supplements. London, 1946–75.

JACK-HINTON, C. *The Search for the Islands of Solomon 1567–1838*. Oxford, 1969.

JACQUEMONT, S. 'Le Mythe du Pacifique dans la littérature', in Rousseau, M., *L'Art océanien*. Paris, 1951.

JACQUIER, H. 'Le Mirage et l'exotisme tahitiens dans la littérature', *Bulletin de la société des études océaniennes*, VII (1944–5), 3–7, 50–76, 91–114.

KELLY, CELSIUS. *Calendar of Documents, Spanish Voyages in the South Pacific 1567–1794 and Franciscan missionary plans for the peoples of the Austral lands 1617–1634*. Madrid, 1965.

'Catholic missionaries in the Pacific', *The Catholic Review*, II, 5, 6, (1946), pp. 257–74.

La Austrialia del Espiritu Santo. 2 vols. Cambridge, 1966.

'Maori and Solomon Islands drawings from the Surville expedition found in Spanish archives', *Journal of the Polynesian Society*, LXXVI, 4 (1967), 459–66.

'New Zealand's first Mass', *The Catholic Review*, IV (1948), 262–76.

KELLY, L. G. *Marion Dufresne at the Bay of Islands*. Wellington, 1951.

KENNEDY, B. E. 'Anglo-French Rivalry in India and the Eastern Seas 1763–1793: a study of Anglo-French tensions and of their impact on the consolidation of British power in the region', unpublished thesis, Canberra, 1969.

KEYS, A. C. 'Zoraï ou les insulaires de la Nouvelle-Zélande', *AUMLLA*, Christchurch, IX (1958), 36–47.

KIMBLE, G. H. T. *Geography in the Middle Ages*. London, 1938.

LA BORDE, J. B. DE. *Histoire abrégée de la Mer du Sud*. 3 vols. Paris, 1791.

Mémoire sur la prétendue découverte faite en 1788 par des Anglois... Paris, 1790.

LA CHENAYE-DESBOIS ET BADIER, *Dictionnaire de la noblesse*. Paris, 1867.

LANGDON, R., *The Lost Caravel*, Sydney, 1975.

LA PEROUSE, J. F. G. DE [see Milet-Mureau N. L. A.].

LE GENTIL DE LA GALAISIERE, G. J. H. B. *Voyage dans les mers des Indes, fait par ordre du Roy, à l'occasion du passage de Vénus sur le disque du soleil le 7 Juin 1761 et le 3 du même mois 1769*. 2 vols. Paris, 1779–81.

LE GOBIEN, C. *Histoire des îles Marianes*. Paris, 1700.

LUTHY, H. *La Banque protestante en France*. 2 vols. Paris, 1970.

MAJOR, R. H. (ed.). *Early Voyages to Terra Australis*. London, 1859.

McCORMICK, E. H. *Tasman in New Zealand, a bibliographic study*. Wellington, 1959.

[McKEEFRY, P.] 'The First Mass in New Zealand', *Zealandia* (24 Feb. 1939).

McNAB, R. *From Tasman to Marsden*. Dunedin, 1914.

Historical Records of New Zealand. 2 vols. Wellington, 1908–14.

MALLESON, G. B. *History of the French in India*, 2nd ed. Edinburgh, 1909.

MARCHAND, L. R. 'The French discovery and settlement of New Zealand 1769–1840: a bibliographical essay on naval records in Paris', *Historical Studies*, X (1963), 511–18.

MARKHAM, C. (ed.). *The Voyages of Don Pedro Fernandez de Quiros 1595 to 1606*, 2 vols. London, 1904.

MARTIN-ALLANIC, J. E. *Bougainville navigateur et les découvertes de son temps.* Paris, 1964.

MAYR, ERNST. *Birds of the South-West Pacific.* New York, 1945.

MENARD, ABBÉ. *Une Servante des pauvres, la Mère Elizabeth de Surville.* Tours, 1887.

MENDIBURN, M. DE, *Diccionario historico biografico del Peru.* Lima, 1931–35.

MERRILL, ELMER D. *Plant Life of the Pacific World.* New York, 1954.

MILET-MUREAU, N. L. A. (ed.), *Voyage autour du monde...de M. de la Pérouse,* 3 vols. Paris, 1797.

MILLIGAN, R. R. D. 'Ranginui, captive chief of Doubtless Bay, 1769', *Journal of the Polynesian Society,* LXVII (1958), 181–203.

MILLIGAN, R. R. D. and DUNMORE, J. 'The Misnaming of North Cape', *New Zealand Geographer,* XIX, 2 (1963), 178–81.

MONNERON, P. A. 'Mon Odyssée', *La Revue de Paris,* (Aug. 1907), pp. 569–96.
  Réponse de M. Pierre Antoine Monneron, député de la colonie de l'isle-de-France à l'Assemblée nationale, à M. Berthelmot et autres et par occasion à M. Arthur Dillon, député de la Martinique. Paris, 1791.

MORRELL, W. P. *Britain in the Pacific Islands.* Oxford, 1960.

NICOD, E. 'Monneron aîné, député de la sénéchaussée d'Annonay', *Revue historique du Vivarais,* IX (1896).

OEXMELIN, A. *Histoire des aventuriers qui se sont signalés dans les Indes,* 2 vols. Paris, 1688.

PICARD, R., KERVIS, J. P. and BRUNEAU, Y. *Les Compagnies des Indes.* Paris, 1966.

PINGRE, A. G. *Mémoire sur le choix et l'état des lieux où le passage de Vénus du 3 Juin 1769 pourra être observé.* Paris, 1767.
  Mémoire sur les découvertes faites dans la Mer du Sud avant les derniers voyages des Anglois et des François autour du monde. Paris, 1778.

PREVOST D'EXILES, ANTOINE-FRANCOIS. *Histoire générale des voyages,* 20 vols. Paris, 1753. 2nd edn in 25 vols, 1758.

PRICE, A. GRENFELL. *The Western Invasions of the Pacific and its Continents.* Oxford, 1963.

PRIESTLEY, H. I. *France Overseas through the Old Regime: a study of European expansion.* New York, 1939.

RAINAUD, A. *Le Continent austral: hypothèses et découvertes.* Paris, 1893.

REID, A., 'The French in Sumatra and the Malay world 1760–1890', in *Bijdragen,* CXXIX, (1973), 195–237.

ROBERTSON, G. *The Discovery of Tahiti: a Journal of the second voyage of H.M.S. Dolphin.* ed. by H. Carrington. London, 1948.

ROCHON, A. M. (ed.). [Crozet's] *Nouveau Voyage à la Mer du Sud commencé sous les ordres de M. Marion...On a joint à ce voyage un extrait de celui de M. de Surville,* Paris, 1783.
  Voyages aux Indes orientales et en Afrique pour l'observation des longitudes en mer. Paris, 1807.

SAINT ELME LE DUC. *Ile de France*. Mauritius, 1925.

SEN, S. P. *The French in India: first establishment and struggle*. Calcutta. 1947.
The French in India 1763–1816. Calcutta, 1958.

SHARP, ANDREW. *The Discovery of the Pacific Islands*. Oxford, 1960.
The Voyages of Abel Janszoon Tasman. Oxford, 1968.

SKELTON, R. A. *Explorers' Maps*. London, 1958.

SMITH, B. *European Vision and the South Pacific 1768–1850*. Oxford, 1960.

SONNERAT P. *An Account of a Voyage to the Spice-Islands and New Guinea*.
London, 1781. [French ed. Paris 1776].

SOULIER-VALBERT, F. *L'Expansion française dans le Pacifique-Sud: Tahiti et
dépendances 1768–1908*. Paris, 1908.

SPATE, O. K. 'Terra Australis. Cognita?', *Historical Studies* [Melbourne], VIII,
(Nov. 1957), 1–19.

STOCKDALE, J. *The Voyage of Governor Philip to Botany Bay...to which are added
the Journals of Lieutenant Shortland...with an Account of their New
Discoveries*. London, 1790.

TAILLEMITE, E. (ed.). *Bougainville et ses compagnons autour du monde 1766–1769*,
2 vols. Paris, 1977.

TARLTON, K. 'The Search for and discovery of anchors lost in 1769 by the
French explorer de Surville at Doubtless Bay, New Zealand', *Nautical
Archeology*, VI, 1 (1977), 64–70.

TAYLOR, N. M. 'French navigators in the Pacific', in *The Pacific: ocean of islands*
(ed. C. L. Barrett). Melbourne, 1950.

THEVENOT, MELCHISÉDECH, *Recueil de voyages de M. Thévenot*. Paris, 1681.
Relations de divers voyages curieux, 2 vols. Paris, 1696.

VINCENT, DERRIC. *The Lilies Wither*, a play in 3 acts and a prologue;
cyclostyled text. Kaitaia, 1975.

WAFER, L. *A New Voyage and Description of the Isthmus of America* (L. E. E.
Joyce, ed.). London, 1934.

WARD, J. M. 'British policy in the exploration of the Pacific 1699–1793',
Journal of the Royal Australian Historical Society, XXXIII 25ff.

WEBER, H. *La Compagnie française des Indes (1605–1875)*, Paris, 1904.

WROTH, L. C. *The Early Cartography of the Pacific*. New York, 1944.

INDEX